In tribute to Hubert Durt

THE THOUSAND AND ONE LIVES OF THE BUDDHA

THE THOUSAND AND ONE LIVES OF THE BUDDHA

Bernard Faure

UNIVERSITY OF HAWAI'I PRESS
Honolulu

Originally published as *Les mille et une vies du Bouddha* by Éditions du Seuil, 2018

Printed in the United States of America

First printing, 2022

Library of Congress Cataloging-in-Publication Data

Names: Faure, Bernard, author.
Title: The thousand and one lives of the Buddha / Bernard Faure.
Description: Honolulu : University of Hawai'i Press, 2022. | Includes bibliographical references and index.
Identifiers: LCCN 2021060221 | ISBN 9780824891909 (hardback) | ISBN 9780824893538 (paperback) | ISBN 9780824893545 (pdf) | ISBN 9780824893552 (epub) | ISBN 9780824893569 (kindle edition)
Subjects: LCSH: Buddhism—Historiography. | Gautama Buddha.
Classification: LCC BQ897 .F38 2022 | DDC 294.3072/2—dc23/eng/20220223
LC record available at https://lccn.loc.gov/2021060221

Publication of this book has been assisted by a grant from Frances Wu and Paul Yin, C-BEAR Monographs Publication Subvention, Columbia University.

University of Hawai'i Press books are printed on acid-free paper and meet the guidelines for permanence and durability of the Council on Library Resources.

Cover art: Scroll of Buddhist images (12th century) by Zhang Shengwen.
Detail. National Palace Museum, Taipei.

CONTENTS

FOREWORD

It is more than likely that Bernard Faure needs no introduction to readers of this book. Over the years, he has been amazingly productive and has been deservedly celebrated for his distinguished studies of various aspects of Chinese and Japanese Buddhist cultures (Chan/Zen in particular), as well as his significant works on Buddhism and sexuality, Buddhism and violence, Western conceptualizations of Buddhism, Buddhism and neuroscience, etc. But he has not heretofore given us a book-length study of the life story of the Buddha. It is a delight, therefore, to welcome this English version of *Les mille et une vies du Bouddha,* which was first published in French in 2018. From my perspective, *The Thousand and One Lives of the Buddha* is an important milestone in the field that will not only transform the way we think about the Buddha's life, but will change the ways we go about studying it.

As is well known, traditional Buddhist lives of the Buddha are filled with events that can be thought of as supernatural or "mythical." Beginning in the late nineteenth century, various Western scholars sought to strip his life story of these elements in an effort to get back to the "historical" Buddha. Things that these demythologizers deemed to be unbelievable, such as the miracles that testified to the Buddha's greatness, or even the recollections of his previous lives (*jātakas*), were simply omitted. Episodes such as his birth, great departure, enlightenment, first sermon, and death were recounted, but denuded of their supernatural trappings. Or, if these trappings were mentioned, they were quickly and mockingly dismissed as the fictitious products of excessive devotionalism. The image that was thus projected was of a Buddha who was a rational, socratic teacher—a great person perhaps, but a more or less ordinary human being, limited, like the rest of us, by the constraints of space and time.

Unlike these early scholars, buddhologists today (with some exceptions) are not very sanguine about the possibilities of knowing anything for certain about the historical Buddha. They point to the gap of several centuries between the supposed lifetime of the Buddha and the first writings about him. They show how even the oldest layers of these writings, as well as the earliest examples of Buddhist art, already emphasize the Buddha's marvelous, supernatural qualities. They criticize the demythologizers for ending up as remythologizers, creating a Buddha that appealed to them, by eliding one that did not.

Even so, the *idea* of a historical Buddha dies hard, and these same skeptical buddhologists, having made clear their doubts, are nonetheless usually willing then to accept certain basic "facts" about the Buddha, things that "there is no good reason to deny given a lack of any contradictory evidence." I myself have succumbed to this, affirming, for example, that the Buddha was born; that he lived in northern India, sometime between the sixth and the fourth centuries BCE; that this was a time of social and cultural change when groups of religious renunciants were being formed; that he was one such renunciant; that having left his family, he sought and found enlightenment; and that he formed a community that looks back to him as its founder. This may well be a minimally acceptable "history," but it is also a very thin and generic biography, hardly doing justice to the richness and appeal of what we know from Buddhist sources about the life of the Buddha.

In this book, Faure wants to shift our focus away from the *idea* of a historical Buddha. This is not because he believes that the Buddha never existed as a person, but because he sees that our latent historicist inclination detracts from the way we go about understanding the traditions about him. The life story of the Buddha, he tells us at one point, "is one of the great myths of modern times," and we should treat it as such, with modes of analysis geared toward its mythic nature. In so doing, we can view the whole of the Buddha's life—with both its factualized fictions and fictionalized facts—as a made-up narrative, or rather as a series of made-up narratives. Once the question of the *history* of the Buddha has been bracketed, it need not be reintroduced, and we can turn our attention to what we are left with: myths and legends, or, more simply, *his story.*

The primacy of story is already clear in the title of this book with its allusion to the great Arabic collection of tales *One Thousand and One Nights* (a.k.a. *Arabian Nights*). Faure does not comment on his choice of title, but one of its implications is clear. We know from scholarship that the *Arabian Nights* is a disparate compilation of tales by many authors, translators, and storytellers from many different cultures and traditions, which developed over many centuries. There is no single or original *Thousand and One Nights,* but multiple versions of it of varying lengths. The only thing that holds them all together is the frame story featuring Scheherezade, the putative narrator of the stories, told to her husband in order to sustain his longing for more (and to keep herself alive). Buddhist accounts of the life of the Buddha don't have a Scheherezade (unless it be the Buddha's disciple Ānanda), but they are often similarly captivating. And it is worth thinking of them as an anthology of tales (or rather as many different anthologies) rather than as a Western-style biography. Like the *Arabian Nights,* they were taken from different sources that were composed in different times and places and put together by a process of *bricolage,* to use Lévi-Strauss's term for mythmaking (which Faure also invokes). The Buddha's life story thus has its origins (and to some extent its continuation) in fragments. To be sure, some Buddhist *bricoleurs* attempted to arrange these fragments in sequential order, starting with the Buddha's birth or his previous lives, and ending (in the case of the "complete" lives) with his death and his ongoing existences in relics and images. In this, they have been followed by many Western biographers. But, in other cases, the put-together anthologies are more chaotic, filled with flashbacks, jump-arounds, repetitions, lacunae, partialities, and excursi. Indeed, with few exceptions, most traditional Buddhist sources on the life of the Buddha are much less well ordered than we like to think. This is important because, from Faure's perspective, one of the things that comes along with historicism is the notion of a linear biography.

In this light, a major challenge in writing a book on the life (or, more appropriately, the "lives") of the Buddha is how to keep its fragments distinct and separate without hopelessly losing one's readers, who, most likely, have an epistemological attraction to chronologically ordered narratives. In meeting this challenge, Faure succeeds magnificently. He first focuses on cycles of tales that arose around certain pilgrimage sites, Lumbinī, Bodhgaya, Kuśinagara, etc., presenting them as though they were acts in a play. He then presents a select number of "secondary episodes," some connected to other pilgrimage sites, and others "floating," that is, assigned to different times and places in the Buddha's life by different sources. These are followed by separate chapters on past lives of the Buddha and stories concerning the Buddha's relationships with his own family members, with Māra, and with ritual celebrations in different Buddhist communities. In laying out these narratives, Faure does not hesitate to tap a wide range of sources, citing early and late Sanskrit, Pāli, Chinese, and Japanese versions of particular scenarios, among others, as well as their interpretations by various scholars and writers.

This use of multiple sources not only helps to keep the fragmentariness of the Buddha's life story in mind; it also reflects the critique of historicism that Faure marshals. For hand in glove with the hypostatization of a historical buddha (whether conscious or not) has been a tendency, in Western scholarship, to privilege certain kinds of records—Pāli or Sanskrit sources (or perhaps their translations into Tibetan or Chinese)—over Southeast or East Asian (or Western or Middle Eastern or modern) vernacular ones. This bias seems to reflect a desire to get closer to a supposed point of origin, a putative historical figure or context. However, once the mythic nature of the Buddha's life story has been recognized, once his lives are seen to be completely "storical," all stories about him are legitimate, regardless of their date or cultural provenance or language they were written in.

Faure drives this point home in the third part of the book, where he returns to some of the episodes already dealt with in Part Two but now discusses more systematically how they are iterated in different eras (classical, medieval, and modern), vernacular sources (Chinese, Japanese, Middle Eastern, Western), and media (literature, art, and film). Along the way, he validates the inclusion of often neglected sources such as the illustrated lives of Śākyamuni from the Ming dynasty (e.g., by Baocheng), parodic portrayals of the Buddha's parinirvāṇa (e.g., Itō Jakuchū's painting of the *Vegetable Nirvāṇa*), Tibetan, Indian, and Japanese stories featuring legendary antagonists of the Buddha (e.g., Gozu Tennō), Shinto-inspired critiques of the Buddha legend (e.g., by Hirata Atsutane), Persian and Arabic renditions of it (e.g., by Rashid al-Dīn), and medieval Christian reworkings (e.g., the tale of Saints Barlaam and Josaphat, included in Voragine's *Golden Legend*), to name but a few. The panoply of examples ends with a chapter on presentations of the Buddha legend in comic books (*manga*), feature films, and science fiction. In this openness to all sources regardless of date or provenance, there are echoes, perhaps, of Lévi-Strauss's assertion that all versions of a myth—even its retellings and relatable narratives—should ideally be considered in its analysis. Unlike Lévi-Strauss, however, Faure does not seek to pull all the pieces together as parts of some unitive "structural message." To do so would betray their fragmentariness. His aim here, moreover, is not to be encyclopedic, but to be pioneering in endorsing the need and encouraging the usefulness of considering such "continuations" in any full study of the lives of the Buddha. As he puts it in his epilogue, rather than reduce these narratives to historicist, structuralist, or functionalist explanations, it behooves us first to savor them. In this way the Life of the Buddha remains an "open story."

THE THOUSAND AND ONE LIVES OF THE BUDDHA

INTRODUCTION

Like the Life of Christ, the Life of the Buddha has been told so often that a potential reader is justified in wondering what difference another book on this subject might make. To answer this question, and to justify this book in part, it is necessary to consider that the Buddha's "life" has been the object of two main types of discourse so far, hagiographical and historicist. Unlike biography, which follows chronology and is based on the historical method, hagiography folds in multiple ramifications like a stream exploring all the anfractuosities of the terrain, following the line of greatest slope. It is intended for believers for whom any event in the life that is narrated can be seen as an object of faith or a model to be imitated. For ordinary Buddhists, everything in the Life of the Buddha makes sense, and the question of true and false is rarely asked. Yet the details of this Life, and the figure of the Buddha himself, were not always accorded the same importance in different times and places.

The historicist approach that presided over the development of Buddhist studies remains dominant today. According to it, everything in the Life of the Buddha is a priori suspect. It is therefore necessary to strip it of its legendary garments—to distinguish between the true and the false, or rather the probable and the improbable—in order to find the real facts beneath the fabric of legends. In this way, historians try to separate the wheat (historical fact) from the chaff (fabrications of mythical thought). In reality, virtually nothing is known about the figure known as the Buddha, and historical reconstructions are just as pious and imaginative as the myths and legends they claim to supplant.[1]

Far from being a faithful transcription of a full existence, the Life of the Buddha was originally a blank, which generations of hagiographers and historians have endeavored to fill, turning it into a palimpsest. Hagiography (pious history) and history (usually impious), though apparently opposed, stem in fact from the same source. Unlike the Buddha of their dreams, hagiographers and historians abhor emptiness—at least that of the blank page.

Another type of approach has recently gained ground in Buddhist studies. This is the literary approach, from whose perspective the Life of the Buddha is a kind of epic or romance of awakening. It has the merit of insisting on a narrative dimension, but in focusing on the Buddha's previous existences (the *Jātakas*) and the fictional character they entail, it hesitated to apply its method to the question of the ultimate existence of the "historical" Buddha. I retain from this approach its creativity, and the idea that infinite variations on the same motif, like a kaleidoscope whose changing combinations one never tires of admiring, have value in themselves. However, the Life of the Buddha is not simply a Buddhist version of the Thousand and One Nights, even if some resemblances may be glimpsed.

The approach I adopt is that of the history of religions, which inherits its orientation from the previous ones but differs from them on certain points. In my opinion, the Life of the Buddha belongs essentially to the domain of legend or myth, and therefore lends itself to a literary, structuralist, and cultural analysis. However, we should not underestimate the importance of this life story as a model. For the vast majority of Buddhists, the Buddha remains above all an object of faith. As the art historian Jurgis Baltrušaitis (1903–1988) wrote, "The illusions and fictions that are born around forms respond to a reality, and they in turn generate forms into which images and legends are projected and materialize in life."[2] Let's go one step further: the thesis I defend here is that the truth of the Buddha is probably more accessible in legend than in historical facts. This re-reading of the founder's Life also implies a re-evaluation of Buddhism as a religion and philosophy.

For the historian of religions, the historicity of the Buddha is not a problem. Even if everything in the life of this character is more or less invented, it is nonetheless "true" on a more essential level. Indeed, it constitutes the paradigm on which Buddhist faith and practice are based.[3] By giving a certain amount of credit to these, while remaining subject to the rules of historical objectivity, the historian of religions comes close to the believers' point of view and is thus better able to understand it. But as a historian, he nonetheless retains his critical spirit. The point is therefore not to question the historicity of the Buddha, but simply to show that while it remains the indisputable origin for elements of the Buddhist tradition, it has not been for this tradition as a whole the determining factor that it is for Western historians.

In spite of the many attempts to reduce it to a linear trajectory, the Life of the Buddha is essentially multiple and proliferating, just like the Buddhist tradition itself, diffracted into multiple schools. To allow this multiplicity to unfold, it is required that we first put the historicist method in brackets to adopt an indirect approach. Moreover, since the Buddha has cast a long shadow over the centuries, his cultural influence is not limited to Buddhist communities or to ancient India. It extends to the whole of Asia, and now to the West, and is also found outside Buddhism proper in sometimes unexpected places, like comic books, Western novels, and science fiction.

Most scholarly works on the Life of the Buddha, despite their critical stance on its legendary aspects, display a certain epistemological naivety in their presumed capacity to determine the ground of its historicity. Moreover, they risk costing readers the pleasure—also naive, certainly, but a fruitful naivety—universally found in telling, hearing, or reading stories. If one throws myth and legend to the wind, seeking to keep only the facts, one may discover there is practically nothing left. In this, the distortion of the materials is not less than that of hagiography, for in a kind of reverse alchemy the historicist works at transforming the gold of the imaginary into a leadenly prosaic reality. Is it not time instead to rehabilitate the mythological narrative while taking care to avoid the error committed by comparative mythologists (from Émile Senart to Mircea Eliade)—the error of imposing an essentially Western reading grid, or set of criteria, on non-Western traditions?[4] The important task still remains of showing how myths and legends have rewritten themselves in new settings, transforming a living tradition in which no single era can be privileged any longer.

Still, the legend of the Buddha took off in India, and any history of Buddhism must begin with India, because, as Paul Mus liked to say, "India produced it, India will explain it." True, but India does not explain everything. In studying the development of Buddhism and the legend of the Buddha, India loses some of its primacy as other Buddhist cultures claim symbolic centrality in turn. This means we will leave behind a purely Indian, "primitivist" reading grid obsessed with the search for origins to embrace non-Indian traditions and, at the other end of Asia in particular, the Japanese tradition.

The first part of the book, which is essentially critical, examines the approaches that have been adopted by scholars so far—namely, the mythological approach (still the first, but long discredited because of its outdated assumptions); the historicist approach, which is still dominant; and a third approach, which claims to adopt a "middle way" between the first two but in fact clearly favors historicism. In all of these cases, researchers have grounded their approach in the Indian tradition because, in seeming closer to the sources, it appeared more authentic. But in doing so despite the paucity of reliable documents, they have only replaced one mythology with another. The main point I argue in this first part is that, once one is freed from the historicist stance and can take the Life of the Buddha for what it is—namely, a literary document—one no longer has any reason to limit the scope of one's inquiry to India and can turn to other cultures, especially those of East Asia, for which the Life of the Buddha played an equally important role.

The second part of the book deals with the Indian Life of the Buddha in a more thematic way, looking at its narrative aspect and the constraints imposed by the biographical genre. It is based on the often-heard observation that the biographical format, which seems so natural to us, required nearly six centuries before it could impose itself in the case of the Buddha, and that, once realized, it was rapidly transformed and sometimes even dissolved. For a Buddhist, the Life of the Master begins well before his birth, and it continues during multiple previous existences and well after his death (or parinirvāṇa), through his relics, which are another form of his presence. Yet, even should we wish to limit ourselves to his last existence, taken in the Western sense of a journey from life to death, another problem arises: the man who was to become the Buddha actually "died" twice: at the moment of the supreme awakening, a kind of initiatory death by which he stripped himself of his self; and at the moment of the parinirvāṇa, his final extinction. The first biographies, consequent on this point, stopped at the awakening. It was only late in the day that the awakening and the parinirvāṇa were connected. With the development of the Great Vehicle (Mahāyāna), which contrasts the purely human Buddha with a superhuman or transcendent Buddha (even a multitude of metaphysical buddhas, infinitely reflecting the life of the historical Buddha), the biographical question takes on a new dimension.

After discussing these biographical problems, I keep the narrative to a loosely chronological thread while giving free rein to the episodes in it that seem to me to be the most significant. Consequently it is, if you like, a selective biography, where not only the most important episodes of the Buddha's career are highlighted (birth, youth, leaving the family, asceticism, victory over Māra, awakening, and preaching), but also the accompanying legends that developed around characters such as his mother Māyā, his wife Yaśodharā, his cousin and rival Devadatta, and, *last but not least,* his sworn enemy Māra.

The third part considers the Life of the Buddha, no longer from a biographical point of view, but as a paradigm for the lives of eminent monks—a kind of *imitatio Buddhaei* (as Christian worship was intended to be an *imitatio Christi*) that developed later—and for the ordinary religious practices inherited by all. I thus take up some of the highlights from the Life of the Buddha to show how they gave rise to ritual practices such as ordination, meditation, and funeral rites throughout Asia.

The fourth part radically shifts the center of gravity: spatially, from India to East Asia, and temporally, from antiquity to the medieval and modern worlds. In this decentering, Japan, as both the farthest place from India geographically and culturally and the culmination of the Mahāyāna tradition in Asia, seemed to me to be the place of greatest interest. In this part, I focus mainly on Japanese narratives that feature a sometimes unexpected Buddha, who in some texts more resembles Prince Shōtoku (Shōtoku Taishi, 574–622) or Prince Genji of the *Genji monogatari* than the Indian prince Siddhārtha. These narratives multiplied in medieval Japan right up to the threshold of the modern age and are a striking example of how the Life of the Buddha adapted to the new cultures encountered by Buddhism in its expansion eastward.

But Japan does not have the last word. To complete the circle, the last section of the book looks at rival conceptions of Buddha, from Islam to Christianity, starting with the legends of Barlaam and Josaphat but also attending to the emergence of a modern, "humanist" Buddha.

As a living tradition, the Life of the Buddha, in spite of the impoverishment to which Western historicism and neo-Buddhism have subjected it, has continued to develop, as it were, in the interstices of these great ideological blocks—like the weed that grows between cobblestones. This is why it seemed useful to me to delve into fields as unusual as *manga,* film and novel, and science fiction. All these popular versions are, in my opinion, part of the same creative spirit that has shaped, for so many generations, the Life of the Buddha as both a model of existence and an object of devotion.

Those who support orthodoxy (assuming there is one, or even several) will no doubt denounce what will seem to them a crime of lèse-majesté, an attack not only on Buddhist morality but on scientific *doxa.* But it is time to question certain dogmas that for too long have stifled the free development of Buddhist studies and contributed to masking the richness of this tradition. The method adopted here lets the narrative depart from the narrow framework of the canonical tradition and gives it, as it were, a free hand. But it also brings out the luminous figure at the center of the narrative in all his glory, and seeks to make us understand the immense prestige he has enjoyed until today, together with the treasures of imagination that Buddhist cultures have lavished upon him.

PART ONE

MYTH AND HISTORY

The story of the Life of the Buddha is also the story of his biographers and their biases. Unfortunately, we know nothing about most of the early biographers, only that they were in fact hagiographers. The work of modern biographers, on the other hand, is more open to inspection, and the story it tells is that the Buddha's Life is inseparable from the interpretations that have been given to it. Modern interpretations seem to follow a pattern: after opposition to mythological and historicist interpretations, initially represented by Émile Senart and Hermann Oldenberg, comes a "middle way" that proposes to respect both legend and historical facts. But attaining this accord has been easier said than done. Yet for all the differences between waves of interpretation, one trait subsists: the will to sustain a linear biography, not only from birth to death, but from before the Buddha Śākyamuni's life (meaning his past lives) to after it (the posthumous course of his relics and the community he founded). It is this bias that must be brought into question.

1

THE LEGEND OF THE BUDDHA BETWEEN HISTORY AND MYTH

Buddhism is often presented academically in the order of the Three Refuges (or Three Jewels): Buddha, Dharma, and Sangha. According to this traditional sequence, the Buddha first was awakened, then began to teach the Dharma (the Buddhist Law or doctrine), and a community of disciples (the Sangha) gathered around him. In reality, without questioning the existence of a founding figure, it is the Buddhist institution that should come first, because it was the Sangha that created and modified the images of the Buddha and his doctrine that have come down to us. From this perspective, the Buddha is not a starting point but an end point, or rather a moving plurality of end points. The order of the Three Refuges should therefore be reversed,[1] though not without a certain circularity, for the image of the Buddha served as a model for practice and for an idealized Dharma and Sangha that constituted the horizon of the concrete Sangha. The Life of the Buddha became an "institution" in the sense that it was instituted by ecclesiastical orthodoxy rather than simply being based on the testimony of reliable witnesses.

For Western authors, the Life of the Buddha was very often treated as only a pretext to consideration of his doctrine—judged infinitely deeper than the religion that derived from it. The latter, with all its miracles, was mostly treated with indifference when it wasn't being condemned for its excesses and deviations from the original message. This book takes the opposite tack, that of sticking to the legendary narrative. But a few words must be said at the outset about the Buddhist teaching insofar as it was intimately linked to its presumed founder's life, the account of which evolved in accordance with doctrinal changes.

THE TWO VEHICLES

For a long time, commentators have contrasted two forms of Buddhism, or two "vehicles"—the so-called Lesser Vehicle, or Hīnayāna, and Greater Vehicle, or Mahāyāna, the first based essentially on texts in Pāli, the second on texts in

Sanskrit. This terminology is partly rejected today, and "Lesser Vehicle" has been replaced by terms without a pejorative connotation, the most common being Nikāya Buddhism—from the term designating certain groups of Pāli texts, and by extension the schools of ancient Buddhism. One of these schools spread throughout South and Southeast Asia (excepting Vietnam) under the name Theravāda, while the Greater Vehicle became the predominant form of Buddhism in Tibet, Mongolia, and the whole of East Asia (China, Korea, and Japan). Recently, the distinction between the two has been called into question from a sociological standpoint, as not designating socially (or geographically) distinct groups, such as those from different monasteries. Doctrinally, however, the distinction remains relevant in that it designates two doctrines that were sometimes radically different in their mythological, cosmological, and soteriological conceptions.

In many ways, Mahāyāna was a rewriting of early Buddhism and thus a reinterpretation of the Buddha as an ideal—insofar as that could be gleaned from the narrative of his life. Essentially, what the development of that narrative and its evolution over the centuries reflected was a doctrinal evolution as to the nature of the Buddha (and what the texts call his "buddha-nature"). In this context, we should probably speak of the two lives of the Buddha, in the sense that the Buddhist narratives of the *nikāyas* and those, often later, of the Mahāyāna reflected two different principles. The first group of narratives described the slow and painful ascent of the Bodhisattva (the future Buddha), through many past lives and during his last human life, to the ultimate truth. In the second group of narratives, this truth somehow came down to earth, and the Buddha's life was seen as but a shadow of a higher reality. Everything makes sense in this life, but the meaning differs in each case. In the first, the Buddha's life is an exemplar, offering a guide for future generations. In the second, each episode takes on a symbolic meaning—that is, with the rise of Mahāyāna, between the first and the fifth century CE, a radical change took place in the notion of the Buddha's (and all buddhas') life span: one now had to consider that the Buddha is basically eternal, and his earthly life is only an appearance, a "skillful means" (*upāya*) to save living beings.

With the emergence of the notion of a transcendent Buddha, the Buddha's "biography" and the problem it presented were posed very differently. The Tibetan historian Tāranātha (1575–1634) summed up the question well:

> It would be good, in my opinion, if those who state that their biography concerning Tathāgata derives "from the Three Caskets" [of the Buddhist canon] could differentiate between the texts of the Basic Vehicle and those of the Greater Vehicle. . . . It would be wrong to confuse the different levels, because it would result—and this is not desirable—in a text that belongs neither to the Greater Vehicle nor to the Basic Vehicle.[2]

For Tāranātha, it was clear that the Greater Vehicle, which taught the ultimate truth, is superior to the Basic Vehicle (read "Lesser Vehicle"), which reflected conventional truth. However, as a historian, he had to base his research on conventional truth—namely, that the Buddha lived at such and such a time and place: "Such elements are a matter of the Basic Vehicle and not of the Greater Vehicle. The latter reports precisely those activities of the Buddha that are inconceivable [such as miracles] and therefore very difficult to inscribe in specific events, periods, and places."[3] This distinction is crucial in that it points out the limits, but also the presuppositions, of the historicist approach.

THE LEGEND OF THE BUDDHA

As a preview, here in a few sentences is the gist of the legend of the Buddha. Most of the sources begin it at the moment when the being who is still called the Bodhisattva (he will become the Buddha only at the time of his supreme awakening), residing in Tuṣita Heaven after many terrestrial existences, gets ready to be reborn one last time to save sentient beings in this world. His conception is, as it should be, immaculate, as is his birth. The mother he has chosen, Māyā, is the wife of Śudhoddana, the king of a small kingdom in northern India. One night, she dreams that a white elephant penetrates her right side. In the morning, she finds herself pregnant, and ten months later she gives birth, in a grove in the park of Lumbinī, not far from the town of Kapilavastu. As soon as he is born, the child declares: "I alone am the World-honored One." But this happy event is overshadowed by the death of Māyā, seven days after the birth. The child is therefore raised by Māyā's sister, Mahāprajāpatī Gautamī, the second wife of Śuddhodana. Following predictions that the child will become either a universal monarch or a spiritual guide for humanity, his father decides to keep him in the palace to protect him from the harshness of reality and thus prevent any spiritual seeking. At the age of sixteen, the prince marries the lovely Yaśodharā, who soon gives him a child, Rāhula. Everything seems to push him toward a traditional career as a monarch. But his destiny awaits in the form of four encounters that occur during one (or more) excursion(s) out of the city: he meets an old man, a sick man, a corpse, and an ascetic (see plate 1). The first three encounters make him suddenly aware of the ephemeral, painful nature of existence; the fourth makes him glimpse the possibility of deliverance. Thus, at the age of twenty-nine, Prince Siddhārtha leaves the palace, abandoning his duties and prerogatives. For six long years he practices a severe asceticism, which leads him to the brink of death. After finally grasping the inanity of such practices, he opts for a "middle way" between pleasure and asceticism. He then has to undergo the assault of the evil one, Māra, from which he emerges victorious. From then on, nothing can stand in the way of his ultimate awakening, during which he reaches the four degrees of concentration (*dhyāna*), obtains knowledge of his past lives, and realizes the four "noble truths." He will spend the rest of a long life preaching his doctrine and gathering around him a community of disciples, effecting many conversions through his teaching and miracles. He dies at the age of eighty in a grove of *sāla* trees near the town of Kuśinagara, and the funeral gives rise to a succession of miracles. After the cremation of his body, his relics are divided among the kings of the neighboring principalities, and placed in stūpas which become objects of worship. In particular, the four stūpas commemorating his birth, awakening, first sermon, and parinirvāṇa seem to have become, from very early on, flourishing places of pilgrimage where the legend was becoming distilled while still settling. The Buddha's life thus took on an increasingly "monumental" aspect, in every sense of the word. By visiting these sacred sites, believers could relive each episode of the master's glorious life and anchor their imagination in these specific places. But the stūpas were also, and above all else, reliquaries. The relics of the Buddha were believed to have magical properties, and contact with them or even mere proximity increased the pilgrims' chances of happiness in this world and salvation in the next.

The history of early Buddhism is essentially that of a community of believers and pilgrims. The most eminent among them was to have a tremendous impact on the development of the new religion. It was King Aśoka (304–232 BCE), the third ruler of the Maurya dynasty, who extended his rule—and religion—to the whole of India. Aśoka made a pilgrimage to the presumed birthplace of the Buddha, the small town of Lumbinī in present-day Nepalese Therai, and erected a memorial pillar there. But, according to legend, he also built eighty-four thousand stūpas throughout India (and East Asia) to hold the relics of the Buddha. Without him, Buddhism might have remained a minority religion, like Jainism, which resembles it in many ways.

Relic worship played an essential role—just as much as, or perhaps even more than doctrine—in the expansion of Buddhism in Asia. However, with the emergence of a modernist construction of Buddhism in the nineteenth century came a trend toward demythologization, which discounted the history of the relics and images of the Buddha. The miracles performed by the Buddha, who now was presented as a social reformer, were no longer mentioned either.[4] Evidently, as the Buddha's story is constantly being reappropriated for ideological purposes, one might infer that, far from being closed, it continues to evolve.

IN SEARCH OF THE HISTORICAL BUDDHA

The linguist and Indianist Eugène Burnouf (1801–1852), one of the first Westerners to study Buddhist legend, emphasized the human personality and historical importance of the Buddha. "He lived, taught, and died as a philosopher, and his humanity remained so indisputably a fact recognized by all, that the legends, to which miracles cost so little, did not even try making him a god after his death."[5] As early as the second half of the nineteenth century, in reaction to what it perceived as "fabrications," a wave of historicism sought to reduce the legend of the Buddha to its simplest expression in the hope of rediscovering its historical substratum. Historians of Buddhism were encouraged in this direction by the efforts of biblical scholars to find the historical Jesus behind the Christ—efforts that culminated in the works of Alfred Loisy (1857–1940), who was excommunicated by the Vatican in 1908. Fortunately for the historians of Buddhism, there was no such thing as a Buddhist Vatican.

A Powerful Metaphor

Let us approach historicism through a recurring (not to speak of tenacious) metaphor, that of the *core*. For Ernest Renan (1823–1892), it was "only rather late in the day that the question was asked whether this legend, colored with brilliant reflections, contained a nucleus, or whether, like a soap bubble, it lacked a solid mass." This dilemma was quickly passed over, however, and only the "historical core" hypothesis was retained. Another metaphor, that of the grain of sand around which the oyster makes its pearl, could just as well have been used, but it would have made the legend too positive—a gem—and Buddhism a bivalve.

What credit can be given to the legend of the Buddha? According to E. J. Thomas, "The question remains for consideration whether we are justified in selecting from this legend the portions that appear credible, or whether the whole legend is not the invention of a period."[6] The goal was to bring out the "real" life of the Buddha, like the gold nugget that would fain be rid of its mythological dross. Thomas added: "For us, even with stricter methods of criticism, it is still more difficult to make a clear distinction between what may have been gradually incorporated and the original nucleus. But the nucleus is there, even though we may never succeed in separating it, or in deciding what the earliest form of it may have been."[7]

Most of the biographies we have of the Buddha are thus founded on dual criteria of credulity and skepticism—that is, the imperatives to retain any episode that presents itself in a realistic guise and to reject anything that smacks of the marvelous. The German historian Hermann Oldenberg (1854–1920) stands out in this regard: "If we now abstract from the traditions those of the categories indicated, which are wholly unhistorical, or are at least suspected to be of unhistorical character, we then have left as the very pith of these stories regarding Buddha a thread of facts, which we may claim to be a perfectly reliable, though, it may be, a very meagre, historical acquisition."[8] This methodology, paradoxically, led to both a proliferation and a rarefaction of discourse.

The metaphor of the nucleus can also be found in Alfred Foucher's description of the Buddha's "civil status," based on the "relatively recent date of his birth; names of his country, his birthplace, his family, his father and mother: so much information whose authenticity increases for us because it has resisted to the end the corrosion of later devotion. Let us treasure this small historical nucleus and, for the rest, let us leave the field free to the imagination of hagiographers without fear. . . . Afterwards, they will not fail to multiply in profusion the miraculous prodigies, premonitory dreams, celestial interventions, and exceptions to natural laws: they will never succeed, however, in completely erasing from the biography of the Buddha the indelible traces of his human personality and his historicity."[9] As André Couture notes, Foucher remained conscious of the limits facing the scholar: "Despite efforts to uncover a historical core or the initial fact, he must sometimes give up the task of disentangling the real from the fabulous.[10]

Unfortunately, there is no method that can separate the "man Gotama" from the Buddha of the legend. Those who claim, like Foucher, that this character "must" have existed carry on as if such a method does exist without ever explaining why they believe it is (or should be) so. It is therefore incumbent that the usual pattern be explicitly reversed: as far as we can judge, there did not exist, in early Buddhism, a simple biography of the Buddha on which legendary elements could have been grafted. At the beginning, we only find a number of legends that are not yet unified in a biography, even a basic one. Or, to resort again to the metaphor of the "core": there is no factual nucleus around which multiple legendary layers could have grown, the last one forming a shell. Similarly, there are no criteria for separating the historical fact from the many layers of myth and legend. The Life of the Buddha is like an onion, which can be peeled without ever revealing a kernel. This was already understood by Émile Senart, who wrote in his *Essay on the Legend of the Buddha:*

> The stories . . . are mixed of two elements: some visibly legendary and marvelous, others realistic or at least possible. . . . But an alternative arises in the presence of such dissimilar features: either the historical data are the primitive nucleus and the central focus, the legendary elements being a later work, in some way incidental, without the necessary cohesion; or, conversely, the mythological features form a whole linked by a superior and anterior unit to the character on whom they are here fixed, historical data, if there are any, being associated with them only by virtue of a secondary reworking. It is at the first point of view that we have stopped so far. The practical consequence has been that it is sufficient to remove all the implausible details; the rest should be regarded as proven history. I would like to show that, to this way of looking at things, it is decidedly appropriate to substitute the second one.[11]

But what's bred in the bones will come out in the flesh. As we shall see, despite Senart's warnings (but also as a reaction against certain excesses of his mythological method), most researchers could not help trying to find a historical Buddha, the only true one in their eyes. Once the Buddha is given a "civil status," as Foucher does, it becomes possible in principle to extract the historical facts from the myth. But this is begging the question. It seems just as fair to say that it is *not* that the basic elements have taken on the trappings of the myth, but rather that the myth from which these elements were extracted has ended up being passed off as history. How can we continue to believe in the truth of these elements when it turns out that none of our sources can serve as evidence? Is it because these elements, far from having the factual character they are believed to have, are in fact a construction, an abstraction drawn from mythical stories about a character named the Buddha? They are no more historical than the rest—the weed is no longer really a weed, but a rich grass. It is precisely the scientists who come to sow *discord* (another name for ryegrass) in the field of an otherwise fertile tradition. On the other hand, if one persists in affirming the historicity of these basic elements in the case of the historical Buddha, why not do the same for the other buddhas of the past whose biography is broadly the same? In reality, the narrative of the Buddha's Life, as it has come down to us, obeys certain narrative constraints, including a belief in karmic retribution.[12]

A JANUS-FACED BUDDHA

As Alfred Foucher noted: "We are dealing with a personality which is not only out of the ordinary, but which is truly two-faced, depending on whether we consider what it must have been in everyday reality or, on the other hand, what it has become in the imagination of its followers." For Foucher, the case was heard: "The Buddha was therefore an ordinary human being with his halo of more or less incommunicable experiences; it is no less true that he was transformed by the imagination of his followers. These two faces of the Buddha are historical: texts and archaeological remains tell us about them. And these two levels of reality demand to be appreciated for what they are."[13]

In spite of its claims to objectivity, moreover, the biography of the "historical" Buddha lent itself to all sorts of recuperative efforts. In the nineteenth century, he became a kind of Protestant reformer opposed to the excesses of Hindu Papism, or a militant revolutionary for an egalitarian society. As Michel Strickmann notes: "While Mahāyāna and Tantrism had transformed him [the Buddha] into an omnipotent cosmic deity, the English school of Pāli studies redesigned his portrait as a respectable Anglican agnostic, a proto-Victorian sage."[14]

At first glance, the thesis that the Buddha's legend is merely the embellished image of a real person seems reasonable. The texts of the Pāli tradition, in particular, claim to be based on certain historical data, and we also see in the monastic codes (the Vinaya) obvious efforts to present the Buddha as a pragmatic (or even down-to-earth) character, concerned about what people say. Historians point out, not without reason, that it is easier to mythologize a biography than to demythologize a legend. Criticism in search of authenticity has therefore focused on demonstrating the historicity of certain facts that seem to run counter to the Buddhist ideal. For example, according to Oldenberg, we must consider as true all the stories that are presented to us as if by chance, without responding to a didactic purpose or to introduce pathetic situations.[15] Thus, the dubious circumstances of the Buddha's death—following a poisoning due to the ingestion of pork—might at first sight sound more plausible than his miracles precisely because they are scandalous for a Buddhism that is in principle vegetarian. On the basis of this simple detail, Mettanando Bhikku and Oskar von Hinüber believed that this poisoning, too rapid for the development of an infection, instead indicates that "the Buddha suffered from mesenteric infarction caused by an occlusion of an opening of the superior mesenteric artery."[16] A "reality effect," however, is not reality itself, and there is nothing to suggest that we are not also dealing here with a pious invention—that is, a "salvific expedient" (*upāya*) intended to illustrate the truth of impermanence.

Historians tend to consider the events of the Buddha's old age as more authentic than those of his youth. Even more, they see the clearly legendary aspects, as described in late texts such as the *Lalitavistara,* as embellishments—a hagiography that would have perverted the early biography. In doing so, biographers forget that the reverse process—of simplification—is also plausible. It is indeed naive to believe that the seemingly realistic character of an anecdote like the fatal indigestion of the Buddha can be taken as a proof of its historicity. In fact, such anecdotes are probably just as artificial as legends. They often have no other interest or motivation than to justify obscure rules, and they have generally had no impact on Buddhist tradition—unlike legends, which are properly *legenda,* stories "to be read" (or recited).

Historical research swears by the original documents. In this case, it is essentially based on a reading of Pāli texts—edited for the most part at the end of the nineteenth century by the Pāli Text Society—and of some Sanskrit texts expurgated from their mythological "slag." On the other hand, texts deemed apocryphal because they were compiled outside India, and are essentially related to the Mahāyana, have been refused any claim to teach us anything about the "authentic" Buddha. Thus, referring to the *Mahāpadāna,* Thomas Rhys Davids stated:

> We find in this tract the root of that Birana-weed which, growing up along with the rest of Buddhism, went on spreading so luxuriantly that it gradually covered up much that was of value in the earlier teaching, and finally led to the downfall, in its home in India, of the ancient faith. The doctrine of the Bodhisatta, of the Wisdom-Being, drove out the doctrine of the Aryan Path. A gorgeous hierarchy of mythological wonder-workers filled men's minds, and the older system of self-training and self-control became forgotten.[17]

Yet it is among these "weeds" that we find some of the most beautiful jewels of Buddhist imagination and thought. Incidentally, the first Pāli texts are also "apocryphal," in a way, since they date from several centuries after the parinirvāṇa. The first known manuscript dates from the fifth century CE. It is this methodological bias that the Sinhalese anthropologist Stanley Tambiah criticizes when he evokes the "Pāli Text Society mentality."[18]

In contradiction to their own method, some historians believe they are allowed to jump over the centuries—roughly from the first century CE to the fifth century BCE—and do violence to sources that are essentially hagiographic or mythological, in order to transform them into so-called historical documents. Some go even further, since they form, from these later sources, the hypothesis of a basic text that would faithfully reflect the authentic life and teaching of the Buddha. However, in the present state of the documentation—but perhaps in a more essential way—it is not possible to rely on these Pāli texts to obtain any testimony on the real events of the Buddha's life. It is not simply that we have not yet found the key that would open the door to this biography, it is rather that there is no key—or at least that this key only opens the way to other fictions and not to a "historical" reality.

In the absence of a basic text that would reliably tell the life of the Buddha, most historians agree on a biography that is reduced to its simplest expression. But paradoxically, such a biography loses all historical character and becomes a simple archetype that could be valid for any Indian ascetic—Buddhist or not—or for any Buddha past or future. Ironically, we come back to the much derided thesis of Émile Senart, minus its solar mythology. Far from the "real life" of the Buddha having acquired, with time, a legendary character, it is on the contrary the legend that has been transformed into the rudiments of history, into an abstraction empty of content that wants to pass itself off as a set of facts. In response to those who make it their business to "pierce the mists of Buddhist legend," we must therefore ask ourselves why, in the absence of any proof, we are so keen to believe that these mists are indeed hiding someone, and why any skepticism in this area is considered misplaced.

However, let us take the historians at their word. What remains of the Life of the Buddha once the legend has been sifted by the critics? If one sticks to the results of archaeological excavations and the (approximate) Indian context of the time, all that can be said with any degree of certainty can be summed up in a few words. At a not very definite time, five or six centuries BCE, a person named Siddhārtha Gautama (or Gotama), or Śākyamuni, because he was from the Śākya clan, is said to have lived in northern India. Having renounced the world, he had a long period of asceticism and, at its end, a spiritual experience described as awakening (or enlightenment), which earned him the name of Buddha, the Awakened One. He is also said to have founded a monastic order that developed and spread throughout India, mainly due to the conversion of King Aśoka. Later, the new religion spread throughout the rest of Asia, not without considerable changes as it came in contact with new cultures.

This biographical note, although plausible, is also perfectly generic. In reality, the Life of the Buddha is both a doctrinal digest and a paradigm of Buddhist practice. All buddhas and Buddhist saints are supposed to go through the same stages as the Buddha Śākyamuni: a spiritual crisis, followed by renunciation of the world and an ascetic existence, which leads to awakening and the attainment of supernormal powers (*abhijñā*), years of preaching, jealousies over his success and criticism of a corrupt society, then a death foretold and a funeral resulting in a cult of stūpas and relics.

Moreover, this critical biography does not take into account the fact that, for the vast majority of Buddhists, a completely different "Life" of the Buddha has been passed down over the centuries, a history made up of a multitude of stories of diverse origins, which prove to be far superior to the so-called facts—which are, basically, what Bruno Latour calls *factish,* a hybrid of fact and fetish.[19] It is to these narratives, in their aim and effects, that Buddhism owes much of its vitality over the centuries and up to the present day. For ordinary Buddhists, who did not have access to philosophical or doctrinal texts, the Life of the Buddha in words or images, as they heard it told or saw it represented in monasteries, was the main means of identifying with their tradition. This Life had not passed through any hypercriticism, so it was rich in prodigies of all kinds. There is therefore no reason to despise the stories, quite the contrary. Without them, Buddhism would perhaps be only a minor current of Hinduism today; or at worst a word empty of referent and meaning. All in all, a frankly mythological fiction seems better than a historical fiction that is all the more insidious because it does not speak its name.

BIRTH OF A BIOGRAPHY

To the methodological presuppositions of historians, we must add epistemological or cultural presuppositions that have led us to approach the life of the Buddha with a Western conception of biography that is ill suited to account for the life of such a person. His biography, in its broad outlines, is so well known to us that it seems to go without saying. A deceptive impression. It is too easily forgotten that the story, even in its simplest form, was constructed and the result of a slow percolation of numerous elements. Just like the origins of the doctrine, those of the Buddhist legend are multiple and do not constitute in any way the "piously preserved" memory of a great man. We must therefore reject the idea that the biography of the Buddha was "dispersed" in many passages of the Vinaya texts before finally being "reunited" by historians. It emerged gradually, like a melody against a background of noise, from a profusion of heterogeneous material from a wide variety of document types and literary genres. These materials were subsequently homogenized, unified as far as possible by the compilers, for the needs of the biographical cause (a bit like a skeleton reconstituted from bones of different origins). The elaboration of the Buddha's biography from scattered fragments actually brings to mind the discovery of the Piltdown man (1910), announced as the missing link between ape and man, and unmasked as a deception—human skull and jawbone of a great ape—only in the 1950s. It also evokes literary criticism as practiced in the imaginary world of Jorge Luis Borges's Tlön: "The critics often invent authors: they select two dissimilar works—the *Tao-te ching* and the *1001 Nights,* say—attribute them to the same writer and then determine most scrupulously the psychology of this interesting *homme de lettres.*"[20]

DEVELOPMENT OF THE LEGEND

According to André Bareau, there was a rudimentary biography during the Buddha's lifetime: "Shortly after [the extinction], the numerous gaps in this primitive biography were filled by various and increasingly numerous legends, either invented from scratch or borrowed from the rich Indian folklore."[21] From such beginnings, the account of the Life of the Buddha certainly evolved, and it is possible to follow, in broad outline, the stages of this evolution. For Étienne Lamotte, it developed in five phases: first there were "biographical fragments" in various canonical texts in Pāli or in Sanskrit; then "fragmentary biographies"; autonomous but incomplete "lives"; "complete biographies," composed outside India and in languages other than Pāli or Sanskrit; finally, in some Sinhalese chronicles, "amplified compilations," providing a tighter—though incomplete—chronology. As John Strong notes, "These sources are interesting for the local twists and turns they give to the stories about the Buddha, and also for the way they attempt to answer some of the problems and questions about the Buddha's life that the more 'classical' sources, whether deliberately or not, had left unanswered (or even asked)."[22]

The prevailing opinion among Indianists is that the biography of the Buddha must have developed from an event that had made a deep impression on his contemporaries, namely, his extinction or parinirvāṇa, whose account therefore very likely remained close to historical reality. From there, hagiographers supposedly went back to the youth and awakening of the Buddha, and then, to fill the gap between these two summits, they invented all sorts of stories of conversions and miracles. There seems to have been in fact two cycles, even two different traditions, one centered on the awakening and the circumstances leading to it, the other on the final extinction. Lamotte opted for a slightly different sequence, however. According to him, the successors of the Buddha were interested first in his awakening, before going back to his birth and the beginnings of his preaching.[23] Once the biographical gaps had been filled, the Buddha's life developed progressively upstream, with the previous lives of the Bodhisattva, going back further and further in time; and downstream, with the history of the posthumous destiny of the Buddha's relics and that of his community.[24] At the same time, as Lamotte noted, the sequence of events after the first sermon became ever tighter, resulting in a veritable chronology of summer retreats (during the rainy season), the account of which was increasingly stripped of marvelous occurrences.[25]

As a thesis, the "developmental" model is not without value, but it has the disadvantage of suggesting that one could, by going into reverse, return to the sources, to an "original" Buddhism and to the Buddha himself. Whether historians like it or not, the Buddha remains the virtual, and not the real, focus of a cumulative biography whose diversity and richness should be emphasized. As far back as one can go, we are always *in medias res,* and the events that precede are only recounted—or rather invented—after the fact. It therefore seems better to linger on the irreplaceable panoramic views that are offered at such and such a detour along the way. From this nomadic perspective, the antiquity of a text or tradition no longer implies its intrinsic superiority. The narratives of the Life of the Buddha are no longer perceived as more or less exact reflections of the events in the life of a historical character, but as a place of creativity and change. In other words: "Si non e vero e ben trovato" (Even if it is not true, it is a good story).

Small narrative streams make large biographical rivers. The Life of the Buddha as it has come down to us—like a long, meandering river fed by numerous tributaries, periodically overflowing from its deep bed—reflects the cultural abundance of twenty-five centuries of history. In the course of time, with the multiplication of sources, there has been a proliferation of events, people, and places. Conversely, recent biographies, influenced by Buddhist modernism (or neo-Buddhism), are sometimes almost empty of substance and reduced to a kind of narrative skeleton that no longer has much to do with the traditional Buddha and Buddhism. Indeed, what is the basis of such a biography? Essentially, a written tradition several centuries later than the presumed time of the Buddha (i.e., around the beginning of our era), taking up diverse and fluctuating oral traditions, which had also given rise, from the second and third centuries BCE, to a fragmentary iconography (Indian bas-reliefs of Sanchi, Bharhut, etc.). Nevertheless, it was not until about seven centuries later that a more or less complete "biography" was produced. Yet historians acted as if this ideal biography had always been there, as a watermark, and they made it the framework of their own biographies. Then they impoverished their account by stripping it of all that seemed legendary while insisting on place names and historical context to produce what Roland Barthes called a "reality effect."[26] In this way, they brought to the forefront anecdotes that had little value to tradition while ignoring episodes that inspired generations of Buddhists. Despite their sophistication, they seemed to pass over any recognition that their version of the "facts" was just as constructed, and therefore ideological, as that of the tradition. Of course, they were not alone, and everyone could see the Buddha at his or her door. Thus, if the miracles of the birth and youth of the Bodhisattva found a certain success with the laity, the emphasis for the monks was on the great departure and the advent of preaching. The Therāvadin, for example, tried to establish a chronology of the beginnings of the Buddha's preaching and were less interested in the Buddha's youth. The Sinhalese chronicles, in particular, framed their account of the Buddha's life with the mythical story of the various lineages that led to it and the later history of his doctrine and relics. The existence of the historical Buddha was thus embedded in the casket of an infinitely longer sacred Life and an infinitely larger sacred history, that of an immemorial Buddhist tradition.

Even after the parinirvāṇa, the story (or rather the legend) continued. Parallel to the elaboration of biographies that were more or less complete (going from birth to the awakening and/or extinction), different fragments and cycles (stories involving the relics, stūpas, or images) emerged and developed independently, sometimes overshadowing the Buddha's life itself. Sinhalese chronicles such as the *Thūpavaṃsa* and the *Dhātuvaṃsa,* for example, gave a colorful story of the Tooth of the Buddha. Other sources reported the adventures of the Emerald Buddha, an icon that became the palladium of the Thai dynasty. Buddhism adapted to new countries by proclaiming that the Buddha had visited them, leaving his shadow or footprints as proof of his presence—in Sri Lanka, Central Asia, and Korea. Foucher was one of the first to have compared the development of the Buddha's legend with the geographical expansion of Buddhism, but he drew up an additional argument against the legend: "Later, when his religion spread throughout the [Indian] peninsula and conquered Ceylon and Gandhāra, it was inevitable that the legend gave the devotion of the inhabitants of these new holy lands the satisfaction of believing that their ancestors had once received the visit of the Blessed One. . . . But these tales have just as much value as those that make Jesus Christ travel to Brittany."[27]

According to the Sinhalese chronicles (*Dīpavaṃsa, Mahāvaṃsa*), the Buddha visited Ceylon (Sri Lanka) three times during the first eight years after his awakening. The *Treatise on the Great Perfection of Wisdom* states: "The Buddha Śākyamuni, born in Jambudvīpa, lived in Kapilavastu but frequently visited the six major cities of East India. One day, he went flying to South India. . . . Another day, he went to North India, to the kingdom of Yueche; he subdued the dragon king Apalāla; then, going to the west of the kingdom of Yueche, he subdued the [demon] Rākṣasī and stayed in his cave, and the shadow of the Buddha has remained there, as it is, until now."[28] Further avenues were opened with the Buddha's observations that certain episodes in his life took place outside India—for example, his statement that Vulture Peak, the setting for his preaching of the *Lotus Sūtra,* had been magically transported through the air to a faraway land. One of the scriptures of Mahāyāna, the *Laṅkāvatāra-sūtra,* takes the Buddha to the island of the Rākṣasa demons to give his teaching to Rāvaṇa, their king.[29] In a late Thai text, Ratanapañña Thera's *The Wreath of*

Garlands from the Conqueror's Times (Jinakālamālīpakaraṇaṁ), the Buddha flies from Benares (now Vanarasi) to Hari-puñjaya in northern Thailand.[30] All the chronicles of the great Thai monasteries begin with the visit of the Buddha to the monastery. In a way, the Life of the Buddha became the *commons* wherein a host of different motivations came to be merged and concealed—instrumental (origins of the Vinaya rules, framework of the sūtras), sentimental or poetic (*Buddhacarita*), political (legitimization of a dynasty), sectarian (history of the sangha), nationalist (transmission of the Dharma in Sri Lanka and Thailand), and so on. Thus it was not only a point of arrival, but also a point of departure for new discourses touching on mythological, ritual, and other dimensions.

So if the narrative remained important in Mahāyāna, we can also see developing in it a tendency that could be described as anti-narrative, which accepts the narrative of the Buddha's life but strips it of its content, making it a kind of external decoration (as on the balustrades of Sanchi's Indian stūpa), an ornament that is legitimized by the presence of a higher principle, the true, timeless, cosmic Buddha enshrined as the relic at the heart of the stūpa. We find there, in another form, the principle of the two truths, esoteric and exoteric, of Mahāyāna.

FOR ANOTHER APPROACH

As we have seen, the historical method claimed to be different from hagiography. However, one would be condemned to understanding nothing of Buddhism if one were to ignore the hagiography or try to reduce it to the biography of a "historical" Buddha. As Michel de Certeau remarks: "It is also impossible to consider hagiography solely in terms of its 'authenticity' or 'historical value': this would be equivalent to submitting a literary genre to the laws of another genre—historiography—and to dismantling a proper type of discourse only in order to engage its contrary."[31] To reject as late fabulations the legends that developed around the Buddha is to underestimate the creativity of generations of Buddhists who sought to express, through a lovingly concocted image, their highest aspirations and deepest visions. Moreover, these "affabulations" offer us valuable information, if not about the Buddha himself, at least about the thoughts and ulterior motives of the individuals, groups, and cultures that developed them. The fact that these stories were invented—as if all the "facts" that constitute a biography were not constructed—does not diminish their value; on the contrary, they attest to the inventiveness, the genius, of those Asian cultures—beginning with India—that were able to give life to a multiform ideal.

Just as it is impossible to disentangle the biography of Śākyamuni from his legend, it is virtually impossible to reconstruct the Buddha's original teaching. Even assuming that the oral tradition remained faithful to it, given the incredible diversity of the later tradition, it is reasonable to assume that Buddhist doctrine evolved considerably over the four centuries between the written record and its living source. According to tradition, the first texts were written in Pāli toward the end of the first century BCE, but in fact the oldest known Pāli manuscript dates from the fifth century CE, while the oldest Sanskrit manuscripts, recently found in Gandhāra, date from the first two centuries.

Even the theory of the Four Truths, generally held to be the heart of the first sermon, does not appear in the early sources. In other words, whatever the original Buddhism—the *verbatim* teaching of the Buddha—may have been, the only accessible Buddhism is that of his self-proclaimed heirs, and their inheritance, by the very fact of its transmission, was undoubtedly changed in the process. The simple idea of an initial inheritance, preserved more or less intact beneath later accretions and capable of being rediscovered, seems doubtful at best. The Buddha's doctrine could as easily have been wholly or partly invented by his so-called heirs, a probability, even if true, that still would not take away any of its soteriological or philosophical value.

Despite its claims to universality, Buddhism supposedly reflects the religious experience of a charismatic individual. If so, how was the truth of the Law (Dharma) to be established before the appearance of the Buddha Śākyamuni? Theravāda solved the problem by denying its historicity, which was accomplished through the proliferation of mythological narratives dating back to time immemorial. As his past lives multiplied, the Buddha was effectively "de-historicized": he was no longer the individual Śākyamuni but a series of characters who appeared in different times and settings, though bound by the same karma.

The majority of Western writings on the Buddha and his doctrine accepted as obvious the historical character of the central figure, thus confusing the biography of the Buddha with investigating the origins of Buddhism. In other words, by positing the existence of a pure or original Buddhism to which one could try to get closer in time and space, the resulting approach led to the devaluing of both non-Indian Buddhism and subsequent developments in the narrative of the Buddha's life. It is the consequences of these presuppositions on our conception of the Buddha and his teaching that need to be questioned now.

Most researchers claim to be searching for a middle way between hagiography and historicist reductionism, but their search for an "authentic" life, anchored in concrete events, leads to an impasse. And it is not simply for lack of documents, as one might think. In wanting to make the Buddha a *man,* one should, logically, concentrate more on his fatal indigestion than on his awakening, because the latter remains, essentially or by nature, beyond the reach of biographers. It is a non-event from a biographical point of view. Therefore it has hardly attracted the attention of historians.

The accounts that constitute the Life of the Buddha are a protean genre that over the centuries has persisted in overflowing the Procrustean bed of biography, turning the life story of the historical Buddha into just one of his many transformations. There are others, equally worthy of study, that make the Buddha a paradigm of religious practice, a divine or cosmic being, even a character in a novel. But before turning to these, it will be useful to gain some perspective on the course and stakes of Western historiography, which for so long has put these other guises beyond the pale.

In the pages that follow, I begin by giving a historical overview of the studies that marked, in the twentieth century, the Life of the Buddha. Since this field was dominated from the outset by the sharp opposition between mythological and historical approaches, one might just as well describe this evolution as the progressive occupation of structurally determined positions in order to focus on the structures of thought rather than the history of the (perhaps illusory) "progress" of that thought. That is, if the understanding of Buddhism requires a detailed knowledge of its history, historicism, by taking the Buddha's history back to its origins—necessarily virtual given the state of documentation—is the obstacle that has to be removed in order to survey that history's development. In other words, to deconstruct a biographical approach that masks the discontinuities and tensions within the Buddhist tradition, we must insist above all on the nonlinear character of the Buddha's Life.

2

A BIT OF HISTORIOGRAPHY

Before returning to the methodological biases that have plagued studies of the Life of the Buddha, we must quickly review the main theses that have dominated this field. Buddhist studies took off in the mid-nineteenth century with the work of Eugène Burnouf (1801–1852) and the first triumphs of philology and historicism.[1] While Burnouf was on the whole respectful of Buddhism, limiting himself to deploring certain (Mahāyānist) "deviations" from the "authentic" Buddhist tradition in Pāli, that constraint was dropped by his disciple, the philosopher Jules Barthélémy Saint Hilaire (1805–1895), who rejected Buddhism en bloc, and whose popular book *The Buddha and His Religion* (1862) had a resonance at least as important as that of his master.[2] After reading his extremely simplified and polemical interpretation, the German philologist and orientalist Friedrich Max-Müller (1823–1900) wrote: "Here, in simple terms, is the life of the Buddha. It seems to us much more touching in the eloquent pages of M. Barthélémy Saint Hilaire than in the bombastic accounts of Buddhist legends."[3]

A PROBLEMATIC DICHOTOMY

Methodologically, the two main approaches to the subject were inaugurated by Émile Senart, "the most brilliant of mythographers," and Hermann Oldenberg, "the champion of historiographers who have tried to uncover the dry framework of history under the prolix coating of myths."[4] The controversy that brought these two into opposition has more than a purely historical interest, for it was this opposition that determined from the outset the terms of the ensuing, rather sterile debate on the biography of the Buddha, giving these two tutelary figures a quasi-mythological character. Following them, researchers divided into two camps: mythologists such as the orientalist Johann Hendrik Caspar Kern (1833–1917) and the art historian Ananda Coomaraswamy (1877–1947), relying on Sanskrit sources, and philologists or historians such as Thomas William Rhys Davids (1843–1922) and Caroline Augusta Foley Rhys Davids (1857–1942), relying on Pāli sources. In between the two was Max-Müller, who, though he was full of praise for comparative mythology à la Senart, nonetheless considered myths to be "diseases of language."

The subsequent emergence of Edward Joseph Thomas (1869–1958) in the 1920s began a tendency to emphasize the inadequacy of the two approaches and the need to compare, not only Indian (Pāli and Sanskrit) sources, but also Chinese and Tibetan. In the 1940s and 1950s, new, less doctrinaire attempts were made by Ernst Waldschmidt (1897–1985), Alfred Foucher (1865–1952), Erich Frauwallner (1878–1974), and Étienne Lamotte (1903–1983). Nevertheless, the historicist approach returned in force from the 1960s onward with the work of André Bareau (1921–1993) in France, Heinz Bechert (1932–2005) in Germany, and Richard Gombrich (1937–) in England.

Émile Senart and the Mythological Approach

Historians of Buddhism have tended to view the Buddha's life as if it existed in a purely Buddhist setting, often neglecting the relationship between Buddhism and other Indian religions. But for Émile Senart (1847–1928), the correct method for a biography of the Buddha "could only be the comparative method."[5] Although he became the example not to be followed, he was not entirely wrong when he emphasized the essentially mythological nature of the received account of the Buddha's life. According to him, "the legend of the Buddha does not represent a real *life,* even one colored by certain fanciful inventions; it is essentially the epic glorification of a certain mythological and divine type that popular respect has been able to fix like a halo on the head of a perfectly human, perfectly real cult founder."[6] For Senart, it was not so much the life of the historical Buddha that was masked by the many legendary additions, but an older myth in which the Buddha was perceived as a solar deity, a myth that was later reduced to human dimensions. At the same time, Senart denied (or rather relativized) the importance of the Pāli canon dear to historians, in which he saw a belated attempt to make a fabric of legends and myths a little more plausible. As Donald Lopez notes, "For Senart, the Buddha of the Pāli canon is a demythologized myth, an attempt to make the myth a man."[7] This is not to say that Senart was denying the possibility that a real individual served as a basis for the image of the Buddha that was constructed; his position was simply that "a Buddha may have lived; the Buddha known to us never existed."[8]

In particular, Senart criticized what Louis de La Vallée Poussin termed the "method of subtraction"—of arriving at historical truth by subtracting the legend, thus conceiving of historical truth as a sort of zero degree of the narrative. For him, in contrast, the mythological elements formed a coherent system that anticipated incorporation in the Life of the Buddha. He accepted the existence of historical elements in the Buddha's life, but believed that they belong to different traditions.[9] The fact that Pāli sources seemed less inclined to the miraculous did not, in his opinion, guarantee their authenticity: "A priori, this brevity, this apparent simplicity of the Pāli data admits a double explanation. It may come from the fact that these versions are more primitive, more authentic; it may also come from the fact that they have been reworked and simplified."[10] A rather similar point of view was recently supported by Gregory Schopen, a historian who cannot be suspected of having any sympathy for the mythological approach.[11]

We can see in Senart a structuralist *avant la lettre* who based his method on Indian conceptions of the Buddha, not on Western conceptions. It is regrettable that he felt obliged in the end to impose his interpretations—with less nuance (but no less imagination) than a Lévi-Strauss. His method was indeed reductive, sometimes turning into an interpretative delirium. But it would be wrong to retain only what can be caricatured and to throw the baby out with the bathwater, as almost all subsequent researchers have done. Senart himself, moreover, warned us against such a view: "It suffices that these data be generally recognized as mythological; no matter what naturalistic foundation they rest on. . . . Does this mean that I intend to present the Buddha as an astronomical entity, and Buddhism as a sidereal religion, as a naturalist mythology? No competent reader will attribute such a ludicrous viewpoint to me."[12]

Senart found some defenders among his contemporaries, notably Ernest Renan, who described him as follows:

> [He] showed that the narrative account that has hitherto been considered the life of Buddha is less a legendary biography than a mythological concoction, made up of earlier elements, most of them of naturalist origin. Placing the Buddhist legend in its Hindu context better than had been done, [he] tried to prove that this legend was only the development of the cycle of ideas that Brahmanism had grouped around Vishnu Narayana. . . . He did not deny . . . the existence of a real character that served, if not as a substratum, at least as a prop for the legend; but he believed that euhemeristic attempts to discern, in such a case, the myth from the real are sterile. According to [him], the legend of the Buddha does not allow us to affirm the existence of Shākyamuni any more than the *Mahābhārata* and the *Puranas* allow us to affirm the existence of Krishna. He only thought that we have given Shākyamuni too much historical consistency, that we have complacently transformed, by arbitrary cuts, a fabric of formulas conceived a priori into a more or less plausible form of history. . . . The point at which Mr. Senart completely triumphs is when he develops the idea that the Buddha legend does not in some way belong to Buddhism, that it is an accommodation, a new version of ancient popular traditions unified earlier in the Vishnu cycle, with a human being taking the place of the divine master of Vishnuism.[13]

Among Buddhist specialists, Louis de La Vallée Poussin was one of the rare ones to defend Senart: "The legend of Śākyamuni, or, more precisely, of the Buddha—because the historical personality disappears behind the type—is not a legend strictly speaking, the glorified memory of a very wise and revered master."[14] The discrepancy, he explained, was this: "A slow transformation of the remembrance of Śākyamuni, leading to the divine type of the Buddha, would seem less implausible if, in the canonical or deuterocanonical literature, we were dealing with accidental or incoherent data. . . . But . . . the legend is made up of elements which are certainly not euhemeristic, and which form a block. It was visibly fed by the torrent of sources that overflow in Vishnuite, or, in general, Hindu mythologies."[15]

Perhaps the time has come to rehabilitate certain aspects of Senart's method. To be sure, his "mythologism," insofar as it imposes its own mythology on the materials, today seems dated and simplistic. But he did at least look for the logic of the myth, which historians generally consider to be a senseless hodgepodge. However, he was still under the spell of the comparative mythology of his time, which tended, unfortunately, to amalgamate all cultures.[16]

Hermann Oldenberg and the Historicist Approach

Hermann Oldenberg (1854–1920) defended the reliability of Pāli sources and rejected Senart's theses in the same gesture. He attacked Senart in the first part of his major work, *The Buddha, His Life, His Doctrine, His Order,* accusing him of denying the Buddha's historicity: "[Has] Buddha ever lived? . . . That ingenious student of Indian antiquity who has occupied himself most closely with this question, *Emile Senart,* answers it with an absolute NO."[17] A few pages later, however, Oldenberg seems to qualify his position: "In Senart's opinion, Buddha, the real Buddha, did exist, it is true: his reality, he admits, is a logical necessity, inasmuch as we see the reality of the Church founded by him; but beyond this bare reality there is nothing substantial."[18] Oldenberg points out the weaknesses of his opponent's resolutely mythological interpretation: "Senart seeks to trace step by step in the history of Buddha's life, the history of the life of the sun-hero: like the sun from the clouds of night, he issues from the dark womb of Mâyâ; a flash of light pierces through all the world when he is born; Mâyâ dies like the morning-cloud which vanishes before the sun's rays. Like the sun-hero conquering the thunder Demon, Buddha vanquishes Mâra, the Tempter, in dire combat, under the sacred tree; the tree is the dark cloud-tree in heaven."[19] And he concludes: "We may say in a word: the components which go to make up the history of the attainment of Buddhahood, and, we may add, countless similar narratives in the legends of Buddha, are not to be explained by reference to the mythology of the Veda, and still less to that of the Edda, but by the dogmatics of the Buddhist doctrine of deliverance and the external conditions and habits of Buddhist monastic life."[20]

Oldenberg violently rejected Senart's thesis, who saw in the life of the Buddha a version of the archetypal account of the life of the sun god. According to Oldenberg, the identification of the Buddha as a solar hero is based on mythological lucubrations. This clear-cut difference is due, as he himself pointed out, to a different interpretation of the sources and, in particular, to a different evaluation of the Pāli canon, which he held to be the only one to provide credible information on the historical Buddha and his doctrine.[21] It is for this very reason that Senart's attempt, based on Sanskrit sources such as the *Lalitavistara* (3rd–4th cent. CE), was for Oldenberg doomed from the start. He remarks: "But would it be allowable for anyone who undertook to write a criticism of the Life of Christ, to set aside the New Testament and follow solely the apocryphal gospels or any of the legendary works whatsoever of the Middle Ages?"[22] Oldenberg concedes that his "scientific" position is based on his intimate belief: "It is, therefore, evident that the narrative concerned *may be* a myth. . . . But showing that a thing *may be a myth* is not equivalent to showing that it *is* a myth."[23] Later, he adds: "In this sense it is quite possible that this narrative may cover a real fact. . . . Let each individual come to a conclusion, or refrain from coming to a conclusion, as he thinks proper; let me, for my part, declare my belief that, in the narrative of how the Sakya youth became the Buddha, there is really an element of historical memory."[24]

While Senart was mainly interested in popular Buddhism, Oldenberg sought "true" Buddhism in the practice of monks, which was in principle focused on the search for deliverance. Louis de La Vallée Poussin, for his part, noted that Buddhism was from the outset the religion both of the masses and of the clergy, the dividing line running within the clergy itself, a lax and urban clergy standing against forest ascetics. He criticized Oldenberg's work on this point: "The Buddha takes on too precise a physiognomy in this book, being partly Socratic, partly evangelical, not at all Hindu; the Buddha's teaching is rationalized: all mysticism, ecstasy, and supernatural powers are excluded—and at the same time it is simplified: the technique of the path of deliverance is almost ignored. . . . Any traditional datum which, from the point of view of myth or dogma, fits uneasily into the framework of this overly well composed book, is, if not concealed, at least politely dismissed; the epic or supernatural scenes and features are volatilized in a radical euhemerism. Oldenberg's Buddhism is one in which, by his own admission, the dogma of the Buddha is unimportant—hence a Buddhism cut off in its vital parts."[25]

Thomas Rhys Davids

Despite these criticisms, Oldenberg's influence proved to be lasting, and it partly explains the lack of interest, until recently, in the vernacular traditions of Southeast Asia, considered irrelevant because they were local and late. This influence can be found notably in the English scholar Thomas William Rhys

Davids (1843–1922), one of the founders of the Pāli Text Society, who made the texts of the Pāli canon available long before those of the Sanskrit and Chinese canons, and at the same time determined the major directions of Western "Buddhology."[26] On many points, Rhys Davids merely repeated and developed Oldenberg's arguments. He believed that the Pāli texts reflect the authentic teachings of the Buddha: "In one breath we are reminded of the scholastic dulness [sic], the sectarian narrowness, the literary incapacity of the Ceylon Buddhists. In the next we are asked to accept propositions implying that they were capable of forging extensive documents so well, with such historical accuracy, with so delicate a discrimination between ideas current among themselves and those held centuries before, with so great a literary skill in expressing the ancient views, that not only did they deceive their contemporaries and opponents, but European scholars have not been able to point out a single discrepancy in their work. It is not unreasonable to hesitate in adopting a scepticism which involves belief in so unique, and therefore so incredible, a performance."[27]

The method Rhys Davids recommended is to "compare the different versions of each episode in order to reach its earliest forms; it is then to discuss this narrative in order to determine whether, or to what extent, it can be explained in its entirety by hero-worship, simple poetic imagery, misunderstanding, a desire to edify, the application to Gotama of pre-existing stories, solar myths, etc." It is here, in the most difficult part of the inquiry, that he thought there would always be a great deal of disagreement, but he believed that substantial progress could be made.[28] Like Oldenberg, Rhys Davids criticized Sanskrit works such as the *Buddhacarita* (2nd half of the 2nd cent.) and the *Lalitavistara,* which can in no way be regarded as "historical biographies" and therefore should not be used by a historian worthy of the name. At most, the historical value of these texts "is the very instructive way in which they show how far the older beliefs about the life of the Buddha had been, at the time when these books were composed, developed (or rather corrupted) by the inevitable hero-worship of the followers of his religion."[29] Such fixation on a purely textual corpus, one limited to Pāli besides, is what scholars such as Alfred Foucher and Étienne Lamotte would come to question.

FOUCHER AND THE ELUSIVE "MIDDLE WAY"

Toward the middle of the twentieth century, new biographical attempts were made by Alfred Foucher, who took up the Life of the Buddha on the basis of new types of material, namely, archaeological and iconographic discoveries; Étienne Lamotte, who undertook the translation of an enormous Buddhist Summa Theologica, the *Treatise on the Great Perfection of Wisdom* (Ch. *Dazhidulun;* hereafter abbreviated as *Treatise*), attributed to Nāgārjuna (2nd cent. CE); and André Bareau, who subjected the texts to close criticism.

Foucher's *The Life of Buddha* remains a classic, in many ways emblematic but problematic as well. I will therefore indulge in making extensive references to it. Foucher presented himself as a "reader of images," and the back and forth that he orchestrated between texts and monuments clearly privileged the latter. In his view, "the figurative tradition has the appreciable advantage over the written tradition of having reached us (except for accidental mutilation) as it came out of the artist's hands, while the texts have undergone many tendentious revisions under the pen of their overzealous compilers."[30] He even thought that figurative representations may, at a certain point, have generated texts,[31] and argued that the scenes of the Life of the Buddha are arranged according to topography and not according to chronology, which is subordinate to it.[32] In Foucher's mind, his knowledge of the terrain gave him an advantage over his colleagues (and rivals): "None of the European exegetes . . . has, as far as we know, begun by accomplishing the eight great Buddhist pilgrimages."[33] Where so many others had failed, he believed himself capable of providing a credible biography—while remaining conscious of the limits of his method: "Mythologists had warned us: by stripping the Buddha of the sumptuous mantle of his legend, one exposes oneself to find underneath only a sort of badly squared joist, good at most to crystallize around itself the beliefs and myths which floated in suspension in its environment."[34]

Foucher too criticized Senart's mythological interpretations, which he considered outdated: "To take Senart's thesis in all its rigor, the Buddha would no longer be a historical figure, hardly an entity, a postulate, a pretext for crystallizing around itself a whole set of mythical narratives; and these narratives, familiar to all our Indo-European mythologies . . . , would relate uniformly to the marvelous adventures of the solar hero." The theme of the solar hero allowed him to give free rein to his sarcastic verve: "We know how far we've come since then, after we realized that the theory of the solar myth was a key to every door and a saddle for every horse. How easy it was, for example, to season in this way the biography of Napoleon and show that he was born on an island in the sea (Corsica), setting the East ablaze with the first fires of his glory (the campaigns of Italy and Egypt), and then pursued his triumphant career amidst the signs of the zodiac represented by his marshals until finally defeated in a supreme struggle against the powers of cold and darkness (the retreat from Russia), he agonized and died at the bottom of the southern ocean (in St. Helena)."[35] Thus, concluded Foucher, "it was all right for Oldenberg to claim the rights of history against the intransigence of this purely mythological conception."[36]

One cannot fail to be struck by Foucher's style, whether one likes it or not. For my part, I confess that I have developed a taste for it, although it is too often put at the service of a certain orientalist condescension. Witness this passage, rich in metaphors, which deserves to be quoted in extenso, not only for its style but also for the way it poses the problem—rejecting in advance the reductionism that will inspire the rest of his work:

> Thus, we can better understand why European criticism has naturally adopted two very different attitudes in the face of this inextricable mixture of reality and ideal, truth and fiction, history and myth. It was, if such a comparison may be permitted, as if faced with one of those almost impenetrable thickets made of tangled, centuries-old trunks, multiplied boughs, intertwined branches and vines—what to do in the presence of such a massif? Just go around it, figuring out its canopy or its luxuriant efflorescences, recognizing in them the spontaneous products of Indian soil . . . in short, look in the Buddhist legend for a pretext to compose a herbarium of the mythical flora of the Ganges basin? The result is certainly not lacking in interest; but it is to condemn oneself in advance to ignoring the true meaning of the giant of the forest that carries without weakening, like a royal mantle, this moving network of parasitic vegetation. Do we want instead to pierce this enigma? We will have to proceed quite differently, to resolutely carry the axe in this curtain of legendary fictions that have climbed to the summit and covered from top to bottom the historical personality that serves as their support; but when everything has been cut down and ransacked around it, isn't it to be feared that we may discover that the central tree has been dead for a long time, exhausted of sap by its foreign grafts and suffocated under the exuberance of weeds? So much so that the critic would be or should be the first to regret, facing the emaciated skeleton thus brought to light, the triumphant ornament of which he has taken it upon himself to strip it.[37]

In a slightly different metaphorical vein, Foucher wrote: "The Sanskrit poets credit the beautiful Indian wild goose with the gift of separating milk from water, however intimate the mixture may be: what historian will discover the secret of disentangling in such a mixture of real and fabulous facts the exact part of each of them?"[38] The question is purely rhetorical, for in various passages Foucher suggested that he was precisely that historian.

Another common metaphor employed by historians of Buddhism comes from the archaeological register. Taking this metaphor to heart, Foucher believed that, "just as the excavations of archaeologists must not stop before reaching virgin soil, so philologists must push their excavations deeper and deeper through the heap of Scriptures until they finally reach, if possible, the historical tuff."[39] But what if it were not possible? What can pure philology and historicism bring to the historian of religions, for whom, even if there may be some "historical tuff," there is no "virgin soil"? For whom, in the field of culture, there is no bedrock under the sand of beliefs on which a solid edifice could be built, for there is nothing but sand. The historical tuff itself would still be a heap of cultural debris. As Senart saw it well, Buddhism, in a sense, essentially began long before the Buddha.

Foucher's use of metaphor was not simply a stylistic effect; it almost always signaled a value judgment.[40] As Nalini Balbir notes, "There is a fine line between the rewriting of the Indian text and the commentary of the scholar, whose personal culture penetrates discourse."[41] Foucher's attitude as an author was thus the very opposite of benevolent neutrality. Remarks such as the following testify to this: "And this is how, from one version to another, by aiming at the sublime, one falls into the ridiculous."[42] Or again: "You can see that no cliché is missing. But here, in addition to banality, there is ineptitude."[43] His condescension expressed itself in numerous passages, including the following: "Thus immunized in advance to the mental agitation of the hagiographers, we can approach their writings without blind faith or angry mistrust and try to untangle in the endless fabric of wonders the few bits of truth that are mixed with all the fictions."[44]

As Balbir points out, these value judgments may engender a certain discomfort in the reader, and they seem to contradict the scientificity of Foucher's project.[45] The middle way that Foucher claimed to adopt, however, was intended to guarantee scientific objectivity. About the controversy between Senart and Oldenberg, he wrote:

> If Senart's mythological interpretation, taken to the extreme, tends to dissipate the Buddha's personality into thin air, Oldenberg's euhemerism leads to a no less serious misunderstanding of this figure who, arbitrarily isolated from his environment, becomes incomprehensible. Both seem to be both right and wrong, right in what they admit, wrong in what they omit. In E. Senart's Buddha, it is man who is missing; in H. Oldenberg's, it is the god.[46]

Foucher returned to this point on several occasions:

> We take this biography for what it is, that is to say, for a mixture of history and legend, truth and fiction; and without indulging, like H. Oldenberg, in excesses of rationalist exegesis, or yielding, like E. Senart, "to the inebriation of comparative mythology," we will simply try to reconstruct, with the help of written documents and figurative monuments, the way in which the Indians of 2000 years ago conceived and represented it themselves.[47]

Foucher rejected both extremes, adopting what he believed to be a middle way. It would suffice, in his view, to negotiate a path between mythology and euhemerism, or faith and hypercriticism, a way between seeing the Buddha as a god and seeing him "simply as a man."[48] In fact, the middle way he presented, with some false modesty, as a "particular little path" resembled the famous Middle Path advocated by the Buddha: "Consequently, there remains no other alternative but to guard against the dizzying twists and turns of comparative mythology no less than the platitudes of euhemerism and to follow midside a particular little path. And if it seems excessive to some to pretend to tread a middle path in this way—that middle path which the Master formally recommended to his disciples on every occasion—let it be pleaded that there is a precedent."[49] A beautiful program, certainly, but perhaps not as easy to carry out as to announce.

Based on his training as an archaeologist and his experience in the field, Foucher proposed to accept the Buddhist fact in its entirety. But he stopped short of explaining how one could do so while still considering legends to be "distortions." Fully imbued with the scientific spirit of his time and its reductive method, he sought to extract from the preponderance of data a "coefficient of reduction," a standard that would allow one to "assess the excess of the texts." Unfortunately, as he had to concede, "there are not enough elements to establish this kind of reduction coefficient."[50] And he resigned himself to never discovering the historical bedrock: "Let us say it in advance and without any ambiguity: there is almost nothing in their lucubrations that deserves credit; and if such and such an episode happens to have a background of verisimilitude, the variations in the texts about it betray its irremediably fictitious character." Accepting the legend, albeit reluctantly, he found a psychological justification for it: "Does this mean that the legend must be rejected outright as a useless jumble? In all sincerity, we do not think so. Admittedly, we only read in the Buddhist Scriptures a hopelessly romanticized life . . . but this reading, too often disheartening because of its ridiculous exaggerations, happens to be attractive at times. Of course a novel is not history: this does not prevent it from sometimes containing more psychological truth, or even objective reality, than many methodically constructed treatises." And so he mixed water into the wine of historians, and added condiments to the bland food of biographers: "One should not bring an overly rigorous spirit to these matters. After all, what we allow ourselves to call historical truth is too often only the conjecture on which bona fide researchers have come to agree: the unanimity of hagiographers will give us, at least in this case, what might be called traditional truth. However repugnant it is to the logical mind of a Frenchman to admit that there can be several kinds of truths, this one already constitutes a very appreciable acquisition; and finally we remain free to accept it only by mixing in it the grain of salt that is appropriate."[51] Which he never failed to do, even if his hand on occasion was a little heavy.

Although he often wielded the criterion of verisimilitude, Foucher nevertheless pointed out its fragility: "For verisimilitude and implausibility can both be, especially in religious matters, sometimes the face of the true and sometimes the mask of the false."[52] He thus seemed to be revising the historical method downward: "Let us resign ourselves to knowing about him [the Buddha] only the little that we can learn of the character of every man simply by hearing him speak and, above all, by watching him act. This is precisely what we have just tried to do together, according to the testimonies that have been preserved."[53] Yet, while pretending to renounce the "historical tuff," he persisted in finding the historical Buddha behind the legend: "Here is all we know, or think we know for sure, about the one who is still called the Buddha. . . . Nothing could be more historical, in the usual sense of the word, than this sketch; and nothing less sensational."[54]

Showing great optimism, Foucher believed that the confrontation of the various sources allowed him to re-establish the historical truth: "Presented differently according to the milieu and the addressees, neither of these arrangements deserves full credit in advance. The only encouragement their contrast gives us is that a double distortion in a direction opposite to the truth should make it easier to re-establish the facts than the presence of a single false testimony." Here again, we can note the terms used and the value judgments they imply: distortion, truth, re-establishing the facts, false testimony.[55]

However, Foucher's doubts did not prevent him from finally endorsing the "historical" bias, and making a bet that he could only lose. His biography of the Buddha is a work of fiction, an interlacing of legends and historical, sociological, or doctrinal insights—anything but an objective biography. And with good reason, for as he himself noted: "Nothing, when it comes to this unique being, can be left to chance. He deliberately chose his hometown, his caste, his family, his mother; and it is not without reason that she died after seven days."[56] But without chance, there are no events, let alone a biography worthy of the name. That, however, did not stop Foucher from lending the Buddha a psychology that is surprisingly similar to that of a modern rationalist thinker. The precise portrait he drew, in the manner of a La Bruyère, gives us the impression that he knew him personally:

> A gentleman to the tips of his fingernails and pure of any hint of charlatanism or fanaticism; endowed with incomparable fortitude and perfect serenity; an austere moralist, but without excess, and helpful to others; a free and judicious thinker, as much an enemy of idle metaphysics as of vulgar superstition; as founder of a religion imbued, in its secret despair, with the spirit of mercy, the Buddha [Śākyamuni] was the first—the first at least that the world is entitled to remember—to denounce in the selfishness of desire the source of malice and hatred, and to preach to his fellow men an infallible remedy for their worst miseries in the gentleness of mutual love. If only they had better heeded his word![57]

AVATARS OF THE MIDDLE WAY

Most Western historians, following Foucher, advocate a middle way between myth and history, or more precisely between the making of myth and the making of history.[58] On condition, however, that the mythology in question is that of the Buddhist tradition, not that of specialists in comparative mythology. As Strong puts it: "What is needed is a middle way between remythologizing and demythologizing, between myth-making and history-making, between seeing the Buddha as a god and seeing him as 'just a man.'"[59] But in fact, it is difficult to stand on this crest line, and most authors end up falling back into the historicist rut, according to which the legend is merely the ornamentation surrounding a real life, which can be found by clearing away all the accumulated garbage, the scum of the centuries. Foucher himself ultimately believed, as did Oldenberg and Rhys Davids, that the purpose of research is to gather the bits of information that such sources give us and to link them into a linear narrative. This method is still favored by contemporary historians, who aim to give us the definitive biography of the "historical" or "human" Buddha. If the anthropologist Stanley Tambiah could still denounce "the Pāli Text Society mentality" a hundred years after its founding, it was because that mentality showed no signs of stopping. Like Gulliver's Big-Enders and Little-Enders—arguing over which end of an egg to break—scholars continue to debate how best to conceive of Buddhism—by one end (legend, ergo Buddha's divinity) or by the other (history, ergo Buddha's humanity).

Étienne Lamotte

According to Bareau, we have moved beyond that quandary: "The person and life of the Buddha appear to us only through a thick fog of legends, which explains why Western orientalists were still so divided about them, not so long ago. To mention only extreme opinions, some of them accepted the whole of the tradition judged by them the oldest, not without much imprudence, and were satisfied to eliminate the implausible elements, such as stories of wonders and divine intervention, while others wanted to see in the Buddha a mere solar myth. Today, the comparative and meticulous study of all the ancient texts that have come down to us leads to a much more nuanced judgment and more certain results."[60]

Étienne Lamotte (1903–1983) was one of those scholars who sought to resist the "obsession with origins," concentrating his vision on the development of a legend that started with a man (the historical Buddha) and ended with a god (the divinized Buddha). His *History of Indian Buddhism,* though unfinished, remains a classic, both in its knowledge of the sources and in its clear and elegant style. In concluding that mythological and historicist (rationalist) methods are both insufficient, he proposed a seemingly more modest goal, which he called "methodological reversal." Accordingly, the study of the Buddha's biographies "first informs us about the hagiographers themselves, and the context in which they lived. We have no direct knowledge of the period in which the Buddha lived, which seems to escape the investigations of history. And in this field, the criterion of plausibility is very difficult to handle."[61]

Like most of his colleagues, Lamotte presupposed that the development of a tradition goes from the simple to the complex. But the opposite movement, from the complex to the simple, will not necessarily lead back to the origin, which, as we know from Foucault, is always already complex. Moreover, it is impossible, in the current state of knowledge, to go back beyond the reign of King Aśoka, that is to say, more than a century after the presumed date of the parinirvāṇa. But that impossibility is perhaps due to deeper reasons than the absence of materials, which archaeology can always hope to discover. Nevertheless, when Lamotte retraced the life of the Buddha, he apparently succumbed to the spells cast by factual signs (the names of people and places) and fashioned a life of the Buddha that, however sober, nonetheless is in part constructed, fictitious, and in fact mythical. Despite his more nuanced approach, it ultimately represents the same bid to paint a minimalist portrait of the master, whose biography would consist in the lowest common denominator of the texts considered to be the oldest.

André Bareau

After Foucher and Lamotte, the main contribution to the biography of the Buddha was that of André Bareau (1921–1993). It offered, for the first time, access to Buddhist sources concerning the decisive periods of the Buddha's life that had been preserved only in Chinese translations. Like Foucher and Lamotte, Bareau sought in principle to "remain on the middle road between pure acceptance of all the plausible elements provided by the canonical sources . . . and a finicky hypercriticism."[62] Like them too, however, he finally fell into the very same historicism against which he had warned us. He took care to observe that, while the oldest texts should contain historical elements, "such is not the case, and the simplest episodes are in fact *reconstructions*."[63] Yet he himself often lost sight of this perception. In his view, while proven historical facts were indeed lacking for the childhood and youth of the Buddha, things were different for the period of his maturity, the significant events of which remained in collective memory: "Although many of the stories in which he appears were invented several centuries after the parinirvāṇa, as their in-depth study proves, one is very tempted to see them as a reflection of the memory, piously and carefully preserved, of the singularly powerful personality that was certainly that of the Blessed One."[64]

Bareau deduced that the youth of the Bodhisattva had nothing memorable about it. The modest and rough circumstances of that youth would explain, according to Bareau, the virtues of the man who became the Buddha.[65] Of the latter he painted a portrait that he thought was "realistic": coming from the warrior caste, this was the "son of a modest squire whose family was attached to the Brahmanic clan of the Gautama." Contrary to the legend, in which the crown prince of a rich and powerful king luxuriated in opulence and idleness, indulging in every pleasure and ignoring all suffering and pain, the future Buddha must have had a raw youth, exposed to many dangers. But this had the happy result of forging his character and enabling him to acquire the qualities that would later make him the founder of one of the world's most important religions.

From that point on, Bareau continued, "we can safely say that he did not physically resemble in any way the portrait that sculptors and painters have been giving us for some twenty centuries, which was inspired only by his legend. . . . No, the Buddha was not this prince of high lineage, visibly accustomed to a life of opulence, refined luxury, and idleness; he was a former warrior, impecunious, trained from adolescence to bravely face deprivation, fatigue, and danger, who then became a true ascetic, leading an austere and vagabond existence, feeding only on alms. He was thus a man with a thin and nervous body, but solid and resistant, with a thin, if not emaciated face, with a tanned and probably even dark complexion from life in the open air, with a skull carefully shaved to obey the rule that he himself had decreed, and with a lively gaze, whose attitudes and gestures were certainly full of assurance and energy."[66]

To give a plausible explanation for Śākyamuni's renunciation of the world, Bareau imagined that, having experienced a violent emotional shock, he wanted to leave the places that reminded him of his misfortune.[67] Without realizing that he was begging the question, Bareau appealed to the (presumed) psychology of the Bodhisattva to decide which textual version to rely on. The hypothesis he adopted was that of the death of Yaśodharā after the birth of Rāhula. That death allowed him to look at Gautama's departure in a completely different light and to absolve him of the accusation of fleeing from his family responsibilities.[68] The image we have been given here is that of the conversion of a warrior (like Ignatius of Loyola or Aśoka). We also have room for an alternative psychological explanation, that of the trauma created by the loss of his mother (who Bareau believed was still alive at the time of the great departure). These two women are almost absent from canonical texts, suggesting that both had died before the Buddha's return to Kapilavastu. But of course this is pure speculation, and the plausible, which Bareau considered to be a sufficient criterion of authenticity, is no more convincing here than the marvelous.

Moreover, Bareau's desire to make Buddha a kind of philosopher forced him to practically deny the dazzling reality of the awakening:

> Nothing proves . . . that this important discovery took place in a few hours, while the ascetic Gautama was meditating, sitting at the foot of a tree in a precise place. . . . It is even highly probable that it was the result of long and deep reflections which would have followed one another over

> the course of several months or several years. . . . In this case . . . , awakening would be the phenomenon by which the Buddha finally came to a clear awareness of the doctrine, the fruit of his meditations, which he had long carried in his mind in a kind of mental gestation until it was perfectly formed, mature and complete. This kind of delivery is a fairly common and well-known phenomenon.[69]

However, having given a long description of the "historical" Buddha, Bareau felt obliged to mention the other side of the tradition:

> Very different, let us repeat, is the Buddha of the legend. . . . The work of the hagiographers will have continued more or less slowly until today, when one can see with astonishment on the walls of certain modern "pagodas" painted representations of episodes that one would look for in vain in the texts of past times. . . . Although legendary scenes are scattered throughout the life of the Blessed One, it is above all his childhood and youth, the period of his life of which no memory has been kept, to which the hagiographers' imagination gave free rein . . . , with a devotion touching on sycophancy.[70]

Bareau's anti-religious prejudices stand out in his conjoining of devotion and sycophancy. Not surprisingly, the Buddhist taste for the marvelous does not find favor in his eyes: "The Buddha, we are told, was reluctant to use his powers to convert people. Such methods would not have had much evidential value." Still, this statement is surprising given the importance of the miracles performed by the Buddha in converting his future disciples.[71]

Despite its methodological bias, Bareau's work furnished important insights into the development of Buddhist texts and schools and the relationships between them, giving researchers the means to write a history of Buddhism downstream, *after the Buddha,* as historians such as Étienne Lamotte and John Strong have begun to do. Such a history should allow us to take full measure of the richness and creativity of the Buddhist tradition. It is all the more regrettable, then, that Bareau, for his part, persevered in the more risky approach inherited from his predecessors, which consisted in going back upstream to arrive at a hypothetical urtext and the historical Buddha from which it supposedly emanated.

Richard Gombrich

The Theravāda specialist Richard Gombrich (1937–) continues to believe, as in the best days of historicism, that one can jump with both feet beyond the era of King Aśoka to that of the Buddha himself. In an article published in 2003, he responded to those who denounced his "obsession with origins" by accusing them of "postmodernism"—the supreme insult under his pen. According to Gombrich, there are two good reasons to be "obsessed" with the origins of Buddhism. The first is that this obsession, authorized by a careful reading of Pāli scriptures, allows us to understand the Buddha as "one of the most brilliant and interesting minds in all human history"—a kind of philosophical Einstein.[72] The second is that by showing how the original meanings have been changed, we can give Buddhism a history.[73]

Gombrich proclaims the authenticity of the oral tradition, which in his view must go back to about 150 years after the Buddha's death (ca. 405 BCE). He also holds that the teachings attributed to the Buddha are indeed his own. In his estimation, it is not the high spirituality of the words attributed to the Buddha that attests to their authenticity, but rather the humor that the Buddha shows toward his rivals, the Brahmins. This humor would have been ill advised in the mouths of his respectful disciples. Therefore such words ring true—they are too personal to be the work of a later editorial board. Is not belief a more appropriate response than criticism of authenticity?[74] To the objection that these texts were written long after the Buddha's death, Gombrich replies that the teachings they contain would not have been preserved if they had not been recorded during the Buddha's lifetime. To be preserved, they had to exist. The argument is perfectly circular. He recommends that we stick to the *lectio difficilior* of the texts. And if we were to take this advice at face value, the strangest aspects of the legend should be counted the most authentic, contrary to the opinion of the historians who seek to reduce everything to the plausible.

The reason it is so important to go back to the origin, writes Gombrich, is that it allows us to get closer to "one of the strongest intelligences that ever existed." To support this view, he adduces the theory of "co-dependent origination" (*pratītya-samutpāda*), which he wants to see as the quasi-original doctrine of Buddhism as well as an answer to the Vedic cosmogony. But this argument confuses a doctrinal register (we can show that *pratītya-samutpāda* is specific to early Buddhism, if not to the Buddha himself) with a biographical one (we should be able to show that certain biographical features refer to the historical reality of the Buddha). Moreover, the theory itself does not seem to be as original as Gombrich claims. As Steve Collins points out, we should abandon this old-fashioned and quixotic search for an original urtext, as well as the notion that the Pāli canon is equivalent to primitive Buddhism, and remember that we don't have the slightest piece of evidence that can be dated with certainty to before the time of Aśoka.[75] As for the alleged biographical facts that lend support for the Buddha's doctrine, they cannot explain the fascination with which so many generations have beheld his character. Both doctrinally and biographically, Gombrich's position is profoundly reductive. Indeed, the cost of transforming the Buddha into a simple philosopher is nothing less than his "scandalous" dimension.

Hans Penner

Among the recent biographers of the Buddha, Hans Penner (1934–2012) has earned a special place. In his book *Rediscovering the Buddha* (2009), he challenged historicism and sought to rehabilitate the mythological approach—just as I am trying to do here. In passing, he offered a proper critique of the Pāli Text Society mentality, noting that there is no document proving the existence of the Buddha. All that historians have at their disposal are myths and legends, which they refuse on principle to consider relevant. On the basis of archaeological data, Penner showed that the *Jātakas,* or past lives of the Buddha, were included in the Buddhist legend from early on, as can be seen on the stūpas of Sanchi and Bharhut (2nd–3rd cent. BCE). They are not, therefore, the late products of an overflowing popular imagination, as had been assumed, but fundamental structural elements of Buddhism and of the biography of the Buddha.[76]

According to Penner, the quest for the historical Buddha is also that for a pure and authentic Buddhism. However, ideological preconceptions too often contaminate objective research. This quest for the Buddha is part of a wider undertaking, a quest for the origins of religion. Hence the importance of interpretive frameworks that emphasize the ethical and philosophical—rather than ritual and mythological—aspects of the Buddha's teaching. For Penner, what these explanations have in common is the use of Pāli sources: "This presupposes a huge leap of faith from the second or third century A.D. back to about the sixth or fifth century B.C. and the magical transformation, sometimes called "demythologization," of documents that are clearly mythical into documents that are or reflect actual historical events and developments."[77]

When he questioned the equation between the Pāli canon and early Buddhism, Penner clearly distanced himself from the historicist approach that seeks to elaborate a biographical blueprint by rejecting mythological accretions. According to Penner, "It is not the basic outline that takes on the character of myth, but the myth from which the basic outline is extracted that has taken on the character of history! The motto of the received tradition, 'the outline must be true,' is clearly based on the 'metamorphosis' of myth into history."[78] Furthermore, since the outline in question is fundamentally the same for the present Buddha as for all past buddhas, its historical value is almost nil. The Life of the Buddha is part of an immense cosmological system and cannot be understood apart from the system of all his predecessors.[79] But how can one write a biography when this "Life" spans innumerable previous existences in many cosmic periods? In what way, Penner wondered—showing himself to be a worthy heir of Senart—is the search for the historical Buddha different from that of the historical Rāma or Krishna? This question, thus rephrased, is both stimulating and troubling, for we know how Hindu nationalism is investing these deities with a historicity they never had. Unfortunately, Penner's untimely death prevented him from developing these insights further.

John Strong

Another recent attempt, and probably the most interesting of those we have reviewed, is that of John Strong (1948–). Strong, too, pretends from the outset to go beyond the false myth-history alternative. He believes, however, that there is nothing fundamentally wrong with the "minimalist" portrait given by historians of the Buddha, and declares himself ready to make it his own. With, however, one important caveat: this is not how Buddhists themselves tell the Life of the Buddha: "These narrations may contain 'fictions' about the Buddha—legends and traditions that have accrued around him—but these 'fictions' are in many ways 'truer,' or at least religiously more meaningful, than the 'facts.' They are certainly more plentiful, more interesting, and more revelatory of the ongoing concerns of Buddhists."[80]

While giving a lot of space to legends, Strong sometimes gives in to the demands of the "biographical imperative." Moreover, he does not draw all the conclusions from his premise that, if one wants to "give mythology its due," there is no longer any reason to give preference to Indian sources. His Buddha remains a little too Indian, even if the sources used are not always Indian. The middle way he proposes between history and myth, or rather between "making history" and "making myth," comes up against a major obstacle. For, if it is impossible to say anything verifiable about the Buddha's life, one always ends up wanting to negotiate an impossible middle way between stories (myths and legends) and other "histories," which, despite their realistic style and plausibility, have nothing factual or historical about them and are also essentially mythological in nature. Strong himself was the first to recognize this, and his recent book on the Buddha's relics shows that he is giving increasing importance to non-Indian (and especially Japanese) traditions.[81]

3

AN UNFINDABLE BIOGRAPHY

After this brief overview of Western historiography, we must ask about alternative approaches—as Penner and Strong have already begun to do. Buddhist sources cannot simply be treated as if they were administrative archives. Awareness of the discursive constraints to which they are subject, as literary sources, must be matched with a recognition of the claims of the biographical genre that has determined the form they have taken. In the following pages, I attempt to show how the biases of Buddhist historians have formed a network that ended up enclosing a supposedly historical but purely fictitious Buddha in its meshes. This review of the fundamental methodology of Buddhist studies must be undertaken if we wish to understand the crucial role played by the Life of the Buddha in the Buddhist tradition. To do so, it is required above all that we discard the "obsession with origins."

QUESTIONS OF CHRONOLOGY

The temporal framework in which the Buddha's life is placed is essential, since it is on that placement—at least in part—that his historicity depends. One can certainly grasp the importance of the dates of the Buddha, or rather, the date of the parinirvāṇa, an event that should have been engraved in the minds of his contemporaries—if it took place at all. For it is from that date that we derive the dates of his birth and awakening, and the chronology of every significant event between these markers (and beyond, with the first Buddhist councils).

The date of the parinirvāṇa was a problem for East Asian Buddhists from early on but for very different reasons from those experienced by Western historians. One reason was that the parinirvāṇa was considered the triggering event for the progressive stages in the decline of the Buddhist Law predicted by the Buddha, and traditional Buddhists wanted to know where in that great eschatological scheme they found themselves. According to Tibetan chronology, the Buddha lived from 961 to 881 BCE, but those same dates ran from 1061 to 949 (or 878) BCE in the East Asian chronology—and not from 566 to

486 BCE, as the Theravāda tradition had it, the dates accepted until recently by Western historians.

The important dates in the Buddha's life have always had (and still retain) particular importance, not only in giving rise to commemorative rites and celebrations, such as those that marked the 2,500th anniversary of the Buddha's death worldwide, but also as a political and ideological matter of concern. In Japanese chronicles such as the *History of the Legitimate Succession of Divine Emperors* (*Jinnō shōtoki*), by Kitabatake Chikafusa (1293–1354), the Buddha's birth is reported as having occurred 290 years before the reign of Emperor Jinmu, that is, in 370–368 BCE.[1] Elsewhere, it was held that Buddhism was introduced in China during the reign of Emperor Ming, 1,016 years after the parinirvāṇa, and 488 years before its official introduction in Japan, which occurred in 552 CE, during the reign of Emperor Kinmei. Combining these dates, we get 952 BCE as the date of the parinirvāṇa.

The Meiji "Restoration" of 1868—in effect, a kind of Cultural Revolution—led to the development of a new Japanese Buddhist history aimed at underlining the human character of the Buddha and presenting a Buddhism compatible with modernization.[2] Numerous studies of the biography of the Buddha, the geography of ancient India, and the Buddhist councils were created to meet the need of Japanese Buddhists to rediscover the origins of their faith in accordance with scientific criteria.[3] It was crucial, then, to arrive at a reliable chronology—accurate to the year, month, and day—to establish the historicity of the Buddha. The enormous energy expended in this undertaking shows the depth of the Japanese scholars' motivations, and the importance of what was at stake for them.[4] The Japanese historian Nanjō Bunyū (1849–1927) listed no fewer than thirty-two theories concerning the dates of the Buddha, based on his research in Tibetan, Mongolian, Indian, Burmese, Sinhalese, Chinese, Japanese, German, and English sources. This list was later increased to forty-eight.[5] Although it was generally agreed that the Buddha had lived for eighty years, this span had not yet been firmly established for the Japanese historians of the Meiji period. Other hypotheses, all drawn from canonical sources, were proposed, involving spans of seventy-eight, seventy-nine, eighty-two, and eighty-five years.[6] To further complicate matters, there was the belief, as implausible as it was widely held, that all the major events in the Buddha's life occurred on the same day in different years, making it possible to celebrate their anniversaries on the same date. Moreover, another very old tradition said that the parinirvāṇa took place three months after the end of the rainy season—in other words, around the winter solstice—or several months before the date later chosen to celebrate (together) the Buddha's birth, his awakening, and his extinction.

In the West, the Buddha's dates have been the subject of heated debate, especially after the data on which they were based proved to be problematic. Perhaps the most striking example is the collection of essays on the subject that

Heinz Bechert assembled in a three-volume work, *The Dating of the Historical Buddha,* published from 1991 to 1993 following a symposium held in Göttingen that brought together, in his words, "scholars from all over the world to examine the question from every conceivable position, discipline, and language."[7] The dates proposed for the parinirvāṇa ranged from 486 to 261 BCE. A compromise was eventually reached stating that the Buddha died around 400 BCE. Yet Bechert himself, in his introduction to the work, admitted that none of the dates were agreed upon. According to the most commonly accepted "long" chronology, the Buddha was born in 566 BCE, at Lumbinī, and died in 486, at the age of eighty, near the village of Kuśinagara. According to Pāli sources, King Aśoka was enthroned 218 years after the Buddha's death. Since the date of this enthronement, chosen by historians on the basis of epigraphic documents, is 268 BCE, a simple subtraction was sufficient to establish the date of 486 BCE for the extinction. Nevertheless, it was in accordance with the traditional Theravāda chronology that the 2,500th anniversary of the parinirvāṇa was celebrated in 1956. Furthermore, a decision of the Fourth World Buddhist Congress, meeting in Kathmandu in 1956, set the Buddha's birth date at 544 BCE—also in accordance with the Pāli tradition. This date was adopted throughout Asia for essentially political reasons: it was considered important for Buddhists from all countries to present a united front.

But there is another, "short" chronology, based on Sanskrit sources, that places the enthronement of Aśoka only one hundred years after the Buddha's death—the date of which is therefore set at 386 BCE. The round figure of one hundred, a little too symbolic, is obviously questionable. Richard Gombrich, basing himself on another Sinhalese chronicle, the *Dīpavaṃsa,* states that the enthronement of Aśoka took place 136 years after the Buddha's death, which therefore must have taken place around 404 BCE. From this, other dates can be calculated, such as his awakening and his return to Kapilavastu six years later. Even so, how can we fail to see that all these dates rest on a fragile—or even nonexistent—basis? The complicated chronological calculations that historians make rely on texts that are known to have been compiled long after the events reported. As K. R. Norman cautions, "It is clear that we must guard against trying to use uncritical material critically. . . . References to a long or short chronology only make sense in a context where we think that the numbers are meaningful, i.e., correct."[8] That seems to be common sense itself, but common sense in this area is not the most fairly distributed property in the world.

As Gananath Obeyesekere notes, in the absence of accurate records the chronological interval in Sinhalese chronicles such as the *Mahāvaṃsa* has been filled with numbers that derive from numerological categories: "Rhetorical devices took the place of chronological accuracy, but these rhetorical devices did not violate the norm of specificity. That the *Mahāvaṃsa* concern with chronological specificity was successful is very clear from the fact that modern historians have been seduced into thinking that chronological specificity indicates accuracy."[9] Thus, Aśoka was enthroned 100 years or 218 years after the parinirvāṇa; and the monk Mahinda introduced Buddhism to the island of Ceylon (Sri Lanka) 236 years after this event. From a methodological point of view, the approach is strikingly naive. In fact, all that can be said for certain is that the conventional date of 486 BCE chosen for the parinirvāṇa is no longer admissible, and that basically we don't know, to the nearest century, when the Buddha lived (if this is indeed the case). One century, even in a supposedly unchanging and nonhistorical society like traditional India, is a lot, especially when one claims to give oneself a chronology.

HISTORICITY OF THE BUDDHA

To want, in spite of the difficulties, to comb through the texts in order to draw out information on the Buddha and his doctrine, one must believe in the human reality of the Buddha and the possibility of going back to him. One must seek, as Bareau says, to discern the "silhouette of the unmistakably historical figure" that looms behind the "golden mist" of the legend.[10] Some metaphors are themselves rather misty.

The question of the Buddha's historicity, as Senart had raised it, no longer seems to be relevant for most researchers today.[11] Lamotte reflected the general opinion when he wrote: "Buddhism would remain inexplicable if one did not suppose at its origins a strong personality who was its founder. But this is a postulate, not to say an act of faith, rather than a result of historical research."[12] The only historical reality is that of the legend and its development. If it is important that there be a presence at the source of these myths, it is a virtual presence. But perhaps the question has been asked incorrectly, inasmuch as the historicity of the Buddha has never been, for the Buddhist tradition as a whole, the determining element that it is for Western historians. Buddhist discourse instead developed around an absence, and hagiography and ritual are only there to produce a semblance of presence.

Even the idea of a "developing" legend is problematic, because it implies a zero point constituted by a historical substratum, the bedrock. Yet all that can be observed are various states of the legend, some more realistic than others, some dealing with a human Buddha, others with a transcendent Buddha. Very early, if not from the beginning of the oral tradition, the Buddha is clearly presented as transcendent. From his very birth, his life is structured by legend. The four encounters, the six years of asceticism, the awakening, the first sermon, and the conversions he makes: so many narrative devices that have little to do with real events.

The received tradition found its most complete expression in the statement of one of the participants at the seventh World Sanskrit Conference, held in Leiden in 1987: "In the nineteenth century, not all European scholars were even prepared to accept that such a historical person as Gotama the Buddha ever existed . . . though such an extremity of skepticism now seems absurd."[13] Still, marshalling evidence for a historical Buddha would seem to require that new and indisputable elements have been added to the file, which is not the case. One is instead met with the mere repetition that the Buddha "must" have existed to justify the existence of Buddhism even though a normative statement, however often repeated, cannot constitute proof. Whatever one thinks of the "historical" reality of the Buddha, what is significant is the way tradition has remembered him, the role that his life has played in the "cultural memory" of Buddhism.[14] This is the pragmatic interpretation—in the sense of William James's pragmatism, which holds that the importance of a belief or philosophy depends on its practical implications, on the impact it has had on minds and on society.[15]

THE QUESTION OF THE SOURCES

The question of the historicity of the Buddha does not exactly overlap with that of the reliability of the sources, although the two are obviously linked. Because of both their hagiographical nature and the contradictions between them, the textual sources—as objects of belief—are hardly credible. The Life of the Buddha, as found in the oldest sources, already obeys a number of narrative constraints, including a belief in karma and in previous existences.

The Buddha's sermons, as reported in canonical scriptures, contain very few autobiographical elements—and for good reason: autobiography had yet to be invented as a concept. It took several centuries for what could be called one or several "biographies" to emerge, although these texts seem to be more concerned with the lives of past buddhas than with that of Śākyamuni. Even when that is not the case, the account of the Buddha's life often stops at his awakening and first sermon, and remains strangely silent for the rest of his life. We will return to this point in a moment.

The search for origins, so dear to historians, is based on a methodological principle that is rarely questioned, namely, that the oldest sources are the most reliable or authentic sources—and its corollary, that the simplest texts are the oldest. Thus, for a long time, Pāli texts were preferred over Sanskrit texts. But often these texts were considered authentic, not by external criteria, but because they seemed to better correspond, from the standpoint of internal criticism, to the idea of a "primitive" Buddhism. We can already see that this reasoning is circular. Foucher himself, an expert on the subject, warned against this simplistic view, which, in his opinion, characterized the Pāli Text Society: "What has recommended the canon of the Elders to the eyes of many is its relative sobriety. . . . From there to the conclusion that the *simplicior* version is also the oldest and truest only required one step, which was quickly taken. . . . . The Pāli canon is no less full of marvels than that of other sects."[16] Today there can be little belief in the anteriority—therefore the superior authenticity—of the Pāli canon, which took form several centuries after the presumed parinirvāṇa of the Buddha and thus is no older than the Sanskrit canon.

Another methodological principle, often invoked, is that the agreement between the Sanskrit *Āgamas* and the Pāli *Nikāyas* implies that we are in the presence of ancient data, prior to the schism that separated the tradition of the Theras (the future Theravāda) from that of the Mahāsāṃghika (the future Mahāyāna). Thus, according to Bareau, everything on which all the sects agree must be prior to the schism.[17] In other words, the concordance between various versions of an event in the life of the Buddha shows that they "derive from a common original, to which they have remained faithful for the most part, and which may date back to the time of the Blessed One, thus roughly reflecting a historical truth."[18] This argument implies that all communication between the sects had been definitively interrupted, forbidding them to reconcile on certain points of doctrine. But nothing is less certain, and any concordance could on the contrary reflect a later development of tradition, an attempt at a posteriori reconciliation (this is precisely the role of councils).[19] This does not mean that these sources are devoid of value, but simply that this value is not the one that has been attributed to them up to now. They are, to take up the distinction elaborated by Michel Foucault, "monuments" aimed at perpetuating the memory of an event rather than "documents" allowing us to reconstruct the past in its factuality.[20]

Main Sources

The first extended biographies of the Buddha do not seem to have been compiled until the second century CE. The three main sources are unquestionably the *Acts of the Buddha* (*Buddhacarita*), the *Extensive Play* (*Lalitavistara*), and the *Book of Great Events* (*Mahāvastu*). They offer an almost complete, or at least coherent, "life," even if they do not reach the ultimate episode, the parinirvāṇa. As Lamotte noted, their authors "like to imagine the Buddha not only as a wise man, but as an extraordinary being, adorned with the thirty-two marks of the Great Man."[21] To them one must add the *Mahāparinirvāṇa-sūtra,* which gives a long account of the parinirvāṇa, and some sections of the monastic code (Vinaya) dating from the fifth century CE. Since these texts belong mainly to the Mahāyāna, they have not found favor in the eyes of historians, who have endeavored to show their contradictions or textual filiations, in the manner of historians of Christianity comparing the Gospels.

Finally, there are later accounts of the Buddha's life, composed outside India (in Sri Lanka, Southeast Asia, Tibet, or East Asia) in various languages (Pāli and Sanskrit, but also Tibetan, Thai, Khmer, Mongolian, Chinese, Korean, and Japanese). Their interest is not only the touch of local color they add; in many cases, they try to answer questions that canonical sources had left out, deliberately or not.[22] Such for example is the case of the *Nidānakathā* in Pāli (3rd–4th cent. CE), which focuses on the Buddha's earlier existences.

The *Acts of the Buddha* (*Buddhacarita*), an epic poem in Sanskrit by the monk Aśvaghoṣa, is probably the most famous Life of the Buddha.[23] Poet, playwright, musician, and Buddhist thinker, Aśvaghoṣa lived in the second half of the second century, almost certainly as a member of the Dharmaguptaka school.[24] He is an outstanding storyteller whose style has affinities with great literary texts such as the *Mahābhārata* and the *Rāmāyana*. He seems to have come from a Brahmin family, but he was nonetheless a fervent Buddhist, well versed in the Buddhist doctrines of his time. The text, which realizes a compromise between the divinity and the humanity of the Buddha, is lyrical and reads like a play (especially in Sanskrit, less so in the Chinese translation). Its structure reflects that of the four events and the four places of pilgrimage (Kapila, Bodh Gaya, Vanarasi, Kuśinagara). Omitting the traditional references to the Buddha's previous lives, it begins directly with his birth as Prince Siddhārtha and ends with the great departure. What distinguishes it from other Lives of the Buddha is not only its poetic style, but also the structured narrative, in which the events, more densely woven, form an artistic whole.

The *Extensive Play* (*Lalitavistara*) probably dates from the third or fourth century CE.[25] It is said to come from the Sarvāstivāda school, although it shows a strong influence from early Mahāyāna. It was translated into Chinese in 308 under the title *Sūtra of Universal Awakening* (*Puyao jing*) and had a great influence on Chinese Buddhism. It emphasizes the purity and transcendence of the Buddha—who has paradoxically already attained his awakening in his past lives—as well as the supernatural events that marked his life. Its narrative begins in Tuṣita Heaven, from which the Bodhisattva will descend for a final human rebirth. His stay in the maternal womb, transformed into a palace, is described in great detail. The episodes recounted from his youth are broadly the same as in other sources. Māra's assault, when it comes, is dissociated into several episodes that do not integrate well. Māra is defeated by the earth goddess, but the Buddha, *after* his awakening, must undergo a second assault by the daughters of Māra. The story ends with the first sermon and the Buddha's return to Kapilavastu, omitting the parinirvāṇa cycle.

The *Book of Great Events* (hereafter the *Mahāvastu*), was written in hybrid Sanskrit between the third and fourth centuries CE and first published by Émile Senart between 1882 and 1897.[26] As a kind of anonymous preface to the texts of monastic discipline (Vinaya), it gives extensive treatment to the events of the Buddha's life and already prefigures in many ways the Mahāyāna. Thus the Buddha, while going through a variety of human trials, is in no way affected by them. Unlike most of the "biographical" sūtras, whose narrator is his cousin and favorite disciple, Ānanda, here it is the

Buddha himself who tells his disciples about the events running throughout his career as a Bodhisattva that preceded his awakening. The text begins with the life of the Buddha Dīpankara, which only serves as a pretext for the prediction made to the young practitioner Sumedha that he will in turn become, in a distant future, a buddha under the name of Śākyamuni. Then one passes without transition to the rebirth of the Bodhisattva in Tuṣita Heaven, and to his last birth in human form. Curiously, the episode concerning his ascetic practice is very detailed. Other episodes are also developed, providing the pretext for the narration of past lives that constantly interrupt the thread of the story. This pseudo-autobiography of the Buddha in fact serves as a *pre*-text for the narrative of his previous existences (*Jātakas*), which occupies half of the text, with numerous repetitions and variants. For example, the birth of the Bodhisattva and his victory over Māra are told no fewer than four times. Two versions of the great departure are also given. The first is very sober: Siddhārtha simply concludes that palace life is too full of distractions to allow him to carry out his spiritual quest, and so decides to become an ascetic. The second version, much richer in detail, corresponds more closely to the traditional story. Yet the narrative structure of the *Mahāvastu,* with its constant backtracking and repetitions, departs from the more linear makeup of the two previous biographies and resembles nothing so much as a postmodern novel.

It is also necessary to say a few words about pictorial sources. Despite the aniconic tradition of early Buddhism, scenes from the Life of the Buddha appeared quite early, around the second century BCE, on the balustrades of stūpas at Sānchī and Bharhut (in present-day Madhya Pradesh), or Amaravati (in present-day Andhra Pradesh). The pictorial tradition thus provides a transition between ancient oral and textual traditions. It reached its peak between the third and tenth centuries in the wall paintings of the caves of Kizil and Mogao (Dunhuang), on the Silk Road. There is also a later illustrated scriptural format that merges pictorial and textual traditions. It is represented by Japanese works such as the eighth-century *Illustrated Sūtra of Cause and Effect* (*E-ingakyō*), and Chinese works such as the *Origins of the Śākya Clan* (*Shishi yuanlu,* 1425).[27]

It is not always easy to distinguish between purely narrative and symbolic images. Some narrative scenes—for example, those of the victory over Māra or of the first sermon—became symbols detached from the narrative, which led to their proliferation (e.g., in Southeast Asia). Visual art follows its own rules apart from the needs of textual illustration even though texts can often provide the key to certain iconographic motifs. Just as a narrative technique may have given rise to certain hagiographic themes, which were then illustrated, certain purely technical imperatives of Buddhist sculpture or painting may have given rise to representations of the Buddha, which then had to be justified from a narrative point of view.

THE BUDDHIST MARVELOUS

The question of the Buddhist marvelous has caused a lot of ink to be spilled. As we have seen, historians have sought to eradicate everything that seemed miraculous, and therefore suspicious, in the accounts of the Buddha's life. In the best of cases, they have sought to explain miracles as literary clichés in order to arrive at a more sober and credible account. Eugène Burnouf, in his presentation of the *Lotus Sūtra,* a Mahāyāna text fertile in miracles that he was the first to translate, wrote: "Here is an example of the incredible nonsense to which the passion for the supernatural can lead."[28] The profusion of miracles also inspired Renan to comment: "Like hashish, these lush dreams suppress time and space. To the extreme boredom that they produce at first, soon follows sleepiness. . . . If the authors of these strange tales wanted to compose a powerful narcotic, the forerunner of nirvāṇa, it must be said that they succeeded perfectly."[29] T. W. Rhys Davids defined *Jātakas* as "fairy tales, parables, riddles, and comic and moral stories."[30] For Foucher, the marvelous was only the shell, or the dross, of the authentic Life of the Buddha. The question was then approached with a more open mind by Lamotte, who, it should be pointed out, was a Catholic priest before becoming an Indianist: "In fact, from the earliest documents, the legend of the Buddha appears to be broadly constituted; the marvelous is an integral part of it, and there is no evidence that the episodes that seem reasonable and normal to us are historically better established than the miraculous events that offend reason."[31] Lamotte had seen the flaw in the historicist perspective even if he did not always know how to avoid it.

An argument derived from this dichotomy between ordinary facts and the miraculous is the thesis that the development of Buddhist legend represents a concession, on the part of an allegedly rationalist clergy, to the "childish" mentality of the people—thus maintaining the old dichotomy between monks and laity. Lamotte thought he could explain the rise of Mahāyāna by the growing influence of lay circles. In his view, "If monks, dedicated to a life of study and meditation, can resign themselves to seeing in their founder only a wise man who has entered parinirvāṇa, lay followers, faced with the difficulties of the world, demand something other than a 'dead god' whose 'remains' (*śarīra*) can only be venerated. They want a living god, a 'god superior to the gods' (*devatīdeva*) who continues his salvific action among them, who can predict the future, work miracles, and whose worship is something more than a simple commemoration."[32]

Today we know that the origins of Mahāyāna are complex, and we are beginning to realize that in matters of credulity, some monks matched pious lay people. It is indeed in monastic circles that one can observe, as Max Weber already discerned, a tendency to rationalize religious practices, but it would be an exaggeration to transform the distinction between clerics and lay people into a rigid dichotomy. Moreover, as Lamotte himself acknowledged, it was within the monastic schools that the notion of a transcendent Buddha developed, leading to his divinization."[33] About this, Lamotte wrote: "This Buddha of a new kind is no longer as talkative as the *śramana* Gautama of Kapilavastu. He no longer expounds at length dogmatic, technically advanced sūtras, but frequently intervenes to reveal to his listeners their past deeds or to announce their future rebirths."[34] Lamotte added: "Seen from this angle and perspective, the last life and previous lives of the Buddha Śākyamuni appear in a more legendary than historical aspect. It is no longer a simple biography . . . , but a real saga with all the subjective elements that this literary genre contains."[35] Let us take away from these remarks the insight that the legends relating to Buddha are not the product of a "popularization," but constitute the fundamental structure of Buddhism as a religion. From this point of view, the distinction between Nikāya Buddhism (the former Hīnayāna) and Mahāyāna is not relevant.

GEOGRAPHY AND HISTORIOGRAPHY

The Life of the Buddha, like those of the Christian saints, is more spatial than temporal; it is a "composition of places." According to Michel de Certeau, "Hagiography is marked by a predominance of precise indications of place over those of time. In this way it also differs from biography, following a law of expression that characterizes this . . . genre: discontinuities of time are crushed by the permanence of that which is the beginning, the end, and the foundation. The history of the saint is translated into a course of places and changes of scene; they determine the space of a constancy."[36]

Geography sometimes comes to the rescue of historiography. The first accounts of the Buddha's life are in fact found in what we could almost, if we did not fear anachronism, regard as tourist guides—Buddhist equivalents of our Baedeker, Michelin Guide, Petite Planète, or Guide du Routard. Buddhist ascetics—starting with the Buddha—were, as it were, the first backpackers. Foucher was the first to insist on the importance of the Buddhist places of remembrance: "One can establish the fact as a law: in India, before their recording by writing, only the memories attached to a given place or object have survived."[37] Unable to offer a precise chronology of the Buddha's life, he had to emphasize geographical precision:

> A chronological arrangement of the scenes is impracticable, and a social classification of their characters is contraindicated; yet we still have a last resort: it is to see if it is not at least possible to establish a geographical distribution. . . . A glance at all the preserved memories quickly reveals that most of them remain grouped, like planetary systems in a diffuse nebula, around one of those second-sized stars that complete the number

of the eight pilgrimages, namely, the holy cities of Śrāvastī, Sānkāśya, Vaiśālī, and Rājagṛha. They thus constitute four minor cycles.[38]

In addition, Foucher gave a very original interpretation of the Buddha's (physical and spiritual) itinerary and doctrine: "It seems that the community had preserved, accurately enough for us to be able to follow him on the map, the memory of the Master's itinerary between Kapilavastu . . . and Bodh Gaya. . . ."[39] He developed this thought in a striking manner:

> How the Bodhisattva would have reacted to contact with Iranian dualism and the religious conceptions of Zarathustra, we will not attempt to guess; all we want to show here is that, having gone in the direction of the northwest, he would have always found himself trapped in forms of civilization that were already rigidly fixed. Prisoner of a social milieu and of a circle of ideas totally different from those in which he would move with such ease and lasting success, he would have been lost forever to history.[40]

Here Foucher defined an interesting watershed: the river Sadānīra (the current Gandaki), which separates the western and eastern regions of northern India. To the west, the land of "meat and wheat eaters and drinkers of alcohol"—in other words, the followers of Brahmanic orthodoxy; to the east, the "vegetarian and water-drinking populations of the great rice field, friends of abstinence, mercy, and peace," who protested before any animal sacrifice and rebelled against Brahmanism. "It was, it goes without saying, toward the latter that the heart and mind of the Bodhisattva inclined, and it was from them that he drew most of the elements of his doctrine."[41] Thus, like Caesar crossing the Rubicon, the future Buddha supposedly sealed the fate of his doctrine by crossing the Sadānīrā. Without denying the importance of geography and culture on the evolution of a particular form of spirituality, one might still find such an unremitting determinism to be naive and reductive, if not ludicrous.

In the absence of precise dates, the multiplication of geographical references in the modern biographies of the Buddha seems to testify to the historicity of the character. However, as Hans Penner notes, one could invoke equally precise references in the case of figures as clearly mythical as Vishnu or Rāma.[42] These references are trompe-l'oeil effects. As Gregory Schopen has shown, based on a late Vinaya text from the Mūlasarvāstivādin school, the *Kṣudrakavastu,* they are generic references, acting as fillers in case of ignorance or oblivion. The Buddha, in this text, tells his disciple:

> Upāli, those who forget the name of the place, et cetera, must declare that it was one or another of the six great cities, or someplace where the Tathāgata stayed many times. If they forget the name of the king, they

> must declare it was Prasenajit; if they forget the name of the householder, say that it was Anāthapiṇḍada; [again,] if they forget where an old story took place, say that it was Vārānasī; or the name of the king, say that it was Brahmādatta.[43]

In this light, it is not surprising to see the name Śrāvastī so often mentioned in the canonical literature, since it was the city where King Prasenajit resided. Similarly, among the 547 *Jātakas* included in the *Introduction to the Commentary on Jātakas* (*Nidānakathā*) attributed to Buddhagosa (5th cent. CE), more than four hundred take place in Vārānasī during the reign of Brahmādatta.[44] This, Schopen concludes, casts doubt even on the allegedly oldest texts—for example, the collection of Pāli *Jātakas,* most of which begin with the words "in Vārānasī during the reign of the king Brahmādatta"; or the early sūtras and Vinaya texts, where Śrāvastī, Prasenajit, and Anāthapiṇḍada predominate. In other words, it seems that all these texts were written in accordance with the same rules as the *Kṣudrakavastu*.[45] If one replaces the name of the king by Prasenajit, and the name of the place consequently becomes Śrāvastī, then it is clear how obedience to these rules could quickly lead to a literature of sūtras and Vinaya texts dominated by Śrāvastī, and a literature of *Jātakas* dominated by Vārānasī. We can conclude, with Schopen, that these supposedly "ancient" texts reflect the application of editorial rules that are much later in date, perhaps even from the fourth and fifth centuries CE.[46] We must therefore be wary of the "reality effect" they induce, and take them for what they are, texts obeying a narrative logic rather than documents to be included as part of the Buddha's biographical record.

BIOGRAPHY AND ITS CONSTRAINTS

If hagiographical writing imposes certain constraints, biographical writing imposes others, and the gap between the two genres is not always well perceived by historians. Oldenberg, however, saw the artificiality of imposing biographical constraints on Buddhist material. He wrote: "Here it must be premised as a cardinal statement: a biography of Buddha has not come down to us from ancient times, from the age of the Pāli texts, and, we can safely say, no such biography was in existence then. This, is, moreover, very easily understood. The idea of biography was foreign to the mind of that age."[47]

We must accept this too quickly forgotten insight of Oldenberg's as a starting point. It can be summed up in a few points: (1) There is no original or authentic biography of the Buddha, since the very concept of a biography did not exist at the time. (2) This concept, as a late and to a large extent Western idea, imposes on the narrative the ideal of a "unified whole" running from beginning to end (usually, from birth to death) (3) in accordance with a linear arrow of time. Consequently, most accounts of the Life of the Buddha have taken on a form (or been "formatted") to meet these requirements even when the standard biographical format is verifiably Procrustean.

Before examining the extent to which the Life of the Buddha conforms to (or departs from) Western biographical criteria, it is useful to note how context determines its importance in relation to doctrine. There are two main types of works in Buddhism: those that see the life and doctrine of the Buddha as two sides of the same reality, according to a model characterized academically as "the man and his work"; and those that emphasize the life itself in keeping with a biographical model—even if it means adding a few references to the doctrine in the biography. If the Life of the Buddha has frequently served as a simple prologue to the exposition of the Buddhist teaching, we should not lose sight of the fact that it has its own, too often ignored, dynamics. It is not, as Edward Conze thought, "a gospel for the busy householder," one that has "little to do with the fundamental teachings of Buddhism."[48] Such a misconception might explain why some historians have little interest in the accounts of the Buddha's past lives—even the German sociologist Max Weber could find little in the Buddha's biography but "mythologies swollen to fabulous dimensions."[49]

Nevertheless, the Life of the Buddha is not an ordinary biography; it is a quasi-sacred narrative that legitimizes Buddhist philosophy and ritual, and is in turn informed by them. Not a "weed" to be extirpated, then, but the narrative rationalization of a founded religion. All the canonical teachings are legitimized by the narrative (including past lives and precursors of the Buddha), and they are as important to monks as they are to lay people. All Buddhist texts, regardless of their doctrinal or philosophical content, unfold within the framework of the Life of the Buddha. What guarantees their authenticity is the preliminary statement of a supposedly reliable witness, the Buddha's cousin and favorite disciple, Ānanda: "Thus have I heard . . ." The narrative has its own persuasive power, and it often proves to be more motivating than the teaching. As Michel Serres remarked in another context:

> The Acts of the Apostles, the Epistles of St. Paul, confessions, reveries, memoirs and autobiographies . . . swarm . . . with a thousand stories in which the hero describes and goes through hazards and avatars, despair. . . . [This] custom of telling one's life in fine detail plunges, in fact, deeper than abstractions and quintessences. The narrative prevails over the concept.[50]

The narrative of the Life of the Buddha, as it developed in Asia, responded to narrative constraints unknown to Western-style biographies. Let us therefore take up the points raised by Oldenberg and confront them with the reality of Buddhist narrative practices.

There is no original or authentic biography. We have seen how historians tried to reconstruct an "original" biography of the Buddha by looking for the historical facts behind the legend. But despite their efforts to circumscribe the earliest texts, the only "biographical" elements that are available come from relatively late textual or iconographic sources. It might seem natural, to us, to organize the events of the Buddha's life in chronological order, from birth to death, and many biographers and historians tried to do so with varying degrees of success. Yet it was not until several centuries after the Buddha's death that the first "complete" biographies appeared. The Buddha's life, originally so poor in events, became plethoric.[51] At some point, this life story, which already existed implicitly in iconographic representations, passed through a sort of "percolation" threshold, becoming transformed into a complete biography. We cannot say enough about the contingent and quasi-miraculous character of that evolution, which seems to us, in retrospect and fictitiously, so natural. The biography so formed was not the shadow cast, through the centuries, of a real biography, but the result of a long concatenation of scattered fragments, histories, and traditions of geographical, social, and historical data. The result was a fiction that served as a framework for the "realistic" narratives composed by historians.

The concept of a biography imposes the ideal of a "unified whole" extending from birth to death. The biography of the Buddha does not form—far from it—a unified whole. In order to obtain a "complete" biography, two independent cycles (that of the parinirvāṇa, elaborated early, and that of the birth and youth of the Bodhisattva, a later development) seem to have been connected after the fact, and in a rather artificial way. The biography may thus have developed in reverse: from the end (the parinirvāṇa) to the beginning (the youth of the Bodhisattva). In most accounts of holy lives, the only fact that is more or less certain concerns the death of the saint. Starting there, hagiographers try to work back in time, going into increasingly obscure areas of the saint's life, where they can give free rein to their imagination and tell us about all kinds of wonders. *Hic sunt dracones.* The Life of the Buddha was no exception: upstream of the parinirvāṇa, hagiographers invented a glorious youth, then his previous existences, interspersed with tales of victories over dragons, before extending the narrative from the life of Śākyamuni (including his previous existences) to those of past buddhas. According to some observers, it was actually the prior existences of past buddhas and of the Bodhisattva, as reported in the *Jātakas,* that provided the model for the Buddha's biography.[52] In any case, these *Jātakas* often became the real springboards of the story: in the *Mahāvastu,* for example, the Bodhisattva's past lives are constantly invoked to explain this or that event in his present life.

In principle, the awakening (*bodhi*) should represent the culmination of Śākyamuni's life, since that is what makes him, precisely, the Buddha (or Awakened One). However, tradition hesitated on this point and gave as much if not more importance to the parinirvāṇa. Perhaps the reason was that the Life so formed was the composite product of two narrative actants—the Bodhisattva (Śākyamuni before the awakening) and the Buddha (the same after)—or of two moments—the spiritual quest, culminating in the awakening; and the preaching, culminating in the parinirvāṇa—which in retrospect were fused into one. The Buddha was therefore "historical" only up to a certain point, namely, the moment of his awakening, after which he somehow doubled, and his essential being became identified with a supra-historical reality, the Law or Dharma. According to the Mahāyāna, even if he appeared to continue his earthly destiny, in reality it was a transcendental principle, a higher consciousness that was incarnated in him and now guides beings.

Thus the problem that the Life of the Buddha poses to the biographer is that it is an ellipse with two centers or, if you like, two distinct narratives, each leading to a kind of apotheosis: awakening and parinirvāṇa. The difficulty lies in the fact that the Buddha was said to have attained awakening (i.e., a type of nirvāṇa) at the age of thirty-five, and only passed away much later, at the age of eighty. His life is first and foremost the story of a quest, which should end, in the manner of fairy tales, with a formula such as "And he lived happily for the rest of his days." But how, then, to conceive and tell of the sometimes monotonous continuation of those days? The Buddha was resolved to teach his new doctrine, but at the same time his life became rather monochrome (at least to narrate) even if it was spiced with a few miracles. It was a long series of journeys, punctuated by summer retreats, during which he had to face the problems posed by an ever-growing community. Gone was the superb heroism of solitary asceticism. As the community developed, it also lost the beautiful cohesion of its beginnings, and the danger of schisms emerged. Devadatta's schism was only the symptom of a complex and partly obscure situation. We understand better the reasons the Buddha may have had for hesitating to preach, as it would mean leaving the serene heights of awakening to return to a prosaic and tormented reality. Accordingly, the account of the period linking the first sermon to the parinirvāṇa has struck some historians (like Foucher) as only filling, while others have considered it the quintessential part of the Buddha's Life. In any case, with the parinirvāṇa, the story seems to come to an end, marked by the cremation of the Buddha's body. But the narrative is stubborn, and its end is always postponed. Even though it is cloaked with the sense of an ending, the parinirvāṇa itself is not yet the final extinction.[53] The Buddha lives on (*sur-vit*) in his relics, and there is another nirvāṇa, the "nirvāṇa of the relics," which in Theravāda is supposed to mark the Buddha's true disappearance from this world and the concomitant possibility of another Buddha's appearing in it.

This raises another problem for the biographer: where does the Buddha's life—or rather, in Buddhist terms, the psycho-physiological "series" called Śākyamuni—begin and end? The historian, for whom every biography has a definite beginning and end, might now have the unpleasant sensation of being confronted with a narrative without beginning or end—much less head or tail. He or she stares at a considerable (and indeed staggering) extension of the narrative domain. Unlike the earthly existence of Śākyamuni, marked by his birth and death (or parinirvāṇa, for Buddhists), the Buddha's Life takes place in a cosmic and temporal framework that is far broader than a single human life. Therefore any account of his Life, while it may strive to respect a certain chronology, cannot presume to achieve the linearity expected of a Western-style biography. This straight-line pattern is so ingrained by now that we forget it took several centuries to impose itself in the case at hand.

The Life of the Buddha, refracted by innumerable textual or iconographic mirrors, developed in multiple ramifications; it was the product of an arborescent evolution that led to a profusion of meaning. Certainly the irresistible tendency of almost all biographers, from the authors of a "Complete Life"—Indian, Chinese, or others—to modern historians, has been to give or rather construct from scratch a roughly chronological account, made up in part of non-narrative elements (such as doctrine). It is tempting to let oneself be carried by the narrative stream. But that would be to forget a little too quickly that this linear pattern is not a description of "facts" but rather the result of a long elaboration, a collection of disparate elements, and that its linearity is therefore more or less illusory. And this elaboration is not finished, it is an ongoing process. The Life of the Buddha is an open biography, and historical biographies are only a continuation of it.

The concept of a biography follows a linear arrow of time. The Life of the Buddha as we know it only came into being through the efforts of hagiographers and historians, who sought to fill in the gaps and anchor it in a little-known Indian society. So great is our thirst for storytelling, however, that it hardly matters—as Sheherazade understood so well. This narrative, far from being linear, constitutes a complex network, a sedimented structure, clearly visible in texts like the *Mahāvastu.* Here we can see a "deconstruction" taking place *avant la lettre.* The Buddha's last life acquires its meaning only through its relationship with his past lives. Śākyamuni is both an individual (with specific biographical data) and a type—that of the Buddha, endowed with the thirty-two marks of the great man. And always the question of the narrator and the narrative voice arises. Who is speaking? It is usually assumed to be Ānanda, the beloved disciple who declares at the beginning of every sūtra, "Thus have I heard . . . ," but this is patently a narrative device and not the account of an eyewitness. It is known that the Buddhist sūtras developed over a period of several centuries (between the 1st cent. BCE and the 5th cent. CE), and anonymous authors are hidden behind that initial invocation—some of them, especially in the Mahāyāna tradition, perhaps evincing the "revelations" obtained in the course of their own visionary experiments.

Even when it seems to assert its linear character, the narrative of the Life of the Buddha presents an "accordion-like" structure that compresses some episodes while unfolding others, depending on the circumstances. Each event, even those of secondary importance, can be brought into the foreground to provide a speaker with a (if not *the*) key to the Life of the Buddha. In some cases, the narrative can also present a layered structure. In the *Mahāvastu,* for example, this structure creates a circle of biographical legitimization: the text begins in the present, goes back to the past, and returns to the present, thus identifying past and present. As a group of monks discuss the Buddha's past existences, the Buddha, who listens to the conversation with his divine hearing, joins them and talks about the six buddhas who preceded him. He takes the example of Vipaśyin, the first of them, and lists his thirty-two marks; he recounts Vipaśyin's life up to the moment when, exhorted by the god Brahmā, he decided to teach. After that, he gives some indications about himself—probably the longest "autobiographical" section of the whole canon, although it is buried under textual layers relating to the biographies of other buddhas. This is information that he never gives about himself in sūtras.

We can thus observe two opposite tendencies in the development of the Life of the Buddha. First, there is a more or less linear narrative tendency (at least in its aim), which seeks to link all the biographical elements into a single narrative, and to connect all the dotted lines into a single continuous line, according to a principle that could be summarized with the formula, "Narrative abhors a vacuum." New episodes are constantly added, which can in turn give rise to illustrations. Opposing this narrative tendency is another that consists in reducing the life of the Buddha to certain paradigmatic episodes (or vignettes) and reorganizing them thematically. This tendency, which could be described as *kaleidoscopic,* has the effect of repeating certain events in the Life of the Buddha in incessant variations. The narrative thread is interrupted, or rather the grand narrative breaks up into various small narratives, each of which is classified by theme. It is this second tendency that allows us to deconstruct the Life of the Buddha rather than reproduce it in the wake of all the biographers—hagiographers or historians, the difference is not so great—who preceded us. These two tendencies broadly cover the opposition between narrative and structure. Structure engenders narrative, but narrative is not reduced to structure; it has an important performative and ritual dimension.

In sources such as the *Mahāvastu,* the temporality of the Buddha's last human life is intertwined with the timelessness of the myth: the highlights of this life are transported *in illo tempore,* but also at a precise moment in a life that should serve as a model. Subsequently, we move from a continuous narrative to a modular narrative, which already appears in the *Divine Exploits* (*Divyāvadāna*), a collection of Sanskrit tales that seems to date back to the second century CE.[54] A further step is taken with thematic biography, as it develops in China in such works as the *Origins of the Śākya Clan* (*Shishi yuanliu*), an illustrated life of the Buddha dating from 1425.[55] The division into chapters leads to the establishment of synoptic tables that allow the various biographies to be compared (and reconciled if necessary). The Life of the Buddha, thus fragmented into modules consisting of a short text and the corresponding illustration, loses the continuity of his experience that texts such as the *Buddhacarita* and the *Lalitavistara* had somehow succeeded in suggesting; on the other hand, this discontinuity is partly filled by the multiplication of fragments or vignettes. But such division, which makes each episode, duly recorded, an event similar to all the others—reducing, for example, Māra's assault or the Buddha's awakening to the same length as minor episodes—has the effect of flattening this existence, reducing it to a coded series, perfectly manipulable for preaching, according to the liturgical needs of the Buddhist community.

On the iconographic level, there is a similar distinction (and sometimes confusion) between narrative representations illustrating a particular episode in the Life of the Master and "iconic" representations, offering the ideal image of a Buddha who has reached (or is about to reach) awakening, having already transcended temporality. These seem to have become the most important, but it further appears that some iconic representations interpreted as "bodhisattvas" (or as the future Maitreya Buddha) are in fact narrative representations of Siddhārtha in meditation, before the great departure.[56]

Paradoxically, the spiritual experience of the Buddha, accumulated over many existences, leads to a realization that removes all reality from that experience (since it is revealed as an illusion, showing the emptiness of the self that lived it). As a result, it acquires an uncertain ontological status as a limit-experience, since in principle there is no longer a subject to undergo it. The Buddha is not an ordinary individual, he is no longer strictly speaking an individual, and this is what makes him the supreme agent. Ultimately, it is his very experience—the course his own life has taken leading to his awakening—that allows him to understand the emptiness of any personal narrative. It is the biographical narrative itself that reveals this truth, namely, that every biographical narrative is null and void, because there is in fact no self or subject to which it can be applied.

In the Buddhist tradition there is a constant tension between narrative and anti-narrative tendencies, with the awakening or the parinirvāṇa as the end of the narrative, a climax that flattens the whole landscape before it. In a sense, there can be no historical Buddha, because awakening, the anti-narrative, is supposed to abolish all personal history. Historians, however, have persisted in denying that such an awakening is possible, seeing it as a kind of intellectual achievement, which cannot produce a radical mutation. For them, the Buddha is not a superhuman, much less a god; he is only a sage or a philosopher among others, a *primus inter pares*. As Louis Marin used to say, "Narrative is a trap."[57] It is all the more so for a Buddha whose essential activity lies in principle beyond worldly phenomena, and therefore beyond any narrativity.

In short, the biography of the Buddha is a late, laborious construction, one that, barely finished, seems once again to fragment, unravel, and multiply all over again. The narrative biography, constantly interrupted by the narration of previous existences, never manages to "thicken." No matter how much one tries to fill the intervals between "events" to give the appearance of continuity, the whole retains an artificial character. If the narrative still retains all its prestige, it is at the level of the sub-elements, not of the whole. Certainly, the idea of a life is fulfilled—giving the illusion of a continuous and unstoppable flow that carries the Buddha from birth to awakening and extinction; and once achieved, the model becomes self-evident, providing historians with a ready-made framework. But alongside this complete and linear biography, other partial, and in a way multidimensional, biographies continue to proliferate.

Our Western conception of a biography is poorly adapted to the concept of multiple "lives" or to the paradoxical continuities of a self that is different in each of its past lives, not to mention the theory of "no-self" (*anātman*) that undermines the very existence of an (auto)biographical self, replacing it with a psychophysical series. In the *Great Discourse on Lineage* (*Mahāpadāna Sutta*), for example—the same Pāli text that Thomas Rhys Davids called the "weed" of Mahāyāna—the Buddha is only a nodal point, albeit an important one, within a network formed by many past buddhas.

Yet the narrative of the Buddha's life is also normative, including in particular a ritual imperative that serves as a paradigm for Buddhist practice. In certain contexts at least, the narrative sometimes tends to assert itself as such, carried forward by its own movement, or by what might be called narrative pleasure; it no longer aims simply to account for an event—biographical or otherwise—or a doctrine. The two tendencies are not mutually exclusive, however, and at the very heart of this narrative lies a tension between narrative and doctrine. But, as Michel de Certeau points out, opposites are compatible in the *same* text as long as it is *narrative*. Temporalization creates the possibility of making consistent an "order" and what is heterogeneous to it. In relation to the flat space of a system, narrativization creates a thickness that makes it possible to place, *next to* the system, its opposite or remainder.[58]

BACK TO MYTHOLOGY

Despite all the claims to objectivity by historians, the historical Buddha is undoubtedly one of the great myths of modern times. One could almost believe, as used to be said in novels and films, that any resemblance between this figure and an actual person, living or dead, is purely coincidental. At the same time, it is difficult for people to call themselves Buddhists without believing that the Buddha existed, or even still exists—in one way or another. But this Buddha has little to do with the historical figure whose qualities as a philosopher or religious reformer have been vaunted for about a century and a half.

Recognizing the primacy of myth radically affects the historical discourse on Buddhism. By expunging from the Life of the Buddha all mythological elements, or rather by retaining only those that do not offend against reason, historians have been able to believe that they have found in the historical Buddha a kind of Socratic or Stoic sage, a rational and philosophical mind. Carried away by their demystifying enthusiasm, they have made a clean sweep and now find themselves empty-handed, reduced to telling legends they despise in the hope of recognizing in them, from afar, the echo of a historical fact.[59]

The "Life" of the Buddha, as it has come down to us, belongs essentially to the hagiographic imaginary. Even if we thought we had detected some vestiges of memorized facts, these (hypothetical) traces—we know what tricks memory can play—do not allow us to elaborate even a canvas. Yet it is such a canvas that historians have been quick to trace and fill with "facts." Whether the Buddha existed or is only a myth, the mythological Buddha is very real—since all Buddhism derives from it. All in all, then, I prefer the imagination of hagiographers, which is explicit, to that of historians, which is insidious, because it is masked.

Once we admit that the account representing the Life of the Buddha is the stuff of literature, legend, or mythology, we no longer have to worry about the subtle dosages to be observed between the historical dough and the leaven of the imagination. The historical Buddha is likely to remain out of our reach for a long time (if not forever); nevertheless, there is no valid reason to privilege, as we have done up to now, only the stories that seem to belong to a "primitive state of the legend" and to approximate so-called raw historical facts. For the historian of religions, all myths and legends are more or less equal. If one assumes that the myth itself is a set of partial myths, one can be content to keep a more developed version or a composite set of several variants—insofar as this is indeed how the myth proceeds, through a properly Lévi-Straussian *bricolage.* And one can, one must, abandon any claim to exhaustiveness, since the myth is by nature open, always in the process of creating itself and creating us—without point of origin, and therefore no alpha, but no omega either. What we can learn from the structuralist lesson is that all the variants of a myth are equal and that there is no original myth. The latter is only a virtual origin. The Buddha as we can reconstruct him according to tradition will always be a virtual Buddha.

Whatever the historicity of the Indian prince named Gautama or Śākyamuni, the Life of the Buddha is a founding myth, it is even one of the great myths of human history. Therefore, to understand it, we must return to mythology, but not the comparative mythology of Émile Senart or Pierre Saintyves (1870–1935), who saw naturalist myths everywhere and reduced the legend of the Buddha to a solar myth.[60] The structuralist method, in its Lévi-Straussian and Dumézilian variants, is more appropriate in that it reveals certain mythological structures underlying the Life of the Buddha. It does, however, put in brackets (or in equations) what is most important, namely, the narrative itself, in its eminently temporal aspect, its becoming. In this sense, it is also reductive and should only be used as a supplementary method to account for certain elements of the Life, and not as the key that explains everything.

Approaching the myth in its historical development, as a living process, is thus the only way forward if we want to avoid any taint of (mythologizing or historicizing) reductionism. In reaction against the historicist approach, which reduces the Life of the Buddha to a kind of *curriculum vitae,* I have chosen to deploy the range of possibilities and to consider the *Lives* of the Buddha in their diversity, as a tribute to the creativity of humans, their traditions, and their cultures. Yet variety, which usually results in enrichment, can sometimes lead to the opposite result, as when certain polemical accounts of the Buddha's life are too clearly intended to demean the character. Such is the case with the descriptions of the Buddha by Christian missionaries: they cannot be blamed for their lack of imagination—they go so far as to make him an African with frizzy hair. But in essence, their narrative is a hijacking of meaning and not so different from the "historical" narrative, even though the latter consciously takes the opposite view.

The man who may have inspired the legend of the Buddha Śākyamuni sank into the dark abyss of time, like a stone to the bottom of the sea. But the waves produced by this event are still spreading on the surface of human culture. Trying to understand the mystery of this event from a historicist point of view is obviously a misunderstanding. Diluting the event into a more or less timeless myth is another. The Buddha's life is above all a story, and whether it is mythological or realistic is in the end of little importance.

At this point, I hope I have shown how the simple pieces of evidence that usually support the notion of a "biography" of the historical Buddha vanish as soon as one looks a little closer, leaving room for a discursive proliferation that seems to taunt historians (as well as mythologists, even if they are a little better equipped to account for it). In the following pages, I try to loosen the biographical constraints and lighten the narrative links, hoping to untie the thread (or strings) of the narrative. Whether I can succeed given the grip of the thread (and weft) of the narrative on our comprehension, I leave it to the reader to judge. Our lives—together with our memory and our very identity, according to the cognitive sciences—are organized according to this narrative principle. It is difficult to imagine that it could be otherwise.

This must be the reason it is so difficult to grasp the idea that it took several centuries for a complete biography of the Buddha, from birth to death, to come into being. Far from being self-evident at first, the Life of the Buddha, once established, has commanded our vision of him. Here again, perhaps the obviousness of that observation is false, the result of a confirmation bias that prevents us from seeing counter-examples—however clear in the case of China. Ancient cultures, without rejecting the biographical principle, did not attach as much importance to it as we do, although they were no less fond of stories of all kinds. Even more so, Buddhist practitioners, whose practice was centered on experiences close to what we today call mindfulness, perhaps preferred momentary experiences over a Bergsonian *durée.* After all, wasn't a clear focus on the present moment the best way to get closer to the not-self advocated by the Buddha? But it may not even be necessary to rely on Buddhist doctrine to deconstruct the Buddha's biography: modern narrative studies make the sequence of events a structural element. On the philosophical side, Galen Strawson's thesis opposing two types of individuals—some who prefer narrative, others who do not—leads to the same result.[61] In this light, paradoxically, we have sought to present a "Life" of the Buddha that is not a biography and not even a true fictional narrative. As Antonio Muñoz-Molina notes: "Fiction . . . is an art of limits. . . . Departures, arrivals, and dates provide a beginning and an end to stories, but the future lasts a very long time and the past is as long as the future."[62] The structuralist approach advocated by mythologists since Lévi-Strauss must itself ultimately be outgrown to reflect the fascination exerted by the Life of the Buddha as a paradigm of Buddhist faith and practice.

PART TWO

THE LIFE OF THE BUDDHA AS NARRATIVE AND PARADIGM

If historical discourse strives, in its best moments, to stick to the complexity of reality, the historicism that has dominated Buddhist studies is reductive by nature. In its view, the Life of the Buddha becomes a signifier, each element of which must be able to point to a "historical" signified. Hence the temptation to eliminate all apparent (or sometimes real) nonsense. But while flying toward the meaning, our thought forgets to linger on the pleasure of the text.

In the next chapter, I try to resist this slope, sometimes contenting myself with giving the stories that recount episodes from the Life of the Buddha without interpreting them, exploring their nooks and crannies to bring out the narrative qualities of these stories without trying too quickly to go beyond them toward a meaning that overlooks them. While my goal is to resist the historicizing discourse, I occasionally fall back into old habits and suggest reading keys or compare different versions and interpretations given by specialists.

4

THE LIFE OF THE BUDDHA IN ACTS

Very early on, the Buddhist tradition sought to summarize the Life of the Buddha in four or eight key moments. One may wonder whether it was a biographical totality that was cut apart in this way, or a series of independent anecdotes that were gradually aggregated into a larger whole to constitute a biography. As we saw, Foucher had clearly seen that this biography was elaborated with a geographical logic around four major holy places: those of birth (Kapilavastu or Lumbinī), awakening or bodhi (Bodh Gaya), the first sermon (Sarnath), and the final extinction or parinirvāṇa (Kuśināgara). Anchored on these sites, the four high points of the Buddha's Life then became "attractors" around which real legendary cycles developed. Between these cycles, in their interstices, as it were, ancillary narratives emerged, which sometimes reinforced the narrative thread and sometimes subverted it. These side paths, no longer obeying temporal logic, are tiny uchronias, parallel or minuscule lives that make it possible to deconstruct the linear biography and show the nodal proliferation of cycles, which have their own dynamics, like nodes on a network. Despite the advances logged in Buddhist studies, it is still difficult to provide a precise chronology of the development of the episodes.

Without knowing too well why or exactly when, four new places, and thus four new "acts" or "events" were added relatively quickly to the first ones, forming an intermediate sequence between the youth of the Bodhisattva and his extinction: Sāmkāsya, the place of his descent from Trāyastrimśa Heaven; Śrāvastī, where, among other things, the miracle of the multiplied bodies took place; Rājagṛha, the place of the submission of the elephant Nālāgiri; and Vaiśālī, the place where a monkey made a gift of honey. These eight sites were associated with liturgical texts entitled "Homage and Offerings to the Eight Sites," the recitation of which allowed for "paying homage from afar" in lieu of the pilgrimage itself.[1] Each of these eight acts in turn attracted other secondary episodes, some of which became more important: the four encounters that caused the Bodhisattva to renounce the world, his great departure, his six years of austerities, and his victory over Māra. Let us note here a point to which I will return, namely, the existence of "floating" episodes that are not fixed chronologically, such as the Bodhisattva's first meditation under the jambu tree, during which he obtained a foretaste of the awakening to come.[2]

From very early on, the Ganges basin in northern India was understood to provide the setting for the Buddha's last existence, and one can find there four stūpas that commemorate the four acts. Subsequently, the accounts of his earlier existences in the *Jātakas* helped to raise the prestige of regions where Buddhism developed later, and where it was more difficult (but certainly not impossible) to locate events in the life of the "historical" Buddha. Thus Mahāyāna Buddhism invented (in the sense of discovering relics of the Buddha) a series of sites in Gandhāra and the Indus basin where some of these earlier existences were supposed to have taken place. It is these holy places that Chinese pilgrims such as Faxian and Xuanzang rediscovered over the centuries.[3]

According to Édouard Chavannes, "There are thus two Holy Lands of Buddhism, one in the Ganges basin, the other in the basin of the Middle Indus. Chinese pilgrims pass through the first before reaching the second (road of Kashmir and Udyāna), and many stop at the first (Peshawar, Taxasila). This middle basin of the Indus is the cradle of Mahāyāna."[4] Most of the new sites in northwest India commemorate the "gifts of self" performed by the Bodhisattva in his earlier lives. In Suvastu, for example, the Chinese pilgrim Faxian (337–422) saw a stūpa marking the place where, in the form of King Śibi, the Bodhisattva offered his flesh to a kite. A few days later, Faxian visited another stūpa erected on the very spot, it was believed, where the same king Śibi had offered his eyes.[5] In Taxasila, he also described the place where, in the form of King Candraprabha, the Bodhisattva offered his head to a brahmin. Further on, Faxian visited the place where the Bodhisattva offered his body to a tigress. We will return to these stories of self-sacrifice and their importance in the Buddhist tradition. These four places were marked by stūpas that were local replicas of the four great stūpas of northern India. Like them, they became the objects of popular veneration.

In the sixth century, another Chinese traveler, Song Yun, on an official mission to India, also described the sacred sites of Buddhism. Crossing Udyāna, he saw the place where the Bodhisattva, in the form of Prince Vessantara, had given his children to a Brahmin; nearby, the Bodhisattva had sacrificed his body to feed a starving tigress and her cubs. A stone on which the Buddha walked could also be seen in the vicinity of the city. Strangely enough, the dimensions of this stone varied: "It is sometimes long and sometimes short."[6] Farther south, Song Yun described various places that commemorate other "self-sacrifices" of the Bodhisattva.[7] In Gandhāra, he described the place where the Bodhisattva cut off his head. On the West Bank, he was shown the place where the Bodhisattva, having taken the form of a monstrous fish, was stranded and fed men with its flesh during twelve years of famine. He also visited the places where the Bodhisattva offered his eyes and flesh. In the city of

Nagarahāra, he saw several bodily relics of the Buddha.[8] He also visited the Buddha's Shadow Cave: "If one enters the mountain at a depth of fifteen paces and looks from a distance, then all the distinctive marks [of the Buddha] appear clearly; if one comes closer to look, they become darkened and invisible."[9]

In the seventh century, the Chinese priest Xuanzang (602–664) described the same places in more detail and added others, such as the monastery of Mahāvana (Great Forest) where the Bodhisattva, in the form of King Sarvadatta, gave his head to a beggar; or the stūpa that marks the place where, having taken the form of the god Indra, he transformed himself into a huge python that gave up its life to alleviate a famine and an epidemic in the valley.[10] Xuanzang's tears in front of these places expressed a feeling of dereliction, the regret of arriving too late in an orphaned world. When he visited the Buddha's Shadow Cave, he first of all noted with regret that the shadow is no longer visible, but after a tearful recitation of texts and multiple prostrations, he briefly glimpsed the form of the master; then, after still more prostrations, he obtained a clear vision of it. The journeys of the Chinese pilgrims were thus part of a circuit, among places full of meaning, rich in memories, and heavy with "presence"—but at the same time marked by absence.[11]

CYCLE OF BIRTH

Numerous sources begin the Life of the Buddha just before his birth.[12] The *Lalitavistara,* for example, expands on the Bodhisattva's activities in Tuṣita Heaven and the preparations for his last birth, including his choice of the correct time and place, and the criteria for choosing his future parents. Just as the Bodhisattva is said to possess the thirty-two marks of the great man, his mother-to-be possesses the thirty-two marks of the perfect mother: she has a deep navel; her thighs, even and well-made, are like the trunk of an elephant; her legs are like those of an antelope. "As she is in a body that seems to be the product of illusion, she has been given the significant name of Mâyâ."[13] It turns out that Śuddhodana and Māyā have already been his parents for five hundred past lives.

The Bodhisattva is now about to descend into the womb, but he has not yet determined in what form. He asks the advice of the other gods, who recommend various human, divine, or animal forms—including that of a rabbit. It is finally the white elephant, symbol of sovereignty, that prevails. The Bodhisattva then causes eight auspicious signs to appear. At this moment, Māyā chooses to purify herself, and she asks the king to declare a general amnesty. The conception, or "descent from Tuṣita Heaven," takes the form of a dream in which Māyā sees a majestic white elephant with six tusks penetrating her right side (fig. 1). In a variant, she dreams that she flies to the highest of the heavens, climbs a great rocky peak, and a multitude of beings prostrate themselves at her feet.[14]

FIGURE 1. The dream of Queen Māyā. 2nd–3rd century. Ghandāra (Pakistan). Carved panel, schist. British Museum (1932,0709.1).

In Chinese sources, it is no longer the Bodhisattva who takes the form of an elephant; he simply descends into the bosom of Māyā, mounted on a white elephant.[15] The first translations from Sanskrit into Chinese, such as the *Mahāvastu,* keep the image of the Bodhisattva-elephant. Nevertheless, the wrong interpretation—the Bodhisattva "mounted" on an elephant (and not like an elephant)—eventually came to the fore, probably because it was less offensive to Chinese minds, although the change is usually explained by appeal to the more "pragmatic" mentality of the Chinese. Foucher, for example, writes: "The Chinese thought they could solve the problem by imagining that the Bodhisattva had entered his mother's womb 'mounted on an elephant.' "[16] It is tempting to see this as a modification aimed at reducing the slightly too erotic aspect of the scene. Chinese translators, no doubt influenced by a certain prudishness in the Confucian tradition, often watered down passages of Buddhist texts that are a little too explicit—they did not have the possibility, unlike their Western counterparts, of translating them into Latin (or to leave them in Pāli or Sanskrit)!

In most sources, we go directly from Māyā's dream to the birth of the Bodhisattva without being told much about her pregnancy. However, some texts look more closely at this interval. In the *Lalitavistara,* it is the Buddha himself who, at the Jetavana monastery in Śrāvastī, tells his disciples about his intrauterine sojourn. Ānanda asks him how he was able to spend ten months in his mother's womb, the female body being reputed for its impurity. The

Buddha then describes in detail his uterine life, which he actually spent, without contact with the maternal womb, in a sumptuous palace where he was visited by the gods who came to hear him preach the Law. As Foucher notes: "It is inside this incorruptible tabernacle that for ten months he sat cross-legged in the Indian manner, already the size of a six-month-old child and provided with the thirty-two marks of the Great Man. It is from there that, by transparency, he illuminated the whole universe."[17]

The *Mahāvastu* also insists on the prodigious virtues of Māyā during pregnancy. The comings and goings of the gods do not cause her the slightest discomfort; on the contrary, she feels a constant sense of well-being. Thanks to the qualities of the Bodhisattva in her womb, she achieves perfection: virtue, purity, knowledge, and wisdom. All those who approach her are revived or healed. Renan describes the scene as follows: "The Bodhisattva, in his mother's womb, was always immersed in meditation, sitting cross-legged. His mother saw him in her bosom; she felt neither heaviness nor desires; she had no bad dreams; she saw nothing that was not pleasing in form, sound, smell, or taste. Meanwhile, the people of Kapilavastu were virtuous and happy; they lived in innocence and pleasure."[18]

At the end of her pregnancy, Māyā gives birth standing upright, without difficulty, holding onto the branch of a tree in the Lumbinī park. The Bodhisattva exits his mother's body as he entered it, through the right flank and not vaginally (fig. 2). This is probably a pious attempt by hagiographers to prevent him from being soiled at birth. It is also possible that they wanted to take into account the Indian tradition that the trauma of passing through the narrow gate erases the memory of past lives.[19] But the Bodhisattva, if he seems at first to remember his past lives, will soon forget them and rediscover them much later, at the moment of awakening. Foucher, like most Indian commentators, is relieved when the child appears: "At last the Child Buddha is born; and here we are out of this scabrous mixture of mythology and obstetrics, of gynecological details and pious scruples."[20]

The birth is said to have taken place in the park of Lumbinī, halfway between Kapilavastu and Māyā's parental house, where she wanted to give birth. The name of Lumbinī is not mentioned in the oldest sources, despite the tradition that makes it the birthplace of the Buddha. This tradition is based on the fact that King Aśoka himself visited this place and had a commemorative stele erected there. This same stele was recently rediscovered by archaeologists, with great media publicity.[21] Immediately, promoters hastened to throw out plans for the international city that would rise on the spot to allow a large-scale commercial exploitation of the legend of the Buddha. Lumbinī has since been recognized as a UNESCO World Heritage Site, and the "exact" place where the Buddha was born can be viewed within the Great Goddess Temple (Mahādevī). It is thus on the basis of a stele, so to speak, that the entire Life of the (historical) Buddha rests, and this is the reason that Lumbinī (now

FIGURE 2. Queen Māyā giving birth to the future Buddha. Early 19th century. Kathmandu valley, Nepal. Gilded bronze and copper alloy with polychrome inlay. Musée Guimet (MA1779).

Rummindei), a small and uninteresting town in the Nepalese Terai until these latter-day developments, has become a flourishing place of memory, a kind of utopia or theme park where Buddhists of all walks of life and of all nationalities can live and congregate side by side. A few years ago, an international colloquium was held there precisely on the "Birth of the Buddha," resulting in a scholarly publication.

The choice of Lumbinī has puzzled both old and new commentators. According to Bareau, the Buddha was more likely to have been born in Kapilavastu, some fifteen kilometers away. The transfer to Lumbinī is possibly explained by the hagiographers' desire to associate Māyā with a fertility goddess whose temple was located there. Many commentators have noted that the posture in which Māyā gives birth is reminiscent of that of the tree deities (*yaksinī*) who were worshiped as fertility goddesses. As Strong notes, one source mentions that one of these goddesses resided in the tree under which the Buddha was born.

According to the *Lalitavistara,* in the tenth month, Māyā asks the king to let her go to the park at Lumbinī. There she chooses a beautiful tree, under which the buddhas of the past were born. The tree bows toward her, and she grabs one of its branches as a sign of blessing. At this moment the child chooses to be born. When he emerges from his mother's right side, without causing her the slightest harm, he is received by the gods Indra (Śakra) and

Brahmā, who bathe him in two streams of water—one hot, the other cold—while the uterine palace is taken by the gods and removed to heaven, to Brahmā's world. In Indian descriptions, the water for his bath comes either from jars held by the gods, or from the trunks of elephants, or, most frequently, it is poured by two *nāgas,* aquatic spirits represented in the form of snakes (but sometimes also in anthropomorphic form). This is notably the version used by the *Lalitavistara,* where the Buddha explains to Ānanda how, at the time of his birth, two *nāgas* made two streams of water appear, one cold, the other warm, and sprayed him with them. In Chinese translations, these two *nāgas* become nine dragons, a traditional imperial symbol. Thus the art of each region used the symbols that represented the purifying power of water to confer royal status (the anointing rite known as abhiṣeka).

A variant describes the scene as follows: "[Indra], in order to hide this modest woman from the eyes of the men, caused a violent storm, and the soldiers, assailed by bursts of rain, dispersed. The lord of the gods, hidden in the guise of an old midwife, remained alone with the queen. The Bodhisattva was born without causing his mother a moment's suffering: he came out of her right side without any more effort than you make to open a door, go through it, and close it behind you. The body of [Māyā], intact, did not bear the slightest trace of injury. . . . The child was not naked: bodhisattvas, naturally adorned with dignity and modesty, are born draped in celestial garments."[22] This trait, which was known to St. Jerome, perhaps reflects an Indian belief that when a fetus dwells on the right side of the maternal womb, it will become a boy; and a girl, when it dwells on the left side.[23]

The miraculous birth is often depicted in bas-reliefs that do not include any images of the child. Māyā is depicted as a nearly naked fertility goddess in a dance posture, holding the branch of a tree. As early as the beginning of the second century CE, in the Gandhāra region, a very small child is shown miraculously emerging from the right side of his mother's body. In the more prudish Chinese and Japanese representations, Māyā is depicted fully clothed, and the child emerges from her long right sleeve.

According to the *Treatise,* the Bodhisattva, at the moment of his birth, walked seven steps and contemplated the four regions, and then pronounced these words: "I have been born, my births are over: this is my very last existence. I have obtained deliverance, from now on I will save beings."[24] This statement is about the same as what the Buddha will say at the moment of awakening. In the meantime, however, he seems to have forgotten his omniscience.[25] It is likely that this omniscience, first perceived as resulting from his awakening, was later projected back to the moment of birth, to enhance the prestige of the future Buddha (fig. 3).

The birth of the Bodhisattva is accompanied by that of several other characters who will play an important role in his Life—namely his future wife Yaśodharā, his future servant Chandaka, his future companion Udāyin, his

FIGURE 3. Birth of the future Buddha, by Hanegawa Chincho. 1705–1715. Japan. Hand-colored woodblock print. Art Institute of Chicago (1966.163).

future disciple Ānanda, his future elephant, and his future horse. Various signs presage his extraordinary destiny. When, shortly after his birth, he is brought to the temple to be presented to the tutelary goddess of the clan, it is she who, against all odds, pays homage to him. Having witnessed this prodigy, the child's father, Śuddhodana, in turn prostrates himself before him, calling him a "god superior to the gods" (*devatīdeva*). Commenting on this passage, Foucher, in his usual ironic vein, writes: "As all the desires and needs (*artha*) of Śuddhodana are thus fulfilled (*siddha*) by the grace of his supposed offspring, he decides to call him Sarva-artha-siddha or, more briefly, Siddhārtha: which is roughly equivalent to saying in French that, faced with the prosperity brought into his house by the little prince, the king decides to call him Prosper."[26]

The king then asks soothsayers to examine the child's body, on which they find the thirty-two characteristic marks of the great man. They conclude that the child is destined to become either a "king who turns the wheel [of the Law]" (*cakravartin,* or universal monarch) or, if he leaves the family to accomplish his spiritual quest, a buddha—*the* Buddha. The king is saddened because he fears that his son will leave, and decides to do everything possible to prevent him from doing so. This fear is an essential plot device, since it prefigures the four encounters episode. If the king had not cloistered his son, the latter, having grown up knowing the harsh realities of life, would not have experienced a salutary shock on his first outings.

The *Lalitavistara* then mentions, as if it were a detail, the death of Māyā seven days after the birth of her son. She is reborn directly in Trāyastriṃśa Heaven, at the top of Mount Meru (or Sumeru); or, according to the Theravāda tradition, in Tuṣita Heaven, an upper level of Buddhist cosmology.[27] "But don't think," the Buddha explains to his disciples, "that it is my fault that my mother died. It is the same for the mothers of all the buddhas, to spare them suffering when their son leaves home." Moreover, says the *Mahāvastu,* it is precisely for this reason that the Bodhisattva, from Tuṣita Heaven, had chosen as his mother a woman whose days were numbered. For it would not be fitting that the one who bore such an incomparable being should later enjoy the games of love. The *Buddhacarita,* for its part, attributes the death of Māyā to the excess of joy she feels in front of the almost divine perfection of the newborn baby![28]

CYCLE OF AWAKENING

From one cycle, let us jump directly, over the Bodhisattva's youth, to another, the moments that precede his awakening. The first gift he accepts, at the end of his long asceticism, is that of a young village girl named Sujātā. The *Mahāvastu* specifies that she was the mother of the Bodhisattva during five hundred previous existences.[29] In the *Introduction to the Commentary on Jātakas,* we read that Sujātā had asked the deity of a banyan tree to give her a son. Having obtained the fulfillment of her wish, she sent her maid to make an offering of milk rice to the deity, and the maid, dazzled by the beauty of the Bodhisattva, took him for the deity.

In the *Lalitavistara,* the Bodhisattva bathes in the Nairañjanā River before eating his meal. In other sources, having finished eating, he throws his bowl into the river, making a vow or "act of truth" (*satyakriyā*): "If I am to become a Buddha on this day, may this bowl go upstream!" Of course, that's what happens. The bowl is collected by a *nāga,* an aquatic deity that lives at the bottom of the river and has already seen three bodhisattvas do the same thing in the same place in the distant past. The *nāga* then realizes that a fourth bodhisattva is on his way to awakening. The offering of Sujātā, which somehow sets in motion the process of awakening, is particularly nutritious, since it will allow the Bodhisattva, who has meanwhile experienced his awakening and become the Buddha, to fast for forty-nine days. He divides the offering into forty-nine "pellets" (*piṇḍa*), a term used for rice offerings made to the dead. This seven-week period is also known throughout Asia as the liminal period between death and rebirth.[30]

The *Treatise* quickly passes over the steps that lead the Bodhisattva to awakening: "The Bodhisattva, renouncing asceticism, ate the milk soup of a hundred flavors, and his body regained its fatness. After bathing in the water of the Nairañjanā River, he arrived under the tree of awakening, sat down on the diamond seat, and took the following oath: 'I will remain with my legs crossed until I have achieved omniscience; until I have achieved omniscience, I will not tire of this seat.'"[31] Other sources, however, describe in more detail his progress from the river to the Bodhi tree.[32] This intermediate sequence contains a number of important elements, both symbolically and narratively. Some sources first mention a strange episode in which, before beginning his triumphal march, the Bodhisattva is suddenly reduced to the utmost distress by his opponent, Māra. While he is bathing in the river, Māra suddenly raises the height of its banks. About to drown, the Bodhisattva is saved in extremis by a tree deity (another one), who extends the branches of the tree down toward him.

The obstacles now cleared, the gods celebrate his progress toward the Bodhi tree (fig. 4). Along the way, he meets the *nāga* king Kālika, who predicts his imminent awakening. Near the tree, a grass cutter named Swastika gives him eight sheaves of *kuśa* grass to sit on. In the Pāli tradition, having reached the Bodhi tree, he still has to find the exact spot on which to sit. He tries facing successively south, west, and north, but each time the earth trembles, seemingly unable to support his weight. It is only when he sits facing east that he finds a stable base for his awe-inspiring meditation. He has truly reached the "seat of awakening" (*bodhimaṇḍa*), the navel of the world; so it is a kind of enthronement. Māra will then appear on stage, a little late, to challenge him.

FIGURE 4. Śākyamuni at the Bodhi tree. 2nd–3rd century. Ghandāra (Pakistan). Sculpture, schist. Cleveland Museum of Art (1997.151).

Victory over Māra

The victory over Māra (Māravijaya), the ruler of the world, is one of the most famous motifs in the Life of the Buddha, although, because of its openly mythological character, it has barely aroused the interest of historians. Some recent biographies of the Buddha do not even mention it, even though it had achieved considerable renown early on, including iconographic representation on the stūpa of Sanchi (in present-day Madhya Pradesh) in the third century BCE. Moreover, as Senart remarks: "The struggle between these adversaries is not a mere accident in the life of Śākya that can be disregarded if need be; it is—and this is what marks its true nature—absolutely necessary to his mission, it is inseparable from it."[33] Senart further opposes the common interpretation—probably inspired by Christianity—that wishes to see the episode as a Temptation of the Buddha: "Let it be noted that, in all versions, Śākya is in reality the aggressor; when he isn't represented as provoking his adversary directly, it is he who threatens to destroy Māra's power. This aspect obviates the idea of a 'temptation,' in the theological sense of the term, and gives us a true sense of the action: all the texts show it to be the struggle of two rivals fighting for the empire."[34] Put differently: "The idea of temptation, of a moral trial—far from being, as it ought to be, the central focus around which borrowed prodigies would cohere—has never been able to capture the point of the episode." According to Senart, this episode is instead analogous to the battle between the devas (gods) and asuras (demons) for world domination in the Hindu tradition.[35]

The Māravijaya theme has issued in multiple versions, and the *Mahāvastu* alone contains no fewer than four. Māra first tries to dissuade the Bodhisattva: "What good is this effort to you? Go home and become a universal king. Perform sacrifices, accumulate merits."[36] In another version, when the Bodhisattva sits under the Bodhi tree, Māra comes to laugh at him ten times. In response, the Bodhisattva roars fourteen times. Māra answers with sixteen laments, before launching his army. The Bodhisattva then touches the ground, and the earth resounds, terrorizing the demons (fig. 5). Then he enters a series of meditations that will lead him to his awakening.[37] A weird detail in this panoply: the Bodhisattva defeats Māra and his armies by the simple sound of his cough.[38] He exults: "Māra is defeated, the enemies are defeated, I am rid of every tie to existence." Māra then attacks the Bodhisattva at the head of his army, "uttering appalling shouts and threats; but the Bodhisattva extends his right hand, touches his head, his seat, then the earth, which resounds deeply, and immediately the entire army of Māra is dispersed, falls to the ground, and faints away."[39] The passage is repeated with a variation: "For seven days Māra and his people remain paralyzed, disfigured, at the feet of the Bodhisattva."[40]

FIGURE 5. Māra's attack. 2nd–3rd century. Ghandāra (Pakistan). Slate relief. Berlin State Museums (I 10198).

In other versions, Māra is more persistent. As in any fairy tale worthy of the name, he returns three times before admitting defeat. He first appears at the head of his army of demons, who shoot their arrows at the Bodhisattva—but the arrows turn into flowers. Then the Bodhisattva performs a series of wonders, sitting, standing, walking in the air, emitting water and fire (as he later does in Śrāvastī to confuse "heretical" Brahmins).[41]

It should be noted here that the gods, who had celebrated the Bodhisattva's progress to the Bodhi tree, cautiously slip away at the critical moment. In some versions, they even join the army of Māra, whose subjects they still are. After the Buddha's final victory, they hurry to congratulate him while Māra, abandoned by all, sits in a corner, drawing signs on the ground with his staff. In still other versions, the Bodhisattva calls on the ten perfections (*pāramitā*) for help, personified as warriors who put the battalions of Māra on the run, leaving the latter alone to face his opponent.

In a second stage of the battle, it is Māra's daughters who take the initiative (see plate 3). They intend to console their father by bringing him the

Bodhisattva "like a captive elephant, lassoed by their charm." Māra tries to dissuade them, but "disobeying their father, the beautiful celestial nymphs dare to tease the perfected Buddha as they once did the Bodhisattva: but this time their hubris cannot go unpunished. Suddenly they are transformed into decrepit old women, and it takes nothing less than their sincere repentance and the infinite leniency of the Buddha for them to regain their pristine beauty."[42] The iconography has retained this motif of the transformation of Māra's daughters into old women, which found an echo in monastic misogyny.

Finally Māra, in a third and final stage, challenges the Bodhisattva in words, calling him an impostor. The earth goddess, who in some versions had already intervened to rout Māra's armies, again plays a decisive role. When the Bodhisattva calls on the earth as his witness, it responds with a seismic tremor and manifests as a young woman who testifies to the merits he has acquired through rites and practices conducted in countless previous existences.

In the Pāli biographies, the earth is rarely personified, and the Buddha overcomes Māra by himself. In Sanskrit biographies, on the other hand, it takes the form of a goddess who plays an active, even combative role.[43] Among these, the *Buddhacarita* is the only source that does not mention her. In the *Mahāvastu,* the earth goddess emits a powerful roar that overturns Māra and his armies. (In other versions, there is both a roar and an earthquake.) In the Vinaya of the Mūlasarvāstivādin (a branch of the early Sarvāstivāda school), the goddess emerges from the earth, filling the scene with sound and fury, but Māra is humiliated rather than terrified. The *Lalitavistara* mentions two deities, one of whom holds a bowl of water to sprinkle on Māra. It gives two versions of the Māravijaya: in the first, the earth trembles six times and resounds when the Buddha's hand touches it (like a bell struck by its clapper), and the earth goddess, with her innumerable retinue, emerges from the ground and testifies to the merits of the Bodhisattva. In the second version, a voice resounds in space and threatens Māra, who loses consciousness. The goddess of the Bodhi tree, out of pity, sprinkles him with water to bring him back to himself. The earth is thus personified in the first case, but is replaced in the second case by the goddess of the Bodhi tree.

In response to his opponent's challenge, the Bodhisattva explains that Māra attained his rank as ruler of the world through the merits produced by a single sacrifice, whereas he himself has accomplished innumerable water libations in many previous existences. However, the mention of the countless libations, which turn into a tidal wave sweeping Māra's armies away, seems to bring us back to the realm of Brahmanic sacrifice. Furthermore, it is not clear whether the virtue of the Buddha is of the same nature (and simply greater) than that of Māra, or of a fundamentally different nature.

Georges Dumézil gave a structural interpretation of Māra's assault in light of the Indo-European ideology of the three functions (sovereignty, war, abundance). Although the traditional order of the three functions is modified here, Māra's three assaults seem to correspond to the three areas they govern: war (the assault of Māra and his armies), justice (Māra accuses the Bodhisattva of usurpation), and fecundity (the seduction attempt by Māra's daughters). Māra thus seeks to arouse three weaknesses in the Bodhisattva—fear, abdication, and sensual desire—any one of which would disqualify him as ruler of the world. In other words, he aims to reintegrate the Bodhisattva into one of the three major social roles that constitute Indian society: the warrior, the priest, and the householder. The Bodhisattva rejects these roles, of course, and affirms his transcendence of the social order.[44] For Dumézil, the transmission of this trifunctional structure from Brahmanism to Buddhism does not emerge either from popular beliefs or from a purely priestly transmission. Rather, it is to be seen as the influence of cultivated intellectual circles, "well informed of tradition, but free."[45] Dumézil's analysis is ingenious and quite relevant. However, by reducing Māra's assault to an ideological structure, it misses the very value (or even fascination) of the narrative. If it was only a question of presenting the theory of the three functions in a veiled, allegorical way, the episode would probably not have been so celebrated, especially outside the Indo-European area. The scene should not be read simply as a rejection of worldly power by the future Buddha, but as a power struggle between two pretenders to the throne. As Senart saw it, it is a question of who will occupy the diamond seat under the Bodhi tree. By attaining awakening, the Bodhisattva, who has become the Buddha, establishes himself as the ruler of the world. The renouncer has become the ultimate conqueror.

The gesture of the Bodhisattva touching the earth is the predominant motif in Southeast Asian Buddhist statuary. This motif, however, has lost its narrative character, to become a mere representation of the Buddha's awakening, in the same way as—and in competition with—the representation of the Bodhi tree. It is, on the other hand, rarely represented in the Far East.

The Awakening Itself

Canonical texts describe the three night vigils in which the Buddha attains his awakening. In the first vigil, he remembers his past lives and understands the emptiness of his self (*anātman*). This should mark the end of the narrative, since there is no longer, strictly speaking, any active subjectivity—but this is not the case: on the contrary, all the details of the Buddha's many past lives will be revealed. In the second vigil, he understands how beings are reborn through the mechanism of karma, the law of retribution, in differing conditions. In the third vigil, he understands how to disengage from the deep tendencies binding beings to the cycle of births and deaths (see plate 4).

From a narrative point of view, the awakening scene does not compare with that of the Māravijaya, which marks the dramatic climax of the

Buddhist legend. Moreover, it cannot be understood independently of the episodes that frame it. Should we entertain the idea that the awakening episode has two sides: the victory over Māra, and the awakening itself? The victory over Māra can be seen as the critical moment, on which everything else depends. Once the obstacles created by Māra are removed, there is nothing to prevent the Buddha from reaching awakening. In the *Lalitavistara,* the two moments are quite distinct and the subjects of two different chapters. But according to Foucher, they simply represent two ways of telling the same story. The first, in mythological dress, reflects the popular point of view; the second, demythologized, the monastic point of view. In other words, only the second should be considered authentic, the first being at best a pictorial description of the "scholastic train of thought" and other mental processes that led the Bodhisattva to his awakening.[46] This interpretation is not entirely convincing. Indeed, if the progression from the Māravijaya to the awakening does not seem to be a problem for the Buddha Śākyamuni, insofar as the defeat of Māra constitutes the necessary (and sufficient) condition for the awakening, this is not a universal rule, as shown by the example of a very ancient buddha named Mahābhijñanabhibū, for whom the two moments were not consecutive, but separated by many cosmic periods (*kalpas*).[47]

After the awakening, the Buddha remains immersed in concentration (*samādhi*) for one week. During this time, a strong storm rages, and a seven-headed *nāga* king named Mucalinda (var. Mucilinda) protects him by wrapping itself around his body and spreading its sevenfold hood over his head (fig. 6). When fine weather returns, Mucalinda unrolls its coils, freeing the body of the Buddha, then magically takes the form of a young Brahmin who prostrates himself at the feet of the master. Representations of this episode, like those of the Māravijaya, are very common in Southeast Asia, especially in early thirteenth-century Cambodia, during the reign of King Jayavarman VII (r. ca. 1181–1219), where the *nāga* was venerated as a royal symbol. The episode symbolizes the Buddha's domestication of the forces of nature (represented by the *nāga*), but at the same time the image of the two entangled bodies evokes a quasi-identity. For the pilgrim who encountered this image in a dark corridor of one of the Angkor temples, the Buddha must have seemed to fuse with the water deity, suggesting that the Buddha himself participates intimately in this chthonian power.

CYCLE OF THE FIRST SERMON

How can we justify the lapse of time between the awakening and the first sermon? Most accounts tell us that, during the seven weeks following his awakening, the Buddha hesitated to preach, wondering if anyone would listen to him: "My Law is deep, difficult to fathom, and difficult to know. Those who are

FIGURE 6. Buddha sheltered by the *nāga* king Mucalinda. 11th–12th century. Kathmandu valley, Nepal. Schist. Art Institute of Chicago (2014.1030).

attached to the things of the world are incapable of understanding it."[48] This initial hesitation disconcerted many commentators. The sources in fact disagree on the length of time that elapsed between the awakening and the first sermon. The Pāli Vinaya speaks of four weeks, the *Mahāvastu* and the *Lalitavistara* of seven. According to the latter version, exactly forty-nine days after his awakening, the Buddha, at the invitation of the god Brahmā, agreed to preach the Law. But according to the *Treatise,* the sermon preached in Benares (Vārānasī) did not take place until the fifty-seventh day. This extra week was filled by the Buddha's journey from Gayā to Vārānasī.[49] To justify this delay, the *Treatise* invokes precedents: "There are bodhisattvas who, after having achieved their awakening, do not immediately turn the wheel of the Law. Thus the Buddha Dīpankara, during the twelve years following his awakening, only emitted rays of light, and since there was no one to understand him, did not preach the Law."

Some have seen this delay as an obstacle created by Māra. Others claimed that the Buddha's preaching could only be done in response to an invitation to preach, because "the Buddha has no attachment to or love for his Law; it is out of compassion for beings that he preaches when he is invited to do so; if he is not invited, he will not make the wheel of the Law turn."[50] Thus it is in response to the repeated exortations of the god Brahmā that he finally resolves to preach. According to Georges Dumézil, this exortation is divided into three parts, which correspond, like the three attacks made by Māra, to the three Indo-European functions:

> This sort of incantation in three steps—look, get up, travel the world—challenges the Blessed in three aspects, in three qualities that he has just acquired with the *bodhi.* He is the *visionary* who, from the height that doctrine constitutes for him, can contemplate and understand the state of the world; he is the *warrior* who, victorious in the battle waged against ignorance and the resulting attachment, can help others in their own battle; he is the *caravanner* who, having been able to pay his debts, is now master of his itinerary and his action. This formula, the last two terms of which are unexpected, expresses a trifunctional conception of the omnipotence of the new Awakened One, a conception that is a transposition to the spiritual realm of that which founds temporal kingship.[51]

Dumézil's interpretation seems interesting to me, and it is a pity that he limited himself to a few isolated episodes, without seeking to apply it to the Life of the Buddha as a whole (as he did for the Indian epic, the *Mahābhārata*).

The Buddha's reluctance to preach seems to contradict the cardinal virtue of Buddhism, compassion. Moreover, this virtue is hardly evident in the stories of the Buddha's Life. In the early texts, the Bodhisattva's quest is motivated by his desire to find an escape from old age and death. According to Lambert Schmithausen, in exhorting the Buddha to preach, Brahmā implicitly asks his own worshipers, the Brahmins, to recognize the superiority of the Buddha and his doctrine.[52] Another common, but less charitable interpretation is that the Buddha acted with the ulterior motive of improving his reputation by urging Brahmā to invite him to preach—an idea difficult to reconcile with his detachment from worldly values.[53] In most sources, the Buddha's predominant concern seems to be for himself—before, during, and immediately after awakening.[54] If he hesitates to preach, it is for fear of disappointment that his listeners have failed to understand him. For the Mahāyāna tradition, this is indeed what happens when he preaches the *Avataṃsaka-sūtra* for an entire month, a sermon in which he gives direct expression to the ultimate truth. Faced with the incomprehension of his disciples, he first takes refuge in silence, then, yielding to Brahmā's exhortations, resolves to preach a simpler doctrine. Gradually, as the level of his listeners rises, he starts to preach higher truths: first that of the *Vaipulya-sūtras,* which represents a transitional phase, the beginning of Mahāyāna; then that of emptiness, as found in the *Prajñāpāramitā-sūtras;*

finally, again, the ultimate truth, but this time expressed in the *Lotus Sūtra,* the scriptural authority of the Tiantai school founded by the Chinese monk Zhiyi (538–597).

In the eighth week after his awakening, the Buddha receives a food offering from two merchants, Trapuṣa and Bhallika. In exchange, he gives them a lock of his hair and nail clippings. This episode is more important than it seems, since it inaugurates the transmission of Buddhism outside India (especially in Southeast Asia) and the cult of relics. It merges with the offering of four bowls by the four heavenly kings. When these deities offer four golden bowls to the Buddha, he refuses to accept, because doing so would not be suitable for a renouncer; they then offer him four bowls made of other precious materials in succession, and he refuses each one. Eventually he accepts four bowls of stone, which he magically merges into one.[55]

Strictly speaking, the Buddha's first sermon was the one he gave to the two merchants, but tradition considers that this title belongs to the sermon he gave to his five former disciples at the Deer Park in Sarnath, near Vārānasī.[56] This place was to become one of the four great centers of Buddhist pilgrimage in India. According to the *Lalitavistara,* the Buddha, seeking recipients for his doctrine, first thought of his two ancient masters, Udrāka and Ārāḍa Kālama, but these, he learned from the gods, had died three days earlier.[57] He then thought of his five companions during his ascetic practices and decided to join them in Sarnath. Seeing him coming, and convinced that he had betrayed their ascetic ideal, they prepared to treat him with contempt. But they were seduced by his majesty, and became his first disciples (fig. 7).

The first sermon is seen as one of the founding events of Buddhism. For Lamotte, it is the key to the entire subsequent development of Buddhist doctrine. Yet from a narrative point of view, it offers little interest. Its importance seems to lie above all in the fact that it anticipates and summarizes the Buddha's long teaching career. In the *Lalitavistara,* it is only toward the end of his sermon that he mentions the Four Truths, which will become the philosophical heart of Buddhism. Before that, he gives a long and surrealistic description of the beings who gather to witness the preaching of the Law, the same Dharma that all the buddhas of the past have expounded. He also gives a long explanation of the thirty-two marks of the Buddha. As a result, the new doctrine seems somewhat drowned in the mass of mythological elements, and it is difficult to make it the central point of the narrative, as modern biographers would wish. In the *Mahāvastu,* the first sermon is strangely divided into three parts, as if they had originated as independent sermons. The first part includes a discussion of the Four Truths, followed by a long description of an earthquake and its effects. The second and third parts, which are not found in the *Lalitavistara,* focus on the teachings of no-self and impermanence.[58] The *Buddhacarita* gives a somewhat more detailed account of the event but does not refer to the Deer Park, although this setting has become an integral part of the canonical

FIGURE 7. Buddha preaching the first sermon at Sarnath. 11th century. Bihar (India). Black stone. Metropolitan Museum of Art (20.43).

biography of the Buddha. The *Nidānakathā,* for its part, gives us a very succinct account and does not even mention the Four Truths. This is surprising—all the more so since this sermon is not mentioned in early Chinese biographies either, which seems to indicate that it represents a late tradition.[59]

The possibility that the first sermon did not emphasize the dogma of the Four Truths sheds new light on the supposedly original doctrine of the Buddha, since it is in fact this dogma that most Western authors, and the neo-Buddhist adepts who have followed them, consider to be the foundation stone of the entire edifice of Buddhist doctrine.

CYCLE OF EXTINCTION

The last highlight of the Buddha's Life, the extinction, or parinirvāṇa, is separated from the previous one by a long interval, which hagiographers have retrospectively filled with conversions, preachings, and miracles—including the

Buddha's stay in Trāyastriṃśa Heaven, the miracles of Śrāvastī, and the return to Kapilavastu. These events are described in detail in the *Mahāparinirvāṇa-sūtra,* which is known to us in six different versions, one in Sanskrit, another in Pāli, and the other four in ancient Chinese translations. In spite of its apparently biographical character, this text actually presents us with a transcendent and therefore ahistorical Buddha. It has been the subject of a series of in-depth studies by André Bareau, who, after a long and meticulous comparison of sources, considers the account of the parinirvāṇa almost entirely legendary, and limits himself to concluding that "the Blessed One died, very old and ill, during a journey, very close to the humble village of Kuśinagara, where he had stopped, exhausted, a few hours before."[60] Compared with this, the legend is fortunately more detailed.

But we have to go back a bit, to the moment when the Buddha, now in his eighties, decides not to "push his body" anymore—which he compares to an old cart. He has served his time and resigns himself to his impending extinction. A little later, however, we learn that it could have been avoided if his disciple and confidant Ānanda had had the presence of mind to ask him to stay in this world. The text also attributes responsibility to Māra, who convinces the Buddha that it is time for him to leave, and to the blacksmith Cunda, who unintentionally poisons him. To wit: Māra, intervening once again, finally succeeds in getting the Buddha to fulfill the promise he made, somewhat thoughtlessly, on the eve of his awakening. When Māra urged him to enter nirvāṇa on this occasion, the Buddha replied that he would not do so until he had made many conversions and trained many disciples. Māra now argues that all this has been accomplished, and there is nothing to hold the Buddha back anymore. The Buddha finally agrees and enters a concentration (*samādhi*) in which he extinguishes his vital principle. Although he will remain in the world for another three months, in fact he is already dead to this world. When he announces the news to Ānanda, the latter collapses. Instead of consoling him, the Buddha holds him responsible for his departure, explaining that he could have held him back by asking him to stay in this world, since as a Buddha he is perfectly free to come and go between worlds. As the fatal moment approaches, the Buddha accepts a final offering of food from the blacksmith Cunda, which will be the immediate cause of his death. In some traditions, to avoid having the onus fall on Cunda (and thereby showing more compassion for him than for Ānanda), the Buddha explains that the fatal foodstuff is only the instrument of an inexorable karma.

The question of the Buddha's last meal has been the subject of much debate. The eminently "realistic" circumstances of this death by food poisoning constitute for most historians a clue as to the authenticity of the episode. Foucher, for example, writes sardonically, "The Blessed One, the Predestined, the Perfect One, died miserably in an obscure village from an attack of dysentery following a digestive upset caused by eating pork. What a comedown for the sublime Being who, a century or two later, would be exempted by his devotees from any human failings! But also what a guarantee of authenticity to have a fact that it would have been in the legend's interest to conceal or disguise!"[61]

This rather infamous end, however, offended not just the greatness of the character but also the vegetarianism of his disciples. Commentators were therefore divided on whether the fatal dish was meat or vegetarian. Some tried to interpret the term, which seems to refer to pork, as actually referring to a mushroom-based dish.[62] Bareau, more circumspect, rejects both interpretations: "We are here in the midst of a legend. . . . Let us recall in passing . . . that Indians of good caste, such as the Buddha was, have a deep dislike of mushrooms and not much less for pork; it would therefore have been as incongruous to offer him one or the other of these dishes to honor and delight him as it would have been to serve slugs and locusts to the pope at a banquet at the Elysée."[63]

When the "eye of the world" closes, all of nature participates in the mourning. According to the *Dharmasaṃgraha-sūtra:* "When the Buddha entered Nirvāṇa, the earth shook six times, the rivers flowed upstream, a strong wind blew up a storm, black clouds rose on all four corners of the horizon. There was thunder and lightning, hail and rain fell in showers, and here and there stars fell. The lions and wild beasts began to howl; men and gods wailed loudly. At the same time, plants, woodlands, grasses, trees, flowers and leaves suddenly cracked. Sumeru, king of the mountains, trembled on its foundation. Waves rose on the sea, the earth shook with a great tremor. Mountains and cliffs collapsed, trees broke, and smoke rose from every point on the horizon. There was great panic. Ponds and rivers were stained with mud. The stars appeared in broad daylight. Men began to weep, gods mourned, goddesses drowned while swallowing torrents of tears."[64]

The monks themselves, though accustomed to more restraint, join in this cosmic desolation (see figs. 8–9 and plates 5–6): "[Overwhelmed] with grief, [they] would fall unconscious or throw themselves on the ground, or whirl around staggering, screaming and sobbing without being able to control themselves. . . . Like large trees with roots torn out, branches and twigs cut off, or like snakes cut in half, turning and twisting without knowing how to join their sections together, such were these monks."[65]

There were a few exceptions, however—as in the following story: "There was a monk named Upānanda in the community at that time, who said to the monks: 'Stop! Don't grieve! With the Blessed One passed away, we have our freedom. That old man was constantly telling us: "Do this! Do not do that!" From now on, we will do what we want.' "[66] It was on hearing these words that the arhat Mahākāśyapa resolved to gather the main disciples of the Buddha to codify his teaching in what became the First Council.

FIGURE 8. The parinirvāṇa of the Buddha. 3rd century. Ghandāra (Pakistan). Schist. Metropolitan Museum of Art (2015.500.4.1).

FIGURE 9. The parinirvāṇa of the Buddha. 2nd–3rd century. Ghandāra (Pakistan). Slate relief. Berlin State Museums (I 80).

The parinirvāṇa is often represented in sculpture. But the Buddha, lying on his right side, became a figure more iconic than narrative. The narrative aspect is preserved, however, in monumental sculptures such as that in Cave 158 at Dunhuang, where we see the Buddha with Tibetan and Chinese kings at his feet, some of whom, in pain, seek to mutilate themselves, while one of the Buddha's great disciples, Subhūti, sets himself on fire. The scene was often depicted in paintings as well. Among the most famous representations are the beautiful paintings of Tongdosa monastery in South Korea, and various Japanese *nehan-zu* (images of the nirvāṇa), which we will return to later.[67]

Before entering the parinirvāṇa, the Buddha says to his disciples: "Those who wish to perform funeral rites for my body must apply the rules for the funeral of a holy *cakravartin* king. These rules are as follows: wrap the body in a number of pieces of cotton cloth, place it in an iron vat full of oil, cremate it on a pyre made of fragrant pieces of wood, place its remains in a burial mound raised at a large crossroads."[68] As Bareau notes, the vat full of oil does not seem to be justified by practical considerations such as conservation. In fact, it is not at the beginning of the seven days, but at the end, just before cremation, that the Buddha is placed there.

The body of the Buddha is then transported around the city, passing each of its four gates. The symbolism of the four gates would become significant in later Chinese sources, echoing the symbolism of the four encounters and the four events of the Buddha's life: birth, awakening, first sermon, and parinirvāṇa.

The cremation episode itself offers multiple developments. When the disciples try to set the pyre on fire, it refuses to light and the body cannot be cremated for seven days. This is attributed to the absence of Mahākāśyapa, who had gone on an alms tour. When he arrives on the scene and asks to see the body of the master, the other close disciple, Ānanda, answers that it is not possible. A strange occurrence now takes place: the feet of the Buddha—whose body is enclosed in several shrouds—suddenly pop out from the coffin, and Mahākāśyapa is able to pay homage to his master by circumambulating the coffin three times. The funeral pyre then ignites spontaneously and burns for several days and nights. The Chinese and Japanese traditions add another episode to the same theme, that of the Buddha sitting in his coffin to console his mother, who has come down from Trāyastriṃśa Heaven. If filial piety remains the central theme of this episode, it also shows that the Buddha, although he has entered parinirvāṇa, is not dead in the ordinary sense of the word, since he can still sit up in his coffin without being perceived as a vampire or a zombie (or their Asian equivalents). In China and Japan, this episode came to take precedence over the last homage of Mahākāśyapa to his master from around the seventh century.

The story could end there. But that would be counting against the genius of narrators in search of a narrative. The cremation of the Buddha leaves a residue of mysterious power, the relics (*śarīra*), whose fate will lead us on to new narratives. But before going there, we must interrupt the linear stream of the narrative to return to a number of secondary episodes that occupied on occasion, even without the same official recognition, as important a place in the Buddhist imaginary as the four events we have just examined.

5

SECONDARY EPISODES

To the four events comprising the birth, awakening, first sermon, and extinction, four others were added to form the canonical eight events or eight acts of the Buddha's Life. In the East Asian traditions, a different list emerged, consisting of the descent from Tuṣita Heaven, the stay in the womb, birth, leaving the family, defeat of Māra, awakening, first sermon, and parinirvāṇa. Before examining the additions, we must also mention a number of episodes that played significant roles in the Buddhist imaginary even though they were not accorded the same status. These include the various wonders (or "floating episodes") that marked the Bodhisattva's early years: his first meditation, his four fateful encounters at the city gates, his departure from the royal palace, the wonders he performed after his awakening in the city of Śrāvastī, his return to earth after a stay in Trāyastriṃśa Heaven, and his return to Kapilavastu, along with the additional wonders accompanying the conversions he performed during his long career as a preacher.

YOUTH OF THE BODHISATTVA

The *Lalitavistara* describes the main moments of the Bodhisattva's youth as follows. Having grown up quickly (within the space of a chapter), he is brought before his tutor to learn writing. But he has nothing to learn from him, and confuses him by asking him which of the sixty-four types of (Indian) writing he is going to learn from him—the poor man has never even heard of most of them. The king's advisers, remembering the prophecy, advise the king to quickly find a wife for his son. Śākyamuni, yielding to his father's request, lists the qualities he is looking for in a woman. Gopā (or Yaśodharā, according to the source) is finally chosen, but to deserve her he must distinguish himself in the arts (both letters and the martial arts). The list of arts and techniques in question includes the language of birds and animals, and the knowledge of perfumes. The Bodhisattva will have to face young noblemen, including his cousin Devadatta, who are determined to win the competition. It begins with writing and mathematics, in which the prince excels. He dazzles the spectators with his knowledge of arithmetic and cosmology, and then with his physical prowess (jumping, swimming, and the like). Moving on to the serious events in this world of warriors, the martial arts are next: wrestling, where he effortlessly triumphs over Devadatta, and archery—where, like Odysseus, he bends his grandfather's bow, which no one could accomplish after his grandfather's death, and each of his arrows hits its target. Yaśodharā is conquered. The king decides to unite these two beings, "as pure as the mixture of cream and milk."[1] The prince's easy victory prefigures his future victory over Māra.

The question of marriage having been settled, the Bodhisattva spends his days in luxury and voluptuousness. The king has had three palaces built for him: one for the rainy season, another for the winter, and a third for the summer. He entertains himself there with the women of his gynaeceum. Some sources, more prudish, are content to describe the extraordinary luxury he enjoys without insisting on the palaces' sensual pleasures. However, the gods become impatient, finding that he is spending too much time in the women's quarters. They therefore decide to remind him of the vows he had made during his many previous existences. Here is interspersed a long litany of past lives during which the Bodhisattva had already renounced the world, in the presence of the past buddhas. A sermon on the transience of all things is given to him in passing: "These countless kalpas have been exhausted by you, and these buddhas have gone into nirvāṇa. All the bodies that were yours and their names, where did they go? . . . When a kalpa ends . . . , old age, suffering, sickness, and death will all come to your door, terrible and accompanied by a great fear that is unbearable." It is these harsh realities of existence that the Bodhisattva will soon rediscover—having seemingly forgotten them in the meantime. But the message, repeated like a refrain, is not forgotten: the time has come for him to leave the family and to renounce his princely life. The gods await him, eager to lend their support. Thus, explains the Buddha to his disciples, "the Bodhisattva, when he was in the midst of the women's quarters, was not deprived of hearing the Law, was not deprived of meditating on the Law in his mind." Let there be no mistake, palace life is not all pleasure: "While in the midst of the women's quarters, he was waiting for the time when he could bring to maturation the elemental substance of beings."[2] Soon all the women of the gynaeceum were converted: "So then, by the Bodhisattva who had gone into the midst of the inner quarters, these eighty-four thousand women were fully matured."[3] Even the sound of the musical instruments and the songs of the women of the gynaeceum that reach the ears of the Bodhisattva are diverted from their frivolous meaning, as if they were exhortations to leave the palace without further delay.

THE FIRST MEDITATION

While all the efforts of biographers aim at elaborating a stable chronology, there is one episode that stands out for its "floating" or atemporal character, placed as it is during the adolescence (or even early childhood) of the Bodhisattva or, alternately, in his adulthood, just before the great departure. It is the episode of the first meditation, under the jambu tree. As Bareau notes, this episode and that of the four encounters never appear side by side in the texts. He concludes, a little quickly: "We see that the two episodes are two versions of the same fact, *undoubtedly real in any case,* namely, the event that was the determining cause of the Buddha's renunciation of secular life" [emphasis added].[4] While Bareau may reject as pure legend all the events concerning the youth of the Bodhisattva, he makes an exception for the first meditation. His reasoning is that the story, with the exception of a late version that adduces the jambu tree's miraculous immobile shadow, is in no way intended to make the Bodhisattva appear superhuman.[5] For him, this pastoral episode, which shows us the king as a landowner obliged to supervise the work done by his people in the fields, is probably based on an accurate recollection.[6] One can only admire the logical rigor of Bareau's argument once its historicist premise is admitted. Unfortunately, the essential narrative role of the meditation under the jambu tree leads one to question this interpretation and to see it instead as a structural device of the narrative, making it all the more difficult to accept as a real fact.

The *Lalitavistara* places the episode during the Buddha's youth. The Bodhisattva goes with other young men to a village of ploughmen. After observing their labor, he sits under a jambu tree and enters into meditation. Five ascetics, who happen to be flying over while exercising their supernormal powers, are suddenly stopped in mid-air by the force emanating from the Bodhisattva's meditation. They then pay homage to him. Meanwhile, the king, having noticed the absence of his son, has sent his servants in search of him. One of them finds the youth and realizes that, while the shadows of the other trees have moved, only the shade of the jambu tree under which the Bodhisattva sits remains motionless, protecting him from the sun. The king, hearing of the miracle, comes to prostrate himself before his son. The latter, coming out of his meditation, promises his father to shower him with blessings. Then he returns to the city, but he has already made up his mind to leave the palace.

The episode is in fact composed of two parts: a trial and a miracle. The miracle is that the jambu tree's shadow stops changing in order to protect the Bodhisattva's meditation. This miracle remained famous in Buddhist legend—and it was known even in the West, since Flaubert mentions it in *The Temptation of Saint Anthony.*[7] The trial consists, for the Bodhisattva, in contemplating the spectacle of the sufferings of the animal world, ruled by the laws of killing, and the sufferings of the human world, ruled by the rigors of labor (imposed in this case on the ploughmen and their oxen). It is thus an encounter with active pain, which complements the passive pain represented by old age, sickness, and death that the Bodhisattva will discover in his four encounters. Meditation leads him to the recognition of suffering, which the Buddha will make the first of the Four Truths. But it also leads, by a kind of grace, to his experiencing the first of the four levels of meditation (the four *dhyānas*). In the *Latitavistara,* the Bodhisattva experiences the four levels in their totality, which introduces an anachronism, since it is precisely this experience that will constitute, much later, his awakening. In one of the first versions of the story, the Bodhisattva reaches the first *dhyāna,* then he reflects on the evanescence of things and recites stanzas (which resemble the Four Truths). This last part is abandoned in later texts, and the meaning of the episode changes: it simply explains how the Bodhisattva found, as if by chance, the method of the first *dhyāna,* but not why he renounces secular life. This renunciation is explained by the episode of the four encounters. It is the latter that has been retained by tradition, although the pictorial sources show us the crucial role played by the first meditation. In the *Mahāvastu,* the first meditation under the jambu tree is followed by a repetition of this meditative experience in the palace, which is one of the reasons the two scenes are sometimes combined iconographically. This depiction of the "pensive prince" in his palace became particularly popular in East Asia, even to the point of supplanting that of the first meditation; but the two types of images represent essentially the same idea, the realization of universal suffering and the desire to transcend it.[8]

In the *Buddhacarita,* this meditation takes place when the Bodhisattva has become a young adult, and it has been integrated into the cycle of the four encounters. When the prince goes out on three occasions through the east, south, and west gates of the city on an excursion to the parks, he successively meets an old man, a sick person, and a corpse; after each meeting he returns to the palace without completing his excursion. The fourth time, out of the north gate, he reaches the park. But by the side of the road he sees ploughmen and feels compassion for them, and he sits under a jambu tree to meditate. It is at this point that the fourth encounter—with a wandering monk—takes place.

The first meditation is not only a decisive element in Śākyamuni's decision to renounce the world; it is also his memory of it that allows him to break the deadlock he reaches after six years of austerities. It thus prefigures the final meditation that will lead to his awakening. From an iconographic point of view—in both cases, he is sitting under a tree—it very much resembles it, and this resemblance is not fortuitous. The only difference is that Śākyamuni is still depicted as a prince in the representations of his meditation under the jambu tree, whereas under the Bodhi tree, he has become the Buddha.

THE FOUR ENCOUNTERS

The events of the four encounters make up a crucial episode in the Life of the Buddha, the one that determines him to renounce the world. We have seen that, on the four occasions when he left Kapilavastu, the Bodhisattva was confronted with an old man, a sick man, a dead man, and a wandering religious, respectively. The episode actually appears in the life of a past buddha, Vipaśyin, and only the Vinaya tradition, after the fifth century, links it to Śākyamuni. As we have just seen, in early sources such as the *Lalitavistara* and the *Buddhacarita,* the meditation under the jambu tree played this role. Although in most sources the four encounters occur at intervals relatively distant in time, in some they take place on the same excursion. The Vinaya tradition locates the encounter with the ascetic on the third excursion, just after the vision of the corpse. The ascetic, as described, looks like a Buddhist monk (*avant la lettre*). In the *Mahāvadāna-sūtra,* the prince renounces the world immediately after meeting the ascetic, without even returning to the palace.[9]

The psychological shock experienced by the Bodhisattva in the face of the harsh realities of life is somewhat surprising. Some commentators have not failed to wonder about the amnesia that seems to have struck him in his youth. He who was so clear-sighted at birth is now forced to rediscover truths he should have known better than anyone else.[10] It is clear that we are dealing here with a narrative device explaining his decision to leave the palace. The Bodhisattva, once reduced to the human condition, becomes a model of the conduct typical of people who can forget a long series of previous existences, such as the one that led Śākyamuni to this crossroads of his present life.[11] Later tradition, in glorifying the Buddha, tended to minimize the human significance of his life, and at the same time the episode of the four encounters.

THE GREAT DEPARTURE

Back at the palace, the Bodhisattva, still troubled by his encounters, perceives a hidden meaning in the songs of the women of his gynaeceum—a meaning that is suggested to him by the gods to encourage him to leave. After meditating for a long time, he falls asleep, and the women stop their music and dancing. They fall into a deep sleep—induced by the gods—and when he wakes up in the middle of the night, he discovers them lying around him in unflattering poses. The hagiographers, somewhat misogynistic, took malicious pleasure in describing them in luxurious detail. The Bodhisattva sees them as "ignorant women," "idiots attached to beautiful vases full of vomit," "excited dogs in the middle of bones," "fish caught in the mesh of a net," and "moths throwing themselves into the flames."[12] This episode is especially developed in the *Buddhacarita,* which contrasts the diurnal beauty of the women of the gynaeceum with their nocturnal ugliness. Here Aśvaghosa uses all the vocabulary of erotic poetry and then changes register, even if it offends good taste, by comparing women to corpses. Confronted with this display of unsightly flesh, which reveals the true nature of women, the Bodhisattva is overcome with nausea. The gynaeceum now appears to him as a veritable mass grave, and realizing the defilement of the body and its impermanence, he decides to leave the palace immediately.[13]

King Śuddhodana, following premonitory dreams, has decided to close the gates of the city. But in vain: the gods intervene and plunge all the inhabitants into a deep sleep, leaving the Bodhisattva free to prepare his departure. He goes to take leave of his father but finds him asleep. He then bids farewell to Yaśodharā. The scene is reported in quite different ways depending on the source. In Pāli texts, his son Rāhula has already been born, and the mother and child are asleep when he goes to their room. He resists his desire to take his child in his arms, for fear of weakening his determination. In Sanskrit texts, it is precisely on this night that Rāhula is conceived. This event is quite bizarre. Indeed, Siddhārtha decides to impregnate Yaśodharā to prove his virility. He is said to have reflected: "In times to come, the misguided might imagine that I left sixty thousand extraordinary women behind and chose to give up my life because I was not a man. That notion would kindle all sorts of rumors detrimental to the truth."[14] This enactment of the scene must be placed in the context of the Indian family ideology of the time, which held that a son could not leave his family before producing an heir capable of observing the cult of the ancestors in his place. We are told that King Śuddhodana is reassured when he learns that Siddhārtha has left an heir to the throne. In other words, by fulfilling his marital duty, the Bodhisattva is in fact fulfilling his filial duty. It is this aspect that Chinese biographies have emphasized, forgetting to mention that the Buddha later has his son ordained, thus depriving the throne of his heir. In any case, once the marital duty is fulfilled, both spouses fall asleep, and each of them dreams. But while the auspicious dreams of Siddhārtha foretell his awakening, those of Yaśodharā are ominous. Awakened with a start, she tells them to her husband, who reassures her that he will never abandon her. A pious lie: at dawn, he has disappeared. But their fates will remain intertwined, since during the six years that the Bodhisattva will spend practicing austerities in the forest, Yaśodharā will do the same at the palace. Rāhula, the child born of their union, will remain the link between their two lives.[15]

In canonical versions, Śākyamuni depart without taking leave of his young wife or does so only to put his conscience at rest. In the iconography of Southeast Asia, on the other hand, a very particular moment in this scene has been retained—the one where he goes to find Yaśodharā and finds her asleep, her child next to her. In Japan, too, this scene will give rise to melodramatic complications that underline the difficulty the prince has in tearing himself away from the woman he loves. Yaśodharā awakens, and the two spouses shed torrents of tears.

So in the middle of the night, Siddhārtha gets on his horse Kaṇṭhaka and sets off, accompanied by his squire Candaka (see plate 2). The horse neighs with grief, but the gods "disperse" his cry. In some variations, the city gates open by themselves; in others, Kaṇṭhaka flies over the walls. In one source, the Bodhisattva turns to take one last look at his hometown and vows that he will not return until he is awakened. Sometimes Māra tries to dissuade him by promising him that within a week he will become the king of the universe; in other instances, it is one of his cousins who describes the grief his departure will cause. But nothing helps. Siddhārtha, moreover, is strengthened in his determination by the encouragement of the gods, who make flowers rain down on him.

In the early morning, having traveled a good distance from Kapilavastu, he takes leave of his two companions. He first strips himself of his princely jewels, which he entrusts to Candaka to be returned to the palace, and cuts off his own hair with a dagger. The gods collect the hair and take it to heaven for worship. He then exchanges his clothes for a patched monastic frock, given to him by a hunter passing by—who happens to be none other than the god Indra. According to some sources, Kaṇṭhaka thereupon dies of grief and is reborn among the gods. The Bodhisattva also sends back the gods who have accompanied and helped him so far. He is now alone, exposed to wild beasts and demons—in fact, all the dangers of the forest.

ASCETICISM

According to all sources, six long years of mortification followed. The Bodhisattva first takes as his masters two famous ascetics, Ārāḍa Kālama and Udraka Rāmaputra, but soon leaves them, convinced that their techniques will not lead him to the supreme goal. He then moves to Uruvilvā, in the kingdom of Magadha, and engages in extreme ascetic practices—including breath control and fasting. Foucher provides us with a colorful description of this period:

> Committed to complete immobility, he did not move, either to seek shade or sunshine or to shelter himself from wind or rain. He did not move a finger to protect himself against horseflies, mosquitoes, and various reptiles. And perhaps, O reader, do you think that after a few days the place must have become untenable . . . ? You would be wrong to think so: know that during all these years no functional waste, no natural excretion of any kind, liquid or solid, was discharged from any of the openings of the body of the Predestined One.[16]

This harsh ascesis leads the Bodhisattva to the gates of death. That's when Māra comes to tempt him for the first time.[17] Here is how the *Treatise* presents the scene: "It is said that at the time when the Buddha was practicing the six years of austerity, King Māra came to him and said: 'Noble warrior (*kṣatriya*), of the thousand parts that are in you, only one is still alive. Rise up quickly! Go back to your country—by generous donations, earn merits, and you will find, in present and future existence, the path to human and divine happiness. It is not possible for you to increase this painful effort. If you do not listen to my affectionate advice, if you persist in your error and do not rise up, I will lead my great armies here and come to destroy you.' "[18] But the Bodhisattva does not waver in his resolve, and Māra, despondent, finally withdraws. Only later, when he realizes that the Bodhisattva is on the verge of awakening, does he pull himself together and decide to throw all his forces into battle.

At the end of his austerities, the body of Śākyamuni has become so emaciated that it is blackened and devoid of the thirty-two physical marks of excellence (figs. 10–11). The gods consider him already dead, and news of his death reaches his mother Māyā in Trāyastriṃśa Heaven. She descends from her heavenly abode in the middle of the night, and seeing her son lying on the ground, laments. Awakened by her tears, the Bodhisattva recognizes her at last and comes back to life. It is at this moment that he agrees to break his fast. Reassured, Māyā bows down before him and returns to Trāyastriṃśa Heaven.

Realizing that asceticism, far from leading to his awakening, has only put his life in danger, the Bodhisattva recalls in good time his first meditation under the jambu tree and decides to resume that method of practice. But first he needs to regain his strength. Sometimes it is the god Indra who suggests the way forward, taking the form of a three-stringed lute player. When he plucks the first string, which is too taut, the sound is too high pitched; when he plucks the second string, which is too loose, the sound is too dull, barely audible. It is only when he plucks the third string, neither too tight nor too loose, that he obtains a perfect sound. The Bodhisattva now understands that his body, like the lute, can only give its full measure when it is neither too tense (bent on mortification) nor too slack (given to pleasure). It is this new, well-tempered practice that will enable him to overcome Māra and take all the steps toward awaking.

MIRACLES AT ŚRĀVASTĪ

Miracles are a pervasive aspect of all past buddhas and the Buddha of our cosmic era, Śākyamuni. Without them, Buddhism would not have had the prodigious impact it has had on the lives of the people of Asia. Despite generally forbidding his followers from displaying their supernormal powers (*abhijñā*), the Buddha does not deprive himself of the ability to use them when needed. The most famous demonstration occurs during the so-called miracles at Śrāvastī, a popular theme in Southeast Asia but one that has been relatively ignored in East Asia.

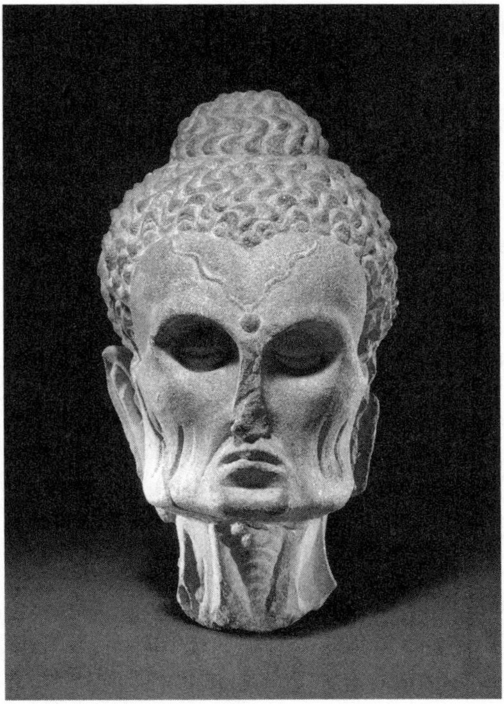

FIGURE 10. Head of the fasting Buddha. 2nd–3rd century. Ghandāra (Pakistan). Carved schist. British Museum (1907,1228.1).

FIGURE 11. The fasting Buddha. 3rd–5th century. Ghandāra (Pakistan). Sculpture, schist. Metropolitan Museum of Art (1987.218.5).

Śrāvastī, where most of the Buddha's sermons (sūtras) are delivered, was an important site, not only for Buddhists, but also for Jains. As Strong points out, one could see this episode as a way for Buddhists to assert their dominance and establish Śrāvastī as a bastion of their faith. The event takes place at the beginning of the rainy season, just before the Buddha's ascension to Trāyastriṃśa Heaven. It is motivated by the challenge of six heretics or "masters of error" (*tīrthika*). This term, often used in Buddhist texts, in fact covers a number of ascetic movements, among them a strand of Jainism. It seems that these ascetics have gotten wind of the rule enacted by the Buddha forbidding his disciples from displaying their powers, and they resolve to embarrass the Buddha by challenging him to a magical competition. To their chagrin, the Buddha takes up the challenge, saying that the rules that apply to his disciples do not apply to him. Issuing this challenge was a considerable gamble, and one wonders why the *thīrtikas* took the risk, since each of them knows that he himself does not possess such powers. In fact, we are told, it was Māra, taking the appearance of one of them, who convinced each in turn that the others possessed such powers and therefore they risked nothing in challenging the Buddha on this ground.

The miracles of Śrāvastī actually comprise three distinct prodigies (and various related wonders): the instantaneous growth of a mango tree, the multiplying of the Buddha's doubles in space, and the dual emission of water and fire from his body. The Pāli sources insist on the mango tree incident. Learning that the Buddha has declared that the competition will take place under a mango tree, the heretic masters have all the mango trees cut down or uprooted from the place. But a gardener finds a mango. When he gives it to the Buddha, he is told to plant the kernel. Instantly a mango tree starts to grow, shooting up to a height of twenty-five meters, and King Prasenajit places a guard in front of the tree to prevent it from being cut down.

The mango tree miracle, despite its popularity, is only a preliminary to what comes next. As part of the preparations, seats for the contestants are installed at a very great height, since flying is in principle only a game for them. This forces the heretics to humiliate themselves by using ladders, unlike the Buddha, who can easily preview, so to speak, his power of levitation. During the first week, the Buddha transforms the field into an enchanted site, a kind of Buddhist Disneyland. He summons five great demons who destroy the seats and pavilions of the *tīrthikas,* while his bodyguard, the *yakṣa* Vajrapāṇi, terrifies them. In their frantic flight, one of them drowns in a pond. The story could end there (and indeed it does in a Chinese version), but instead it continues with a new series of miracles that reinforce, if need be, the glory and sovereignty of the Buddha. After the elimination of the *tīrthikas,* the show can finally begin.

Usually two great miracles are reported, one involving the gushing of water and fire from the levitating body of the Buddha, and the other involving the multiplying of body doubles, which fill all space. Sanskrit sources emphasize the latter, while the dual miracle (of water and fire gushing out from the Buddha's body) is common to Pāli and Sanskrit sources. As fire gushes forth from the upper body of the Buddha, water is emitted from the lower body; then it is seen from the front and back of his body; from his two eyes, his two ears, his two nostrils, his two shoulders, his two hands, and so on (fig. 12). Then a magical double appears, who sits when the Buddha walks, walks when he sits, and so on. In some versions, this doppelgänger asks questions, and the Buddha answers them. This theme is developed in Sanskrit and Chinese sources that insist on the multiplying of doubles rather than the dual miracle. Foucher notes that the multiplying of doubles was probably judged more important than the dual miracle or miracle of pairs. But this multiplying is also done in pairs, by successive duplications, and not all at once. In the *Sūtra of the Wise Man and the Madman* (*Xianyu jing,* translated into Chinese in the 5th cent.), the Buddha causes a ray of light to emerge from his navel, which divides into two and gives birth to two flowers, on each of which a Buddha is seated. The same thing occurs with each of these buddhas, whose number thus increases exponentially. All these buddhas then start walking in the air, conversing, and performing a myriad of other actions. However, this multiplying of doubles poses a problem, because, as we know, Māra can also take the form of the Buddha to preach a counterfeit of the Buddhist doctrine. Perhaps this is why, notes Strong, the *tīrthikas* must be defeated and driven out before the Buddha can perform his true miracles, so that there can be no doubt that he, and not Māra, is the author.

FIGURE 12. The Buddha's great miracle. 3rd–4th century. Kapisa (Afghanistan). Schist with traces of gilding. Musée Guimet (MG 17478).

The miracles of the mango tree and the multiplying of doubles, distinct in the texts, were combined in iconography from very early on. The miracles of Śrāvastī were included in the bas-reliefs of Sanchi and Bharhut in

Maddhya Pradesh and were later found in the caves of Ajanta (in Maharashtra), as well as in various other strongholds of Buddhism (Gandhāra, Sarnath, Amarāvatī). What is striking, however, is that at no time was there any question of doctrine in this whole progression. The Buddhist Law imposed itself by its miracles, not by its philosophical or spiritual depth.

DESCENT FROM TRĀYASTRIṂŚA HEAVEN

The preaching career of the Buddha is marked by numerous miracles, one of the principal ones being his sojourn in Trāyastriṃśa Heaven (Heaven of the Thirty-three Gods), where his mother, who had departed too soon, was reborn. In his forty-second year, that is to say, seven years after his awakening, the Buddha is said to have gone up to Trāyastriṃśa Heaven in order to preach the Law to Māyā and to the gods. His departure is first perceived by his disciples as an extinction, or entry into nirvāṇa, but it proves a false exit. He returns to earth three months later, on the day of the full moon of October, near the city of Sānkāśya.

We will come back to the Buddha's relationship with his mother. The episode of his sojourn in Trāyastrimśa stands out because it gives birth to the first statuary images of the Buddha. A first version of the story is reported in the fifth century by the pilgrim monk Faxian, who attributes the creation of the statue to King Prasenajit. But the most famous version of the story is the one reported by Xuanzang in the seventh century: "When the Buddha ascended to Heaven to preach the Law to his mother, and had not yet returned after three months, King Udāyana became worried and wanted to have an image of him. He asked one of the Buddha's great disciples, Maudgalyāyana, to recruit craftsmen and go up to Heaven to observe all the characteristic signs [of the Buddha's body] and carve them in sandalwood. Maudgalyāyana recruited thirty-two craftsmen, each of whom was told to carve one of the thirty-two marks of the Buddha. When the Buddha finally came down from Trāyastrimśa Heaven, his statue rose up to welcome him."[19] The *Zengyi ahan jing* combines both versions: Udāyana would have first had the sandalwood statue executed. Then Prasenajit, learning of this, would have had his own statue made in turn, but in fine gold. These were the first two images of the Buddha. There seems to have been a prohibition against representing the Buddha in early Buddhism; but the rule was bent, very early on, by representing him in his Bodhisattva form (in other words, before his awakening). According to tradition, a copy of this statue was introduced into China during the Han dynasty at the time of the Ming emperor (r. 28–75 CE). Another copy appeared during the Liang dynasty under Emperor Wu Di (r. 502–549). Finally, the original is supposed to have arrived toward the mid-fourth century in the Chinese region of Gansu. Xuanzang is also said to have brought back to China a copy of King Udāyana's statue.

While the Buddha's ascension to Trāyastriṃśa Heaven was kept a secret, his "descent" was done in great pomp. The iconography likes to represent him descending, flanked by Brahmā and Indra, along a triple staircase made of precious materials created for this purpose by the gods. This motif was soon established in a kind of triptych with vertically superimposed panels, representing in the higher panel the preaching of the Buddha to the gods, in the middle panel his return on earth, and in the lower panel the resumption of his preaching to humans.[20] As Strong remark, the episode was called Descent of the Gods and not Descent of the Buddha, because on this occasion the gods, usually invisible, became visible to humans.[21] There is thus a temporary cancellation of the separation between the divine and human realms. The return from Trāyastriṃśa Heaven took place at the end of the rainy season, which is also a time of festivals in Asia. Still today in Thailand, the ceremony that marks the end of the rainy season in October is accompanied by a representation of the Descent of the Gods.

RETURN TO KAPILAVASTU

The Buddha's return to Kapilavastu, like his ascent to Trāyastriṃśa Heaven to preach the Law to his mother, reaffirms the family values that the Bodhisattva seemed to have rejected at the time of the great departure. At the same time, it diverts them, since the Buddha takes away the best members from his clan by converting them. Although the usual interpretation of the story is that the Buddha returns home to bring salvation to his relatives, not everyone liked these conversions, as the following passage testifies: "You who have sons, watch over them and guard them! You who have husbands, watch over them and guard them! Now the great ascetic has come to the land of Magadha; he converts Brahmanic ascetics, who follow him of their own free will. Now that he has come here, he will take men with him again."[22] To avoid this danger, the king has decreed that only young people who have obtained parental permission can enter the orders. In a variation, he decrees that each family must have a boy or girl ordained. In any case, the Buddha's community is suddenly augmented with the serial ordinations of Śākya clan members, including his son Rāhula, his aunt and adoptive mother Mahāprajāpatī Gautamī, his half brother Nanda, and his cousins Ānanda and Devadatta.

As the episode concerning Rāhula's conversion shows, the Buddha sometimes uses skillful means (*upāya*) that may seem questionable to achieve a conversion. When his wife Yaśodharā sends Rāhula to claim his inheritance, the Buddha appears in the midst of five hundred replicas of himself, which he has magically aroused. Rāhula, listening only to the voice of blood, goes directly to his progenitor. Yaśodharā, still in love with her husband, has given Rāhula a love potion that he is supposed to give to the Buddha to bring him back to her, but it is Rāhula who drinks it and falls under the spell of his father. The Buddha knowingly takes this opportunity to ordain him as a novice.

The Buddha uses a similar trick with his half brother Nanda. Having come to knock on Nanda's door on the latter's wedding day, he hands him his alms bowl and leaves without saying anything. Nanda tries to catch up with him to return the bowl, but in vain. He is thus obliged to follow the Buddha to the monastery, where he is ordained against his will. Nanda languishes, sighing incessantly after his young wife, the beautiful Sundarī. Seeing this, the Buddha leads him into a forest where he shows him an old she-monkey whose hair has been scorched by a fire, then he leads him to Trāyastriṃśa Heaven, where he shows him marvelous celestial nymphs. On the way back, questioned by the Buddha, Nanda recognizes that there is as much difference between the she-monkey and his fiancée as there is between them and the celestial nymphs, and from then on his thoughts are no longer tormented by the image of Sundarī. However, the Buddha's ploy seems to backfire, for Nanda now dreams of nymphs, and the Buddha must promise him that he will take one of them as his wife if he perseveres in his practice. In a variant, Nanda is seduced by a celestial nymph, who tells him that she will only give herself to a virtuous monk. Only then does he decide to be ordained. However, the mockery of his companions encourages him to devote himself to meditation. He ends up realizing the vanity of beauty and desire, and quickly obtains the status of an arhat. In another—darker—variation of the theme, the Buddha, after showing him heaven, leads Nanda to hell. When the latter, horrified, questions a demon about a particularly cruel torture, the latter answers that it is reserved for a certain Nanda who does not respect the Buddhist Law. Finally convinced, or rather appalled, Nanda begins to practice assiduously and soon becomes an arhat.[23]

As we can see, the Buddha uses the same strategy here—albeit with a diametrically opposed goal—as Māra did in sending his armies of demons or his daughters to frighten or seduce the Bodhisattva; but the tradition retains only the end—justified in one case, but not in the other—not the means. While ridiculing Māra for his outdated stratagems, traditional commentators have not faulted the Buddha's way of doing things, which can be seen as having anticipated (or inspired) the Japanese proverb: "Even a lie can be a salvific means" (*uso mo hōben*).

DEMONS AND WONDERS

The foregoing examples amply show that the Life of the Buddha is replete with wonders and miracles. From the moment of his birth, he receives the help of the gods. On all occasions, the gods encourage him to persevere in the path he has chosen for himself. At each important moment or crossroads, the earth shakes (apparently without causing injury). He explains the reason for this to his disciple Ānanda: "There are eight causes and eight conditions for a great earthquake."[24] In another passage, three causes are mentioned:

"The great earthquake is due to a great cause: when the Buddha is born, reaches buddhahood, and is about to enter parinirvāṇa, the whole universe is agitated; this is the great earthquake."[25] The production of earthquakes is also one of the supernormal powers obtained through meditation. Earthquakes occur, for example, when the Buddha recalls his past lives.[26] In the above example, the Buddha ends his explanation with the following: "Here the Buddha, who wants to unite beings en masse, causes the earth to shake in six ways."[27]

He demonstrates his powers repeatedly, revealing, for example, certain events that have occurred in the past lives of his listeners to illustrate the mechanism of karma. These powers essentially serve him as a means to convert unbelievers. A famous example of a miraculous conversion is that of the dragon Apalāla:[28] In a cave near Nagarahāra lived a fierce dragon king who brought famine and epidemics to the country. The king of that land asked the Buddha to purge his kingdom of this scourge. The Buddha, accompanied by five disciples, went to the mountain and subdued the dragon king. When he was about to leave again, the dragon king, fearing a relapse into his bad ways, begged the Buddha to always remain close to him. The Buddha, agreeing to stay in the cave for fifteen hundred years, projected his body onto a rock, where the dragon could constantly see him preaching the Law. Men can also see him, but only from a distance, because when they approach, he disappears.[29] We saw that the Chinese pilgrim Xuanzang described his visit to this cave. There are other legends about the shadow of the Buddha in other places, all built on the same model.

Another episode often cited in this connection is that of the conversion of Kāśyapa of Urulvila, a fire worshiper. The Buddha asks Kāśyapa for permission to sleep in the hut where he keeps his sacrificial fire; Kāśyapa tries to dissuade him, because this place is protected by a dangerous *nāga*. The Buddha ignores this advice, and during the night a terrible struggle takes place between him and the *nāga*. In its course, the Buddha uses his supernormal powers to tame the *nāga*, which he then locks up in his alms bowl.[30] But Kāśyapa is not so easily shaken in his deepest convictions, and he asks for further proof of the Buddha's supremacy. The Buddha immediately goes to the four corners of the world and brings back a characteristic fruit or flower.[31] Kāśyapa finally admits defeat, and his two brothers and their many followers are converted after him. The Buddha then preaches three kinds of teachings to them, having to do, in order, with supernormal powers, recollection, and preaching the doctrine. The first, the most developed, concerns topics such as the multiplication of one's own body into countless other bodies; the return of these innumerable bodies into a single body; the ability to pass through a wall without feeling any obstacle; the ability to sit cross-legged in space, or to fly like a bird in space; the ability to enter the earth as easily as water, to dive in and out at will, and to walk on water as on land; to emit smoke and fire out of one's own body; to touch the sun and the moon with one's hand; to ascend with one's body to Brahmā's heaven, and to come and go without any obstacles. One will note the detailed character of this first teaching in comparison to the rather banal character of the second, clearly showing the importance of these powers (and the wonders that accompany them) in early Buddhism—and a fortiori in later Buddhism, especially in its esoteric version—to the detriment of the philosophical doctrine itself.

6

PREVIOUS LIVES

The idea that the Buddha's awakening was not simply the result of six years of asceticism, but the karmic culmination of many earlier existences, during which he was still only a bodhisattva (being destined for awakening)—or rather *the* Bodhisattva—appears very early and is developed in the collections of stories known as *Jātakas*—"(Re)Births." Some of these earlier existences appear in iconography as early as the second century BCE and were disseminated in texts such as the *Mahāvastu* before being collected in compilations.

The last life of the Buddha according to tradition is probably the first from the standpoint of the real order of the elaboration of the legend. According to the most commonly accepted theory, the narrative of these earlier existences probably developed after the life of the "historical" Buddha was pieced together, and on the model of the latter; it is therefore legitimate to reverse the apparent chronological order and study them after the latter. However, certain episodes in the life of the Buddha Śākyamuni presuppose those of past buddhas, and one therefore does not have a simple linear evolution. It seems, for example, that the cycle of stories concerning his youth was elaborated on the model of that of the buddha Vipaśyin. From the outset, the Buddha's life is therefore diffracted and refracted.

Even in the early texts, the Buddha obtains recollection of his previous existences at the moment of his awakening. As Foucher notes: "His personal memories, we are told, go back to ninety-one *kalpas* or aeons—that is, ninety-one times 432 million years—in the past."[1] Although the number of his predecessors is usually limited to twenty-four, this number ends up appearing too small in relation to the immense amount of time that has elapsed. This is why some sources appear to outbid each other: in the first, incalculable cosmic period, Śākyamuni is said to have venerated seventy-five thousand buddhas; in the second, seventy-six thousand; and in the third, seventy-seven thousand. Or again: "The Bodhisattva had an extremely long career, during which he served and honored 512,027 buddhas. The first of these was Dīpankara the Elder."[2] The texts do not explain how these numbers were derived, and they remain a good illustration of Indian numerological hybris.

During his long years of preaching, the Buddha often had the opportunity to recount one or another of these past existences in order to illustrate an idea or a moral lesson, or to shed light on a particular situation. In some sources, he uses the same first person to talk about his past existences as he does to talk about his present life. In others, he alternates between first and third persons. This play between the two persons appears to give more vitality and emotional reality to his portrait. The listener is confronted with two parallel narratives—that of a past existence and that of the present life—which come together in the final statement "*Aham eva*"—This is how I was.[3] As Strong notes, the primary purpose of these stories is to add karmic depth to the Buddha's life, as well as a "quality of déjà vu" that helps to give the narrative a "touch of eternity."[4] At the same time, the *Jātakas* allow the tradition to tell the same story several times, exploring it from many angles. Clearly one life was not enough to say all that needed to be said about the Buddha."[5] This projection of the present onto the past allows the Buddha to conveniently increase the spectrum of his experiences without compromising himself too much. However, the character whose actions he recounts is often only a "type" with little individuality.

Even before the appearance of *Jātaka* collections, the tale, when it is quoted in a sūtra or a Vinaya text such as the *Mahāvastu,* functions as a kind of quotation, which enriches (and weighs down) the text, perforates and destabilizes it, mobilizes it, and interrupts the narrative by making it proliferate. Readers in a hurry tend to skip the long quotations; those who take their time and enjoy the text find them useful. The *Jātakas* thus come to form an inseparable part, if not the main part of the Life of the Buddha. They are one of the most popular forms of Buddhist literature, especially in South and Southeast Asia. The genre seems to be very old, and it allowed Buddhism to assimilate an enormous amount of traditional Indian folklore. Any traditional tale could thus be transformed into a *Jātaka* simply by making one of its protagonists a past incarnation of the future Buddha.

In the Theravāda tradition, the *Commentary on Jātakas* (*Jātakatthakathā*), a Pāli anthology of 547 *Jātakas* in prose and verse, is authoritative. But the number of *Jātakas* is potentially infinite, since the Buddha, we are told, has had hundreds of millions of past lives. There are also *Jātakas* in Sanskrit, and translations in Chinese, Tibetan, Japanese, and many vernacular languages. Some of these stories have been translated or summarized from the Chinese by Édouard Chavannes in his monumental book *Cinq cents contes et apologues.*[6]

The oldest *Jātakas* are probably the visual accounts of the Bharhut stūpa (ca. 2nd cent. BCE).[7] Each is a unique narrative that reflects the cultural memory of a specific group, and they should be interpreted in that light. But they are rarely told in isolation and usually appear as parts of more developed literary texts or architectural programs. The Borobudur stūpa in Java is a sculpted example of a unified cycle of *Jātakas* in a monumental setting, perhaps a developed biography of the Buddha. Similar cycles proliferated on the walls of the rock monasteries of the Kucha oasis on the Silk Road before the Tang (5th to 7th cent.) and in Burmese temples from the eleventh century onward. Burma (Myanmar) has the longest and most prolific tradition of visual representation of the *Jātakas*. One example is the ceramic tiles that adorn the upper terraces of the Ānanda temple in Bagan, composing a cycle of 554 *Jātakas*, "prefaced" by the representation of events from the Buddha's last human life on the lower terraces.

We saw that Foucher, despite his interest in visual sources, did not hold the *Jātakas* in high esteem, because of their clearly fictional character, and claimed fidelity to the life of the historical Buddha. The historicist approach, by aiming to reconstruct the complete history of the Buddha, in fact amputates an entire prehistory without which it loses much of its meaning. These past existences have had a profound impact on the Buddhist imaginary, and ignoring them under the pretext that they are purely fictitious is no longer tenable.

Many of these tales derive from a substratum of Indo-European folklore and share features in common with tales from other cultures, especially European ones. What characterizes them is not only the story of the Bodhisattva's spiritual quest, but also the emphasis on his relationships with the other protagonists of the Buddhist legend (Śuddhodana, Yaśodharā, Devadatta, etc.) in a temporal framework extending over many lives.

Some *Jātakas* insist on the humble origins of the Bodhisattva, who evidently was not always a prince. Some tales make him a merchant, a craftsman, even a slave. Sometimes he is reborn in a divine form—as the god Indra, in at least one case; in another, as the god Brahmā.[8] Human rebirths, on the other hand, are rare. Nor was it impossible for him to be reborn in the form of a mere demon (*yakṣa*). In some tales, moreover, he is reborn even lower on the scale of beings, namely, as an animal. As Louis de La Vallée Poussin notes:

> India had conceived a gentler and more human holiness whose heroes are, naturally, mostly animals. It repeated the story of the deer that places its head on the stone of sacrifice to save a doe from its herd, of the monkey that turns its body into a bridge, of the elephant that tears off its ivory to give to the miserly hunter, of the good bear and the ungrateful man. With these noble beasts it associates some princes—a Vessantara who gives up his wife and children, a Śibi who saves a dove by feeding the hawk his own flesh. This pathetic saga found in Śākyamuni its pole of crystallization. It was believed that Śākyamuni had been the hare, the monkey, the bear, the Śibi of the golden legend.[9]

When the Bodhisattva is reborn in animal form, it is almost always that of a noble animal. Thus, he is twice reborn as a *nāga* (the equivalent of a cobra), and once as a lion. There are, of course, some exceptions to this rule—for example, the *Jātaka* featuring a goat that is about to be sacrificed by the disciples of a Brahmin and bursts out laughing at the thought that it will be delivered from pain on the same day, but then starts crying out of compassion for the Brahmin, who will have to undergo karmic retribution in turn after the sacrifice. When asked by the Brahmin for the reason for his strange behavior, the goat declares that he himself was a Brahmin in his previous existences, but then he was beheaded 499 times and this time will be his five hundredth! As this number is symbolic of a totality, one can surmise that this goat, who in reality is none other than our Bodhisattva, is in line to be reborn in human form.[10] Laughter, as we know (or at least we think we know), is a human characteristic, and this story illustrates the idea that it is always a man (in the essentially humanistic Buddhist conception of karma) who transmigrates and can be reborn in animal form—and never the other way around.

Moreover, the Bodhisattva is almost always reborn as a male, which is not surprising when one considers the decidedly misogynistic proclivities of early Buddhism. There are, however, a few exceptions. The very first conversion of the future Śākyamuni takes place when he is reborn as a woman despite the orthodox belief that only men can have bodhisattva careers. He is then a princess, the sister-in-law of an ancient buddha named Purāna-Dīpankara (Dīpankara the Elder), who has a disciple by the name of Pacchima-Dīpankara (future Dīpankara), because he is destined, in the distant future, to become the buddha Dīpankara. In fact, it is to him, and not to her brother-in-law, that the princess makes an offering while resolving to become a bodhisattva. Dīpankara the Elder cannot confer his prediction on her, of course, but he instructs his disciple to do so—in the distant future, when she will be reborn as a man and he himself will have become a buddha. As can be seen, this is a rehearsal, in a past life, of the great scene in which Sumedha receives Dīpankara's prediction. But in this case, the puritan code is safe because the prediction of future awakening is not given to a woman by a buddha: it is only a *promise* of a prediction by a future buddha to a future man. Nevertheless, the door has slightly opened for the admission of women into the Buddhist path.[11]

Another exception is the beautiful Rūpyāvatī, who, during a famine, cuts off her breasts to give them to a woman who is about to eat her own child. Returning home, Rūpyāvatī asks her husband to take food to the woman. He then produces an act of truth (*satyakriyā*, an act invoking the power of truth to bring about a miracle) that restores his wife's breasts. She in turn produces an act of truth, asking to be reborn as a man (apparently she cared less about her breasts than he did).[12] This Buddhist Agatha is the feminine counterpart of King Śibi, who surrenders some flesh from his own thighs to save a dove from the talons of a hawk—but her story is less well known. According to Peter Skilling, this tale "shows us that a woman can aspire to become a buddha and that Śākyamuni himself was born a woman at the dawn of his Bodhisattva career. This means that an ordinary woman can, just like a man, aspire to the state of a future buddha, but that from a certain point on, she will travel the road to this distant goal only as a man."[13] In other words, this exception only confirms the rule of male dominance.

The spiritual career of the Bodhisattva thus extends over thousands, even millions of rebirths. Although his path has been arduous, he has nonetheless, during countless cosmic periods, been fortunate enough to meet other buddhas—no fewer than twenty-four—who have shown him the way and given him hope. To all of them he made offerings, which earned him immense merits. The first of them, whom he met when he himself had taken the form of a young Brahmin named Sumedha, was the buddha Dīpankara. Learning that this buddha was passing through the city, Sumedha looks for an offering to present to him and buys from a young girl five of the seven lotuses she has just picked. When he tosses them to Dīpankara, the lotuses remain suspended in the air, forming a halo around the buddha's head. Sumedha then throws himself to the ground and, making a carpet of his hair to keep the buddha from walking in the mud, vows to become awakened. At this moment, Dīpankara predicts that he will become, in the distant future, a buddha named Śākyamuni (fig. 13). In the Pāli sources, the girl and the lotus offering are ignored, while the *Mahāvastu* passes over the pattern of hair spread out on the mud.

FIGURE 13. *Dīpankara Jātaka* (Story of the ascetic Megha and the Buddha Dīpankara). 2nd century. Ghandāra (Pakistan). Schist with gold leaf. Metropolitan Museum of Art (1998.491).

As noted, the fact that later biographies of the Buddha go back in time before his birth as Sumedha seems to reflect the geographical expansion of Buddhism, which adapted to new countries by proclaiming that the Buddha had once walked there (leaving his shadow or footprints as a permanent record, as in Sri Lanka, Central Asia, and Korea). A further step in the consolidation of the Buddha's legend is taken when it is revealed that an episode in the Life of the Buddha occurred in such and such a place in China, Korea, or Japan. Even better is the affirmation that past buddhas practiced in this place before the Buddha's time (as attested by the meditation stone of the buddha Kāśyapa in Korea and Japan). Going back beyond Sumedha and Dīpankara thus opened the possibility of conversion and future awakening in the absence of any buddha and any prediction of his coming.

PREVIOUS LIVES AND PERFECTIONS

The multiplication of past existences—like the repetition of the same day in the film *The Groundhog Day*—gives the Boddhisattva time to accumulate the virtues necessary for his future awakening. Allegorically, the *Jātakas* are often little more than the illustration of the six (or ten) perfections (*pāramitā*) of the Bodhisattva.[14] As such, they can often seem artificial and monotonous, if not excessive and unrelated to reality—which is the reason they are angrily rejected by Foucher, who writes about the Bodhisattva: "To speak only of his charity, do we want a few examples? Some are admirable in every respect. . . . There are others which may seem rather extravagant, as when he offers his eyes to a blind man, or somewhat excessive, as when he sacrifices his body to feed a starving tigress. Some are even frankly cruel, as when, born as a crown prince, he cannot refuse anything to a beggar, neither his own possessions, nor the treasures of the State, nor his two young children, nor his faithful wife, etc."[15] This last example refers to the well-known legend of Prince Vessantara, to which we shall return.

In these tales, the perfection of giving (*dāna-pāramitā*) is the virtue that stands out most often. The Bodhisattva practices it even during his animal rebirths, as when, reborn as a hare, he gives up his body to feed a traveler. To illustrate the other perfections, let us simply mention the *Jātaka* in which he appears as a boy who cultivates the perfection of morality (*śīla-pāramitā*) by refusing to commit a theft even when his master, a Brahmin, encourages him to do so;[16] or another tale in which an ascetic calmly tolerates the mutilations inflicted on him by a furious king in order to cultivate the perfection of patience (*kṣānti-pāramitā*). Some *Jātakas,* however, also describe how the Bodhisattva, life after life, succeeds in acquiring the thirty-two characteristic marks of the great man (*mahāpuruṣa*), which are in a way the physical counterparts of the moral virtues. What are these marks, and what do they mean?

THIRTY-TWO MARKS

Paradoxically, for a doctrine that affirms the superiority of mind over body and matter, all of the Buddha's previous lives—and a good part of his last incarnation—put great weight in his bodily perfection, symbolized by the thirty-two marks of the great man (along with eighty secondary marks). As John Powers notes:

> These attributes are mentioned and emphasized throughout the Pāli canon, in scholastic treatises, and in Mahāyāna texts, and their pervasiveness and elaboration demonstrate that the authors considered them to be important. The thirty-two physical characteristics distinguished the Buddha from lesser men and were evidence of his superiority to all other beings. Men and women who saw his body were struck by his extraordinary beauty and mention the physical characteristics of a great man as a key factor in convincing them of the validity of his claims to authority.[17]

A priori, the list of the thirty-two marks of the great man is not specific to the Buddha. As Senart was one of the first to point out, it is pre-Buddhist.[18] Moreover, are the thirty-two marks necessary? The oldest *Jātakas* do not mention them, and the link between them and spiritual perfection seems relatively late. For example, the arhat Upagupta, renowned among other things for his ugliness, is said to be a true "buddha without marks."[19] The same is true of the layman Vimalakīrti, who, in *The Teaching of Vimalakīrti* (*Vimalakīrti-nirdeśa,* a Mahāyāna text probably dating to the 2nd cent. CE), presents himself as an old man afflicted by illness, thus denying the very idea of marks of buddhahood. If in early Buddhism these marks constitute proof of long existences spent accumulating merits, in Mahāyana they become less important, because all beings already have within them a buddha-nature. The universality of this truth does not, however, prevent Mahāyāna statuary from preserving the thirty-two marks in their representations of the transcendent buddhas. A careful reading of the *Jātakas* further shows that their purpose is to describe not only the long process of acquiring the Bodhisattva's virtues (the ten perfections), but also the construction, mark by mark, of a perfect body.[20] Indeed, the physical aspect is emphasized in many sources, making it appear to be at least as important as the spiritual aspect (if at all distinguishable). We will therefore observe a close link between the thirty-two marks and the *Jātakas,* which seem in many cases to be only a narrative framework for obtaining these marks of perfection.

Buddhist literature describes the obtaining of a buddha's body as the result of the work of many past lives, including the sacrifice of imperfect bodily limbs, to be replaced, in the next life, with perfect counterparts.[21] In this way, throughout countless periods of time spent in performing meritorious acts and difficult sacrifices, bodhisattvas gradually build up a body—which is necessarily a male body—with the thirty-two requisite marks.[22]

When this very long career is quantified, a bodhisattva is expected to practice the Buddhist Way during three cosmic periods or incalculable kalpas, and then to produce the thirty-two marks during one hundred shorter kalpas. The case of Śākyamuni is an exception, however, since he only needed ninety-one kalpas to acquire the thirty-two marks, thanks to his energy, compassion, and devotion to his master, an ancient Buddha named Puśya. He is often contrasted on this point with Maitreya, another disciple of the same master, who will need the totality of the one hundred kalpas to become the future Buddha.[23] According to the *Treatise,* this is because the future Maitreya, while much concerned with himself, had less concern for beings, whereas the future Śākyamuni had less concern for himself and great concern for the good of beings.[24]

The thirty-two marks are explained in detail by the Buddha himself in a Pāli sūtra, the *Lakkhana Sutta,* which details the various advantages that accompany possession of one or another of them. Some of the marks are, to say the least, strange—if not shocking to canons of beauty inherited from Greco-Roman antiquity. This is all the more astonishing since the first Buddhist sculptures were strongly influenced by Greek art. Art historians have wondered, for example, about the Buddha's webbed fingers, wanting to see this sculptural detail as a late invention meeting purely iconographic criteria; yet sculptors, working with their material, would have needed to reinforce fingers that were too fragile to be free standing, and what began as a technical accommodation became in time a characteristic trait of the Buddha, giving rise to new legends.[25] Although the texts agree in attributing to the Buddha the webbed feet and hands of the king of the swans, Burnouf refused to classify the Buddha in the genus of palmipedes.[26] Historians have tended to overlook these particular marks, but the problem remains, as they were important to the tradition and seemingly reflect the Buddhist vision of a perfect body and a powerful being.

Among the thirty-two marks, let us also mention the drawing of the wheel of the Law on the soles of the feet and the palms of the hands of the Buddha; a golden skin, so soft and delicate that dust or dirt does not cling to it; a protuberance at the top of the skull; a tuft of white hair between the eyes; hair turned to the right; legs like those of an antelope (a trait usually characteristic of feminine beauty); a lion's torso and jaws; eyebrows as long as those of a cow; physical proportions like those of a banyan; a wide and long tongue; and a penis hidden in a sheath. Many of these marks became characteristic features of the iconography. Some of the eighty secondary marks also became important, such as other symbolic signs (*swastika,* etc.) on the palms and soles of the feet, or long earlobes.

In the tenth century, a Japanese work, the *Illustrated Explanations on the Three Jewels* (*Sanbō ekotoba*), described the main marks of the Buddha as follows:

> The crown of his head was like the vast canopy of heaven, and his face was as perfectly round as the full moon. The curls on his head resembled twisted cords of dark blue thread, and the downy hairs between his eyebrows were like strands of polished white jewels. His eyebrows were like two crescent moons, his teeth like a mass of white snow, his eyes like blue lotus blossoms, his lips like red berries. His skin was the color of burnished gold and shone brilliantly, without blemish. On the sole of each of his feet was the mark of a wheel with one thousand spokes, and when he walked he did not touch the ground. All of these marks were the result of his deeds in previous ages, the effect of his practice of the various perfections. Even the heavenly eye of Brahma could not see the top of his head; even the supernatural hearing of Maudgalyāyana could not detect all the nuances of his voice.[27]

The Buddha is usually depicted standing, sitting, or lying down. Depicting him walking could be difficult as walking is deemed unsuitable for a divine being, and not walking is thought to be one of his royal attributes.[28] There are, however, many images of the walking Buddha in Southeast Asia, and the trace of his footsteps is worshiped throughout Asia. There the soles of his feet are said to be perfectly flat. Senart rejects the literal interpretation that "only results in giving him flat feet," and interprets this as the Buddha's ability to flatten everything in his path.[29] According to a Pāli text quoted by Burnouf: "Wherever the leader of the world advances, the low places rise up and the high places become united." Thus, the earth flattens under his steps.

Other marks are even more amazing, such as the "long and wide tongue" and the evidence of cryptorchidism. It is reported that the Buddha, under certain circumstances, "brought out his long tongue and covered his face with it up to the top of his hair."[30] To a disciple surprised by this, seeing it as a proof of levity, he replies that he "stuck out his wide tongue as a witness, for the words spoken by such a tongue are necessarily true."[31] In the same way, when a Brahmin questions his word, the Buddha extends his long tongue and covers his face to the top of his hair. He asks the Brahmin, "You have read the treatises; does a man who has such a tongue lie?" The Brahmin answers: "The man whose tongue can cover his nose does not tell lies; what then of the man whose tongue reaches the top of his hair?"

Tongue and sex are linked in several passages of the *Treatise* where the Buddha shows the mark of his tongue and that of his concealed genital organs: "Some people had doubts about these two marks of the Buddha's body. Then the Buddha brought out his tongue, and covered his face with it. . . . Then he created a marvelous elephant or a marvelous stallion and, while showing it, declared: 'My cryptorchidism is an invisible mark just like that.' Some even say that the Buddha brought out his secret organs and showed them to someone to remove doubts."[32]

Cryptorchidism is defined in the *Treatise* as follows: "The secret part of the abdomen is contained in a sheath, like in a purebred elephant . . . or a purebred horse."[33] The question of the Buddha's penis has aroused quite a bit of curiosity, as shown in a passage from the *Sūtra on the Oceanic Samādhi of the Visualization of the Buddha* (*Guanfo sanmei hai jing*), translated into Chinese in the sixth century. One of Prince Siddhārtha's attendants complains that although she has served him for eighteen years, she has never seen his penis, let alone been able to observe him making love. Her companions join her in declaring that the prince is not really a man. Subsequently, we are told, the prince, during his nap one day, lets his robe open to show his genitals. He then makes a white lotus appear from his penis. Then a whole series of apparitions, first a child and then an adult, emerge from the lotus. Confronted with this prodigy, the women of the gynaeceum are convinced.[34] But this doubt concerning the hidden sex of the Buddha seems to have continued to hover. His disciple Ānanda was excluded from the First Council for having shown, at the time of the parinirvāṇa, this same mark to disbelieving women in order to convert them.

At the end of six years of austerities, the body of the Bodhisattva is described as blackened and emaciated—the very opposite of the perfect, slightly plump body that constitutes one of the thirty-two marks. In fact, all the biographies report that because of the extremity of his austerities, the Bodhisattva lost the marks. The *Nidānakathā* describes this in the following way: "By this fasting, however, he became as thin as a skeleton; the colour of his body, once fair as gold, became dark; and the Thirty-two signs of a Great Being disappeared. And one day, when walking up and down, plunged in intense meditation, he was overcome by a severe pain; and he fainted, and fell."[35] The loss of physical marks is an important part of the Buddha's life story because it shows that wrong practice can lead to physical transformation—just as correct practice can change the body for the better. When the Bodhisattva comes to his senses, he realizes that he needs to eat, and accepts the food offered to him by a young village girl. Almost immediately, he regains his thirty-two marks, and his body regains its golden color. As in Louis Aragon's poem, "Man can take nothing for granted, neither his strength nor his weakness." In fact, the Bodhisattva's physical perfection seemed to go against the fundamental theory of Buddhism, the impermanence of all things, and one can sense in some texts this hesitation between the realization of evanescence and the desire for perfection, even immortality.

In spite of the parallelism that some texts have sought to establish between the Buddha's previous existences, the perfections (*pāramitā*), and the thirty-two marks of the great man, a large majority of the *Jātakas* (especially those involving animals) seem to have no other motive or purpose than the pleasure of the narrative or, at best, the exposition of a simple and fairly down-to-earth morality. In a Pāli text, the *Cariyā-piṭaka,* the Buddha classifies some of his past existences according to the perfections he obtained in them. But this amounts to only a very small number of *Jātakas* (thirty-five out of a total of more than five hundred). Moreover, while the account of these lives is supposed to illustrate the Bodhisattva's progression toward awakening, these rebirths are never classified, as one would expect, in an evolutionary scheme leading from the lowest to the highest animal, then through human (according to caste) and divine (according to Buddhist heavens) hierarchies. Attempts at a posteriori rationalization thus seem to apply only to certain texts, not to the literature of the *Jātakas* as a whole.[36]

ABANDONING THE BODY

In *The Temptation of Saint Anthony,* the Buddha appears before Anthony and Hilarion to declare: "In view of the deliverance of beings, I have made hundreds of thousands of sacrifices; I have given to the poor robes of silk, beds, chariots, houses, heaps of gold and diamonds. I have given my hands to the one-handed, my legs to the lame, my eyes to the blind; I have cut off my head for the decapitated. At the time when I was king, I distributed the provinces; at the time when I was Brahmin, I despised nobody. When I was a solitary I spoke words of tenderness to the thief who tried to cut my throat. When I was a tiger, I let myself die of hunger."[37]

As noted, past lives are intent on achieving perfections. Among these, as we have seen, the perfection of giving is by far the most exalted (in both senses of the word), and extreme generosity is the subject of several famous stories, such as the legend of King Śibi, an earlier incarnation of the Bodhisattva. To test the generosity of this king, the god Indra transforms into a hawk about to seize a dove. The dove takes refuge with the Bodhisattva, who, to save it, agrees to give the equivalent of the dove's weight from his own flesh. But each time he extracts a piece of flesh, the dove's weight increases. Eventually he has to give up his whole body, and the dove still remains heavier than he is. Then, we are told, "the great earth shook six times, the great sea swelled its waves, the dead trees began to blossom, the gods caused a fragrant rain to fall and threw flowers." Indra reveals himself, and asks the Bodhisattva if he felt any regret before his sacrifice. When the latter answers that he did not, Indra refuses to believe him. The Bodhisattva then produces the following act of truth: "When I was cutting out my flesh and my blood was flowing, I felt neither anger nor irritation. I was resolute and felt no regrets because I aimed at buddhahood. If this be the truth, let my body become as it was before."[38] As soon as these words have been uttered, his body becomes as it was before. This act of truth brings a timely restoration of the previous situation. But through it, the meaning of the gift changes from an act of pure generosity, a real sacrifice in which the Bodhisattva puts his life in the balance, to an ordeal he survives: it is now more of a contest between Indra and the Bodhisattva, in which generosity takes a back seat. Some might say that the act of truth allows the Bodhisattva to cash in on both sides and makes his gift more understandable, for it contains the hope of a reward at a lower cost.

The perfection of giving, which is usually thought to be motivated by compassion, is actually about earning merit. When the Bodhisattva sacrifices his body to feed the the tigress, he does not care about the grief of his parents or the karma of the tigress—he only wants to gain merit. Therefore his compassion is not really universal. This form of self-giving, motivated less by generosity pure and simple than by the desire to awaken, was particularly favored in East Asia. A case in point is that of the bodhisattva Sarvarūpasaṃdarṣana, who sets himself on fire in the *Lotus Sūtra.* Another is the "Stanzas on Impermanence" (*Wuchang ji*) from the *Parinirvāṇa Sūtra,* which feature the story of a young Brahmin practicing austerities in the Himalayas.[39] After hearing a demon reciting the first stanza on nirvāṇa, he offers him his body in exchange for the second stanza. Having obtained the second stanza, and before being devoured (at least he believes so), he inscribes the stanza on a rock for the benefit of future generations. But when he throws himself from the top of a tree at the feet of the demon, the latter, revealing his true form, stops his fall and pays homage to him. This youth became very popular in Japanese Buddhism (under the name of Sessen Dōji), where he is often put in parallel with Prince Vessantara.

What impact might these stories have had on the lives of ordinary Buddhists? As Max Müller notes: "We are told that Ārya Śūra, the author of *The Garland of Jātakas* (*Jātakamālā*), to follow the example of the Buddha in a past life, threw himself in front of a starving tigress to be devoured. Let us hope that this too is still only a *jātaka.*"[40] The theme of abandoning the body led to disturbing scenes of self-mutilation and immolation by fire in China, acts that were not redeemed by any act of truth: contrary to the traditional description of sacrifice, where the sacrificer offers up a proxy of his own person (an animal or various other offerings), the faithful in China refused any substitute and offered themselves, following the mythical example of the bodhisattva Sarvasattvapriyadarśana.[41]

The Legend of Prince Vessantara

The *Vessantara-jātaka* (Skt. *Viśvantara-jātaka*) is not only the best illustration of the perfection of giving but also a detailed account of the penultimate earthly life of the Bodhisattva, when he was a prince named Vessantara (Viśvantara), who was also known as Sudana (Excellent Charity). As Steve Collins notes, the story of Vessantara, which is found throughout South and Southeast Asia as well as in East Asia, has become as important—if not more so—than the Life of the Buddha itself.[42]

The story begins when the future mother of Vessantara, Phusatī, who is the wife of the god Indra (as Māyā will be later), having finished her stay in Trāyastriṃśa Heaven, is reborn on earth to become the wife of King Sañjaya. At

Indra's request, the Bodhisattva agrees to descend into her womb. He is born immaculate, eyes wide open. Hardly out of the womb, he asks his mother: "Ma, I wish to make a donation, do you have anything?" As a teenager, he is obsessed with the desire to make donations and even gives up a white elephant revered as the palladium of the kingdom. This gift is a game changer, for suddenly the prince's generosity is seen as a threat to society and is met with general disapproval. The people demand his death, but the king, after much procrastination, condemns him to exile. Vessantara's wife, Maddī, decides to follow him into exile along with their two children. This punishment does not cool the generosity of the prince, however: "On the way, two Brahmins ask him for the horses of his chariot: he surrenders them, but the gods replace them with antelopes; a third asks for the chariot itself: he gives it, and the family must continue on foot. However, the gods shorten the path to the forest that will be their dwelling place, where Indra has had a hermitage prepared for them." As their existence gets organized, Vessantara meditates while Maddī goes into the forest every day to gather fruits. Now enters Jūjaka, a libidinous old Brahmin obeying the whims of his young wife, who has ordered him to bring back slaves. Taking advantage of Maddī's absence, Jūjaka asks Vessantara to give him his children. Vessantara agrees, despite his son's plea. The children try to hide, but Vessantara brings them out of hiding. Then, as if he were setting the price of oxen, he determines the price that his children will have to pay to the Brahmin to be freed. "There was then a frightening phenomenon, one that would give you goose-flesh: when the children were given away, the earth shook."[43] Vessantara, "elated to have given the appropriate gift," observes his children as the Brahmin takes them away propelled with kicks: "Where they were hit, their skin split, the blood flowed; when they were hit, they leaned against each other." With the children gone, Vessantara suddenly realizes the enormity of his action and breaks into tears. He even considers pursuing the Brahmin, perhaps to kill him, but he changes his mind. The children, having succeeded in escaping, return, but he gives them back to the Brahmin, this time with a heavy heart: "The great sorrow caused by the moaning and crying of his children as they left fell on the Great Being, and his heart became hot; unable to draw a breath through his nose, he began to pant; his breath was hot, and tears of blood were streaming from his eyes." But he quickly recovers, saying to himself: "Such a pain has for its cause this single defect: my feelings of affection; I must annihilate them by the practice of indifference." Then, "by the power that his knowledge gave him, he tore off this thorn of sorrow and sat down in his customary posture."[44]

Meanwhile, the gods have held Maddī in the forest, taking the form of wild animals that blocked her way home. When she returns to the hermitage at nightfall, madly worried, she asks the Bodhisattva where the children have gone. Vessantara, instead of explaining what happened, reproaches her for having been away for so long, even accusing her of infidelity. Not until morning does he finally confesss everything to her. He tries to convince her that the gift of children is the ultimate gift, adding that they can always have more children! Maddī finally agrees with him.

The god Indra then decides to put Vessantara's generosity to the test once again. Pretending to be a Brahmin, he asks him for his wife. Vessantara accepts without flinching, and Maddī does the same: "[She] did not frown or show any resentment or tears; he just watched, and she kept silent, certain that he knew what was best."[45] Impressed by Vessantara's generosity, if not out of pity for Maddī, Indra decides to give her back to him immediately, leaving morality intact. In addition, to reward Vessantara, he grants him eight wishes. Vessantara asks that he be able to return to the palace and ascend to the throne. In the meantime, the children have been redeemed by their grandfather, and the Brahmin has died of indigestion! The reunion can finally take place: "Seeing her healthy children from afar, Maddī, trembling like a possessed woman in a trance, sprinkled them with milk from her breasts." All's well that ends well: Vessantara and his family, glorified by their suffering, regain their rank.[46] The tale concludes by saying that its protagonists will be reborn as the main characters in the Life of the Buddha.

Commentators have wanted to see in this narrative, which differs from the others in both its length and its position (it is the last in the canonical list of 547 *Jātakas*), a kind of Buddhist epic, forming a counterpoint to such great Indian epics as the *Mahābharata* and the *Rāmāyana*. Certainly there are striking parallels between the *Rāmāyana* and the *Vessantara-jātaka*. In particular, Vessantara can be considered an analogue of Rāma, and his wife Maddī seems close to the devoted and submissive Sītā. Other concordant elements appear in the course of the story: in both, a prince is banished by his father and goes into exile with his wife. The couple travels far away, undergoes cruel hardships, and finally settles in a forest. The difference is that Maddī, if she had really become the companion of a Brahmin for a time, would have suffered, back at the marital home, all the pain in the world to prove her innocence. She would have been forever tinged with doubt, as Sīta was when she was reunited with Rāma, after having been abducted by the demon Rāvana (who had respected her, however). Hence the leniency shown by Indra when he reveals his true identity. But the *Jātaka* is not simply the counterpart of an Indian epic; because of the intransigence of its hero, it places itself on a higher plane. Its unrealistic nature is what has proved both its weakness (in the eyes of classical Hinduism and most Western commentators) and its strength (in the eyes of Buddhist believers).

Moreover, as Eugen Curtin notes, Vessantara is, after the Buddha himself, one of the greatest "seismic" personalities in the Buddhist canon, because each of his gifts causes earthquakes.[47] It is precisely in relation to these earthquakes that King Milinda asks the monk Nāgasena about Vessantara. According to Curtin, the exorbitant character of Vessantara's gifts is directly related to the very difficult and often poorly understood seismic issue. The earthquakes occur seven times, punctuating the saga of Vessantara: first when he vows to give his heart, his eyes, his flesh, and his blood to whomever asks for them; then when he gives the white elephant, when he distributes all his possessions before going into exile, when he gives his children and then his wife, when he meets his parents again in the forest, and finally when he returns to the royal palace.

In most of the Indochinese peninsula, there is an annual Vessantara festival when monks recite the entire story, in vernacular language, for a period of twelve to eighteen hours.[48] The temple where this performance takes place is transformed for the occasion into the retreat where Vessantara lived with his family during his exile. During the ceremony, painted scrolls are also paraded to aid visualization of the story. The legend has also spread to the Himalayan region and East Asia. A Nepalese version differs from the Pāli version principally in the fact that it does not offer a *happy ending.* In contrast to the fate of the two main protagonists of the *Vessantara-jātaka,* Viśvantara and Madrī are never reunited. Viśvantara, continuing his life of austerities and meditation, does not return to the paternal kingdom. What's more, his father too becomes an ascetic, leaving the throne to his grandson Jālini. On this point, it is obvious that the legend reflects Hindu influences.[49] This Viśvantara, while in principle still a Bodhisattva, is already revered as a Buddha in his own right. The life presented here appears clearly closed in on itself, whereas in the Pāli version it is still only the penultimate stage of the Bodhisattva's spiritual quest.

The same version, reduced to the extreme, can be found in the Chinese translation of the *Bodhisattvāvadāna* (*Pusa benyuan jing*). Here again, the children are redeemed by the king, while the prince continues to live with his wife in exile. There is therefore no reconciliation between the king and Viśvantara, no glorious return of the prodigal son. By choosing the eremitical life, Viśvantara paradoxically places himself "beyond every gift." Hubert Durt emphasizes the more important role played by Viśvantara's son, and by the king himself, who in turn embraces the ascetic life at the end of the story, leaving the throne to his grandson.[50] It is also in the Chinese version that the wife of Viśvantara, Madrī, shows the strongest personality.[51] In this she prefigures in certain respects the wife of the Buddha Śākyamuni, Yaśodharā, who practices austerities at home while her husband pursues an ascetic life in the forest.

Over time, Vessantara's excessive generosity has not failed to stick in the popular imagination, giving rise to ambiguous feelings and diverse appreciations. To alleviate the sense of scandal caused by his gifts, the story has been thought to appeal to a supposedly immemorial tradition according to which all bodhisattvas give away their wife and children, a tactic already recognized in the case of the untimely death of Māyā. The story of Vessantara is presented to us as a simple illustration of the perfection of giving, a superlative example of generosity, but clearly not everyone is agreed on this point. Vessantara's extreme generosity was shocking even to an orthodox Buddhist: in *Milinda's Questions,* the Indo-Greek king Milinda (Menander) points out to his interlocutor, the monk Nāgasena, that this generosity, however sublime it may have been, nevertheless caused the suffering of his wife and children. Nāgasena admits this, but asserts that the end (Vessantara's spiritual progress) justified the means—in the same way, he adds, as when someone afflicted is taken in haste to the doctor in an ox cart, one causes the oxen to suffer. The comparison—in the distinction it makes between the patient (the Bodhisattva in search of awakening) and the oxen (the members of his family, reduced to the rank of cattle)—is sobering.

Vessantara appears twice in *Milinda's Questions.* The first time, as we have seen, in connection with a discussion about earthquakes; the second time, when Milinda asks whether all buddhas are supposed to give away their wife and children, or whether this gift is unique to Vessantara. Nāgasena answers that all future buddhas will do the same. Milinda then asks if the children and wife of Vessantara approved the father's decision. Nāgasena answers that Maddī approved it, but that the children were too young to understand the situation—which does not seem to be the case when his son, for example, tells Vessantara that he must have a heart of stone to sacrifice them in this way. Nāgasena adds, in good casuistical fashion, that if they had understood what was at stake they would have approved. Milinda does not sees the matter in this light, maintaining that someone who wants to accumulate merits should sacrifice himself.[52] Nāgasena argues that the fact that the story of Vessantara's generosity has come down to us is proof that his behavior was justified—so we should avoid slandering him by questioning his actions, which by their *sui generis* nature transcend ordinary morality. A bodhisattva is not accountable to anyone, for his understanding of situations exceeds that of the common man. Without fear of contradiction, Nāgasena goes on to state that it was perfectly normal, according to the customs of the time, to pawn or sell one's children when one was in debt, whereas it would have been wrong for Vessantara to give up his own person when he was asked for his children and wife. He also points out that Vessantara did not give his children away gladly, but felt great sorrow because of it. This sorrow was nevertheless alleviated because he knew that his children would be redeemed by their grandfather, and that their misfortune was temporary. Thus Vessantara's gift of his children, which he regards as the ultimate gift, is not in fact irreversible; it is basically a loan. This realization alleviates Vessantara's pain, without suppressing it. Because he is not yet a buddha (or the Buddha), he is still bound to his human emotions, even if he can already project himself into a future where these emotions will no longer affect him. Similarly, in respect of his wife Maddī, the scandal is mitigated by the fact that the listeners of the story know that the Brahmin to whom she is given is none other than the king of the gods, Indra.

One cannot fail to be struck by the contrast between the popularity of this *Jātaka* in Southeast Asia and the unease that the excess of generosity on Vessantara's part arouses in some commentators. As Louis Gabaude notes, "The excessive aspect of Vessantara's gifts is not just the result of Western perceptions and morality; it has been perceived by Indian Buddhists since Milinda—even though the latter, the Indo-Greek king Menander, was in some ways a Westerner. Similarly, the story has been the subject of much debate in Thailand and other Southeast Asian countries."[53] This dispute is perhaps the precise explanation of its popularity and large number of variants, oral, written, theatrical, and iconographic. In the event, some have sought to justify Vessantara's apparent lack of paternal love by pointing out that putting a very high price on the redemption of his children in effect guaranteed that only his father the king could redeem them. That argument seems a little weak.

The interest of the *Vessantara-jātaka* undoubtedly lies in its literary character, which puts it on the same plane as the *Buddhacarita* and the *Lalitavistara*. But it also, and perhaps above all, lies in Vessantara's contradictions: he is, we are told, joyful about giving up his children, full of joy at the idea of accomplishing the ultimate gift; then, when he realizes the enormity of his act, he is overcome with sadness and anger, and even contemplates killing the Brahmin. When his wife returns from the forest, he reproaches her for having delayed too long and even accuses her of having enjoyed gallant affairs; then, after he has finally confessed to her what he has done, he takes refuge in silence and cultivates indifference. Even if one accepts the hierarchy of values embedded in this tale, it is difficult to approve of Vessantara's behavior. And it is this ambivalence that may have led so many commentators to weigh in on the text. Perhaps the enduring success of *Vessantara-jātaka* is related to the impression it gives of having been written by two authors who were at odds with each other—if not by a single, somewhat schizophrenic writer. This tension creates a stereoscopic effect, giving the Bodhisattva a psychological depth and narrative resilience that he lacks in the narratives of his other lives, including the final one when he becomes the Buddha. Still, the main reason for the popularity of the tale is undoubtedly the heartbreaking fate of the children and their mother, and her unblemished, forgiving character. As Jean-Pierre Osier notes, the world of the *Vessantara-jātaka* "owes its consistency to the psychological thickness of the relatives, friends or hostiles, who do not behave as mere satellites, sending back a weakened image of the central star."[54] All the characters are strongly individualized. Even the Brahmin Jūjaka, a mixture of wickedness and ridicule, becomes human when he is ridiculed by his young wife. He is described as "old, ugly, libidinous, greedy, even gluttonous, stingy, pusillanimous, wily, a liar, submissive to those stronger than himself, and cruel to the weak."[55] Likewise, Vessantara's parents are not extras in this opera. Phusatī, his mother, gives free rein to her sorrow during the exile of her son, and she tries to prevent her daughter-in-law and her grandchildren from leaving.[56] King Sañjaya is torn between his royal function and his fatherly and grandfatherly love. Vessantara's son, Jāli, is an extraordinarily sensitive and intelligent child, who seeks above all to protect his sister, the very image of vulnerability.[57] As for Maddī, she is Vessantara's female double. Like him, she pursues her search for perfection to the end. But she is torn between her maternal love and her love for Vessantara, who finally convinces her that "giving one's children is the supreme gift."[58] Like Sitā, the spouse of the Hindu god Rāma to whom she compares herself, Maddī is the very image (at least for a traditional Indian audience) of the model wife, ready to sacrifice herself for her husband. In spite of her immense pain at the loss of her children, she does not think of blaming Vessantara, and she ends up agreeing with his reasons and praising his generosity. She is perfect in her role as a victim, a tragic heroine, a mother, and a loving, pure, and innocent wife. If Vessantara is ambivalent, which is putting it mildly, she is all of a piece. In short, all the secondary characters are more endearing than the hero.

Steve Collins believes that the success of the story lies in the fact that it opposes two opposing conceptions of virtue: the renunciation of the ascetic versus life in the secular world. And it is this unresolved tension that would explain the continuing fascination of the tale.[59] Until the twentieth century, the debate over this tale attracted ongoing interest. But then the tale lost credibility when historicist critics disavowed it as the "word of the Buddha," turning it into a mere fable and an outmoded model of virtue. Also, at a time when Buddhism was becoming increasingly nationalistic and engaged, imitating the model provided by Vessantara threatened a weakening of the social order, a consequence contrary to the national interest. Vessantara is indeed the one who fails in all his social duties, rejecting his dharma in favor of a higher but perhaps illusory Dharma, the Buddhist Law. Well-ordered charity begins at home. Thus Vessantara finally came up against Buddhist modernism. Not surprisingly, the *Vessantara-jātaka* subsequently provided a target for feminist criticism. Vessantara, in his dealings with Maddī, is now held responsible for keeping Indian women in a subordinate role. According to this reading, Maddī also deserves to be considered a bodhisattva.

Osier, in his remarkable study on the subject, tries to justify extreme generosity in the name of a transcendental goal, that is, awakening. Everything that can hinder awakening must be eliminated.[60] Vessantara is not content to just give, he makes an exaggerated or exorbitant donation (*ati-dāna*) that is out of the ordinary and puts him in jeopardy.[61] He represents "the absolute, inhuman requirement of awakening, the aporia of the Great Gift, in opposition to family, conjugal, and state values." To be sure, this extreme gift seems to contradict the Middle Way advocated by the Buddha. But perhaps, like the asceticism practiced by Śākyamuni for six years, taking him to the edge of the precipice, one must push things to the extreme before coming back to reason. Vessantara gives because "giving pleases him." In doing so, he seems to forget that his gifts have consequences, sometimes unfortunate, especially for those who are sacrificed on the altar of his generosity. The road to a Buddhist hell, too, is paved with good intentions. Osier offers an interesting analysis of Vessantara's gift as a paradox. In his view, the gift ceases to be a mechanical princely occupation, to become an increasingly difficult test. The practice of giving is now accompanied by an absolute awareness of the implications of an act that was until then merely conventional and intended in principle to strengthen the social bond. In this sense, the final restoration brings a new Vessantara into a kingdom that is itself renewed.[62]

Vessantara loves his children, since he is capable of contemplating the murder of the Brahmin, but he loves them less than the goal of his quest. Maddī, despite the protests issuing from her motherly love, finally recognizes the merits of his actions.[63] The proof of this is that while the "inner" gift of King Śibi, who gouges out both his eyes to give them to a Brahmin, has no visible effect on external reality, Vessantara's gifts, however external they might seem, give rise to seismic tremors. Sanctioned by the earth itself, they deserve the name "perfection of giving."[64] The choice is indeed between the codified, constrained relationships of what we can call with Collins the "disciplinary dharma," and a behavior that abolishes all existing relationships to place the giver beyond all the codes and regulations made necessary by social life.[65] Is Vessantara's generosity to be seen as a disguised criticism (or correction) of the lingering selfishness of early Buddhism, centered on individual salvation—in other words, a mahāyānist criticism of Hīnayāna? If so, the story should then have been at least as successful in East Asia, where the Mahāyāna dominates. But this is not the case, and Vessantara's "generosity" can hardly be described as altruistic or compassionate.[66]

THE BUDDHA'S NEGATIVE KARMA

The *Jātakas* provided hagiographers with the opportunity to amplify the story of the Buddha's Life, showing its karmic ins and outs. The tales also help to give him a more human face, showing him as suffering from the small miseries of existence as well as the indignities of old age. Significantly, these accounts of the Buddha's previous existences, while essentially aiming to show the virtues of the great man, sometimes also highlight his shortcomings. It is thus the retribution of a negative karma produced by the Buddha in his previous existences that explains the physical and moral sufferings he has to endure at the end of his life—for example, the various accusations he has to face from heretical masters, or the physical evils that accompany him until the end of his days.

Some anecdotes make one smile, such as the "autobiographical" account of the Buddha's realization of the first *dhyāna* during his first meditation under the jambu tree, prompted by a criticism of his habit of taking a nap.[67] Other *Jātakas* contain immoral episodes, showing us the Bodhisattva succumbing to desire. In one of them, having been reborn as an ascetic with supernormal powers, he loses his ability to fly when he is assailed by carnal desire while seeing the queen lying on her bed as he passes over the royal palace.

The nine torments that the Buddha has to endure because of his karma are often mentioned: the slanders of Sundari and Ciñcā, who accuse him of having impregnated them; the wound on the Buddha's foot caused by a rock thrown by Devadatta; another wound caused by acacia thorns; his headaches during the massacre of the Śākya clan; his back pain; the fact that he is reduced to eating barley after a round of almsgiving, or that he returns with an empty bowl on another occasion; and his having to endure six years of austerity before finding the Middle Way.[68] The Vinaya of the Mūlasarvāstivādin reports a list of ten misdeeds committed by the Buddha in his past lives, which causes him ten inconveniences in his last existence (the nine above plus the angry elephant launched against him by Devadatta).

A number of sources mention that in his old age the Buddha suffers from constant back pain caused by the ascetic exercises he practiced during the six years before awakening, as well as stomachaches due to his fasting. He also suffers on several occasions from Brahmins who see him as a rival, and he encounters antagonisms within his own community as well. An often-mentioned example is the schism of Kauśāmbi, which is described in the *Treatise.* When a quarrel arises between the monks of Kauśāmbi, the Buddha goes to their community and tries to pacify them:

> The monks then told him, "May the Buddha, the Master of the Law, remain modest and silent; we cannot fail to respond when we are attacked." The Buddha, now convinced that these men could not be saved, rose into the air in the very midst of the assembly and withdrew into the forest to give himself up to the concentration of stillness.[69]

The best known example is of course the jealousy of his cousin Devadatta. When the disciples of the Buddha ask him why Devadatta has attacked him, he answers that it is not the first time, and he tells them that the cause goes back to a distant past life. In the *Commentary on Jātakas* (5th cent.) alone, no fewer than seventy stories describe the antagonism between the future Buddha and the future Devadatta, and unlike the result in his final life, the Bodhisattva does not always emerge victorious from these confrontations. In *Milinda's Questions,* King Milinda asks Nāgasena about this, and the latter answers that Devadatta was not always evil, and that he accumulated merits in the past that result in his occasional superiority over the Bodhisattva.[70]

In the "Pubbakammapiloti," a chapter of the Pāli *Apadāna,* the Buddha gives Ānanda a list of twenty-two faults he committed in previous existences.[71] Some of them remain vague (a matter of unspecified karma) while others are very specific, although sometimes minor. For example, if he is twice accused (by Ciñcā and Sundari) of having had sexual relations, it is because in the distant past he slandered a religious person in a similar way. In Sundari's case, the situation is aggravated when the Brahmins who persuaded the girl to accuse the Buddha of impregnating her go on to kill her and her body is found near the Buddha's cell. In both cases, he is finally cleared of all suspicion.

The reason he became hated by Devadatta is that he once killed his younger brother in a past life so as to become the only heir to the family fortune. This caused him not only to be reborn in hell for a thousand years but also, in the present life, to be wounded in the foot by Devadatta when the latter tries to murder him.[72] Sometimes crime and retribution can both take place in the same life—for example, it was for taking a queen and her sons prisoner that his own daughter was raped. Although the text remains silent on his exact crime, it implies that he himself committed rape on that occasion. In view of such crimes, others seem quite minor: For example, if Devadatta throws a furious elephant at him, it is because the Bodhisattva, in a previous life when he himself was a coachman, frightened a *pratyeka-buddha* (a person who is awakened by his own effort) for fun; or, if he suffers from a headache when members of his clan, the Śākya, are slaughtered, it is because he once, as a child, enjoyed watching fishermen (the future Śākya) catching fish in nets. Similarly, his back pain is due to the fact that he once, in a past life when he was a wrestler, injured another wrestler's back; or because he once hit a deer in the back. On the other hand, it is for slandering the Buddha Kāśyapa when he was a Brahmin that he has to pursue asceticism for six long years instead of a few months. To this already long list (which, in fact, is singularly short if one thinks of the temporal immensity involved) are added other faults, mentioned in passing to explain his difficult relationship with Devadatta or Yaśodharā. Thus the Buddha explains that the reason he abandoned Yaśodharā is that in a previous life, when he was living with his wife in exile (in the form of Prince Vessantara), he had sent her away so he could eat what little food they had left.

The idea that the Buddha, while perfectly awakened, could still be subject to karmic retribution was a scandal to some. In the *Treatise,* we read: "If the miraculous power of the Buddha is immense . . . , how can he be subject to the retribution of the nine sins?"[73] Commentators, after seeking the karmic causes of the Buddha's torments in order to attenuate the scandal, endeavored to transform them into trials from which he emerges victorious. As Lamotte notes: "The commentators did not try to conceal these embarrassing episodes, but they cleared their Master of all suspicion by justifying these somewhat daring initiatives with excellent reasons. Moreover, they did not fail to find irrefutable evidence in the life of the Buddha of his unshakable ataraxy under any circumstances, whether pleasant or unpleasant."[74] Thus, when the Buddha is falsely accused by Ciñca, he remains perfectly impassive, and does not relinquish his impassibility when the accusation turns out to be pure slander and the gods cover him with praise.

Various compromises have also been sought—for example, it has been argued that, whatever troubles the Buddha must apparently suffer from, he in fact experiences only pleasant sensations; or that, alongside the torments and illnesses resulting from past acts, there are others that are simply due to present physical conditions. The Buddha, we are also told, receives the fruits of his past karma, but this retribution no longer produces future karma. It is therefore not a proof of incomplete buddhahood.

Nāgasena provides alternative explanations in *Milinda's Questions.* Although he sees good and bad karma in Devadatta, he does not seem to admit that the Bodhisattva may have acquired bad karma. Thus, when the Bodhisattva makes an animal sacrifice, it is because he is temporarily insane and therefore, strictly speaking, irresponsible; when he slanders the buddha Kāśyapa, it is because of his Brahmin origins. Nāgasena claims that the Buddha has consumed all his bad karma; his physical pains are therefore not the effect of karma but have purely natural causes. If certain events seem to indicate that the Buddha is not perfect, the cause is the karma of others, not the Buddha's karma. If, for example, Devadatta has always sought to harm him in many past existences, it is Devadatta's problem, not the Buddha's. Some commentators are not satisfied with these far-fetched explanations. Dhammapāla, for example, explains that Sundari's slander stems from the fact that the Bodhisattva, for slandering a *pratyeka-buddha,* spent thousands of years in hell, and that a residual karma afflicts him even now that he has become the Buddha.

In early Buddhism, the gap between the asserted perfection of a Buddha who is still human and the small miseries he faces already constitutes a kind of cognitive dissonance. But in Mahāyāna, the gap between an almost divine Buddha and the karmic indignities he still has to endure is such that a drastic solution is needed: there are two Buddhas, or rather two bodies of the Buddha, one human, the other transcendent; and the first is not real, it is simply a clever way to teach certain truths to humans. According to the *Treatise:*

> The Buddha has two bodies: an essential body and a body born of father and mother. The essential body fills the space of the ten regions. . . . It is through this essential body that the Buddha saves the beings of the universes of the ten regions. To undergo the retribution of sins is the affair of the Buddha of the body of birth. The Buddha of the body of birth preaches the law gradually as if it were a human law. Since there are two kinds of Buddha, there is nothing wrong with the Buddha feeling the retribution of sins. . . . It is therefore by a skillful means, and not in reality, that the Buddha feels the retribution of sins.[75]

In reality, the Buddha is no longer subject, as he was in early Buddhism, to retribution for his past acts.[76] Thus, to justify the apparent impasse to which his six years of asceticism seemed to have led the Bodhisattva, the *Treatise* states: "How now, during his six years of ascetic practices, would he have followed the wrong path by eating only one grain of sesame, one grain of rice, every day? The Bodhisattva in his last life cannot be wrong even for one day; how then could he be wrong for six years?"[77] The torments that the Buddha seems to suffer are explained simply as skillful means (*upāya*), intended to help beings understand the reality of karma. His illnesses are simulated, as are those of Vimalakīrti, his lay double. As Lamotte notes, "The Buddha, superior to the world, conforms to the world and simulates illnesses to console suffering humanity and ensure its conversion through this skillful means."[78]

The *Jātakas,* by reporting episodes from previous existences where the Buddha does not always appear to his advantage, thus adds to his psychological and literary complexity, and in some respects they reveal the sometimes mixed feelings of those who transmitted them. But in the end, morality is saved, and the Buddha emerges greater from his trials.

7

DRAMATIS PERSONAE

As the Buddhist legend grew, particularly with the development of the *Jātakas,* the characters surrounding the Buddha in his present and past lives shifted from being mere extras to real actors in the story. One could almost speak of real cycles with regard to some of them. In the family circle, in particular, tradition has focused on the close relatives of the Buddha: his biological mother Māyā, who died so soon after giving birth to him; his father Śuddhodana, worried about his succession; his aunt and adoptive mother Mahāprajāpatī, who became the first nun; his young wife Yaśodharā, abandoned by the man she loves. The only exception is his son Rāhula, who plays only a minor role.[1]

QUEEN MĀYĀ

The character of Māyā has been neglected by the Pāli tradition, probably because of her untimely death, which elevates her sister Mahāprajāpatī into the foreground. However, Māyā does not disappear from the scene. Death is not enough to erase the motherly love of a Buddha's mother. Even when she is reborn in Trāyastriṃśa Heaven in the form of a god (*deva*), as is the case in some sources, Māyā returns to haunt the Buddhist imaginary as a feminine presence. She plays an important role in several major episodes in the Life of the Buddha, beginning of course with his conception and birth, but also during his asceticism and his stay in Trāyastriṃśa Heaven, and finally during his parinirvāṇa. In short, despite the official reason given for her premature death—namely, to save her from the sorrow of the great departure—she plays in the Buddhist tradition a *mater dolorosa* role that is not so different from that of the mother of Christ. However, in contrast to Mary, she does not seem to have become the object of a cult.

Without a doubt the most "pregnant" description of Māyā is the one that takes in her immaculate conception, pregnancy, and immaculate parturition (which is not, strictly speaking, a delivery, as we saw). The purification that precedes conception varies somewhat according to the source. In the *Mahāvastu* she asks her royal husband for permission to remain chaste for one night—the night she dreams of the white elephant—while in the *Lalitavistara* she stays in a separate room for thirty-two weeks and practices austerities.

Māyā's pregnancy is not the topic of long commentaries in the earliest texts. However, some of them do report her "cravings" as a pregnant woman—for example, she wants to drink water from the four oceans, an allusion to the universal wisdom that her son will obtain, but also to his possible future as a universal monarch or *cakravartin.* These cravings seem to contradict the perfection of a figure presented to us as perfectly pure and free of all desire. Evidently the mother of the future Buddha remains subject to female servitude. It is, moreover, partly to remove her from desire that tradition makes her disappear a few days after the birth of her son.

During her pregnancy, Māyā serves as a kind of "living tabernacle" to the Bodhisattva,[2] and as such she radiates all of the Bodhisattva's curative powers. All those who approach her are healed. At the end of this pregnancy full of wonders, what could have been a difficult birth is not one, since Māyā gives birth standing upright, in a natural setting (the park of Lumbinī), and the child miraculously emerges from her right side without hurting her in any way. In Indian representations of this event, she radiates beauty: half-naked, slim waistline, rounded forms, she embodies the Indian feminine ideal that is also depicted in voluptuous images of the goddesses of vegetation (*yakṣinī*), symbols of fertility with full breasts (see fig. 2). In this regard, a contrast can be noted between iconographic sources (where the *yakṣinī* are presented as symbols of good omen) and textual, essentially monastic sources (where they become negative symbols, threatening monastic purity).[3]

And yet, Māyā dies a few days after this miraculous birth. This death, on which tradition remains silent, was nevertheless a scandal for some, and in retrospect it seems to tarnish the auspicious character of the Bodhisattva's birth. The reasons given to justify it seem awkward, but perhaps they were more acceptable to the people of the time.[4] According to the *Mahāvastu,* the case of Māyā is not isolated: the mothers of all buddhas die seven days after giving birth. Māyā, we are told, "died of joy" at the beauty of the child she had begotten. Her death becomes an apotheosis, since she is immediately reborn in Trāyastriṃśa Heaven. Foucher, in his usual ironic way, reports the following: "Māyā is supposed to reside on the second or fourth level of the heavens—some say in that . . . of the 'Satisfied' gods, others say in the one over which Indra reigns and which, in the manner of a club of American billionaires, bears the baroque name of Heaven of the 'Thirty-three.'"[5] According to most Pāli sources, Māyā now changes sex. The Chinese tradition, however, continues to consider her a woman, one who even becomes the wife of the king of the gods, Indra (who had, shortly before, assisted her during the birth of the Bodhisattva).

The Buddha's Preaching to His Mother

The brief life of Māyā, described as "ten months of pregnancy, seven days of life," is offset by the account of the Buddha's preaching to his mother. After his awakening, the Buddha takes advantage of a monastic retreat during the rainy season to ascend to Trāyastriṃśa Heaven and preach the Law to his mother there. The episode is the subject of several sūtras, the main one being the *Sūtra of the Great Māyā* (*Mahāmāyā-sūtra*).[6] In this text, Māyā, who has become the wife of Indra, is still a beautiful and fertile young woman. When she learns of the Buddha's coming, milk gushes from her breasts and flies to the Buddha's mouth, testifying that he is indeed her son, a scene strangely reminiscent of certain representations of the Virgin Mary's *lactatio* in Christian art.

In Mahāyāna, the character of the Buddha's mother has sometimes been reinterpreted in cosmic or philosophical terms. In the *Gaṇḍavyūha-sūtra,* when the young Sudhana, in the course of his spiritual quest, comes to Māyā in Trāyastriṃśa Heaven, the latter, after describing how the Bodhisattva descended into her in the form of a white elephant with six tusks, adds that her womb could have contained much more than an elephant. Moreover, she adds, it is not only the Bodhisattva who descended from Tuṣita Heaven to be born in her. Countless other bodhisattvas accompanied him, and all of them emerged from the right side of Māyā at the same time, to become buddhas in countless universes. She claims to be in fact the mother of all the buddhas, present, past, and future.[7] However, if in this text Māyā verges on becoming a universal mother, she still keeps specific links with the Buddha Śākyamuni. In other texts of the Mahāyāna, of more philosophical content, her image tends to become more and more abstract. This is particularly the case with the *Prajñāpāramitā-sūtras,* where the term "mother of the Buddha" becomes a designation of wisdom (*prajñā*). Similarly, in the *Sūtra on the Ascension of the Buddha to Trāyastriṃśa Heaven,* it is specified that the true mother of the Buddha is wisdom and that the Buddha was therefore not born of a carnal mother.[8]

Māyā's Descent during the Parinirvāṇa

Countering this abstract reinterpretation of the Buddha's mother, a number of more popular (and often apocryphal) sūtras exalt the maternal and feminine qualities of Māyā. In the literary and artistic traditions, the human relationship between mother and son comes to the forefront. In the representation of the parinirvāṇa in particular, Māyā appears as a real *mater dolorosa.*[9] Hubert Durt has closely studied this episode, which consists of two distinct scenes: the grief of Māyā when she learns about her son's parinirvāṇa and descends from Trāyastriṃśa Heaven to pay him a last homage; and the momentary "resurrection" of the Buddha to console his mother with a sermon on impermanence.[10] At the beginning of the first scene, Māyā has unpleasant dreams in the form of "five lions entering her right flank." These premonitory dreams are obviously a counterpoint to the famous dream of the white elephant at the time of the Bodhisattva's conception. Her worries are confirmed by a disciple of the Buddha, who comes to tell her of his master's extinction. Mourning, she descends from Trāyastriṃśa Heaven with her retinue to pay her respects in front of her son's coffin. The descent of Māyā has become a particularly popular scene in Japanese representations of the parinirvāṇa (*nehan-zu*), where Māyā, in the upper right (or sometimes left) part of the image, descends from Trāyastriṃśa Heaven on a cloud, accompanied by her retinue, to the grove where the majestic body of the Buddha rests.

In the second scene, the Buddha, pulled out of his deep "sleep" by his mother's laments, manifests one final miracle by sitting up in his coffin and preaching the Law to her one last time. In the *Mahāmāya-sūtra,* he emerges from his coffin "like a lion out of its cave." His hands are joined together as a sign of respect for Māyā, whom he asks to dry her tears. At Ānanda's request, he explains that his temporary resurrection is motivated by filial piety. The Buddha preaches sitting inside his coffin just as he preached before he was reborn, from within the maternal womb. One will note the ambiguity of the scene: if the Buddha underscores, as one could expect, the inanity of human attachments, it is a very human and terrestrial value, filial piety, that retains him at the edge of extinction. Indeed, Japanese Buddhists were not mistaken when they emphasized Māyā's pain at the moment when her son disappears forever. This sensitivity to maternal feelings is reflected in Japanese hagiography and iconography. The scene gave birth to a masterpiece of Buddhist painting from the Heian period, preserved in the Kyoto National Museum, *Shaka Coming Out of His Golden Coffin* (*Shaka konkan shutsugen zu*). While filial piety remains the main theme of the episode, it also shows that the Buddha, having entered parinirvāṇa, is not dead in the ordinary sense of the word, since he can still, thanks to his supernormal powers, emerge from his coffin without being perceived as a phantom or specter.

KING ŚUDDHODANA

King Śuddhodana plays a lesser role in Buddhist legend than his wife Māyā, but nevertheless an important one.[11] In his person, contradictory motives intersect: his social importance as a king and father combines with a negative role (at least in appearance), making him what, from a structural standpoint, could be called an obstacle. At the birth of his son, Śuddhodana is troubled by the prophecy of the soothsayers and determined to prevent its fulfillment. On the Festival of the Ploughmen, he is caught up in his ceremonial duties and forgets his son's presence. Left by himself, his son discovers at a single stroke the universality of pain together with meditation. Apprehending the miraculous immobility of the shadow under the jambu tree, Śuddhodana realizes the quasi-divine standing of his son and prostrates himself before him. But still he refuses to let him fulfill his spiritual destiny and tries in vain to hold him back with a surfeit of pleasures and the bonds of marriage.

Śuddhodana is a quasi-Cornelian character, torn between the duties of his caste and his love for his son. If he seems especially concerned about his lineage and the succession to the throne, some episodes also show him as a loving father concerned about his son's health. By a cruel irony of fate, it is by trying to prevent the prince from leaving the palace—by hiding the suffering in human existence from him—that Śuddhodana actually prepares the ground for him. For if Śākyamuni had gradually, from childhood, become aware of the harsh realities of ordinary existence, he would probably not have reacted so violently during the four encounters to the spectacle of human misery, and perhaps he would not have renounced the world.

Even after Śākyamuni's departure, Śuddhodana does not despair of changing his mind. According to the *Treatise,* after the Bodhisattva leaves the palace to pursue the practice of asceticism, "King Śuddhodana, who loves his son, regularly sends a messenger to question him and see how he is doing."[12] He is devastated when he receives false news of Siddhārtha's death as a result of his pursuit. The same scene will be replayed after the awakening when Māra, refusing to admit defeat, turns against Śuddhodana. Thinking he can reach the son through the father, he comes to torment Śuddhodana with an announcement of the death of the prince. Śuddhodana collapses, thinking that the prediction of the soothsayer Ajita at the birth of his son must be false. But then the deity of the Bodhi tree intervenes and announces that the Bodhisattva has emerged victorious from the ordeal.[13]

When the Buddha returns to Kapilavastu after an absence of twelve years, his father's feelings are mixed. He dislikes seeing his son reduced to begging, and he reproaches him for forgetting his princely rank.[14] He is impressed by the Buddha's miracles, however, and ends up recognizing him as his master. Although he is never ordained, he reaches the arhat state shortly before his death, when the Buddha comes to his bedside and gives him his final teachings. At the funeral, the Buddha insists on carrying his father's coffin. Some sources, no doubt judging this role to be inappropriate for a Buddha, tell us that the earth began to shake and he was finally replaced by a god. Thus, in spite of his disobedience to his father's wishes, the Buddha leaves the impression of a pious son. This is particularly true in Chinese and Japanese sources, which, in response to Confucian criticisms, make him a paragon of filial piety. The *Tales of Times Now Past* (*Konjaku monogatarishū*), in the Kamakura period, explains that the Buddha wanted to shoulder his father's coffin "in order to admonish sentient beings in our own latter age against ingratitude for our fathers' and mothers' loving care."[15]

MAHĀPRAJĀPATĪ

After Māyā's untimely death, her younger sister Mahāprajāpatī becomes the child's adoptive mother. When the death of King Śuddhodana leaves her a widow, she asks the Buddha to found a community of nuns where she can take refuge, but her request is denied. She then asks her son Ānanda to intercede on her behalf. The Buddha finally accepts reluctantly, declaring that nuns, because of their feminine imperfections, will have to submit to a particularly rigorous discipline. This story of the origins of the female sangha has often been interpreted as characteristic of the misogynistic mentality of early Buddhism.[16] In any case, Mahāprajāpatī soon attains the dignity of arhat status and dies before her master and adopted son. The Buddha delivers her eulogy at the funeral, where miraculous events transpire, interpreted as proof of Mahāprajāpatī's awakening.

In the *Gotamī-apadanā,* a text included in a Pāli anthology of moral tales, Mahāprajāpatī Gotamī is presented as the female counterpart of the Buddha. As such, she solves the problem of an overly masculine characterization of awakening by offering the model of a female Buddha. According to Jonathan Walters, women's realization of awakening does not depend on the Buddha, but on Gotamī. It was she who made the foundation of the feminine order possible, it was her parinirvāṇa that opened the way to the supreme goal for nuns.[17] However, this statement must be qualified: while Gotamī may have been perceived by some as a female double of the Buddha, she is by no means his equal. As Liz Wilson remarks, she fulfills her roles as wife and mother for most of her life. Her renunciation, according to some sources, does not take place until after the death of Śuddhodana, and perhaps it is motivated as much by her perception of the subordinate status of widows in Indian society as by her spiritual calling. In any case, it has a very different motivation from that of the Buddha.

YAŚODHARĀ

Nearly all sources claim that the Bodhisattva enjoyed a gynaeceum of sixty thousand women (hopefully a highly symbolic figure), although they disagree on the number of his principal wives. Some speak of a single wife, called Gopā or Yaśodharā; others of multiple wives: two (Yaśodharā and Gopā), or even three (Yaśodharā, Gopikā, and Mṛgajā). The author of the *Lalitavistara* knows only one wife, whom he calls Gopā, and who is the mother of Rāhula. The dominant tradition, following the *Buddhacarita* and the *Mahāvastu,* has retained Yaśodharā as the name of the principal wife, describing her as a kind of Buddhist Penelope.

In the early Pāli biographies, this wife is not even named and is simply mentioned as "Rāhula's mother."[18] As we have seen, some sources report that the Bodhisattva impregnated her on the day before his departure, so that no one could doubt his virility. Later, she plays an extremely brief role during the Buddha's return to Kapilavastu: it is she who points out to her son a father whom he has never seen before. But the story is centered on Rāhula, whom the Buddha will soon wrest from his mother's affection to be ordained as a novice.

Bareau wondered about the reasons for the initial silence in the sources regarding Yaśodharā. Always inclined to uncover the historical fact behind the legend, he explains it by citing the possibility that Yaśodharā died shortly after the birth of Rāhula. This hypothesis, which he acknowledges to be fragile, would also, in his view, explain the great departure—at least in a more satisfactory way than the obviously legendary account of the four encounters. The Bodhisattva would have renounced the world after experiencing this brutal loss. As Bareau himself admits, this kind of speculation borders on unadulterated fiction: "In short, I have done only what Buddhist authors from the beginning of our era and the following centuries did, but using different means of investigation."[19]

Yaśodharā, under that name, appears only in late Vinaya texts dating to the fourth and fifth centuries CE. Her role in the *Mahāvastu* is already quite detailed, and in the Vinaya of the Mulasarvāstivadin she is on her way to being divinized. But this same Vinaya mentions three wives. We are told that the Bodhisattva, because of ties contracted in previous lives, chose Yaśodharā from all the girls in the land.[20] Courting her, he tells her: "I have the power, noble lady, to bind you and make you go wherever I want. What could your father do? I can fulfill a thousand women every night. But I have chosen you."[21] The four encounters and the meditation under the jambu tree follow, and the prince decides to leave the palace. When he returns to the city, a young girl named Mṛgajā praises him from the top of her balcony, and he throws her his necklace, which falls exactly onto her shoulders. The king, hearing of this, brings Mṛgajā into the palace as the prince's second wife. Later, returning to Kapilavastu in triumph after cutting off the head of a huge snake that was devastating the area, the prince sees a young girl named Gopikā at the top of a pavilion and falls in love with her. She becomes his third wife.

It is also possible that Yaśodharā and Gopā (var. Gopī or Gopikā) represent two aspects of the same function. Yaśodharā, separated from the Bodhisattva, would represent pure love, while Gopā, who initiates him to sex, would represent carnal love. At least this is what late Tantric sources suggest when they tell us that the Bodhisattva learned all the secrets of sex from Gopā, whose name evokes the Gopī of the Hindu tradition, shepherdesses in love with the young god Krishna.[22] Thus the *Candamahāroṣana-tantra* explains that "along with Gopā, he experienced bliss. / By uniting the diamond scepter [the penis] and lotus [the vagina], / He attained the fruit of bliss."[23] In reference to this kind of text, La Vallée Poussin wrote that the Tantric masters (whom he transforms into "Buddhist sorcerers") "evoke and interpret in their own way this part of the legend of Śākyamuni on which decent history casts a veil: the sojourn in the harem. Śākyamuni became Buddha by practicing Tantric rites."[24]

Most ancient sources, however, chastely evade the sexual implications of Rāhula's birth and exonerate the Bodhisattva of a possible violation of his vow of chastity, recounting how, having touched his wife's belly with his finger, he tells her that she will bear a son. But it is above all the prolonged pregnancy of Yaśodharā, and the ensuing ordeals, that earn her a place in the legend. She now forms with the Bodhisattva a model couple who have accumulated immense merits during many previous lives together.[25]

An Ambivalent Relationship

The meeting of the Bodhisattva and Yaśodharā was, we are told, predestined: it is the retribution of an ancient karma, which the Buddha reveals to his disciples in the form of various *Jātakas*. Yaśodharā is ambivalently represented there, as both chaste and seductive, lonely and dangerous. Yet in all the texts, Yaśodharā is devastated by Śākyamuni's departure. In the *Divyāvadāna,* a Sanskrit anthology of Buddhist tales dating from the second century CE, the link between the two characters is said to go back to an earlier existence, the distant time when the Bodhisattva, in the form of the young ascetic Sumedha, vowed to become awakened.[26] When Sumedha learns of the approach of the buddha Dīpankara, he asks a young girl (the future Yaśodharā) to give him the lotuses she has just picked so that he can offer them to Dīpankara. She accepts on one condition: that he promise to take her as his wife, life after life.[27] The *Mahāvastu* underlines that this promise linked the two beings very powerfully in their next lives. Thus, in an animal existence, the young girl becomes the doe who saves her companion, the king of the stags. It is again she who is reborn as Maddī, the wife of Prince Vessantara. Late biographies present us with Yaśodharā and the Buddha as a perfect couple, bound by invisible links—a bit like two quantum particles—despite the separation. Yaśodharā is born at the same time as the Bodhisattva, and she gives birth at the very moment he is awakened. But, as with all old couples, not everything proceeds without quarrels. Some *Jātakas* tell of the mutual disillusion of both spouses. In the *Mahāvastu,* the Buddha justifies his apparent disregard for Yaśodharā at the time of the great departure by reference to one of their previous lives. He was then a caravan leader who found himself wrongly accused of a crime and then sentenced to death. A beautiful courtesan named Śyāma saw him, and because of their common karma, she fell madly in love with him. By dint of her own ingenuity, she managed to get him released by substituting another prisoner in his place. They became lovers, but fearing that one day she would sacrifice him for a new lover, he thought it safer to run away. That courtesan was in fact Yaśodharā, the Buddha explains, and that is why he had to run away again.[28] A poor excuse, one might say, but it seems to have suited his followers.

Yaśodharā's Pregnancy and Asceticism

In the Pāli tradition, Rāhula is born on the night of the great departure. In contrast, some Sanskrit sources like the Vinaya of the Mūlasarvāstivādin place the conception of Rāhula—not his birth—on the night of the great departure. Her pregnancy therefore becomes a serious problem. In the first case, the child should have been twelve years old or younger when the Buddha returns to Kapilavastu, six years after his awakening (following six years of asceticism). In the second case, he should have been nine months younger, that is, eleven years old. However, sources affirm almost unanimously that he was only six years old. Commentators have resolved this anachronism in their own way. The solution turns out to be simple: all that is needed is for Māyā to have been pregnant for six years! *Quod erat demonstrandum.* According to the *Treatise:* "Yaśodharā, the very night the Bodhisattva left home, knew she was pregnant. The Bodhisattva, after his departure, practiced asceticism for six years; Yaśodharā too was pregnant for six years without giving birth."[29] Another late source reports how the Bodhisattva, pointing to the belly of Yaśodharā, tells her: "In six years you will give birth to a son." Some sources develop a striking parallelism between the Bodhisattva's six years of asceticism and the pregnancy of Yaśodharā: when he fasts, she fasts; when he becomes thinner, she becomes thinner, and the growth of the fetus is retarded; when he eats again, at the end of his long asceticism, she does the same, and the process of gestation resumes. It is precisely at the moment when he is awakened that she gives birth to Rāhula after having carried the child in her womb for six years. The ascetic pregnancy of Yaśodharā, which marks her as an exceptional woman, becomes the domestic counterpart of the asceticism of the Bodhisattva.

During all this time, just as Penelope waited for the return of Ulysses, Yaśodharā has to resist the advances of many suitors, especially Devadatta, the eternal rival of the Buddha. Nevertheless, her prolonged pregnancy breeds gossip: she is suspected of infidelity toward her absent husband, and a punishment is demanded. In the version reported in the *Treatise,* the second wife of Siddhārtha, Gopā, defends her. And when Rāhula is born on the very night that the Buddha is awakened, King Śuddhodana, having witnessed that his grandson resembles him, treats Yaśodharā with indulgence.[30] But in other versions, Śuddhoddhana cannot believe that Rāhula is his grandson, and Yaśodharā has to submit to a trial by ordeal. Placing Rāhula on a large stone, she has it thrown into a pond while pronouncing an act of truth—namely, that if he is the son of the Bodhisattva, the stone will float. The miracle happens. Yaśodharā's ordeal sanctifies her. Then, through her attentive care, she restores the sight of Mahāprajāpatī, who has become blind from shedding too many tears following the departure of her adopted son. This story passed into popular tradition, and it was known as far away as China, where it has been found among the chantefables (*bianwen*) of Dunhuang.

Yaśodharā and Rāhula

When the Buddha returns to Kapilavastu, he converts with his miracles all the women in the gynaeceum except Yaśodharā. Still in the grip of passion, she tries to seduce him by asking their son Rāhula to offer him magical treats, but her ploy turns against her. To explain her attitude, the Buddha tells his disciples a *Jātaka,* the story of the doe who swallowed the seed of an ascetic and gave birth to a child who was raised by the ascetic. This child had deer hooves, and at the age of twelve, a horn grew on his forehead. He too became an ascetic and was nicknamed Unicorn. One day he was surprised by a sudden rain, and in his anger he caused a drought, which did not end until he was seduced by a princess. "This ascetic," said the Buddha, "was me, and the princess was Yaśodharā."[31]

The Buddha quotes another *Jātaka* to explain how his son, who had never seen him before, was able to recognize him without the slightest hesitation among five hundred magically conjured doubles. In a past life, he says, he was a "cunning thief" who broke into a palace and raped the princess. Six years after the birth of his son, he was recognized by the boy, to whom the king had given a garland, ordering him to give it to the man he would recognize as his father. However, the king, admiring the intelligence of the thief, decided not to punish him and instead offered him the hand of his daughter. "The cunning thief was me," explains the Buddha—an admission that does not seem to cause any surprise or indignation among his listeners.[32]

All sources agree that the Buddha had only one son, named Rāhula. According to some texts, the only reason Śākyamuni fathered a son was to prove his manhood to those who might later have doubts: "And it occurred to him: 'To prevent others from saying that Prince Śākyamuni was not a man, and that he left without paying attention to Yaśodharā, Gopikā, Mṛgaja, and his sixty thousand other wives, let us now make love to Yaśodharā.' So he did, and Yaśodharā became pregnant."[33]

The very name Rāhula has received two very different interpretations. The first, that Rāhula means "obstacle," would seem to say a lot about Śākyamuni's paternal feelings. According to the second, the name means "little Rāhu" and is associated with the demon Rāhu, who produced a lunar eclipse at the time of Rāhula's birth—just as the Buddha, at the time of his awakening, is supposed to have eclipsed the sun."[34] Other sources establish a parallelism between the birth of Rāhula and that of Śākyamuni. In this version, Rāhula was reborn in Tuṣita Heaven and chose Yaśodharā (just as the future Buddha chose Māyā) for his birth mother for his last earthly existence. The birth of Rāhula is also immaculate, despite the fact that this seems to contradict the biological paternity of Śākyamuni. However, commentators do not go so far as to say that Rāhula will also become a buddha: even if he is awakened, he will be a mere arhat. The awakening of the Buddha, in contrast, gives him a special status, which is rarely questioned.

Rāhula does not play a big role in Buddhist legend, apart from the episode where the Buddha, back in Kapilavastu, recognizes him as his legitimate son and makes him join the orders. In the *Mahāvastu,* it is Rāhula himself who, having recognized his father, insists on being ordained.[35] After becoming a monk, he proves to be an extremely zealous practitioner. His determination made him a kind of patron saint of novices, but on the whole he was not much talked about. His name appears in the list of principal disciples, and that is about it. We are told that he became an arhat, and no other details about the relationship he may have had with his illustrious progenitor are given. Tradition has it that he died before the Buddha. According to one variant, however, he was still alive at the time of the Buddha's parinirvāṇa.[36]

THE FAMILY ISSUE

The interest shown by traditional sources in the relatives of the Buddha could surprise when the texts insist so much on his "leaving the family" and renunciation of the throne. In contemporary society, these acts constituted serious breaches of filial piety. Worse still, the Buddha incited others to do the same, seducing the sons of good families and pushing them to become monks. This aspect of the new doctrine did not escape the notice of contemporaries: "At that time, the sons of the renowned and distinguished Magadha families practiced religious life under the guidance of the Blessed One. This angered the people: 'He is on a path to kidnap children, the monk Gotama. He is on a path that makes widows, monk Gotama. He is on a path that destroys families, monk Gotama.'"[37] And yet the legend of the Buddha remains a family romance. After the death of his biological mother, Māyā, the Bodhisattva was, we are told, raised by his aunt, Mahāprajāpatī, the sister of Māyā and the second wife of his father, King Śuddhodana. He had no siblings, only a half brother, Nanda, the son of Mahāprajāpatī. He had several cousins, including Ānanda and Devadatta.

By making Māyā disappear just after the birth of his son, traditional sources sought to alleviate the scandal caused by his "leaving the family." Although he would also abandon his adoptive mother Mahāprajāpatī, to whom he owed a "milk debt," the fact that she was not his biological mother (and that as a toddler he also had a string of nannies) made the matter less serious. On the other hand, it was a moral offense to violate his father's authority, although he did seek his father's approval on several occasions before leaving the palace.

Already in the Pāli tradition, various sources re-inscribed the Buddha in the family lineage and the royal lineage. This is particularly the case in Sinhalese chronicles such as the *Buddhavaṃsa,* and their Thai, Burmese, and Cambodian heirs. In the *Mahāvastu,* the Bodhisattva condemns family life with almost Gidian accents ("Families, I hate you"), describing the family home in claustrophobic terms. Nevertheless, the same text, in contrast to Pāli sources, describes in great detail the Bodhisattva's marital relations with Yaśodharā—in the present life but also in past existences. The point here is to emphasize the cost of his renunciation. But this renunciation is still not as total as one might think, since the texts also seem concerned with underlining the filial and conjugal bonds of the Buddha.[38] Thus, the great departure is often followed by a temporary "return," which, while it cannot be said to reconstitute the family, nevertheless underscores the Buddha's relationships with his close relatives.

In the end, one might think that Buddha never really "left the family" (the term for ordination), since the family occupies such an important place in all his biographies. As can be seen from Indian sources, filial piety, which is usually considered a characteristic trait of Chinese society, was also important in Indian society, and it runs counter to the ascetic tendency that is generally emphasized in the same sources. The Buddha, despite his leaving home, is described as someone who watches over the destiny (sometimes even the posthumous destiny) of his relatives. However, it is especially in the Chinese Lives of the Buddha that the filial relationship of the Buddha with his parents is insisted on. Chinese Buddhists, in response to criticism, even sought to promote a specifically Buddhist form of filial piety. Let us close this parenthesis on what could be called the family romance of the Buddha. Indeed, the Life of the Buddha takes place for the most part on another front, where he must face adversity.

DEVADATTA, THE ETERNAL RIVAL

Another major figure in Buddhist legend is Devadatta, the Buddha's cousin and sworn enemy. He may have been referred to as the Buddhist Judas, but he is as different from Judas as the Buddha is from Christ, or Māra from Satan. His hatred of Śākyamuni is said to go back to an episode in their childhood when a duck that the Bodhisattva is trying to save is shot by Devadatta; it gets worse in their youth, when Devadatta competes with his cousin for the hand of Yaśodharā. In fact, it goes back far beyond that, to distant past lives. In the *Commentary on Jātakas* alone, no fewer than seventy stories bear on the karmic relationship between the Bodhisattva and Devadatta. In these, Devadatta frequently appears as a hunter, that is, a being who violates Buddhist morals by killing animals and is condemned to evil rebirths. But in some texts, Devadatta's wickedness increases a notch. The *Sūtra on Devadatta Teaching People to Do Evil,* for example, reports that the Bodhisattva and Devadatta, in a past life, were both kings of the gods, but while the former exhorted beings to do good, the latter, in the form of Māra, incited them to evil.[39]

The Bodhisattva does not always prevail over Devadatta. In *Milinda's Questions,* King Milinda asks Nāgasena why this is the case, and the latter answers that Devadatta has not always been evil, that even in the past he has accumulated many merits. So his character is not entirely negative, and he is sometimes seen doing good deeds. Once ordained, he conducts himself for a long time as a virtuous monk and is one of the great disciples of the Buddha. It is only when the Buddha reaches an advanced age that Devadatta, devoured by ambition, seeks to supplant him. He first asks him to impose an extremely strict regimen on the monks. When the Buddha refuses, Devadatta accuses him of preaching a life of luxury contrary to true morality. Then, having failed to persuade the Buddha to yield the leadership of the community to him, Devadatta conspires with the prince Ajātaśatru and carries out several attempts to kill the Buddha. He first orders archers to shoot their arrows at the Buddha, but the sight of the Buddha's majesty disarms them. He then decides to act alone; on a day when the Buddha is preaching on Vulture Peak, he dislodges an enormous rock and starts it rolling down toward the Buddha. Miraculously the rock is stopped in its course, but a splinter enters the Buddha's foot. On another occasion, Devadatta makes a ferocious elephant charge at the Buddha, but the elephant is suddenly pacified as it nears the Buddha. In a last attempt, while prostrating himself at the Buddha's feet, he claws at him with poisoned nails. But his intention is instantly known to the Buddha, whose legs transmute into rock crystal, breaking Devadatta's nails. According to the *Treatise on the Great Perfection of Wisdom,* this last abortive attempt is the immediate cause of Devadatta's damnation: "Finally, Devadatta coated his fingernails with poison, and under the pretext of paying his respects to the Buddha, attempted to kill him. In trying to flee, he had not yet reached the city of Rājagṛha when the earth suddenly opened up and a chariot of fire came to meet him: Devadatta entered hell while still alive."[40] In another version, his damnation comes after reproaching the Buddha for not imposing a sufficiently rigorous asceticism: Devadatta thereupon provokes a schism, which founders when two great disciples of the Buddha, Maudgalyāyana and Śāriputra, bring the lost sheep back to the fold. Devadatta falls ill with spite. The earth opens up under his feet, and he is thrown into the deepest hell, where he will remain for the duration of an entire *kalpa,* the Buddha predicts, because of the gravity of his faults.[41]

The Buddhist tradition has made Devadatta a kind of scapegoat, accusing him of every evil and turpitude. In the Vinaya of the Mūlasarvāstivādin, the three sins warranting immediate retribution lodged against Devadatta are to have caused the first schism within the Buddhist community, to have made an attempt on the life of the Buddha and wounded him, and finally to have killed the nun Utpalavarṇā, one of the principal female disciples of the Buddha, out of resentment at the alms she received at Ajātaśatru's palace, where Devadatta, fallen in disgrace, had been refused access.[42]

Insult and Hatred

Devadatta's jealousy is usually presented as the principal motive for his actions. Sources point to Devadatta's continuing resentment against the Bodhisattva for taking Yaśodharā, the woman of his dreams, away from him. But there is another, stranger explanation based on the relationship between Devadatta and Prince Ajātaśatru. To turn Ajātaśatru into an accomplice, Devadatta is said to have metamorphosed several times to seduce him: "One day, he changed into a child and came to sit on Prince Ajātaśatru's knees; the prince took him in his arms, kissed him, and gave him spittle."[43] Although the Pāli sources ignore this distasteful detail, it is reported in the *Treatise* as follows: "Devadatta, coveting profit and honors, metamorphosed into a little boy of heavenly beauty and appeared in the arms of the king [Ajātaśatru]. The king kissed his mouth and gave him spit to swallow." This is why, concludes the author of the *Treatise,* "the Buddha called Devadatta a rabid dog, a corpse, and a spit swallower."[44] The affront is such that Devadatta cannot swallow it: "Devadatta felt as if a poisoned arrow had been shot into his chest, and cried out in anger: 'Gautama is not a Buddha! I am the eldest son of King Dronadana, the elder brother of Ānanda and Gautama's cousin. No matter what misconduct I am guilty of, he should secretly reprimand me. But to publicly accuse me of wrongdoing before this great assembly of human and divine beings—is this the proper attitude for a Great Man or a Buddha? He has shown himself my enemy in the past by stealing the woman I wanted to marry, and he has shown himself my enemy in this assembly today. From this day forward, I vow to consider him my greatest enemy in life after life and in all ages to come.'"[45]

Perhaps to repair the apparent injustice of the Buddha's treatment of Devadatta, certain Mahāyāna texts rehabilitate him to some extent. Indeed, the Buddha predicts that Devadatta, having repented at the moment of falling into hell, will also awaken—albeit in a distant future once he has exhausted the consequences of his bad karma. This change of attitude is explained in the *Lotus Sūtra,* which dedicates an entire chapter to Devadatta. In it, the Buddha explains the background of their rivalry and reveals that Devadatta was actually once his master.[46] He recounts that in many past lives he had been born as the ruler of a kingdom who assiduously practiced the six perfections. One day, he received the teaching of the Great Vehicle and the *Lotus Sūtra* from a hermit and became his disciple for a thousand years. This hermit who set him on the path to the supreme awakening was none other than Devadatta, and that is why Devadatta, in his turn, will finally be awakened.[47] Here it is not the Buddha who saves Devadatta, but the latter's merit that leads, in a quasi-automatic way, to a good reward, which in turn leads to Devadatta's final awakening. In Japanese Buddhism, the rehabilitation goes even further: Devadatta becomes the model of the repentant sinner, whose transgression paradoxically constitutes the very instrument of salvation.

A Christic and Historical Devadatta

In all these stories, Devadatta is presented as the instrument of karma, the agent through whom the retribution for acts committed by the Buddha in his previous existences takes place. In addition, he sometimes plays the role of a stooge, a bit like Judas in Christian legend. Obviously he has been demonized by the Buddhist tradition—officially, for being schismatic. What historians have retained from these legends is that Devadatta, in trying to introduce a more rigorous ascetic regimen, sought to cause a schism in the first Buddhist community after trying in vain to convince the Buddha to transfer his leadership role to him. According to Foucher:

> Reading the many pages that the Scriptures devote to him, one soon distinguishes (once again) two traditional currents that exist side by side, not without sometimes mixing or contradicting each other. One current charges him with every crime imaginable for the simple reason that he committed the most inexpiable of all crimes in trying to create a schism or, as they say, a "rupture of the Community": this is the popular version. The other, elaborated in more intellectual circles, exposes in a much more reasoned and plausible way the motives invoked and the means used by him to carry out his criminal plan.[48]

For Bareau, the whole story of Devadatta, once stripped of its legendary embellishments (in this case, one might rather speak of disfigurements), boils down to this: Devadatta created a schism within the community, and he was followed by a fairly large group of monks. This story would likely have preserved the memory of real events, making Devadatta nothing more than a particularly rigorous practitioner.[49] Following Bareau, some historians have therefore tried to "save" Devadatta, relying on the fact that, in the accounts of their journeys to India, the Chinese pilgrims Faxian, Xuanzang, and Yijing all mention a sect of Devadatta's disciples, which evidently was still widespread in their time (between the 5th and 7th cent.).[50] However, nothing proves that such a sect existed at the time of the Buddha. In any event, this historical (or historicized) Devadatta, like his famous cousin, does not yield much interest for an understanding of the later Buddhist tradition, which wanted to see in him a predestined opponent of the Buddha, a sort of human representative of the powers of evil, and an accomplice of Māra, to whom we must turn in the following pages.

Curiously, however, the theme of Devadatta's infernal torments gave rise to a strange misunderstanding on the part of Christian missionaries in Southeast Asia, as witnessed by Simon de La Loubère (1642–1729), Louis XIV's envoy to the Kingdom of Siam. In his description of the "Talapoins" (Buddhist monks), the envoy mentions a certain Thevetat (Devadatta) who, if we are to believe him, is nothing less than a distorted image of Christ, seen through a Buddhist prism.[51] I will return to this issue when we discuss the Western discovery of the Buddha.

8

MĀRA, THE FALLEN DEMON KING

Although it does not figure as one of the eight acts from a narrative standpoint, one of the great moments in the Life of the Buddha is the Māravijaya, his victory over Māra. The character of his antagonist is extremely complex and deserving of attention—if only to fill, at least in part, the gap left by Western biographers who have consistently reduced Māra to pure fiction, a poisonous fruit of the Buddhist imaginaire, or at best an allegory of the negative mental processes that hinder awakening.[1] This psychological or symbolic interpretation, as found in a number of modern authors, claims to make mythology superfluous. According to Trevor Ling, for example, Māra, in serving as a bridge between popular demonology and abstract Dharma theories, belongs to an "animist," or outdated, stage of Buddhism.[2]

Māra represents the figure of the Enemy, and by extension the Buddha's human opponents such as Devadatta and the Brahmins. He oscillates between two poles—real and fictional, or mythological and psychological—symbolized by his external and internal armies. In the Pāli tradition, he is often perceived as a purely fictional being, and the Māravijaya is supposed to describe a psychological event, which Christian authors would call a psychomachy. Buddhagosa, for example, denies the physical reality of Māra, even though the obstacles Māra creates are very real.[3] One must undoubtedly distinguish between the philosophical or purely symbolic interpretation of Māra, of monastic origin, and the mythological narrative, oriented toward popular culture. With Māra, Buddhism is from the outset right in the middle of local culture. But mythology can also flourish in monastic circles, as we can see in Aśvaghosa, the author of the *Buddhacarita*.

MĀRA, MASTER OF THE WORLD

If Māra plays the role of the evil one or the tempter, he is not the Buddhist Satan.[4] One must be wary of transferring Christian notions of evil and sin onto Buddhism. On the metaphysical level, Māra is rather a necessary evil, which opposes or distorts the good.[5] He does not deny life; he represents the principle that presides over the cycle of birth and death (*saṃsāra*), whereas the Buddha denies this cycle by transcending it through awakening and nirvāṇa. Foucher, who describes the Māravijaya as "drowned in extravagance," nevertheless questions the purely negative image of Māra presented in the early Buddhist tradition: "Power both productive and destructive, if he takes in turn the mask of Love and Death, it is because he is the Spirit of Life, and it is because he is the Spirit of Life that in the eyes of the monk he becomes the Spirit of Evil. . . . In metaphysical language, he is the Spinozist tendency of Being to persevere in its being."[6] Foucher defends this Spinozist conatus: "But isn't [Māra] entitled to think, with the vast majority of us, that life is worth living? After all, what he claims against the ascetic's conscientious objections is the right to happiness, inasmuch as this word has meaning here below, the right to action, to property, to love, to marriage, to the joy of perpetuating oneself in children."[7] Māra was therefore not the only one to protest against the new (social and monastic) order—in his eyes disorder—that the Buddha was establishing: "The Buddha's contemporaries had realized this practical conclusion of the Master's doctrine: in the destruction of Māra's empire what he was ultimately pursuing was 'the end of the world.' We soon hear the people of Magadha whispering that 'the ascetic Gautama came to bring the extinction of families.'"[8]

Māra also plays an important role in Buddhist cosmology. Despite his demonic role or nature, he is in fact a god and not a minor one. As stated in *Milinda's Questions:* "Māra (the Evil One, Death) is great, and he is only one. Mahā-Brahmā is mighty, and he is only one. A Tathāgata, an Arahat Buddha supreme, is great; and he is alone in the world. Wherever any one of these spring up, then there is no room for a second. And therefore, O king, is it that only one Tathāgata, an Arahat Buddha supreme, can appear at one time in the world."[9] Again, according to the *Treatise:* "Māra is the Lord of the Sixth Heaven, or of the entire World of Desire, as the case may be: the gods Yama, Tuṣita, and Nirmānarati all depend on him."[10] As Foucher points out, Māra "is a very great and powerful god . . . and his empire extends not only to the lower heavens, but also to the earth and to the hidden depths of the underworld—in short, to the entire sphere of sensual desires and pleasures. . . . As master of this material universe, whose sovereignty is his *raison d'être,* he sees to it that it is constantly reproduced."[11]

Like the Buddha, Māra is called a "god superior to gods" (*devatīdeva*), a title that would rather suit Indra or Brahmā. He is sometimes confused with Brahmā, the arrogant creator who, cosmologically speaking, is nevertheless superior to him.[12] After the awakening, it is Brahmā who comes to convince the Buddha to preach the Law. In doing so, he cedes his role as protector of the world to the Buddha. Unlike Māra, he knows his rank and sticks to it. But sometimes he can also be arrogant. In the *Mahāvastu,* for instance, he appears to the Bodhisattva while the youth is still living in the palace and tries to dissuade him from renouncing the world. In the *Saṃyutta-nikāya,* Brahmā imagines himself to be eternal. It falls to the Buddha and four disciples to disabuse him of this notion, and he ends up apologizing. His role in this incident is therefore quite similar to that of Māra. In the *Buddhacarita,* Māra identifies himself with the old Brahmanic order, and he tries to win the Buddha over to his cause. In a certain sense, then, Māra and Brahmā are two sides of the same coin.

Māra is sometimes represented as a giant whose body measures two leagues, and whose every day is equivalent to sixteen hundred human years. But this giant can also have sexual relations with men and women, and reincarnate in a female womb. He makes his own the pleasure of humans, hence his heaven is called the "heaven of the lord who transforms others." While he is the ruler of the macrocosm, he also possesses a microcosmic power, in the sense that he reigns over the five senses and over the mind or thought. As such, he symbolizes the three poisons (lust, hatred, and ignorance) that give rise to the false notion of the self. However, in principle, he remains subject to the law of karma. According to the *Treatise,* "One still calls Māra the passions, hindrances, and bonds of desire, the wrapping of attachment, the aggregates, the bases of knowledge and the elements. . . ."[13] Or again: "This Māra has three kinds of acts: play, laughter, chat, song, dance, and everything that comes from love; shackles, strokes, whips, wounds, thorns, knives, cuts, and everything that comes from hate; [senseless mortifications] such as burning oneself, letting oneself freeze, tearing one's hair out, letting oneself go hungry, throwing oneself into the fire, throwing oneself into the water, throwing oneself from on high, and everything that comes from foolishness."[14]

In Brahmanism and classical Hinduism, truth and cosmic order merge: evil, or the demonic, is not only that which opposes the truth, but that which subverts the hierarchical order of things. Each being must follow his dharma or law, and in this sense the conversion of a demon to Buddhism is in itself demonic, since it goes against his dharma. Māra was right or at least had his reasons, which the Buddha does not know or refuses to know.

In the *Buddhacarita,* when Māra intervenes, he does so as a representative of established order, in this case the Brahmanic order. He tells the Bodhisattva: "Up, up, honorable Kṣatriya, fearful of death. Follow your own duty and abandon this practice of release. Having conquered the world with arrows and sacrifices, proceed to gain the heavens of Indra."[15] This sounds like the words of the god Krishna to Arjuna in the *Mahābhārata* (*Bhagavad-gita*).

Māra's antagonism toward the Buddha can be interpreted in two different ways: as a reflection of his fear that the world he rules over will be emptied of its inhabitants, who, following the Buddha, will gain access to the transcendental spheres, or as a response to what he perceives as the Buddha's attempt to usurp his title as ruler of the world. Māra is first and foremost an autochthonous deity (literally, "born from the earth"). He is the ruler of our world, the world of desire, whereas the Buddha aims to destroy this world.

Some sources depersonalize Māra by insisting that his name designates not a person, but an administrative function, which can be performed by various individuals in retribution for their karma. Thus, in the *Māratajjanīya,* the arhat Maudgalyāyana quickly recognizes the presence of Māra because he himself was Māra in a past life (just as the Buddha was the god Brahmā). Thus, three different conceptions of Māra can be distinguished: as a real (individualized) character; as a function; and as an allegory of passions and becoming. In the first two cases, Māra is supposed to have a very real existence; in the third, he is only a symbol.

In the Life of the Buddha, however, it is a well-individualized Māra who appears to us. As a preamble to the Māravijaya episode, Māra is presented as a father. It is not he who attacks the Bodhisattva, it is the Bodhisattva who defies him, sending him nightmares as he is taking a nap among his people in his palace. Following this blatant aggression, Māra holds a meeting with his sons and ministers, asking their advice on how to respond. In the *Buddhacarita,* Māra has three sons, one of whom advises him in vain not to attack the Buddha; after his father's humiliating defeat, he comes to ask the Buddha to forgive him. Māra also has three daughters, who are only briefly mentioned in this text—although they play an important role in other sources, taking the initiative to go and tempt the Bodhisattva (who turns them into old women).

The Māra of the *Buddhacarita* is only a caricature. It pales in comparison to the almighty (or almost almighty) Māra of Buddhist cosmology—even if in theory the two characters are one. Given his cosmic importance, one can only be surprised by the lightness with which it is treated here. It is, for example, strange that the author did not choose to develop the Māravijaya scene into a slightly more substantial dialogue, since it is, in short, a dispute in which Māra accuses the Buddha of usurping his throne (the diamond seat under the Bodhi tree). Even if the authors seem to accept the mythological version of the facts, the way they depreciate Māra is basically not very different from the demythologizing approach of historians, who purely and simply reject the legend or see it as a psychological fable.

A PERSEVERING DEMON

Many things can be blamed on Māra, but not a lack of perseverance. The Japanese monk Nichiren (1222–1282) mentions Māra's attempts to prevent the birth of the Buddha: "When the Buddha Śākyamuni was conceived by his mother, the queen Māyā, Māra, [the king] of the Sixth Heaven gazed down into Queen Māyā's womb and said: 'My archenemy, the sharp sword of the *Lotus Sūtra,* has been conceived. Before the birth can take place, I must do something to destroy it.' Then Māra transformed himself into a learned physician, entered the palace of King Śuddhodana, and said, 'I am a learned physician and have brought some excellent medicines that will ensure the safe delivery of the child.' In this way he attempted to poison the queen."[16]

Nichiren returns to that point: "When the Buddha was born, Māra caused stones to rain down on him and mixed poison in his milk. Later, when the Buddha left the palace to enter the religious life, Māra changed himself into a black venomous serpent and tried to block his way. In addition, he entered the bodies of evil men such as Devadatta, Kokālika, King Virūdhaka, and King Ajātaśatru, inciting them to hurl a great stone at the Buddha, which drew blood and injured him, or to kill many of the Śākya, the Buddha's clansmen, or murder his disciples."[17]

In all these stories, the Buddha effortlessly triumphs over his opponent. But there is one episode, shortly before the awakening, where Māra comes close to success: when the Bodhisattva bathes in the Nairañjanā River to recover from his long asceticism, Māra magically raises the riverbanks. Without the intervention of a tree deity who lowers the branches of a tree, the Bodhisattva, who apparently cannot swim, could have drowned. In the other skirmishes with Māra, the gods cautiously stand aside, and in the great confrontation they openly take his side—perhaps half-heartedly but they are Māra's subjects.

The story of the relationship between Māra and the Buddha could—or should—have ended with the Māravijaya. But Māra stubbornly refuses to admit defeat. He seeks first of all to take a mean revenge by making King Śuddhodana believe that his son has just died.[18] Periodically, he comes back to try to tempt the Buddha. Most sources intersperse, during the seven weeks following the Buddha's awakening, one or more attempts by Māra to incite the Buddha to pass directly from awakening to parinirvāṇa. He also strives to sow discord among the Buddha's disciples. To deceive them, he affects the most diverse forms, including that of the master himself. A typical example is the episode where Māra, taking the form of the Buddha, comes to a monk who had just heard the Buddha's sermon on the impermanence of all things. The Buddha (actually Māra) explains to the monk that the sermon was misleading, and that he meant just the opposite, namely, that all things are permanent. One can imagine the poor monk's confusion. This doctrinal about-face is reminiscent of certain Mahāyāna theories, to which we will return. In fact, one wonders whether this story is not a disguised criticism of the Mahāyāna, whose followers denied, in the name of a higher Dharma, all the doctrines stated by the Buddha in his first sermons. Māra, from this perspective, would be quite similar to the Buddha of Mahāyāna, the one who preached the *Lotus Sūtra,* for example. It is indeed reported that some of the Buddha's listeners, on that occasion, had openly expressed their doubt.

Among the abortive attempts of Māra should be credited the efforts of the various characters who, long before the dramatic scene of the Māravijaya, seek to divert the Bodhisattva from his goal. Among them are King Śuddhodana's attempts to keep the prince in the palace, and those of the emissaries he sends, after the great departure, to convince him to return home. One of them, Udayin, is particularly eloquent when he tries to incite the young prince to enjoy the life and women offered to him. He explains to him that his spiritual quest is commendable, but that the time for it has not yet come. It was precisely in these terms that Indian society incorporated the ideal of the renouncer, using a model of the successive stages in life (*aśrama*) that might allow an individual to renounce the world once he has fulfilled all his family duties. One will find more or less the same line coming from the mouth of Māra.

Likewise, the courtesans of the royal gynaeceum, in their attempt to seduce the Bodhisattva, play the same role that the girls of Māra will later play. However, they are not held in the same contempt by the Bodhisattva; nor is Yaśodharā, when she tries to hold her husband back at the time of the great departure, or later, when she tries to bring him back to her by magic. The feelings that inspire the Bodhisattva's relatives are never described as having been inspired by Māra, with one exception, that of Devadatta. The same is true of the "heretics": sometimes they are incited by Māra to attack the Buddha, and sometimes the Buddha explains their attacks as residual effects of his own karma. Karma replaces Māra here. Japanese Buddhism, on the other hand, has not hesitated to push to its conclusion the logic that makes Māra the lord of this world: it is he who takes the form of the family relatives who seek to dissuade the practitioner from renouncing the world.

AN AMBIVALENT CHARACTER

Let us return to the Māravijaya, which constitutes, from a mythological point of view, the central episode in the Life of the Buddha. According to Michael Nichols, it lends itself to at least two interpretations. On one hand, the narrative presents the Bodhisattva as a kind of deva, and Māra as a kind of asura, in conformity with the eternal conflict between gods (devas) and demons (asuras) described in traditional Indian mythology. On the other hand, in trying to put an end to the Bodhisattva's asceticism, which endangers the cosmic balance envisioned in Brahmanic texts, Māra actually plays the role of a deva while the Bodhisattva behaves like a demon.[19] The different versions of the Māravijaya may tilt toward one or the other of these aspects, but they agree on the whole.

The confrontation between Māra and the Bodhisattva is about sovereignty over the world and whether the current order of things will be maintained or transformed. It is therefore in the same vein as the battle between the devas and the asuras.[20] The Māravijaya is also a kind of offensive against Brahmanism, paradoxically represented by Māra. By turning it into an analogue of Indra's victory over the asura Māra, the Buddhist authors overthrow the Brahmanic order while preserving certain aspects of it.[21] In becoming a new type of warrior (*kṣatriya*) who defeats chaos (Māra) without even fighting a battle, the Bodhisattva transforms the old warrior path into a purely spiritual one. But at the same time he has a demonic side in that he overturns the established order to establish a new rule.

To meet the challenge represented by the Bodhisattva, Māra first tries to convince him to fulfill his dharma, his dual—royal and familial—function; but the Bodhisattva aims at a higher, absolute Dharma, the very negation of the Brahmanical socio-cosmic order on which Māra's power is based. From Māra's perspective, the Bodhisattva is therefore only a troublemaker. Seen from this angle, the conflict between the two characters is a struggle for the throne—the diamond seat and summit of the world—under the Bodhi tree. Senart has already emphasized this point.

On the narrative level, the duel between Māra and the Buddha is also a *duel* (in the grammatical sense, between singular and plural) or a duo, in the sense that the elements considered form a pair. Māra, when most caricatured, can resemble a sort of Mr. Loyal, whose role is to highlight his partner (although the name, in the circus, also designates the master of the ring). He follows the Buddha as his shadow, precisely because he *is* his shadow. Without Māra, there is no Buddha, and vice versa—the eternal enemies are indissolubly linked. Thus the traditional, overly Manichean account of Māra's defeat masks the real complexity of what is at stake. The real Māra is not the caricature that Buddhist commentators have liked to ridicule.

DEFEAT—OR VICTORY—FOR MĀRA?

Should we, after all, consider Māra to be defeated? He may have lost a battle, but he didn't lose the war. Revenge is a dish—of pork or mushrooms, perhaps—to be eaten cold. The extinction of the Buddha—as a result of poisoning—seems to provide Māra with the final victory. According to the *Treatise,* when the Buddha descends from Trāyastriṃśa Heaven, Māra comes to remind him of his ancient promise, made in the aftermath of his awakening. Māra then seeks to convince the Buddha to enter parinirvāṇa immediately, and the Buddha replies that he will wait until his doctrine and his community are firmly established. But this has already been accomplished, Māra says, so there is no reason to procrastinate any longer. Yielding to his request, the Buddha declares that he will enter parinirvāṇa three months later and rejects his "longevity factors" from that moment on.[22] During the short time he has left, he literally outlives himself.[23] In this passage, the author of the *Treatise* effectively blames Māra for the Buddha's disappearance, contradicting a previous passage where the Buddha, ill and very old, shows his resignation to his impending death.[24] In other sources, the Buddha strangely blames his decision on his disciple Ānanda, who, distracted by Māra, omitted asking the Buddha to stay longer in this world. In either case, the Buddha seems to have lost the initiative at this juncture, and his departure leaves the field open to Māra.

MĀRA'S CONVERSION

From a Buddhist perspective, a true defeat of Māra would imply his conversion. But Māra remains the irreducible enemy. Although defeated in the Māravijaya, Māra is (almost) never converted even though the Buddha and his disciples succeed without too much difficulty in turning dragons and other chthonic or demonic powers that function as Māra's henchmen. He himself never ceases to cast his net over the Buddha and his disciples. The first biographers of the Buddha do not seem to have imagined that the Buddha could convert Māra. He is a demon in the soul (so to speak), and the Buddha can certainly defeat but never convert him. Subsequently, however, the Mahāyāna doctrine of salvation for all seems to have brought it into the realm of possibility. In some currents of Mahāyāna, after convincing the Buddha to enter parinirvāṇa (which will eventually lead to the decline of the Law), Māra feels reassured and offers an incantation (*dhāraṇī*) that will protect future practitioners. Paradoxically, he thus stands on the side of Buddhism. The next step is taken in the *Sūtra of the Heroic March* (*Śūraṃgamasamādhi-sūtra*), where, after Māra ends up converting, the Buddha predicts that he will be awakened. Māra then states that there is no longer any difference between his world and the Buddha's world.[25]

In most sources, the honor of converting Māra belongs to a later disciple of the Buddha named Upagupta. The legend, which in this case is more of a folktale, reports that Māra disrupted Upagupta's sermon three times, first with a shower of pearls, then with a shower of gold, and finally with a theatrical performance. Upagupta realizes that since the Buddha did not convert Māra, he must have left it to him, and that is why the Buddha predicted that he would become a buddha "without marks." In a variant, Upagupta takes the garland of flowers that Māra has given him and passes it around Māra's neck, magically transforming it into the corpse of a dog. Māra, disgusted, tries in vain to get rid of it. Then Upagupta binds Māra with his monastic belt, which also seems to mean ordination.[26] Māra, remembering the Buddha's compassion for him, contrasts it to Upagupta's cruelty. And now, as he feels himself filled with a newfound faith in the Buddha—who here represents the Greater Vehicle, and Upagupta the Lesser Vehicle—Māra vows to become awakened. At this point something strange occurs: Upagupta asks Māra to take the Buddha's form. Indeed, in this late period, Māra is one of the few eyewitnesses of the Buddha's presence remaining. Māra grants him this wish, provided that he does not confuse him with the Buddha.[27] In a variant, King Aśoka, fearing that Māra might disrupt a ceremony celebrating a stūpa, asks Upagupta to protect the Buddha's relics. When the ceremony begins, Māra provokes a storm, then appears taking a variety of forms, including those of a bull, a *nāga,* and a *yakṣa.* Upagupta counters him each time by morphing into a higher being (a tiger, *garuḍa,* and more powerful *yakṣa*).[28] As a result of Upagupta's repeated victories over Māra, he becomes a protector, and it is his name that practitioners invoke for protection against Māra's assaults.

MĀRA IN MAHĀYĀNA

As a master of error, Māra is suspected whenever a suspicion of heterodoxy or heresy arises. This was the case, in particular, with the Mahāyāna, before it managed to establish itself as the new orthodoxy. When the Buddha preaches the *Lotus Sūtra,* some of his disciples, thinking that this revolutionary doctrine is the work of Māra, leave the assembly. This is the type of criticism that Sthiramati's *Mahāyanāvatara* (6th cent.) intended to respond to: "If one says that [Mahāyāna] is truly the word of Māra, Bodhisattva Maitreya must be blocking the way for those who say this. . . . If one says that Mahāyāna is the word of Māra, then this greatly harms the Law of Buddha and all these holy people [the arhats] will have to completely oppose it."[29] Yet the idea that Māra inspires heretics continued to gain ground because of its eminently practical character: heretics are often only those who do not think like us. Thus, according to Nichiren, all the monks in other Japanese Buddhist schools are dupes of King Māra of the Sixth Heaven.

Māra's deceptiveness is difficult to avoid because it is inherent in the human mind: it is indeed the "sixth consciousness" (the consciousness that unifies the five sensory consciousnesses) that becomes Māra, who incarnates in all beings, sometimes even in the form of parents or relatives, to catch them in his net of illusion. But he is particularly interested in monks, in whom he inspires the arrogance and will to power that will lead to their rebirth in the so-called Path of Māra. While the distinction between good and evil was relatively clear-cut in early Buddhism, in Mahāyāna, where nothing is ever simple, it loses its importance: there is a true Māra and a false one, since the bodhisattvas themselves can occasionally act as tempters to convert beings. The logic of nonduality, taken to the extreme, leads to the notion that Māra is in fact (or will become) a bodhisattva. Therefore, in the *Vimalakīrti-nirdeśa,* the layman Vimalakīrti sees fit to warn the arhat Mahākāśyapa: "Reverend Sir, among those who play the part of demon kings in the immeasurable universes in the ten directions, there are many who in fact are bodhisattvas dwelling in inconceivable emancipation. They employ their skill in expedient means to teach and convert living beings by appearing in the guise of demon kings."[30] As a result, we no longer know to which Buddhist saint we should turn, or which demon to repudiate.

Japanese Avatars

As the ruler of the Sixth Heaven, Māra seems to have enjoyed some popularity in Japan. However, Japanese Buddhism remained singularly ambivalent about him. In the *Taiheiki*, the monk Jōkei (1155–1213) has a dream of Māra fomenting the civil war of the Jokyū era (1221).[31] In a play entitled *The Sixth Heaven* (J. *Dairokuten*), Jōkei goes on a pilgrimage to Ise Shrine, and Māra appears to him in a dream to warn that he will come to test him. Jōkei interprets this warning as a favor from Amaterasu, the sun goddess worshiped at Ise. He then has a vision in which Māra appears at the head of his armies but is defeated by the god Susanoo, Amaterasu's brother.

In the militarized society of medieval Japan, on the other hand, Māra had a certain following. Several political figures and warlords vowed to become Māra to take revenge on their enemies. Such was the case with Emperor Sutoku (1119–1164), who took an oath of vengeance, initialing with his blood his vow to become Māra, when he was sent into exile by the retired emperor Go-Shirakawa. Or the *daimyō* Oda Nobunaga (1534–1582), who, according to the Jesuit missionary Luis Fróis, added the signature "Nobunaga, King Māra of the Sixth Heaven" to a letter sent to his enemy Takeda Shingen. But the most interesting example—a Japanese version of the Māravijaya—is the story in which Amaterasu asks Māra to cede sovereignty over Japan to her, and deceives him while doing so by swearing that she will never allow Buddhist monks to enter there. This is the reason, we are told, that Buddhist monks are forbidden to enter Ise shrine. Māra accepts this fool's bargain and, to seal the pact, gives Amaterasu a "divine seal" that will become one of the three regalia of the Japanese emperor.[32]

Māra came to be seen as an ally by defenders of local cults who resisted imperial (and Buddhist) centralization and denounced Amaterasu for having committed "perjury." Thus, even today, there are still shrines dedicated to him in some outlying regions of Japan. In medieval Japan, Māra merged with an indigenous deity named Kōjin (the "wild god"), who was reinterpreted as the fundamental Buddha, transcending the human buddha Śākyamuni and the metaphysical buddhas of Mahāyāna: like the Roman god Janus, he had two faces: Buddha *and* Māra. These were the two faces of the one reality—"Buddha and Māra, same principle."

The biographers' refusal to deal with the mythological aspects of the Buddha's life has led them to minimize, if not completely eliminate, the role played by Māra in the account of the Buddha's awakening, and in so doing, to overlook one of the fundamental features of the Buddhist tradition. Without Māra, the Buddha's personality loses all of its relief, and much of its fascination. This repression of the demonic aspects of the religion in certain monastic circles in the first centuries of Buddhism cannot hide the fact that Buddhism is essentially apotropaic in nature, and like the Life of the Buddha, cannot be understood without the presence, in the shadows, of the great tempter—who is at the same time the great awakener.

PLATE 1. Two of the four encounters: old age (top) and sickness (bottom). 8th–9th century. Cave 17, Dunhuang. Hanging banner, ink and color on silk. British Museum (1919,0101,0.88).

PLATE 2. The great departure. 9th century. Cave 17, Dunhuang. Hanging banner, ink and color on silk. British Museum (1919,0101,0.98).

故裂菩薩身或四方
煙起突爛衛天或往
風脅發震動出谷風
火洞磨暗光所現四
大海水一時涌沸騰

法天人諸龍庵等惡
忿魔眾瞋恚增威勢
孔豆流渟居天眾見
此惡魔惱亂菩薩以
惡悲心而惡傷之所
是來下側塞虛空

魔軍眾亢重亢邊圍
統菩薩欲大惡聲震
動天地菩薩心室顧
異相猶如師子亂於
麻牽哮惡歡言為呼
奇武未曾有也菩薩
決之當威必覺是諸
魔眾手相作切各盡
威力摧破菩薩或角
目切岩或橫飛亂掷
菩薩觀之如童子戲
魔益忿對更增戰力
菩薩以慈悲力故念

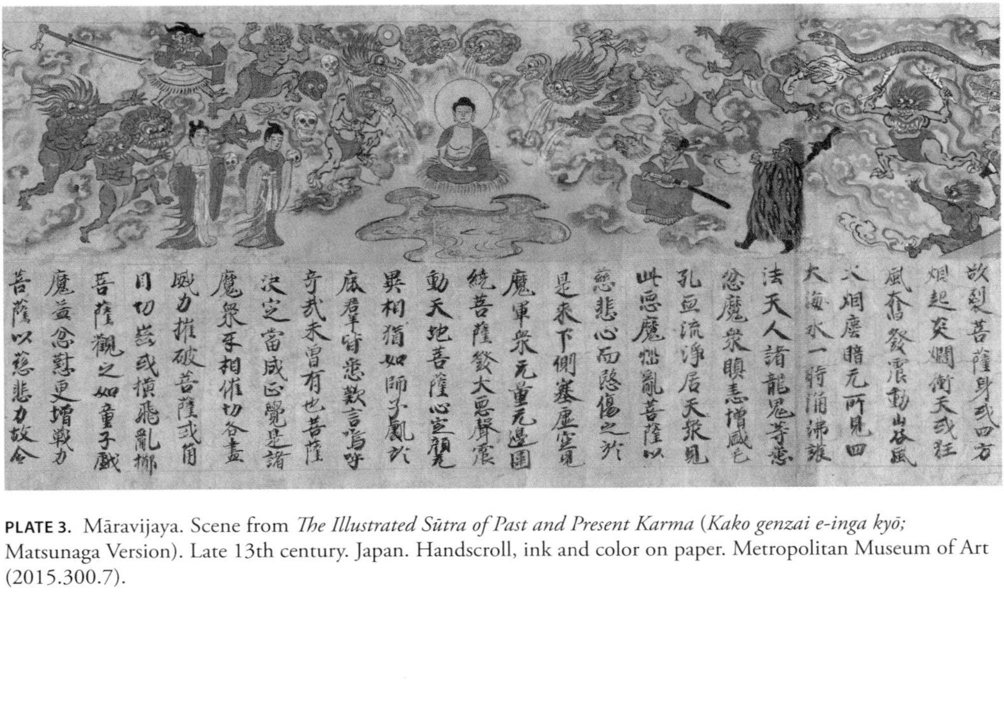

PLATE 3. Māravijaya. Scene from *The Illustrated Sūtra of Past and Present Karma* (*Kako genzai e-inga kyō*; Matsunaga Version). Late 13th century. Japan. Handscroll, ink and color on paper. Metropolitan Museum of Art (2015.300.7).

PLATE 4. Śākyamuni under the Bodhi tree. 17th century. China. Hanging scroll, ink and color on silk. Cleveland Museum of Art (1971.68).

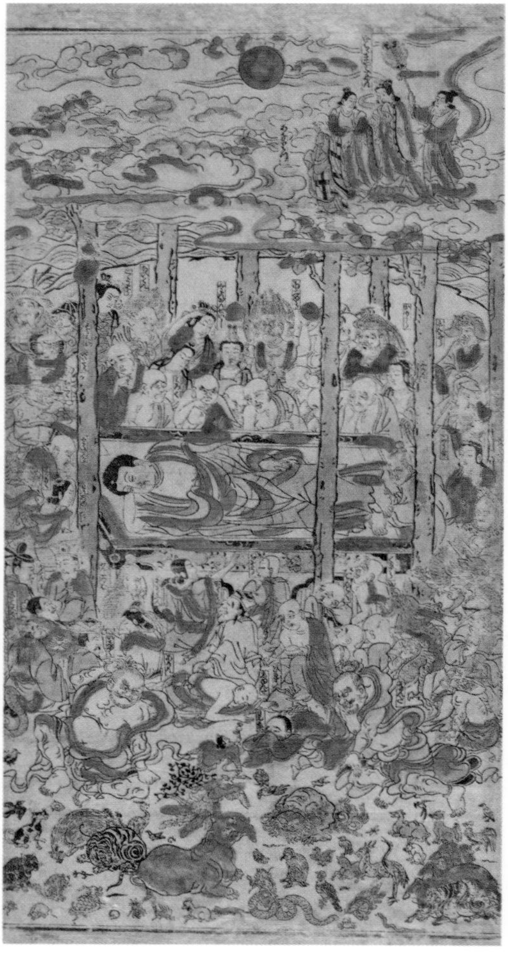

PLATE 5. Parinirvāṇa of the Buddha. Early 18th century. Japan. Color woodblock print. Cleveland Museum of Art (1916.1141).

PLATE 6. Death of the buddha, by Hanabusa Itchō. 1713. Japan. Hanging scroll, ink, color, and gold on paper. Museum of Fine Arts, Boston (11.4221).

PLATE 7. Parodic nirvāṇa. *Ōtsu-e butsu nehanzu,* by Hakuen. 19th century. Japan. Hanging scroll, ink and color on paper. Cleveland Museum of Art (2016.306).

PLATE 8. Prince Siddhārtha. *Shaka hassō,* by Oga Mantei. 19th century. Japan. Color on paper. Courtesy of University Tokyo Academic Archives.

PLATE 9. Prince Siddhārtha (Shitta Taishi), by Utagawa Kuniteru. Center sheet of the triptych *Kudami-jo hōjō-e o okonaite zenkon o hodokosu zu* (Kudami-jo does a good deed by releasing living things). 1847–1852. Japan. Woodblock print, ink and color on paper. Museum of Fine Arts, Boston (11.16221).

PLATE 10. The appearance of Śākyamuni after his death. Page from the *Majma' al-Tavārīik* (Collection of chronicles) by Hafiz-i Abru. 15th century. Herat (Afghanistan). Manuscript, ink, opaque watercolor on paper. Los Angeles County Museum of Art (M.73.5.412).

9

THE LIFE OF THE BUDDHA AS A PARADIGM

The Life of the Buddha, culminating with the awakening and then again with the parinirvāṇa, is above all a doctrinal digest and a paradigm of Buddhist practice. Like the imitation of Christ (or *christo-mimesis*) as described by the Dutch monk Thomas a Kempis (ca. 1380–1471) in his opusculum *De Imitatione Christi,* the Buddhist ideal was a kind of *imitatio Buddhaei* (or *Buddha-mimesis*). All buddhas and Buddhist saints are supposed to go through the same stages as Śākyamuni: a spiritual crisis followed by renunciation of the world, an ascetic phase leading to awakening and the attainment of supernormal powers, a period of preaching, a death foretold, and a royal funeral leading to relic worship. This turned out to be the case with both eminent monks and laymen, such as the Korean priest Wŏnhyo (617–686) and the Japanese priest Myōe (1173–1232); or the Japanese prince Shōtoku (Shōtoku Taishi, 574–622) and the monk-poet Saigyō (1118–1190). On the basis of the *Buddhacarita,* Reginald Ray defines no fewer than thirty-five themes from the Life of the Buddha that informed the later lives of the Buddhist saints. He sees in these themes, not scattered elements, but a paradigm. Even though most of the saints' lives exhibit only a few of these themes, "this paradigm constitutes a coherent ideal guiding Indian Buddhist thinking about saints, and Indian Buddhist saints—mutatis mutandis—tend to approximate it more or less closely."[1] With the idea of a paradigm, we come back to a perspective in which the Life of the Buddha no longer consists in a narrative thread, but rather is constituted of its most significant symbolic moments.

All life seeks to be transformed into a meaningful narrative, and the Life of the Buddha provides a model: even if awakening is only a very distant, almost unattainable goal for ordinary people, it nonetheless provides a meaningful horizon for a succession of lives and deaths, making each death a step in a grand process with cosmic dimensions. By transforming the linear character of the Buddha's life, its ephemeral aspect, into a kind of eternal return, one cancels its temporality. This hesitation between narrative images and iconic representations can be discerned very early on in statuary, as one and the same image may be susceptible to one or the other interpretation. Thus the image of the Buddha taking the earth as his witness can be read either with reference to a specific moment in his life or as a timeless symbol, valid for all buddhas.

BIOGRAPHICAL ORIGINS OF BUDDHIST RITUAL

In the Buddhist tradition we observe a sort of circular causality between legend and ritual: legend becomes the source of ritual, and ritual in turn gives birth to legend. In the *Hoki naiden,* one of the Japanese classics of Onmyōdō (Way of Yin and Yang), the main events in the life of the Buddha and his disciples are interpreted according to the Sino-Japanese calendar and give rise to corresponding Buddhist rituals. We thus learn that because Śākyamuni began his asceticism on a day corresponding to the Chinese cyclical sign of the tiger (*kanoe tora*), this day became auspicious for undertaking study, receiving tonsure, entering the mountains, receiving the precepts, and so on.[2] Likewise, because the Bodhisattva was awakened on the eighth of the twelfth month, again a day of the tiger, this day must be chosen to practice sitting meditation, to enter into concentration (*samādhi*), and to transmit the Dharma.[3]

Birth Rituals

While the Buddha's birth date remained undetermined in the first biographies, it is set on the eighth day of the fourth lunar month in the *Fo suoxing zan,* a Chinese translation of the *Buddhacarita* made by Dharmakṣema (385–433).[4] It remained floating, however, until the seventh century, alternating between the eighth of the fourth month and the eighth of the second month. The *Sūtra of Past and Present Causes and Effects* (*Guoqu xianzai yinguo jing*), translated into Chinese by Gunabhadra in the years 435–443, seeks a compromise by stating that the Bodhisattva entered the maternal womb on the eighth of the fourth month and left it on the eighth of the second month. The latter date is also the date of the great departure, awakening, and parinirvāṇa. An exception is the *Parinirvāṇa-sūtra,* which gives the eighth for entering the womb, the great departure, and the awakening, and the fifteenth for the parinirvāṇa, because on that day (or rather that night) the moon neither grows nor wanes.

On the whole, East Asian Buddhists seem to have preferred the eighth of the fourth lunar month, which became April 8 in our solar calendar. In South and Southeast Asia, on the other hand, the anniversary of the Buddha's birth is set on the fifteenth of *vaiśakha* (Pāli, *vesākha*), the second lunar month (April–May). During the Vishaka ceremony (better known in present-day India as Wesak), on the day of the full moon marking the birth, the awakening, and the parinirvāṇa, the twenty-nine acts of the Life of the Buddha are celebrated, beginning with his birth—symbolized by the bathing of a statue of the infant Buddha.[5] The custom of bathing images of the Buddha on the anniversary of his birth originated in India and was taken up in China in the second century CE. The theme became particularly popular, as a Dunhuang song attests:

> Śākya [muni], the father of compassion, came down to be born here below;
> Here he is, coming out from the right side of the [maternal] womb.
> The nine dragons sprinkle him with water and he is soon washed;
> Beneath his feet marked with thousand[-ray] wheels, auspicious lotuses open up.[6]

The annual celebration of the Buddha's birthday offered rulers of non-Chinese origin a new form of legitimacy. Indeed, the prediction made to King Śuddhodana gave the hope that the child would become a *cakravartin* king—a universal monarch. In an attempt to force the realization of this prediction, some sources describe Śuddhodana as crowning his son on the very day of his birth. The birth of the Buddha thus became a royal consecration, and the status of a *cakravartin* king (translated into Chinese as emperor) was no longer due to the mandate of heaven, as in ancient China, but to the merits accumulated over many past lives. It is understandable why a recently enthroned sovereign would celebrate in great pomp this anniversary of the birth of the Buddha. As early as the third century CE, great processions appeared in China parading a statue of the infant Buddha on a sumptuously decorated chariot, surrounded by automata, along the streets of the capital.[7] One source describes the masterpiece that a craftsman of the capital realized for these processions: an automaton combining dragons sprinkling the Buddha with lustral water and circumambulating monks throwing incense into the fire at each passage, and even more.[8] According to Zong Ling's *Notes on Annual Events in the Jing Region:* "On the eighth of the second moon, the day the Buddha was born and Śākyamuni was awakened, carts, precious canopies, and lanterns . . . for the *baguanzhai* (fast of the eight precepts) are prepared in the homes of the believers. Even today, from the dawn of the eighth day of the second moon, a complete tour of the city is made, holding incense and flowers in one's hands. This is called making a procession around the city."[9]

Canonical texts describe the merits produced by the Buddha's bathing rite on the anniversary of his birth.[10] The celebration of the rite in China, however, was not limited to this occasion or to images of the infant Buddha; it extended to ordinary baths during which images of the Buddha were sprinkled with perfumed water. Such images were perceived as animated, and worshipers behaved before them as if they were a living Buddha. While veneration of the images allowed merits to be obtained, lack of respect for them could have harmful effects. It is reported, for example, that when the iconoclast Sun Hao (3rd cent. CE) mockingly urinated on an image of the Buddha on this anniversary day, tumors developed on his body. These suppurations did not disappear until he repented and took refuge in the Buddha by cleansing the image with warm scented water.[11]

A Buddha Bath commemoration was also held on the fourteenth and twenty-ninth of each month. A large bath was prepared in each temple, and all the monks bathed in preparation for the convocation (*uposatha*) that would take place the next day. The bath that was commemorated, however, was not the first bath of the infant Buddha, but the bath offered to the Buddha and his disciples by Jivāka, the famous doctor and son of the no less famous courtesan Amrapālī. This bath is the subject of a sermon by the Buddha, the *Sūtra on the Baths and Bathing of the Clergy* (*Wenshi xiyu zhongseng jing*), translated into Chinese by An Shigao in the second century CE, in which the Buddha enumerates the virtues of bathing.[12] In some apocryphal meditation treatises dating from the fifth century, we are told that the gods Brahmā and Indra pour a liquid over the meditator's head, and this liquid spreads throughout his body, making him relive, as it were, the Buddha's bathing experience.[13] However, this image of the liquid entering through the head and filling the body is somewhat strange. According to Yamabe Nobuyoshi, the motif of the Buddha's consecration was at one time combined with the old yogic image of water filling the body. In this way, the Buddha's experience was internalized and translated into an experience accessible to the meditator.[14]

In Korea, the ritual bathing of the infant Buddha came to be superimposed on the Lantern Festival around the fourteenth century. Previously, this festival took place during the full moon of the first lunar month and not on the anniversary of the birth of the Buddha, the eighth of the fourth month. While few texts from the ancient period describe this ritual, there are many bronze images of the infant Buddha. But the Korean images, like the Japanese ones, represent him at the moment when he takes seven steps and declares himself to be without equal in the world. He is actually clothed and not naked as in the bathing scene. The origin of these images thus seems more Japanese than Chinese, and the rite itself is undoubtedly late.[15]

In Japan, this rite was known as the Buddha Anointing Ceremony (*kanbutsu-e*), and it took place on the eighth of the fourth lunar month. It is said to have been performed for the first time at court in 606, under the supervision of the regent Shōtoku (Shōtoku Taishi). This imperial ceremony is described in more detail in later texts. An image of the Buddha child was placed on a pedestal, from which threads of five colors ran to a basin of colored water symbolizing the bathwater. The emperor then sprinkled flowers over the image, and the master of ceremonies poured five ladles of that water over it. Then the emperor, ladies of the court, and other courtiers did the same. Similar rites took place in the great monasteries during the Nara period.

In the tenth century, the author of the *Illustrated Explanations on the Three Jewels* (*Sanbō ekotoba*), Minamoto no Tamenori (d. 1011), quotes from the *Sūtra on the Anointment of Buddha Images,* according to which: "All the

Buddhas of the ten directions were born on the eighth day of the fourth month. Between spring and summer great numbers of all kinds of living things are born. At that time it is neither too cold nor too hot, and so everything is wholesome and harmonious."[16] The importance of this ceremony, for Tamenori, lies in the fact that the bath of the infant Buddha had the power to save beings.

The custom continues today, although its meaning has been somewhat lost. It is now part of a festival known as the Flower Festival (Hana matsuri). For most people it is simply a festival celebrating children, and a rite aimed at bringing them luck; or a reference to the cherry blossoms, whose blossoming people follow with a deep aesthetic sense. Very few people know that these actually represent the flowers of the tree under which the Buddha was born, in the park of Lumbinī. Sometimes the infant Buddha is depicted standing on a paper mache elephant, which is placed on a chariot that children will pull around the temple grounds and through the neighborhood. These children often wear a paper wreath identifying them with Prince Siddhārtha. Most often, the infant Buddha is represented by a small metal statue pointing to the sky with one hand and to the earth with the other—an allusion to the words he is said to have spoken shortly after his birth: "In heaven and on earth, I am the only venerable one." The participants in the ceremony pour water or sweet tea on the statue. Because this water and tea are supposed to have magical properties, they fill a small container and take it home with them. Not only is the statue bathed, but food offerings are made to it as if it were alive. This ritual is celebrated publicly in the great Buddhist temples, but also in the intimacy of Zen monasteries. Unlike other Buddhist statues, the infant Buddha statue is used only for this occasion and spends the rest of the year locked up in a warehouse.

The Great Departure

The great departure cycle, that is, the sequence of events that led the Bodhisattva to leave the royal palace, became the paradigm of ordination in Southeast Asia. As we saw, one of the distant causes of the great departure was the Bodhisattva's first meditation, under the jambu tree. The theme of meditation under the jambu tree became central to a number of festivals and rituals in Buddhist India, giving rise early on to a specific image of the Bodhisattva (while images of the Buddha were still forbidden in principle).[17] In China, however, a competing theme, that of the four encounters, was more successful. During the period of the Six Dynasties (220–589), in particular, it became the pretext for a poetic ritual known as the Four City Gates—performed during fasting days. At night, the participants took turns composing poems about sickness (east gate), old age (south gate), death (west gate), and the encounter with the monk, symbolic of deliverance (north gate).[18] But in this elaboration, the theme underwent an important evolution, and the motif of old age—and more precisely that of women—emerged to take precedence over the others. At the same time, the poems adopted a quasi-Ronsardian, even openly erotic tone, and their Buddhist tonality faded. As François Martin points out: "If the general theme of the Buddhist law does not necessarily exclude the precious images dear to the palace poets, for whom falling ill, growing old, dying or renouncing the world perhaps above all means leaving the pleasures of a comfortable life, the most striking thing remains that they succeeded in imposing on the whole jousting game that gallant tone which persists as the trademark of the time."[19]

As noted, on the anniversary of the Buddha's birth, a procession went around the city clockwise, stopping at each of the four gates, starting with the east gate and ending at the north gate.[20] The passage through each of the gates was marked by exorcistic rituals: "The holy banners of the White Law are erected and Buddha's heads are placed at the four gates so that black karma can be wiped out and swept away."[21] The same symbolism is found in Buddhist funeral rites throughout Asia, and the circumambulation of the city or any other symbolic place (such as the altar or the stūpa) should be interpreted as a symbolic recapitulation of the Buddha's Life, ritually leading the practitioner to final deliverance.[22]

What was celebrated in China on the eighth day of the second month, more than a particular event, was at the same time the birth, the great departure, and the awakening—in short, the sum of the determining moments in the Life of the Buddha. But it is clear that the central event, the one represented by the procession around the city, was the great departure, the break with secular existence. This is why many of the prayer texts to be recited that day, although they evoke the whole of the Buddha's life, were entitled "Texts on the Crossing of the Walls" (Yucheng wen).[23] Could not the circumambulation, a symbolic representation of the departure from the palace, also have been a commemoration of the four excursions outside Kapilavastu? One can only be struck by the succession of the four gates, always in the same clockwise direction, their value as high points in the procession, and so on. Although not included in the fixed list of the eight acts, the four encounters occupy a decisive place in the Life of the Buddha: they prepare and announce the flight at the same time as they are the germ of the whole doctrine.[24]

Let's now come to the great departure itself. We have already seen that while the four encounters had disturbed the Bodhisattva, it was the vision of the sleeping women in the gynaeceum that aroused his disgust and motivated him to leave the palace. This vision must be linked to the subsequent episode of ascetic practices—especially the contemplation of impurity (Skt. *aśubhabhāvanā*), a method that involved going to cemeteries (or, even today, to the morgue) to contemplate decaying corpses in order to combat the allure of the senses.

Before leaving the palace, the Bodhisattva takes leave of his father, whom he finds deeply asleep. He walks around him three times, keeping him on his right side (that is, clockwise). Foucher rightly sees in this circumambulation a mark of filial respect, but perhaps the scene should also be interpreted, in the light of later Buddhist ordination rites, as a symbolic exit from the world. As Paul Mus has shown, circumambulating a stupā implies an ascension and ultimately an exit from the three worlds, the final deliverance. Furthermore, according to the monastic code, a candidate for ordination cannot be accepted if he has not received parental permission. This gesture of respect from the Bodhisattva may be tantamount to implicit authorization. But it may be objected that the Buddha was not ordained. To King Milinda, who presents this objection, the monk Nāgasena replies: "The Buddha was ordained by attaining omniscience at the foot of the Bodhi tree. He was not conferred ordination by others in the form he laid down for his disciples as an inviolable rule."[25] In any event, the great departure is clearly equivalent to leaving the family, a term that came to designate ordination.

By renouncing the world, Śākyamuni had in fact preserved (or rather realized) his attributes as universal monarch or *cakravartin* king. Subsequently, the monks' ordination came to be modeled on the ritual of royal consecration, the anointing (*abhiṣeka*) by which the new sovereign is sprinkled with water of the four oceans, symbol of his universal mastery. Like the Western imagery of the two swords, spiritual and temporal, Buddhist ideology came to advocate the harmony of the two wheels of Dharma, the Buddhist Law and the secular law, the Buddha (or Buddhist clergy) and the *cakravartin* king. This theory was to reach its apogee outside India, in medieval Japan.

There is also a certain resemblance between the great departure and the rite of monastic ordination as it is still practiced today in Southeast Asia.[26] This rite consists in adorning the candidate for ordination in his most beautiful finery as he prepares to leave home to go to the monastery. His parents and relatives, playing the role of Māra and his army, pretend to oppose his departure by blocking the door and telling him that he doesn't really want to become a monk.[27] Then, just as the gods rained down a shower of flowers to celebrate the Bodhisattva's great departure, various deities—including Brahmā and Indra—are invoked to protect the postulant, and in some cases it is his friends who play the role of the gods in question. Once at the monastery, the postulant abandons his beautiful clothes to don the monastic frock.[28] Unlike the legendary great departure, ordination has evidently become a rite of passage of sorts for young people who expect to spend some time in the orders before returning to secular life haloed with prestige.

Asceticism

Although the Bodhisattva's long asceticism apparently led him to a dead end, the Buddhist tradition has an ambiguous attitude on this subject. As mortification, asceticism is understood to be a form of bodily abandonment, and without it, the Bodhisattva might not have been able to achieve awakening. The theme of abandoning the body (Ch. *sheshen*), so important in the *Jātakas,* gained renewed popularity in East Asia, especially in Chinese Buddhism. While advocating a more pragmatic ideal, represented by the joyful and pot-bellied monk Budai (known in the West as the Laughing Buddha), Chinese Buddhism continued to affirm the value of asceticism and mortification. The image of the emaciated, cadaverous Śākyamuni also remained popular in India, where it can even be found on postcards. This image of the Bodhisattva is reminiscent of a mummy, and the motif reappears in the image of his disciple Mahākāśyapa, who is said to have entered a prolonged state of concentration (*samādhi*), a kind of suspended animation, to wait in a cave for the coming of the future buddha Maitreya. These two very strong images legitimized for generations of Chinese and Japanese Buddhists the idea of abandoning the body, a consummation that embraced all kinds of self-immolation—including the immolation by fire that still happens today.

In China, the asceticism of Śākyamuni served as a model for the monks of the Chan school, in particular, and it gave rise to certain iconographic themes specific to this school, such as that of "Śākyamuni emerging from the mountains" (J. Shussan Shaka). This theme inspired artists with the image of a more human Buddha, one less distant from the world. It appeared in China during the Song period (12th–13th cent.) but gave rise to opposing interpretations. For traditional art historians, who stick to the conventional biography of the Buddha, it represents the moment when the Bodhisattva, realizing the inanity of his efforts, renounces asceticism and turns to a less extreme type of meditation, which will lead to his awakening. For Zen specialists, on the other hand, it represents Śākyamuni *after* his awakening. At the end point of his asceticism, he has attained the supreme realization and can now return to the secular world to save beings. Instead of representing a disappointed and exhausted Bodhisattva, it supposedly shows the Buddha in all his splendor. If this be the case, however, the meaning of the subsequent meditation under the Bodhi tree is no longer clear. Is this a second awakening? We know that certain "gradualist" currents of Chan insisted on the necessity of deepening a "sudden" awakening through "gradual" practice. The Chan master Zhongfeng Mingben (1264–1325) was inspired to write the following poem on one of these images:

> He who came out of the mountains and went into the mountains:
> It is originally You.
> If we call it "You"
> It's not him yet,
> The venerable master Śākya[muni] comes.
> Ha, ha, ha, ha . . . ! His gaze embraces a huge expanse of clouds!
> Huanzhu Mingben greets him respectfully, with both hands clasped.[29]

In Japanese Buddhism, asceticism is no longer a dead end but the means by which Śākyamuni is awakened. It has become the distant cause of realization, a preliminary but necessary phase. A number of Japanese sources highlight a *Jātaka* in which the Bodhisattva is reborn as a young ascetic in the Himalayas who offers his body to a hungry demon, not out of pure generosity (as in the exemplum of the Bodhisattva's sacrificing himself to feed a starving tigress), but to obtain wisdom in the form of a stanza on impermanence. The positive interpretation is confirmed by the use of these paintings in Zen practice. In Zen monasteries, the Buddha's awakening is celebrated on the eighth day of the twelfth lunar month (today, December 8). On this occasion, the monks practice a particularly intensive meditation session lasting seven days and nights (from the first to the eighth), known as *rōhatsu sesshin.* On the morning of the eighth day, the anniversary of the awakening, a picture of "Śākyamuni emerging from the mountains" is hung in the meditation room while the monks sing the hymn of the Great Compassion. In this context, it is clear that the image represents the Buddha's awakening—and not his disappointment—at the end of his six years of asceticism in the mountains.

In the conventional version, Śākyamuni, famished and naked at the end of his asceticism, takes a piece of cloth from the corpse of a slave. Even if the word is never pronounced, it is in fact a shroud, which he washes to make himself a loincloth. Afterwards, the god Indra offers him more appropriate clothing, but even then the Bodhisattva continues to wear the loincloth underneath, as if to affirm that he still retains his ascetic personality.[30] This act echoes the one that led him, just after the great departure, to exchange his princely clothes for those of a hunter, in order to make himself a monastic frock.

In the *Lalitavistara,* the dead woman from whom Śākyamuni takes the piece of cloth is a servant of Sujātā, the young woman who will offer him rice pudding. The Bodhisattva's act evokes the *paṃśukūla* rite as it is still practiced in Southeast Asia and as it was perhaps practiced, in one form or another, in ancient India. As François Bizot has shown, this rite implies an initiatory death and rebirth.[31] The *paṃśukūla,* as the etymology suggests, is a "discarded cloth," and the term came to designate the monastic frock, which was in principle made from such cloths. In a number of healing rites, the patient is placed inside a pyramidal hut that symbolizes the maternal womb, and the hut is covered with a robe that symbolizes the placenta. Rebirth occurs when the priest tears the robe from the roof of the hut, after which the patient crawls out of the hut. In its structure, this rite seems to date back to a Vedic sacrifice called *dikṣā,* after which it was customary to give the priest (as *dakṣinā,* a reward) the robe that the sacrificer had worn.[32] The two phases of the Indian rite reflect those of the symbolic process of rebirth: during the first phase, the tissue (symbolizing the placenta or amniotic sac) is required for gestation to take place, while during the second, it must be abandoned for birth to take place. In the case of the Bodhisattva, however, this embryological symbolism is coupled with the fact that the tissue taken from the corpse also signifies his status as an ascetic, which he does not intend to renounce altogether, since he retains his loincloth even after he has put on sumptuous clothing that symbolizes his new status as the Buddha.

But the funerary symbolism (which is at the same time embryological, since all death implies rebirth) does not stop there: the whole narrative sequence that serves as a transition between the end of asceticism and Sujātā's offering of food, on the one hand, and the second offering of food by the two merchants Trapuṣa and Bhallika after the Buddha's awakening, on the other hand, can be seen as a prefiguration of the funerary rites and, in a general way, of all Buddhist rites of passage. Such is the case with the *kathina* ceremony in Thailand, marking the end of the monastic retreat during the rainy season. During this ceremony, a mixture of rice pudding is offered to the participants—clearly a replay of Sujātā's offering of rice to the Bodhisattva.[33] Before eating Sujātā's offering, the Bodhisattva had divided it into forty-nine dumplings (*piṇḍa*), one for each of the forty-nine days he would spend sitting in meditation after his awakening. These dumplings are obviously reminiscent of Brahmanical funeral rites, in which a dumpling is offered to each generation of ancestors. Therefore, the number forty-nine, as the maximum number of generations reached by the ritual, could symbolize the power of the Buddha to appease the dead.[34] The same type of interpretation can be applied to the offerings made by the two merchants Trapuṣa and Bhallika.[35] By inserting his action into the ritual offerings made to the spirits, the Bodhisattva also seemed to be inviting a response from the earthly spirits that resided in the forests around Bodh Gaya, and perhaps this is why he was soon under assault from Māra.[36] By going to a place that he knew was haunted by the presence of Māra, Śākyamuni placed himself at the center of a particularly powerful demonic sphere and prepared to confront both desire and fear. This was indeed a direct challenge to the master of the forces of evil, and it is not surprising that he felt compelled to respond.[37]

Victory over Māra

We saw that the victory over Māra represented one of the primary aspects of the Buddha's awakening (the other being his final meditation). The victory constitutes, as it should, the horizon of Buddhist practice. Japanese esoteric Buddhism, for example, offers a ritualistic interpretation of the Māravijaya and the role of the earth deity. The officiant begins by visualizing the image of the earth deity, which he places on a lotus flower. The goddess holds a *swastika* in her right hand and a pilgrim's staff in her left hand. This *swastika* is a Sanskrit letter symbolizing the mind of all the buddhas. Its transmission is the prerequisite for Śākyamuni's awakening, but also for that of the practitioner, since it symbolizes his own mind in all its splendor. A Japanese Life of the Buddha from the fourteenth century explains that just as the Buddha sitting on the seat of awakening defeated Māra by invoking the earth deity, the practitioner wishing to follow the Buddha's practice must first draw a mandala and then place himself at its center. Although he is still far from awakening, he must perceive himself clearly as essentially similar to the Buddha. By identifying himself with the three mysteries (of body, speech, and mind) of the cosmic Buddha Vairocana, he manifests his buddha body. This is why the earth deity must appear to him, as in the mythical past, to bear witness and repel Māra's armies.[38] The victory over Māra not only serves as a model for Buddhist practice oriented toward awakening, but it also becomes the paradigm of the subjugation of demons by Buddhist monks.

The role played by the earth deity has undergone an interesting evolution, especially in Southeast Asia. This deity is known in Thailand under the name of Nang Thoranee, and in Cambodia under that of Phra Thorni (in both cases, a seeming derivation of *dhāranī,* literally "what sustains"). In particular, we see appearing in these countries a theme that does not appear in the Indian legend and is taken up nowhere else: that of the wet hair of the goddess. This representation seems to derive from the *Paṭhamasaṃbodhi,* a text in which the earth goddess Vasundharā twists her wet hair to drown Māra's armies. When the Bodhisattva takes the earth as a witness of his merits, the goddess appears and evokes the countless existences during which he worshiped her by pouring libations of water on the ground. She then presses her wet hair to bring out a trickle of water that, miraculously swelling, turns into a tumultuous river carrying Māra and his armies away. A manuscript of the *Paṭhamasaṃbodhi,* dated 1834, describes Nang Thoranee's address to the Bodhisattva as follows: "My hair is full of the donative water from your past gifts. This shows that I am a witness for you, Lord." And she shouts a hundred, a thousand, ten thousand, a hundred thousand times, deafening the soldiers of Māra with her enormous roar. Then she twists her hair and expresses the water, which flows like a river.[39] It is this episode that Theravāda Buddhists re-actualize when they pour water on the ground during the ritual and take Nang Thoranee as a witness of this meritorious act performed for the benefit of their ancestors.[40]

The image of the earth goddess in the form of a beautiful young woman twisting her hair to wring out the water that will drown Māra's armies is carved on the pedestal of the statues of the Bodhisattva in the classical posture known as "taking the earth as a witness" (*bhūmisparśa-mudrā*). It shows the seated Buddha, his left hand resting on his left leg and the fingers of his right hand touching the ground. It is also found in temple courtyards and parks. With the *Pathamasaṃbodhi,* we have moved from the earthquake of traditional biographies to the tsunami, two phenomena that are closely linked in reality.

In a completely different context, that of medieval Japan, we can mention an apocryphal scripture, the *Sūtra of the Great Incantation of the Earth Goddess* (*Bussetsu jishin dai darani kyō*). This text recounts how the Buddha, who had already entered parinirvāṇa, temporarily comes out of it to explain to his disciples why his funeral pyre refuses to ignite. He tells them that the deities of the earth, which have been neglected for too long, must first be worshiped. The text also reports how, when Māra challenged the Buddha to find a witness to his past merits, the dragon kings of the five directions (the four cardinal points and the center) and the deities of the earth emerged from the ground and came to testify for him. After Māra, defeated, withdrew, the Buddha gave his disciples a series of incantations and rites to worship these deities and obtain their forgiveness when the earth is violated (by manmade constructions, etc.). We will return to this point when we consider Japanese representations of the parinirvāṇa (*nehan-zu*). But before doing so, we must first examine the changes brought about in the narrative of the Life of the Buddha by new conceptions regarding his nature as developed in Mahāyāna and in the esoteric Buddhism of the Diamond Vehicle (Vajrayāna).

10

NEW CONCEPTIONS OF THE BUDDHA

In early Buddhism, the opposition between narrative thought and doctrinal thought was confined to an opposition between the life and doctrine of the Buddha. With the advent of the Mahāyāna, doctrinal thought invaded the biographical sphere and narrativity lost its importance, while, paradoxically, mythology experienced a new rise. The historical Buddha gave way to the metaphysical buddhas, transcending time and space. As a result, the representations (textual or iconographic) of the Life of the Buddha Śākyamuni lost some of their popularity. This evolution had been prepared by the transformation of Śākyamuni himself into a metaphysical Buddha. Historians have sought to describe the process that supposedly led from a "historical" Buddha to a "transcendental" Buddha. Even if one believes that the Buddha has always been transcendent in the eyes of his followers, one can undoubtedly distinguish degrees in transcendence—which clearly increase over the centuries, from the supramundane Buddha of the Lokottaravādin (followers of the Supramundane Teaching), to the transcendent buddhas of Mahāyāna, and finally to Vairocana, the cosmic Buddha of Tantric or esoteric Buddhism (Vajrayāna).[1]

The "historical" Buddha, who had transformed into a kind of superhuman (or posthuman) following his awakening, gradually became a true god. Certain texts, such as the *Lotus Sūtra,* clearly testify to this evolution. Iconography seems to have played an important role, especially at the outset through the description of the thirty-two characteristic marks of the Buddha. So the legend gradually spread to the disciples of the Buddha, the arhats. In China, they gradually became supermen, like the Daoist immortals, and served as models for a new type of Buddhist saint: the *bodhisattva* (literally, "being of awakening"). In the Mahāyāna, the term bodhisattva no longer designates only the future Buddha (Śākyamuni or Maitreya), but a whole category of metaphysical beings such as Avalokiteśvara (Tib. Chenrezig, Ch. Guanyin, Kor. Gwaneum, J. Kannon), symbol of Buddhist compassion; and, following them, all the practitioners of Mahāyāna who vow to become bodhisattvas. The bodhisattva ideal thus supplants that of the arhat, which is perceived as too narrow. Indeed, while the bodhisattva, in his infinite compassion, vows to save all beings, the arhat, we are told, only seeks his own salvation. In reality, the contrast between the two categories was less clear-cut, as evidenced by the cult of the Sixteen Arhats or the Five Hundred Arhats in East Asian Buddhism.[2]

THE POSTHUMOUS BUDDHA

The Life of the Buddha did not end with the parinirvāṇa, as we saw. It continued, paradoxically, with his relics—which become the proof of his immortality. The cult of the relics allegedly began during the Buddha's lifetime, and it was he himself who initiated it, according to the story in which he gives a lock of his hair to the two merchants Trapuṣa and Bhallika, telling them to deposit it in a stūpa. But it is especially with the tradition of the *Parinirvāṇa-sūtra* that this cult became important.

As Strong remarks, the Buddha's relics can be seen as an expression and extension of his biography.[3] They are, in a sense, the eternally living Buddha, as is his (too brief) corporeal incarnation. The planter and amateur archeologist William Peppé, one of the first archeologists to be interested in the Buddhist stūpas, discovered at Piprāhwā, not far from the Indo-Nepalese border, on the Indian side, a soapstone box with an inscription in Brāhmi script dating from the second century BCE. This inscription indicates that the box was a "receptacle of the relics of the Blessed Buddha of the Śākyas."[4] Other relics, even older (4th or 5th cent. BCE), have recently been discovered at the same site.

Relics are a continuation of the Life of the Buddha by other means: this is a somewhat paradoxical method, since, while it allows one to get around the parinirvāṇa, it does not really lend itself to great narrative developments. To be sure, the various adventures of this or that relic are recounted, but, insofar as the subject of these adventures is no longer an individual in flesh and blood (or just bones, in the best of cases), it is more difficult to identify with him. It is thus the Life of the Buddha that confers quasi-magical value on these relics. But they in turn acquire a life of their own, and one could even say, conversely, that the Life of the Buddha is a narrative relic, endowed with the same power as his concrete relics.

A strange story appears in the *Lokapaññati,* a cosmological text in Pāli from the eleventh to twelfth century. This text reports that the relics of Buddha are kept by mechanical robots from Rome and relates the saga of the Indian engineer who had vowed to be reborn in Rome in order to obtain the secret method of building robots. In his next life, he managed to marry the inventor's daughter and obtain the plans, which he secretly passed on to India through his son. The son arrived at Pātaliputra, the capital of Magadha, just at the time of the Buddha's parinirvāṇa. Prince Ajātaśatru obtained the secret and, to protect the relics, had robots built, which he arranged around the stūpa of the Buddha. These robots were still there when King Aśoka visited the place a century later, and they drew their swords, ready to strike him. Fortunately, Aśoka found the engineer's son (still alive!), who managed to disarm them, and Aśoka could then collect the relics and organize their worship.[5]

The precious relic, set like a jewel at the heart of a stūpa that becomes its casket, is no longer a "remainder" of the Buddha's Life, but its culmination. This is why the Life of the Buddha is depicted on the porticoes of the Indian stūpas at Sanchi and Bharhut, or on the bas-reliefs at the base of the stūpa of Borobudur in Indonesia. In fact, as has been noted, the circumambulation that pilgrims accomplish when they visit Borobudur is a kind of spiral ascent of the spirit. The relic, placed at the top and/or the base of the stūpa, is its heart or culmination point. This model also allows us to understand how the Buddha's previous existences are part of a teleological journey: one of their motivations is to obtain the thirty-two marks of the Buddha—in other words, the realization (over a very long term) of a perfect body, which will continue in relics.

According to a local tradition, the arhat Kāśyapa obtained the Buddha's sternum before flying to what is today Thailand, where he deposited it in the Wath Phra That Panon (in the northeast of Thailand).[6] Another major relic, the collarbone of the Buddha, was allegedly obtained by the god Indra and deposited at the Thūpārama (in present-day Sri Lanka). Ceylon thus became the "island of relics." But other Asian countries also boast important relics of the Buddha, such as one of his eyes or fingers (fig. 14).

In Japan, the relics were identified with the mythical wish-fulfilling jewel *(cintāmaṇi)*, based on a passage from the *Treatise* that states: "The *cintāmaṇi* comes from the relics of the Buddha: when the Law disappears, all the relics of the Buddha will be transformed into *cintāmaṇi*. Likewise, after a thousand years, water will turn into pearls of crystal."[7] Various medieval texts refer to an (apocryphal) passage from the *Hikekyō* (*Karuṇāpuṇḍārika-sūtra*) where the Bodhisattva,

FIGURE 14. Reliquary with finger bone of the Buddha. Famen Temple. Shaanxi, China.

in the four hundredth of the five hundred vows he takes before his awakening, declares: "I vow that, when in the future I obtain the Buddha's Way . . . , my relics will be transformed into jewels of crystal."

Since the relics are in a way the posthumous body of the Buddha, this body also has to reach nirvāṇa one day. Thus, there is a "parinirvāṇa of the relics," during which the stūpa-reliquary sinks into the ground, and all memory of the Buddha and his Law disappears. Or the relics gather under the Bodhi tree and reconstitute his body seated in meditation, performing the miracle of the doubles. Their disappearance signifies the end of this cosmic period and the coming of the future buddha Maitreya. The transition between Śākyamuni's "total" nirvāṇa and Maitreya's parousia is assured by the sixteen arhats who are protectors of the Law (and by the bodhisattva Jizō in the Sino-Japanese tradition).[8]

In this context, one can also point out the importance of "contact" relics such as the Buddha's robe and bowl.[9] According to the *Treatise,* the Buddha gave his robe to Mahākāśyapa for transmission to the future Buddha, Maitreya.[10] This story took on great importance in the Chan/Zen tradition, where the Buddha's robe tended to merge with the robe that the Indian patriarch Bodhidharma had transmitted to his Chinese disciple Huike to authenticate his Dharma transmission.[11] Legend has it that shortly after his awakening, the Buddha received four bowls from the four divine kings, which he merged into one. In the fourth to fifth century, this bowl was supposedly kept in a temple in Gandhāra, but it was no longer there when Xuanzang visited the monastery in the seventh century. It had been stolen, Xuanzang reports, by an evil king of Kashmir, then taken to Persia. Sources report its reappearance in various places, including China (from which it is supposed to return to Sri Lanka), or Tuṣita Heaven, or the *nāga* (dragon) palace to await the parousia of Maitreya. According to a tradition reported by Faxian, it will then return to Mount Vinataka, where it will again separate into four bowls; the four kings will retrieve those bowls and bring them to Maitreya, who will merge them into one again.[12]

Shadows and Traces

Two more "relics" of some importance are the shadow of the Buddha and his footprints. The first appears in a number of legends—for example, at the request of Gopāla, a newly converted *nāga* who refuses to separate himself from the Buddha, the latter leaves his shadow in Gopāla's cave, declaring that it has the same powers as he does.[13] This cave became a famous pilgrimage site and is described by Xuanzang among others around the middle of the seventh century. He recounts his disappointment upon entering the cave at not seeing anything there. His guide then showed him where to stand, but he still could not see anything. He prostrated himself a hundred times, but again without success. Overcome with tears, he was blaming himself for his bad karma when his repentance finally bore fruit and the shadow appeared to him.[14] The footprints of the Buddha appeared rather late in Southeast Asia, around the ninth century.[15] The most famous footprint of the Buddha is in Sri Lanka, and this is the footprint described by Marco Polo as the mark of Adam's foot in the earthly paradise (which the myth placed in Ceylon). Two giant footprints (1.30 m wide, 3.50 m long), dating from the seventh to tenth century, were discovered in 1986 in the province of Prachinburi in Thailand. Footprints left by the Buddha have been found as far as Japan, where the oldest example seems to be that of the Yakushiji monastery in Nara. These relics are two inscribed stones, which are considered a national treasure. One has footprints and various inscriptions in Chinese relating to its origin. The other (dated ca. 750) is a slate tablet with twenty-one poems on the footprints. It is one of the oldest monuments of Japanese literature.[16]

THE SUPRAMUNDANE BUDDHA

Given the development of the Buddha's legend, debates about his worldly (i.e., human) or superworldly (quasi-divine) nature have been going on for a long time. The tendency to idealize the person of the Buddha appeared very early.[17] For example, the *Controversial Issues* (*Kathāvatthu*), a treatise of uncertain date belonging to the Pāli Abhidhamma, reports heretical sects who claimed that the fragrance of the Buddha's excrement surpassed all other perfumed things.[18] In schools of ancient Buddhism such as the Mahāsāṃghika (Great Assembly) and the Lokottaravāda (Supramundane Teaching), a purely supramundane Buddha appeared, whose physical body was itself transcendent. Like the true Christian according to St. Paul, this Buddha was believed to be *in* the world without being *of* the world. He therefore could not be defiled by mere things, and the episodes relating to his illness or his wounds were only skillful means (*upāya*) intended for simple souls. Previously, other schools had tried to distinguish two bodies of the Buddha, a physical body and a doctrinal "body" (*dharmakāya*) that soon became a cosmic, transcendental body. With the rise of the Mahāyāna, however, the Life of the Buddha was reinterpreted in a way that can fairly be described as a type of doceticism.[19]

A supernatural, supramundane interpretation of the Buddha's life already appears in the *Latilavistara* and the *Mahāvastu,* from between the second and fourth centuries CE. This tendency becomes more pronounced in the *Treatise:* "Moreover, the Buddha Śākyamuni who was born in the palace of the king apparently assumed human qualities: he endured cold and heat, hunger and thirst, and sleep; he endured criticism, old age, illness, death, and more, but with his mentality, wisdom, and divine qualities, he was no different than a correctly and fully enlightened Buddha."[20] The same is true for all buddhas and bodhisattvas: "Buddhas are not in any way generated by their father and mother; they are produced by their own energy. . . . As for bodhisattvas reaching their last birth, it is known that they are born coming out of their mother's right side without hurting her."[21] The author of the *Treatise* uses a distinction between the two bodies of the Buddha to explain the Buddha's frequent stays in Rājagṛha and Śrāvastī: "It is to dispense benefits to his native land that he frequently resides in Śrāvastī. . . . It is to dispense blessings to the homeland of his Dharmakāya (body of Law) that he frequently resides in Rājagṛha. . . . Since the Dharmakāya prevails over the body of birth, of these two cities, it is in Rājagṛha that the Buddha resides most often."[22] The account of the Buddha's Life is thus emptied of all narrative value while its propaedeutic value is reaffirmed. In this respect, the *Treatise*'s description of the Buddha is reminiscent of another famous Mahāyāna text, the *Lotus Sūtra:* "The Buddha's true body fills all space, his rays illuminate the ten regions; the sounds of his preaching of the Law also fill, in the ten regions, innumerable universes as numerous as the sands of the Ganges; all the members of the great assembly hear the Law simultaneously, and he preaches the Law without interruption."[23]

THE TRANSCENDENT BUDDHA OF THE *LOTUS SŪTRA*

In the accounts of the end of his life, the Buddha, prompted by Māra to enter parinirvāṇa, suggests to Ānanda that, if he were asked, he could remain forever in this world. This already gives us the idea of an immortal Buddha, who enters parinirvāṇa only by convention, to conform to the customs of this world. As we have seen, Ānanda unfortunately did not grasp the opportunity, and the Buddha announces that he will die soon.

The evolution of the narrative of the Buddha's Life also reflects doctrinal speculation as to its nature. Already prepared by the notion of a supramundane Buddha in the Mahāsāṃghika current, the theory of a transcendent Buddha finds its locus classicus toward the beginning of our era in a Mahāyāna scripture, the *Lotus Sūtra* (*Saddharmapuṇḍarīka-sūtra*). In this sūtra, which still enjoys great popularity throughout East Asia, the Buddha reveals to his disciples, gathered around him on Vulture Peak, that his existence transcends life and death:

> In all the worlds the heavenly and human beings and asuras all believe that the present Shakyamuni Buddha, after leaving the palace of the Shakyas, seated himself in the place of practice not far from the city of Gaya and there attained anuttara-samyak-sambodhi. But good men, it has been immeasurable, boundless hundreds, thousands, ten thousands, millions of nayutas of kalpas since I in fact attained Buddhahood.[24]

If the awakening is no longer the event we thought it was, the same is true of the extinction:

> But for the sake of living beings I employ the power of expedient means and say that I am about to pass into extinction. In view of the circumstances, however, no one can say that I have been guilty of lies or falsehoods.[25]

Faced with the disbelief of his listeners, the Buddha calls for the testimony of the countless disciples he has converted since the dawn of time, and they suddenly come out of nowhere. And, as if that weren't enough, another buddha named Prabhūtaratna appears, sitting in meditation in a stūpa that has risen from the ground and is floating in the air. Here is a summary of the episode:

> While the Buddha was preaching the *Lotus of the Law,* a precious stūpa appeared in the air above the congregation. A voice came out of it, warmly congratulating Śākyamuni, who then proceeded to open the stūpa and discover the mummified body of the buddha Prabhūtaratna. . . . He spoke words of praise.[26]

It was probably passages like these that made Renan say: "Everything is driven to absurd hyperbole. Fantastic arithmetic is played out in numbers composed of one unity followed by one hundred and forty zeros. Bodhisattva processions equal in number to the grains of sand of a myriad of one hundred thousand million Ganges all come together from the cracks of the earth to listen to Śākyamuni. It looks like a construction in the air, a castle in the clouds."[27] The scene in which Śākyamuni climbs on board the floating stūpa alongside Prabhūtaratna has exerted a great influence in Asia, both iconographically and doctrinally. The cohabitation of the two buddhas inside the stūpa has become the symbol of Buddhist nonduality. In Japanese esoteric Buddhism, an embryological reading of the two buddhas could even be proposed, one representing the blood of the mother, the other the seed of the father, merging at the moment of conception—while the stūpa itself symbolizes the maternal womb.

This transcendental conception of the Buddha is well summarized in the *Illustrated Explanations on the Three Jewels* by Minamoto no Tamenori:

> [The Buddha] is relied upon by all the beings of all the three worlds, the one revered by all four kinds of creatures. Though he takes various forms, you may not be able to see him; though he speaks, you may not be able to hear him. But when there is an affinity, he will show you his form, as does the moon in the sky when its reflection floats upon the water. In response to your prayers he will let you hear his voice, like thunder in the heavens that echoes your thoughts. His body fills the whole vault of heaven, but for expedience he appears to be sixteen feet tall. His life span is endless and incalculable, but he made it seem as if it came to an end when he reached the age of eighty. . . . Thus, you must know that though the

Buddha chose to hide himself from the sight of mankind for a brief time, he did not disappear for eternity. The Buddha lives always in our hearts. You must never think that he is far away.[28]

To understand the avatars of the Buddhist legend, it is necessary to make a short detour through Buddhology. It is indeed the evolution of the somewhat abstract conceptions of buddhahood and the body (or bodies) of the Buddha that explains, paradoxically, the birth of a devotional Buddhism in which the historical Buddha, Śākyamuni, while always occupying the first place in theory, is sometimes dethroned by other characters in popular piety.[29] The question of the number of buddhas that can coexist in the universe (or rather the Buddhist multiverse) has given rise to much debate. In early Buddhism, it is in principle impossible for there to be more than one Buddha during the same cosmic period. In *Milinda's Questions,* for example, Nāgasena explains to King Milinda that our cosmic system, composed of ten thousand worlds, can only support the qualities of one Buddha at a time; otherwise it would tremble and come to an end. This does not mean that other buddhas cannot exist in other universes, and this is the perspective that Mahāyāna puts forward, postulating the existence of an infinite number of cosmic systems.

This question of the body (or bodies) of the Buddha becomes a pressing one on the occasion of the parinirvāṇa. By losing their master, the community of his followers seemed to have lost everything, and this sense of irretrievable loss explains the scenes of grief surrounding the depiction of the parinirvāṇa. To remedy this, the Dharma transmitted by the Buddha is substituted for the flesh-and-blood Buddha. Like the king of France, the Buddha therefore has two bodies—a perishable body and an imperishable one that is actually the corpus of his doctrine. It is the latter that is called Dharmakāya, or body of Law, playing on the double meaning of *kāya:* "body" but also "corpus," "set," "category." This conception, which is that of early Buddhism, is found even in the Mahāyāna school of Madhyamika; it corresponds to the distinction between conventional and ultimate truth that Nāgārjuna takes up in the second century CE.

But with the Mahāsāṃghika school, resulting from a schism that arose at the Second Council around 334 BCE, we end up with a new conception of a transcendent body of the Buddha that does not perish with the parinirvāṇa. This body is no longer the set of the teachings of the Buddha Śākyamuni, but a body of essences (*dharma*), "the system of abstract notions that analysis can isolate in the transcendental unity of the Blessed One."[30] This "body of essences" (*dharmakāya*) "embraces the universe and transcends it." The buddha-nature is now inherent in all beings—in other words, a buddha lies dormant in each one of us. Soon, an intermediate buddha body between the other two, called the "retribution body" (*sambhogakāya*), appeared in Mahāyāna. The physical body of the Buddha, in this ternary scheme, is called the "metamorphosis body" (*nirmanakāya*), because it is now perceived as a simple projection on the terrestrial plane of the two higher bodies.

In Tantric or esoteric Buddhism, other types of buddha bodies emerge. As Rolf Stein points out: "Indo-Tibetan Tantrism add to these the Supreme Body, said to be of Nature itself or of Bliss (at the top of the hierarchy), and distinguishes between a peaceful, pure form and a terrible form (*krodha*). Sino-Japanese Tantrism takes a further step downwards with an Assimilation Body (Ch. dengliushen; J. tōrūjin), which represents the terrible and 'demonic' form that a Buddha can take to subjugate demons or bloodthirsty non-Buddhist divinities by assuming their form and acting against them."[31] The Buddha should therefore be placed in the forefront of Buddhist and non-Buddhist gods.

Speculations on the superhuman or transcendent nature of the Buddha were reflected iconographically in the gigantism of certain statues. We see this type of image of the Buddha (especially for representations of the final extinction), both in Mahāyāna Buddhism—in Gandhāra (Bāmiyān), China (Yunmen), and Japan (Nara)—and in Theravāda (Sri Lanka, Burma, and Thailand).

A PLETHORA OF BUDDHAS

Thus, we see in Mahāyāna the multiplication of metaphysical buddhas whose domains, often described as pure lands, are hierarchically layered. To these are added their emanations or retribution bodies (*sambhogakāya*), the metaphysical bodhisattvas who also serve as intermediaries between the two levels, relative and absolute, of reality.

By multiplying the number of buddhas, the Mahāyāna dealt an almost fatal blow to the old, linear, and eschatological conception of salvation. Buddhas can now manifest themselves at any time and in any place. They are no longer, like Śākyamuni, the object of irremediable nostalgia, nor do they, like Maitreya, arouse despair in people at having been born too soon. The world has become their playground, the setting for an immense game of hide-and-seek, where the hope of meeting them is still allowed. The most important of these timeless and potentially ubiquitous buddhas, at least those that, carried by popular fervor, did not become too abstract, are probably Amitābha (Ch. Amituo, J. Amida), the Buddha of the Pure Land; and Baiṣajyaguru (Ch. Yaoshi, J. Yakushi), the Healing Buddha. But the place of honor goes to the cosmic Buddha Vairocana (Ch. Dari, J. Dainichi), all the others being basically (at least according to Tantric Buddhism) his hypostases.

After the buddhas come the bodhisattvas, who are considered (depending on the case) to be future buddhas or emanations of the various buddhas. The first instance is represented by Maitreya (Ch. Mile, J. Miroku), the future Buddha, who awaits in Tuṣita Heaven the moment (for us far away, but for him very close) to appear in this world—in just a few billion years. Unlike the

Messiah, Maitreya will not appear at the end of the world, but on the contrary will usher in a new golden age, after our world has been completely renewed. The other major bodhisattvas are Avalokiteśvara (Ch. Guanyin, J. Kannon), Mañjuśrī (Ch. Wenshu, J. Monju), Samantabhadra (Ch. Puxian, J. Fugen), and Kṣitigarbha (Ch. Dizang, J. Jizō). Although the biographies of these transcendent beings remain fairly abstract, those of their human manifestations are less so. Thus Maitreya, for the time being a mere bodhisattva waiting for the hour of his parousia, is already on the job, periodically descending to earth to save humans. One of his most popular manifestations is a tenth-century Chan monk known as Budai ("Cloth Sack") because of the large bag he carried on his shoulder. This pot-bellied and hilarious figure, not unlike the Silenus of the Greeks, has become our Laughing Buddha. This buddha or rather bodhisattva (it is his title of bodhisattva, *pusa* in Chinese, which gave us "pussah"), found in all antique stores, became in Japan one of the Seven Gods of Fortune under the name of Hotei. It forms a striking contrast with certain representations of the Indian Buddha Śakyamuni, emaciated by his long asceticism. While Śakyamuni finally chose the Middle Way between mortification and hedonism, Indian Buddhism has nevertheless remained centered on the rejection of the world and the body; conversely, Chinese and Japanese Buddhism, and in particular Chan / Zen, are characterized by a more positive attitude and a rehabilitation of the world of the senses. However, the contrast should not be exaggerated, and Buddhist China has had its share of renunciators. With the rise of the new deities called bodhisattvas, the popularity of the Buddha Śākyamuni declined after the seventh century, and, as a result, interest in his life story partially declined as well. But, as we shall see, this was only an eclipse, and in medieval Japan, in particular, there was a renewed interest in the Life of the Buddha Śākyamuni, giving rise to the creation of biographies and iconography of a new kind.

PART THREE

THE UNENDING STORY

From the historian's point of view, one could paradoxically say that the Life of the Buddha began with his death, or with what Buddhists prefer to call his parinirvāṇa. It is allegedly from this event, still present in some memories, that the first biographers began to go back in time, seeking to find fragments of this life, a bit like recalling a dream in the morning. From these fragments, they pieced together a biography that was still discontinuous, which the hagiographers soon claimed and cemented into a marvelous narrative. We have seen that this biography, based on a desire for historicity, is questionable. Moreover, the Life of the Buddha continued to be written outside India, in new ways, long after the parinirvāṇa: first with the history of his relics and the invention of his past lives in Southeast Asian Theravāda, but also with the development of the Mahāyāna image of the Buddha in Tibet and in East Asia. I have already mentioned the history of the relics. The evolution of the narrative of the Buddha's Life in Southeast Asia has been well studied, so I will not dwell on it here.[1] Tibetan sources, for their part, generally follow the received tradition.[2] However, some of them are strongly tinged with Tantrism—a ritualistic practice which developed from the fifth century onward in Hinduism and Buddhism, and which insists in particular on the soteriological role of sexuality. After briefly describing the Chinese and Korean Lives of the Buddha, I will focus on the evolution of the Japanese Life of the Buddha, from medieval to early modern times. During the latter period, new versions of this Life kept appearing, no longer legendary but romantic, attesting to another form of the Buddha's survival in an increasingly secularized world.

11

CHINESE LIVES OF THE BUDDHA

In China, the story of the Buddha's Life was reorganized on a taxonomic or encyclopedic basis, "formatting" the biography of Śākyamuni in a way that partly countered the narrative tendency asserted in the first "complete" Indian biographies. But, as we have seen, the development of Mahāyāna, with its many metaphysical buddhas, profoundly changed the prevailing conception of the founder of Buddhism, together with the narrative of his Life.

Thus a characteristic feature of Chinese sources, both Buddhist and non-Buddhist, is their attempt to integrate the Life of the Buddha into Chinese history, fortified with a strong emphasis on specific dates. For example, in the "Treatise on Buddhism and Daoism" in the *Book of Wei* (*Weishu,* ca. 551–554), we read that "the moment of Śākya[muni]'s birth corresponds to the ninth year of the reign of King Zhuang of the Chu [687 BCE]. . . . From that date to the eighth year of Wuding of the Wei, it is said that one thousand and thirty-seven years have passed."[1]

The *Genealogy of the Śākya* (*Shijia pu*) by Sengyou (445–518) is one of the first attempts outside India to give a relatively coherent account of the Buddha's Life. The text does not follow a narrative sequence, however. It is an anthology, in thirty-four chapters, of data relating to the genealogical origins, human existence, parinirvāṇa, and relics of the historical Buddha. This *Genealogy* has had a long posterity in the Chinese encyclopedic tradition. It does not provide any new information and merely systematizes canonical data. As such, it constitutes the precursor of the "objective" and historicist biographies of the Western tradition, a perspective taken up by modern Japanese scholarship. In this respect, it contrasts with the transformation texts (*bianwen*) of Dunhuang, which reflect a creative popular tradition. The latter texts, whose production extended from the sixth to the tenth century, are characterized by their formulaic character—an alternation of prose and verse.

One of the best known of these chantefables, the *Sūtra on the Awakening of the Prince* (*Taizi chengdao jing*), begins with a series of ten *Jātakas* (exempla of King Śibi, Prince Vessantara, etc.). The Bodhisattva is always reborn in the land of Purna (Ch. Poluona), at the center of the universe. At the end of his existence, he gets to be reborn in Tuṣita Heaven. One of the innovations of this text concerns the episode of the four encounters, which here are increased to five.[2] The first encounter takes place at the east gate of the city, where the Bodhisattva observes a man helping a woman about to give birth. The other three encounters follow the normal sequence: an old man (south gate), a sick man (west gate), and a corpse (north gate). Because of the addition of the parturient, it is a fifth encounter, outside the city walls, that allows Śākyamuni to discover the way to salvation. This takes the form of a monk who presents himself, without fear of anachronism or time loop, as a disciple of the Buddha Śākyamuni. Here, the monk seems to transcend the realm of the relative, symbolized by the city and its four gates.[3] This idiosyncratic version seems to have been widespread, and is even found in Japan. Following these encounters, the Bodhisattva leaves the palace to pursue ascetic practice on the slopes of the Himalayas—not in the forest, as Indian tradition has it. Meanwhile, Yaśodharā, who gave birth ten months after her husband's departure, is accused by the king of committing adultery and thrown into a burning pit. The Buddha, by the power of his compassion, turns the burning pit into a pond. Yaśodharā then asks the king for permission to join her husband to practice the Way. Miraculously transforming herself into a man, she obtains the state of an arhat—just like her son, Rāhula. The text ends with the Buddha's awakening, with no mention of Māra's assault. Noticeable here are the Chinese conception of the four evils of existence (including birth) and the Buddhist (and thoroughly sexist) notion of the necessity for a woman to transform herself into a man before reaching salvation. This text already announces the Japanese Lives of the Buddha.

AN ILLUSTRATED LIFE

Artistic representations have greatly contributed to the development of the Buddha legend in East Asia. With the development of printing, illustrated anthologies of the Life of the Buddha were a great success. The best known example is *The Origins of Śākyamuni* (*Shishi yuanliu*), dated 1425, and compiled and illustrated by the Chinese monk Baocheng. It is a compilation made from various sources (no fewer than sixty-five, both canonical and apocryphal). The text consists of 205 (or 208) sections illustrated with short cartouches, ranging from the past lives of the Buddha to his parinirvāṇa and beyond with the sharing of relics and the patriarchal lineage from Mahākāśyapa to the twenty-fourth patriarch, Siṃha.[4] According to the Tiantai school, the patriarchal lineage ended with Siṃha's execution. According to the Chan tradition, it continued until the monk Bodhidharma, the twenty-eighth Indian patriarch and first "Chinese" patriarch. The Life of the Buddha occupies the bulk of the first part, but that part also includes a presentation of the great sūtras and the main doctrines, as well as the patriarchal lineage ending with Bodhidharma, the founder of the Chan school, which forms a transition to the second volume, focusing on the history of Chinese Buddhism. The sequence of events no longer has much to do with the Indian chronology of the Life of the Buddha, who is depicted as an imperial Chinese prince, while the illustrations are often filled with architectural structures, to the detriment of landscapes.[5] The text is governed by a formal constraint: each page contains twelve lines of twenty-four characters each, with the text facing the image. Each event must therefore take place in this specific space. The book opens with the prediction made to Sumedha by the Buddha Dīpankara, and then jumps to the rebirth of the Bodhisattva in Tuṣita Heaven. The description of the birth and youth of the Bodhisattva follows the classical models. The cycle of awakening (which is spread over eight sections) depicts the defeat of Māra, and a number of scenes involve the sons and daughters of Māra. To this, the author has added an unprecedented Indian episode, in which the Buddha challenges Māra to move his water pot and mocks him when he fails. The awakening itself shows the Buddha sitting under his tree in a natural setting composed in accordance with Chinese aesthetics: river, rocks, mushrooms of immortality, constellations.

Unlike Indian sources, most of the text is devoted to the Buddha's teaching, with detailed accounts of various conversions. It is in this area that the work diverges the most from the classical biographies, which often overlooked the preaching period. Here the reader is treated to a wealth of detail from the most diverse sources, often relating to non-events (from a biographical point of view). It is clear, as Foucher noted with regard to Indian sources, that we are dealing with a filling in, and that the chronology of many of these events remains very vague. The text also includes a number of episodes not directly related to the Buddha's life, such as the worship of relics, propitiatory rites, the cleaning of statues on the anniversary of the Buddha's birth (the eighth day of the fourth month), incantations (*dhāranī*) and invocations of the constellation deities, and the preaching of the great Mahāyāna sūtras. The parinirvāṇa cycle roughly follows the canonical tradition while emphasizing the grief of the Buddha's mother. Because of her laments, the Buddha comes back to life for a moment and sits up in his coffin to preach the Law to her one last time. The rest of the book is about the transmission of the Law after the master's death. The last twenty scenes describe the protocol for sharing the relics, the history of the stūpas, the codification—seven days after his disappearance—of the Buddha's sermons, and finally—a typically Chinese innovation—the patriarchal lineage up to the Indian monk Bodhidharma.

Let us note some points of divergence from the Indian Lives of the Buddha. In the illustrated work, the Bodhisattva, "mounted on an elephant, enters the womb" (he is no longer the elephant himself) at the moment of conception. At the time of birth, the child is bathed by nine dragons in contrast to the two jets of water, sprinkled naturally or produced by the two *nāgas* Nanda and Upananda. The importance of the nine dragons theme in China is well known (extending even to the naming of Kowloon, a district of Hong Kong). The scene is repeated when, as a teenager, the prince receives the initiatory anointing (*abhiṣeka*). After that, he goes to see the ploughmen's festival—where his first meditation takes place under the jambu tree. Then we are given a description (although not in so many words and pictures) of his "life in pleasures." The text states that the king his father gave him three thousand wives. However, out of prudishness, no doubt, we only see an aerial view of the palace, without any human presence. But a voice resounds in the sky and tells the prince to put an end to this hedonistic existence.

Among the episodes worth noting for their picturesque or edifying character are the various conversions of low-caste people or outcasts. The sūtra preaching invests the Life of the Buddha with the continuity of his doctrine, with emphasis on the Mahāyāna. Similarly, the mention of eminent Mahāyāna monks such as Vasubandhu (4th–5th cent.) and Bodhidharma, the semi-legendary founder of Chan (Zen), implies that the lives of these figures are, like the Buddha's relics, a posthumous continuation of the Buddha.

This illustrated Life of the Buddha played an important role in the spread of the Buddhist faith, not only in China, but also in Korea, where it is still reprinted periodically,[6] and to a lesser extent in Japan.

12

JAPANESE LIVES

REVIVAL OF THE ŚĀKYAMUNI CULT IN JAPAN

The Life of the Buddha became a significant stake in the rivalries setting the different Japanese Buddhist schools or sects apart, making it necessary to say a few words about them here. During the Heian period (794–1185), two new schools appeared, the Tendai school, founded by Saichō (767–822), and the Shingon school, founded by Kūkai (774–835). The first derived from the Chinese Tiantai school, founded by Zhiyi (538–597), which sought to integrate the doctrines and practices of Indian Buddhism. It is based on the *Lotus Sūtra,* a text in which, it will be remembered, the Buddha Śākyamuni had revealed to his disciples his suprahistorical nature. The Shingon school synthesized the various forms of esoteric Buddhism imported into China by the Indian masters Śubhakarasimha (Ch. Shanwuwei, 637–735), Vajrabodhi (Ch. Jingangzhi, 671–741), and Amoghavajra (Ch. Bukong, 705–774). Shingon esotericism, based on a set of rites concerning the two great mandalas, known as the Womb Realm (Garbhadhātu, J. Taizōkai) and the Diamond Realm (Vajradhātu, J. Kongōkai), strongly marked the society of the Heian period. According to this doctrine, the two mandalas represent complementary aspects of reality, and the universe is none other than the body of the cosmic Buddha Vairocana (J. Dainichi). Ritual identification with it allows one to become a buddha "in this very body" (*sokushin jōbutsu*). The mummification of the school's founder, Kūkai, was explained by this theory, and it became undeniable proof for his disciples of his attainment of buddhahood. Very quickly, under the influence of Shingon, Tendai became tinged with esotericism.

The Kamakura period (1185–1333) saw the addition of three more new schools, those of Zen, Pure Land, and Nichiren. Zen, which takes its name from the practice of sitting meditation, claims to offer direct access to ultimate reality, bypassing ritual (worship of images, etc.) and the study of scripture. Pure Land Buddhism (represented mainly by the Jōdo and Shin sects) is characterized by its devotional attitude, centered on the invocation of the Buddha Amida (Skt. Amitābha). It is based on belief in Amida's vow to lead to his Pure Land in the west all those who have an exclusive faith in him and call his name.

Finally, the Nichiren school, founded by the charismatic monk Nichiren (1222–1282), also relies on the *Lotus Sūtra,* the title of which is recited by practitioners as a kind of mantra.

During the Heian period, the rise of Shingon, centered on the buddha Dainichi, partly eclipsed the popularity of Shaka (Śākyamuni). Interest in Śākyamuni began to revive, however, toward the end of the Heian period. A significant event was the arrival in 985 of the statue of the Buddha allegedly carved for the king Udāyana and brought from China by the monk Chōnen (d. 1016). Enshrined in the Śākyamuni Hall (Shaka-dō) at Seiryōji, a Kyoto monastery, it is in fact a Chinese statue imitating the Indian Gupta style. Because this legendary statue was seen as a double of the Buddha, it was, in principle, an "animated" icon—which perhaps explains why tissue replicas of the main organs of the human body were found inside.[1] Even in Shingon, the Life of the Buddha remained important, but it was reinterpreted in terms borrowed from esoteric Buddhism. For example, we are told that when the Buddha was awakened, two dragons came to bathe him (in the canonical tradition, this event takes place at the time of the Buddha's birth), and that the two dragons are none other than the wisdom kings (*myōō*) Fudō and Aizen, two of the major protective deities of Shingon.

During the Kamakura period, the rival Tendai school also attached great importance to Śākyamuni, but here the emphasis fell on the transcendent Buddha of the *Lotus Sūtra.* The Zen school's two principal variants, called Rinzai and Sōtō, gave a prominent role to Śākyamuni as well, mainly because of the ascetic ideal he still represented. The Nichiren school did the same. The Pure Land school, on the other hand, gave primacy to the buddha Amida.

It is also necessary to mention a singular theory in Japanese Buddhism known under the rubric of "the original nature and its traces" (*honji suijaku*). Initially formulated in esoteric Buddhism, this theory sees in all native Japanese deities, or *kami,* the traces, avatars, or manifestations of metaphysical buddhas and bodhisattvas of Indian origin. Thus, for instance, the sun goddess Amaterasu is said to be the "trace" of the esoteric Buddha Vairocana (J. Dainichi, a name meaning, precisely, Great Sun). Further, the theory also embraced the "historical" or exoteric Buddha Śākyamuni. According to a tradition that was widespread in Japan when Saichō promulgated the Tendai school, Śākyamuni came down to earth in the form of the protective god of Ōmiya Shrine, located at the foot of Mount Hiei and on the border of the ancient province of Ōmi.[2] According to a poem in a Japanese anthology of folk songs from the Heian period, the *Ryōjin hishō:*

> Ōmi's avatar, now that I think of it,
> is Śākyamuni, founder of Buddhism;
> anyone who sets foot on this land, just once,
> would be a companion on Eagle Peak.[3]

But in Tendai there is another deity who is also recognized as an avatar of Śākyamuni. It is the god Jūzenji, represented in the form of a youth (*dōji*) or a young monk. His shrine, adjacent to that of Ōmiya, is known as the Shrine under the Tree (Juge-gū)—the tree in question being the Bodhi tree. In other words, Śākyamuni was awakened under this tree in India during his first descent into this world, while his manifestation "under the tree," in the form of Jūzenji, corresponds to a second descent (unforeseen in Indian tradition), this time to Japan—which thus becomes a sacred land like India.

The Role of Myōe

Perhaps the person who played the greatest role in Śākyamuni's revival in medieval Japan was the priest Myōe (1173–1232), a reformer of the Kegon school, based on the *Avataṃsaka-sūtra* (J. *Kegon-kyō*). Myōe felt intense regret at having been born after the Buddha's parinirvāṇa. In the journal he kept of his dreams, he reports: "One night, I was trying to scrutinize the doctrinal principles (of the *Lotus Sūtra*'s chapter on the Buddha's longevity), and with tears streaming from my eyes, I was overwhelmed by longing for Tathāgata."[4] Myōe dreamed all his life of visiting the places that the Buddha had sanctified with his presence. He actively prepared a plan for a pilgrimage to India in 1202 but had to give it up after receiving an oracle from the deity of Kasuga Shrine, a deity identified with the Buddha Śākyamuni.[5]

For Myōe, Śākyamuni evoked the image of the father. He once addressed a letter he wrote: "To the august precious presence, great saint and compassionate father, the Tathāgata Śākyamuni, Kōben, your beloved son of the posthumous law."[6] Like Śākyamuni pursuing ascetic practice in the wilderness, Myōe decided to test himself, at the age of thirteen, by spending a whole night alone in a cemetery littered with corpses, waiting for the wolves to come and devour him.[7] From then on, every year, on the fifteenth of the second month, Myōe commemorated Śākyamuni's extinction with a ceremony in a setting that evoked the site of the awakening. Before the assembly, he would recite the Buddha's name under a tree, in front of which he had raised a seat of piled stones and a stūpa bearing the inscription: "Homage to the jeweled stūpa of the realization of awakening under the Bodhi tree, near the city of Bodh Gaya in the country of Magadha." By staging the Buddha's absence, he was paradoxically trying to recreate a semblance of presence. At Toganoo, at the foot of Mount Ryōga (the Japanese transcription of Lanka, an allusion to the island of Ceylon, where the *Laṅkāvatāra-sūtra* had supposedly been preached), Myōe reconstituted a number of Indian holy places. For example, the Zenga-in Pavilion, whose name derives from the Nairañjanā River, near the place of the awakening; and the Cave of Buddha's Vestiges, where Myōe practiced meditation in front of a rock bearing the footprints of the Buddha. During an assembly, while he was reciting the Law, he was so moved that he began to tremble and let out a loud cry. His voice and breathing stopped, and all the participants wondered if he was dead. He later explained to his disciples: "The ancient pain [of the Buddha] is my pain, the emotion [he felt] in the past is mine. Although we are two thousand years apart [from this event], it is as if I am now experiencing it intimately."[8]

The liturgical manual compiled by Myōe pays special attention to the emotional and soteriological aspects of the parinirvāṇa assembly, such as "the manifestation of pain at the moment of the Buddha's extinction, the cremation, the karmic link formed at the time of the parinirvāṇa, and the celebration of the Buddha's vow to save all beings." It also lists the many miraculous events that accompanied the Buddha's extinction. At the end of his life, Myōe staged his own death as a replica of the parinirvāṇa. Having vowed to be reborn in Tuṣita Heaven, he lay down on his right side and died.[9] Myōe's case may seem extreme, but it reflects the impact that the parinirvāṇa story had on the medieval Buddhist imaginary.

TEXTUAL SOURCES

I have already mentioned, with regard to this or that episode in the Indian Life of the Buddha, the Chinese or Japanese variants that seemed to signify the altered cultural environments to which Buddhism adapted. Here I would like to explore in greater detail the specificity of the Japanese tradition. Before doing so, it is probably necessary to say a few words about the hagiographic and pictorial tradition of the eight major events or acts (J. *hassō*) in the Life of the Buddha, because it is this tradition that inspires the title of several Japanese Lives. Originally, the eight acts seem to have been associated with eight Indian holy places marked by stūpas. However, a different list of acts spread in East Asia with the rise of Mahāyāna. This list had its origin in two Chinese works, the *Treatise on the Awakening of Faith according to the Great Vehicle* (*Dasheng qixin lun*), an apocryphal text supposedly translated from Sanskrit by the Indian monk Paramārtha (499–569), and the *Commentary on the Four Teachings* (*Sijiao yi*) by Zhiyi (538–597), founder of the Tiantai school (known in Japan as Tendai). In India, emphasis had been placed on the post-awakening period, whereas it is the youth of the Buddha that was emphasized in China and the Sinicized countries in East Asia. The eight acts in question are in fact cycles rather than one-off events, namely: (1) the descent from Tuṣita Heaven; (2) the entry into the womb; (3) the birth; (4) leaving the family (also known as the great departure); (5) the victory over Māra; (6) the awakening; (7) the first sermon; and (8) the parinirvāṇa. To the four acts of the Indian tradition were thus added the two moments of conception (the descent from Tuṣita Heaven, a.k.a. the dream of Māyā, and the entry into the womb), the great departure, and the victory over Māra.

The Life of the Buddha is recounted in numerous collections of Japanese Buddhist legends from the Heian period on. Early Japanese accounts, however, still follow quite closely the conventional Life of the Buddha from India and do not yet constitute independent biographies. The sources used were Chinese, and they were illustrated tales. One of the most famous, the *Illustrated Sūtra of Past and Present Karma (Kako genzai e-inga kyō*, also called *e-ingakyō*), dates from the Nara period (8th cent.). It consists of eight painted scrolls created by adding illustrations to the *Sūtra of Past and Present Karma* (translated into Chinese in the mid-fifth century. It is one of the oldest illustrated scrolls (*emaki*) known. (A later version of the same scroll from the Kamakura period is reproduced in plate 3.)

Later collections from the Heian period do not always show great originality, much less individualized form. Some are written in *kana* (a syllabary associated with the feminine script) as opposed to the Chinese characters generally used for Buddhist doctrinal texts, which were reserved for a male audience. As is well known, the most famous text written in *kana,* attributed to a lady of the court, Murasaki Shikibu, is the famous *Tale of Genji,* whose hero, Prince Genji, is reminiscent of Prince Siddhārtha—albeit a Siddhārtha who would not have renounced the world (or women in particular).

During this period, the Life of the Buddha was still an important part of large anthologies of moral tales, such as the *Record of Miraculous Events in Japan* (*Nihon ryōiki,* 9th cent.). During the Kamakura period, the *Tales of Times Now Past* (*Konjaku monogatarishū*) was a vast collection that still belonged to this literary genre. Now, however, anonymous collections of stories such as the *otogizōshi* began to appear in the circles frequented by popular preachers. This new trend allowed much more freedom to the imagination. Through these collections, the Life of the Buddha gradually departed from the canonical tradition. "The story of a young prince living in ancient India who set out to defeat rebirth in samsara, a story told over so many centuries in so many places," Hank Glassman notes, "is here shaped to the narrative logic of the late medieval Japanese imagination and tuned to the local conventions of emotional response."[10] Despite monastic attempts to return to orthodoxy, the evolution in the Life of the Buddha continued beyond the medieval and well into the Edo period (1600–1868).

Among the innovations coming to the fore is the role played by the theme of the mother's salvation. Although this theme was already present in canonical biographies of the Buddha and those of eminent Chinese monks, it took on central importance in Japan. In the majority of cases, the point at issue is the motivation that drives a person to renounce the world. Buddhism, seeking to appropriate the Chinese notion of filial piety, endeavored to reinterpret this renunciation as a paradoxical way of effecting the salvation of one's parents.

Another difference from the canonical biographies is that the Bodhisattva does not decide to renounce the world following the four encounters. Instead, while in the Spring Garden, he realizes that all beings around him have parents, whereas he alone is an orphan. In a way that reflects the aesthetic vision and sentiments of Japanese culture, it is in the magnificent setting of nature in bloom that the young Bodhisattva becomes aware of the evanescence of all things and the presence of death in this garden—as in Poussin's famous painting *Et in Arcadia ego.* He then asks his adoptive mother Mahāprajāpatī about this, and she reveals the secret associated with his birth that had been carefully guarded until now: it is the premature death of Māyā, only seven days after his birth. Aware of the "wind of impermanence," the young Bodhisattva resolves to be awakened in order to save his dead mother.[11]

Another innovation in the Japanese retelling is the heartbreak caused by the separation of the Bodhisattva from his young wife, Yaśodharā. This theme is not ignored in Chinese biographies—in the Dunhuang *bianwen,* for instance—but it is revisited with particular intensity in the Japanese account. In most Indian sources, Siddhārtha simply disappears without taking leave of Yaśodharā. In Japanese sources, he tries to leave without seeing her again, but then, gripped by love and remorse, he returns and—in a typically Japanese detail—exchanges poems with her under the moon. The *Kakuzenshō,* a ritual collection compiled by the monk Kakuzen (1143–ca. 1213), mentions a significant detail: at the time of the great departure, when everyone is sleeping in the palace, Yaśodharā makes "balls of bliss" (*kangidan*) and offers them to the man of her life.[12] The *Kakuzenshō,* although a monastic work, thus echoes popular sentiment by dwelling on the drama of separation.

The theme of Śākyamuni's asceticism reveals another distinctly Japanese trait. In Indian sources, his ascetic practice takes place in the forest, near the present Bodh Gaya, whereas in Chinese and late Japanese sources, it takes place in the mountains, either in the Himalayas or on Mount Dantoku (Skt. Dantaloka, north of present Pakistan). It is especially in the Chan (Zen) sect, transmitted to Japan at the end of the twelfth century, that Mount Dantoku became the prime location of Śākyamuni's ascetic feats (and awakening). This theme is found in virtually all Japanese Lives of the Buddha after the twelfth century, and it is also the theme that inspired the image, widespread in Zen, of "Śākyamuni emerging from the mountains" at the end of his ascetic retreat. It can also be found in the songs of the aforementioned *Ryōjin hishō* (12th cent.):

> On his journey
> the prince rode the steed Kaṇṭhaka;
> his valet, Chandaka, held the bridle
> on the way to Mount Dantaloka.[13]

Or again:

> Even Prince Siddhārtha, son of the king of Magadha,
> endured six years of austerity
> in the depths of Mount Dantaloka.[14]

The kingdom of Kapilavastu is here confused with Magadha, and Śākyamuni becomes the son of King Bimbisāra. More important, there seems to have been a confusion between the present life of the Bodhisattva and his earlier existence as Prince Vessantara. It is indeed the latter, banished from the kingdom for his excessive generosity, who had taken refuge with his wife and two children on Mount Dantaloka.[15]

These examples provide a first glimpse of the evolution of the Buddha's Life in Japan. To follow more closely how these themes appear and, once asserted in the Japanese imaginaire, take more and more freedom with the canonical and post-canonical traditions, we must quickly review, in roughly chronological order, the main sources.

The Eight Acts of Śākyamuni

According to its preface, *The Eight Acts of Śākyamuni* (*Shaka hassō*), a book attributed to Zen master Eisai (var. Yōsai, 1141–1215), is supposed to date from 1191, the year that Eisai returned to Japan from China.[16] In fact, it is probably later, but in any case earlier than 1273, the date that appears on one of the copies. In it, the author criticizes the Tendai theory concerning the five periods of the Buddha's teaching, which was in vogue at the time and seems to belong to the Pure Land school. The preface states that while the Buddha is in reality eternal, he manifested the eight acts as a skillful means to save beings. It dates the parinirvāṇa according to the Chinese count, stating that 2,140 years have elapsed between that event and the year of the writing of the preface. This would yield the same date, 949 BCE, attested in other Chinese and Japanese sources.

The description of the main events of the Buddha's Life proceeds roughly in accordance with Indian tradition. Note, however, that the four encounters precede Siddhārtha's marriage, the competition with Devadatta comes to the forefront, and the martial skill of the Bodhisattva is blown out of proportion. In the warlike society of medieval Japan, this profane aspect is somehow sacralized. The book has a critical and didactic aspect, and it is relatively discreet about the miracles attributed to the Buddha (with one exception, the conversion of the Brahmin Kāśyapa of Uruvilva). It is largely a factual and demythologizing version of the Buddha's Life, attributed to Eisai, a representative of a school, Chan (Zen), known for its down-to-earth teaching. The work is also characterized by a moralizing tone and numerous references to the scriptures. It ends by reiterating that the eight acts are only skillful means for the salvation of beings, and that the Buddha or awakening is immanent in the mind of humans, even if they cannot see it because of their karmic obstacles. One must therefore contemplate the mind rather than seek happiness in this world. The work certainly lacks originality from a narrative point of view, but it is representative of a persistent tendency, which will form like a counterpoint to the increasingly imaginative medieval Lives of the Buddha.

The Chronicle of Śākyamuni's Apparition in the World

The Chronicle of Śākyamuni's Apparition in the World (*Shaka shusse honkai denki*), an anonymous work dated 1226, is the first independent Japanese biography of the Buddha. Here the Life of the Buddha is reinterpreted in the light of esoteric Buddhism: King Śuddhodana thus becomes an avatar of the Buddha Dainichi (Vairocana) of the Diamond Realm, while his brothers are manifestations of King Māra of the Sixth Heaven, the buddhas of the three periods, and the illusions of all beings, respectively, in an application of the *honji suijaku* (original nature and traces) theory. As in the previous text, the events in the Life of the Buddha are dated according to a chronology based on Chinese eras.

In what will come to be characteristic of the Japanese Lives of the Buddha, the career of the Bodhisattva begins with one of his earlier existences, the *Jātaka* of the Youth of the Snowy Mountains (Sessen dōji)—a young Brahmin who is practicing on the slopes of the Himalayas when he hears a demon reciting the first line of a Buddhist stanza, and is willing to sacrifice his life to hear the second.[17] We then move directly to the last human rebirth of the Bodhisattva. The episode of his descent into the maternal womb contains an interesting detail, but one that will not be retained in later retellings: he descends from Tuṣita Heaven on the back of a bird, not an elephant, to enter the right side of Māyā. Another significant detail, which will be repeated in later works: the Bodhisattva is just seven years old when he vows to leave the palace, because the sight of birds brooding in their nests has led him to wonder about his absent mother and to discover her premature death. It is also at this time, rather than after his birth, that the prediction of his glorious destiny takes place. After this event, the prince's childhood proceeds normally. The four encounters, which have largely become superfluous from a narrative point of view, still take place in the parks of the four seasons, which are described in a highly aesthetic Japanese way. At thirteen, the Bodhisattva tells his father of his desire to leave the palace, but the father refuses to let him go and locks him in a metal citadel guarded by four thousand men. At nineteen, the Bodhisattva renounces the world. Before leaving, he goes to Yaśodharā and announces his intention. As the moon appears in the sky, the two spouses exchange vows in the form of thirty-one-syllable Japanese poems (*waka*). The Bodhisattva feels his resolve weakening, and it is only with great difficulty that he succeeds in tearing himself away from the sweetness of conjugal love.

Śākyamuni then departs for ascetic practice on Mount Dantoku (Dantaloka), where a hermit—actually a manifestation of the buddha Daijizaiō, the teacher of the Buddha Amida—has lived for eighty thousand years. The hermit gives him the novice name Kudon (Gotama), and under his severe supervision, Kudon practices asceticism for twelve years (a duration, twice that of the canonical sources, which matches precisely the time that Tendai monks were committed to spend on Mount Hiei). At the end of this period, his master gives him his spiritual seal—in this case, a text, the *Lotus Sūtra*—and tells him to go to the seat of awakening on Mount Kaya, in the kingdom of Magadha, to preach the Law. As he takes his leave, the Bodhisattva—decidedly very Japanese—recites a poem. Along the way, a youth appears out of nowhere to guide him to his destination. After triumphing over various obstacles caused by Māra and his troupe, the Bodhisattva is awakened at the age of thirty.

In summary, this Japanese Life of the Buddha, while following in broad outline the traditional career of the Indian Bodhisattva, has been adapted to Japanese taste, with particular emphasis on poetic and aesthetic description. On the doctrinal level, although the terminology of esoteric Buddhism seems to serve as an underpinning, it shows a strong influence from the Zen (with its detailed description of asceticism) and Pure Land (with its reference to the Buddha Amida as the ultimate guide) schools. These influences will also be found in the next text.

The Origins of Śākyamuni

Despite its title, *The Origins of Śākyamuni* (*Shaka no honji*), dated 1256, is in fact an apologia for the Buddha Amida, Śākyamuni's main rival in Japanese medieval piety. The work is traditional in its structure, since we find in it—with a few variations—the sequence of the eight acts. However, it takes up and develops some of the innovations of its predecessors, and also reads the events of the Buddha's Life through a Japanese prism. It constitutes both a culmination of the canonical tradition and a new literary departure. As such, it is undoubtedly the most important text in vernacular literature and deserving of a little more attention—all the more so since it has recently been the subject of a superb publication in French.[18]

Its atmosphere is typically that of medieval Japan, and its style is marked by the literary topoi of the time. The character of Siddhārtha is reminiscent in some ways of Prince Genji, the main protagonist of the *Tale of Genji*. Also typical is the theme of the evanescence of things, which had become a cliché in medieval Japan. Another significant detail is the use of Japanese era names, although the story clearly takes place in an Indian setting. This imaginary India is in a way an Other World. But the narrators (and after them the illustrators of the story), when they try to make it exotic, cannot detach themselves from their Chinese and Japanese models.

The plot is basically the same as that of the *Chronicle of Śākyamuni's Apparition in the World,* but each episode is much more developed. The text also opens with the *Jātaka* of the Youth of the Snowy Mountains; then it shifts directly to Śākyamuni's birth. The conception—with the dream of the white elephant penetrating Māyā's side—is passed over in silence. Seven days after his birth (that is, on the very day of his mother's death), the child takes seven steps and then turns west—a detail that alludes to a belief in Amida's Pure Land. In this text again, his spiritual quest is motivated by a desire to save his deceased mother, realized, at the age of seven, through a precocious grasp of the evanescence of all things.[19] The four encounters take place more or less on schedule, but the narrative thread is interrupted by long didactic tirades that reflect popular preaching styles. We then learn that the prince's marriage to Yaśodharā was arranged immediately following these events, as he is not yet thirteen years old, to console him for his discovery of the harsh realities of existence. Previously, he had defeated his cousin Devadatta, one of his rivals for the hand of Yaśodharā, in a series of jousting matches. This scene is considerably simplified, and only the archery contest, very much to the taste of the Japanese of the time, is described in great detail.

The tender feelings that Yaśodharā inspires in him do not divert the Bodhisattva from his resolution—even if the text underlines its difficulty—since he departs only six years later, at the age of nineteen. Before leaving the palace, he comes to take his leave of Yaśodharā. The scene is charged with a specifically Japanese pathos: we are told, for instance, that he "drenches his sleeves with tears." This is a far cry from the coldness of the Indian Bodhisattva.

On his way to Mount Dantoku, demons try to stop him, but he disperses them with magic formulas (another novelty, well in line with esoteric Buddhism). Reaching the mountain, he sends back his squire and his horse, a separation that also gives rise to sentimental outpourings. He then meets a hermit named Ārāda Kālāma, who turns out to be a manifestation of the bodhisattva Kannon (Avalokiteśvara) and claims to have spent eighty-four thousand kalpas on this mountain. Under his direction, the Bodhisattva practices asceticism for twelve years, during which he is constantly insulted and beaten up, in the best Zen tradition of "shoutings and beatings." Thus, the tuft of white hair between his eyebrows (*ūrṇā*), one of the thirty-two marks of the Buddha, is said to have been caused by beatings (fig. 15). At the end of the twelve years, the hermit judges him worthy of receiving initiation, and he gives him a tiger skin robe, as well as the *Lotus Sūtra,* insisting on the fact that all the buddhas have awakened because of this marvelous text, which, as we recall, was the scriptural authority of the Tendai school.[20] He also transmits to him one of the major texts of Amidism, the *Sūtra on the Contemplation* [*of the Buddha*] *Amitayus* (J. *Kanmuryōju kyō*), and reveals to him the supreme arcana—the three syllables of Amida's name. Although Śākyamuni has now attained "perfect" awakening, a supplement still seems required, since his master then sends him to Gāya to preach the Law and receive a second initiation in anticipation of a new perfect awakening. This is an obvious anachronism, resulting from the fact that this text, unlike the Indian sources, seeks to revalue asceticism—as reviewed and updated by Zen.

A youth then guides the Bodhisattva to the rock where all the buddhas have been awakened, which Māra and his troupe are trying in vain to destroy. The youth reveals to him that this rock, a true *omphalos,* is unshakeable, for it

FIGURE 15. Śākyamuni beaten by his master. From *The Life of Shakyamuni Illustrated,* by Katsushika Hokusai. 1845. Japan. Woodblock printed book, ink on paper. Metropolitan Museum of Art (2013.736a–f).

reaches beyond the underworld to the ultimate base of the world. The rock stands in for or replaces the Bodhi tree, and the sacredness of the place now seems to take precedence over the meditative practice that, in the Indian tradition, was the direct cause of awakening.[21] The author then takes the opportunity to give a detailed description of esoteric cosmology. When the divine youth takes his leave upon returning to the Pure Land, he reveals that he too is a manifestation of the bodhisattva Kannon. As can be seen, the earth goddess is no longer mentioned, another departure from the canonical version.

The episode of the Buddha's return to Kapilavastu also presents significant variations, which reinforce the Amidist character of the text. For example, when the king asks him how to escape the cycle of life and death (*saṃsāra*), the Buddha recommends that he recite the three syllables of the name Amida. He then preaches the *Sūtra on the Perfection of Wisdom* and the *Lotus Sūtra,* to adapt, we are told, to the faculties of beings. But the author, having made this concession, feels obliged to add: "That being said, there is nothing to be understood apart from the sacred name of Amida."

Similarly, when the Buddha ascends to Trāyastriṃśa Heaven to preach the Law to his mother, Māyā does not recognize him at first among his disciples. He then suggests that she squeeze her breasts; the milk that spurts out of them goes straight into his mouth, attesting to his filiation. Unfortunately, Buddhist iconography did not represent this episode, as Christian iconography was pleased to represent the Virgin's *lactatio.* The Buddha then preaches the law of impermanence to his mother. But the author, once again, intervenes and inserts in this sermon the thirtieth vow of the Buddha Amida regarding the deliverance of women.

We can see that, at each detour in the story, the author paradoxically puts Amida before Śākyamuni: we might wonder if this is a simple syncretism on his part or rather an attempt at subversion for the benefit of the Pure Land school, to which he obviously belongs. The *Origins of Śākyamuni* thus seems to relativize the importance of Śākyamuni. This tendency, already present in certain Mahāyāna currents, is further accentuated in the theatrical adaptations of the text.

The *Origins* story seems to have been widely known in the Edo period. Its main influence was on the puppet theater (*bunraku*) tradition. While the canonical tradition agreed in describing the auspicious and easy nature of the birth of the Buddha, while noting that his mother, like those of all buddhas, died seven days later, the *bunraku* version is much more realistic. It tells us, for example, that Queen Māyā's waters broke when she tried to pick a flower from a tree in the Lumbinī park: her right flank tore apart and she fell to the ground, writhing in pain. It is this "tearing," from which the child is born, that killed her. The canonical tradition had done its best to quash the suspicion that the Bodhisattva was responsible for his mother's death. Here his guilt is exposed in no uncertain terms.

The *bunraku* version, moreover, emphasizes the ridiculous rather than sublime character of the Bodhisattva at the moment of his awakening. After making a grass seat for himself, he remains immersed in meditation for six years. At the end of this time, during the fifteenth night of the tenth month, he sees the star Venus rising in the sky, and under the effect of this vision he acquires a buddha body. But he has remained motionless for so long that his legs are entirely numb and he does not know what to do. The hermit tells him that he has awakened and prostrates himself in front of him. Then, realizing that the newly awakened one has difficulty moving, he gives him a cane made from the wood of the Bodhi tree. Before taking his leave, he reveals to him that he is the spirit of the *Lotus Sūtra.*[22] In this version, the Bodhisattva apparently does not realize that he has awakened and cannot even get up until his master gives him a cane. The comic nature of the scene, and its devaluation of the Buddha, is characteristic of the parodic literary genre that developed in medieval Japan.

When the Buddha returns to Kapilavastu for a second time, to the bedside of his dying father, his sermon—very different from those of the Indian legend—seems to be inspired by the ideas of Shinran (1173–1262), one of the founders of Pure Land Buddhism. He explains to his father that bad karma is like a forest of poisonous trees, whose very smell is so harmful that those who breathe it in die. But in this forest is also a wonderful tree, whose fragrance fills the air and transforms the forest. Likewise, he says, a single recitation of the name of the Buddha Amida can annihilate a vast amount of bad karma and lead to salvation.

We find the same tendency in the Buddha's sermon to his mother. After spending three months with her in Trāyastriṃśa Heaven, the Buddha explains that he must return to earth. When Māyā bursts into tears at this news, he tells her: "If you make a copy of my appearance and recite the name [of the Buddha] Amida morning and evening, you will surely be reborn in the Pure Land." Śakra (Indra), the king of the gods who has become Māyā's husband, summons the divine craftsman Viśvakarman to make a replica of the Buddha's appearance. All those who venerate the image, starting with the royal couple, will be reborn in the Pure Land.[23]

The Story of Śākyamuni's Eight Acts

The Story of Śākyamuni's Eight Acts (*Shaka hassō monogatari*) is a late work, dated 1666. It was republished several times during the Edo period, and its popularity probably explains why it was translated into English as early as the late nineteenth century by the English missionary John Laidlaw Atkinson (1842–1908). It presents some interesting ideas, although much of its material is derived from *The Origins of Śākyamuni*. This text marks a new phase in the development of the Japanese Life of the Buddha, which has now completely detached itself from canonical sources. Until this point, in spite of literary and pictorial innovations, the Lives of the Buddha had remained part of a traditional narrative framework even if they sometimes rendered it according to interpretive schemes specific to certain currents of Japanese Buddhism (notably the Tendai school). Here we are on a very different terrain.

The Bodhisattva is born as a prince of the kingdom of Magadha, one of the five great kingdoms of India (not the small kingdom of Kapilavastu). The preamble tells us in detail the story of King Śuddhodana's accession to the throne. At the moment of the prince's conception, Māyā sees in a dream a large golden stūpa, whose doors open to reveal the Bodhisattva on a white elephant.[24] He declares to Māyā that he would like to "borrow her womb" to be reborn and save all beings. She objects that she is unworthy of such an honor, being subject to the constraints of her sex. He then explains to her that she was a princess in a previous existence and was unjustly exiled because of a wicked mother-in-law (a theme that we find again later). However, for copying the *Blood Bowl Sūtra* a thousand times, and reciting it ten thousand times, she was given the great honor of being reborn to her present rank. Purified by this act, she is now worthy to welcome the Bodhisattva into her. The reference here to an apocryphal and typically misogynistic sūtra is another characteristic trait. This text has in fact contributed to the belittlement of Japanese women by attributing to them an impurity due to their menstrual blood, and by condemning them to a particular hell, where they would drown endlessly in a pool of blood—unless they obtain the merits accrued through the recitation of this sūtra by monks. The fact that Māyā was able, without the mediation of the monks, to transmute her feminine impurity into supreme purity attests to the power of the sūtra.

This version of the Bodhisattva's birth turns it into a family drama, centered on the fatal rivalry between the two sisters, Māyā, the Bodhisattva's mother, and Mahāprajāpatī, his aunt and adoptive mother, here called Kyodomi (Gautamī), as in the *Origin Story*. The two sisters share King Śuddhodana's bed. The motif of Gautamī's jealousy seems to have been already widespread by medieval times, but here it takes on a new importance due to its literary treatment. The king is delighted with the annunciation to Māyā (by the Bodhisattva riding an elephant, in lieu of the archangel Gabriel), but at the same time Gautamī sees her chances of becoming queen compromised. She calls her confidant, General Ba, and threatens to kill herself and return to haunt Māyā and the child she is carrying. The general dissuades her and orders two mountain ascetics versed in black magic to bewitch Māyā. They make an image of the latter and perform a rite to kill her. The image comes to life and begs for mercy, but Gautamī will not listen. Māyā sinks into despair, although the court doctors try to reassure her. Her condition continues to worsen for two years. Finally, the Bodhisattva appears to her in a dream and reveals the cause of her affliction. He adds that he could very well be born now, but that he prefers to wait so as not to increase Gautamī's hatred and her karmic retribution. He therefore asks Māyā to be patient. Then, in a very strange passage, he grabs her breasts, spreads them apart, and magically penetrates her (frontally this time, and not by the right side). He returns to the maternal womb, which then takes on the appearance of a transparent and luminous jewel.[25] Māyā wakes up, comforted by this vision. She remains pregnant for three years. Her ordeal ends when she learns that the king is going to offer a party in her honor in the park of Lumbinī. She is delighted, and everyone is surprised to see her so radiant. Gautamī herself repents, and this repentance will save her. As Māyā approaches a tree, which hasn't bloomed for three years, it suddenly blooms. At the same time, Māyā's labor begins. The Bodhisattva then speaks to her from within the womb, a golden light illuminates the sky, and the child suddenly comes out from her right side. He takes seven steps, as in the canonical legend, and then he grabs Māyā's breasts, as in her dream, and begins to suckle her. But Māyā has fallen into a deep sleep from which she will not wake up, and the story continues without her.

Even after repenting, Gautamī behaves like an evil mother-in-law to Yaśodharā both during and after Yaśodharā's pregnancy. At the time of the great departure, Śākyamuni asks Yaśodharā for help. She responds by locking the women in the gynaeceum and taking him to the stable, where his squire and his horse are waiting for him. Here Yaśodhara fulfills the role played by the gods in the Indian Life of the Buddha. When the Buddha returns to

Kapilavastu, his son Rāhula offers him, not an aphrodisiac cake prepared by Yaśodharā to seduce him—as in the canonical legend—but the sleeve of his garment, which he had left as a souvenir for Yaśodharā in the elegant tradition of the Japanese court. The honor of becoming the first Buddhist nun also belongs to Yaśodharā, and not to Gautamī. In these details one sees all the importance invested in the relations between the two spouses.

But let us return to the ascetic phase that precedes the awakening. Śākyamuni first becomes the disciple of the hermit Arara (Ārāḍa) on Mount Dantoku. He practices asceticism for three years and studies the three mysteries of Shingon esotericism. Ārāḍa is a harsh master who pounds Śākyamuni with blows, sometimes to the point of making him lose consciousness—and even killing him and then bringing him back to life with his magical powers. Each time, Śākyamuni moves one step forward on the path of initiation. He then goes on to study with two even more demanding masters and spends three years with each of them. His period of asceticism thus lasts a total of nine years, and not six as in the Indian legend. His third master transmits to him the "verse on impermanence" from the *Jātaka* of the Youth of the Snowy Mountains, and it is this verse that serves as a catalyst for his awakening. Through all this, the transmission of the *Lotus Sūtra* is passed over in silence, as is Māra's assault.

The next section is devoted to the Buddha's teaching, which is divided between the doctrines of Tendai and Zen.[26] If, as we have seen, the Tendai school took the *Lotus Sūtra* as its scriptural authority, the Zen school advocated a "special transmission outside the scriptures" (*kyōge betsuden*) and insisted on a rigorous practice of meditation. The Buddha's first sermon takes place, not on Vulture Peak, as in the other Lives of the Buddha, but at the Jetavana monastery in the city of Śrāvastī, shortly before the Buddha enters parinirvāṇa. This is followed by the story, well known in the Zen tradition, of the transmission of the Law to Mahākāśyapa. The Buddha ascends to the pulpit and holds a flower in his raised hand. While all the monks prostrate themselves, Mahākāśyapa stands up and leaves. The Buddha calls him back, and handing him the flower, declares that he transmits to him the "merit of Mahāyāna." In the Zen version, often quoted by the monk Dōgen (1200–1253), the other monks are perplexed by the raised flower, and Mahākāśyapa alone smiles—to which the Buddha says: "I possess the eye of the Dharma of the true Law (*shōbō genzō*) and now pass it on to Mahākāśyapa." But this text, unlike the Zen version, ignores the mind-to-mind transmission that became one of the characteristic ingredients of the Zen tradition.

Like the *Origins of Śākyamuni*, *Śākyamuni's Eight Acts* was a great success in Japanese theatrical circles until the end of the Edo period, and it was mainly through this medium that it spread to the public (see plate 9).[27] The main instrument of this success was Chikamatsu Monzaemon (1653–1725), the great *bunraku* playwright, who in 1685 adapted the Life of the Buddha in a play entitled "The Assembly for the Birth of the Buddha Śākyamuni" (*Shaka nyorai tanjō-e*). The popularity of the play was such that it was performed again two centuries later, in 1922. It rehearses familiar (and familial) themes, such as Gautamī's jealousy toward her sister Māyā; the important role played by the faithful servant Udāyin and his wife Kichijō; and the harsh trials to which the ascetic Arāda Kālāma subjects Śākyamuni.[28] While drawing on some of the motifs from the *Eight Acts,* Chikamatsu adds his own inventions to appeal to his urban audience. He insists on values such as self-sacrifice and honesty, but especially on the battle scenes. We see Devadatta joining forces with Gautamī to eliminate Māyā, who dies at the birth of the Bodhisattva. The infamous Gautamī goes so far as to accuse Śākyamuni of having killed his own mother by choosing an unnatural way to be born: "Humans and animals both have just one gate from which to emerge into the world. To fail to take that route and to be born rending apart his mother's side . . . is first among the Five Heinous Crimes. Could we possibly elevate him to the rank of King of the Five Regions of India? I have made Devadatta my adopted son. That newborn might be my nephew, but he is a foe of my sister's."[29] Then, turning to General Ba, her damned soul, she orders him to strangle the newborn baby. Fortunately, Udāyin and Kichijō manage to prevent the crime.

The awakening episode, in particular, is highly developed, and it crowns the Bodhisattva's asceticism. Under the blows of his master, the Bodhisattva has entered into a deep concentration. When he emerges from it, he secludes himself in a cave, above which stands the Bodhi tree. The hermit then prostrates himself before him and reveals to him that he is in reality a manifestation of the Buddha of the *Lotus Sūtra.* Yaśodharā and Udāyin, who have witnessed the scene, prostrate themselves in turn before the cave, whose door opens to reveal the Buddha in all his splendor. Here the text uses the same expression (*ara omoshiro ya*) employed in classical Japanese mythology when the sun goddess Amaterasu, after locking herself up in the celestial cave, reappears before the assembly of the gods. Thus Chikamatsu fuses in a single climactic scene the Life of the Buddha and the myth of Amaterasu. Senart, for whom the Buddha was a solar hero, would have appreciated a motif that identifies the awakening of the Buddha with the return of the sun at the end of a long night of ignorance.

Toward the end of the Edo period, *Śākyamuni's Eight Acts* gave rise to a number of commercial versions, published in the form of illustrated booklets. The best known and longest, at fifty-eight chapters, is undoubtedly *Śākyamuni's Eight Acts, Yamato Library* (*Shaka hassō Yamato bunko,* 1845) from Ōga Mantei (1818–1890), a true cloak-and-dagger novel that is more reminiscent of the works of Alexander Dumas than of Indian or Western biographies of the Buddha. The master and his disciples are depicted almost identically, so much so that the reader can only distinguish them by the first ideogram of their names, inscribed on their sumptuous robes. The Buddha, with his long hair floating on the nape of his neck and his scepter (the symbol of authority of the Chinese masters), more resembles Prince Genji or Ariwara no Narihira (825–880), the Japanese Don Juan, than an Indian ascetic. With the exception of his ascetic period, the environment in which he evolves is that of the Japanese imperial court in medieval times. Oga Mantei's parodic work spawned other romanticized lives of the Buddha such as *Shaka's True Record, or The Origin of the Eight Schools* (*Hasshū kigen Shaka jitsuroku*) by Umebori Kokuga (1828–1886), and it was even subjected to a pornographic adaptation, published in 1860.

Since we have already mentioned the importance of illustrated texts, let us now turn to iconographic sources—and in particular to a widespread iconographic theme, the parinirvāṇa or final extinction. The transformation of the Buddha from a sacred figure in the Kamakura period to an almost caricatural character in the Edo period can indeed be observed in the evolution of this a priori tragic theme.

13

THE ILLUSTRATED NIRVĀṆA

With the revival of the cult of Śākyamuni during the Kamakura period (1185–1333), illustrations of the Buddha's Life (*butsuden-zu*), and especially the illustration of nirvāṇa (*nehan-zu*), became increasingly popular. As early as the end of the tenth century, Genshin (942–1017), a monk of the Tendai school and a proponent of Amidist devotion, composed a liturgical manual with instructions for the annual commemoration of the parinirvāṇa (*nehan kōshiki*), to be held in conjunction with Amida-oriented ceremonies. This commemoration, traditionally set for the fifteenth of the second lunar month, was based on the canonical narrative of the parinirvāṇa, as described in the *Mahāparinirvāṇa-sūtra,* and painted scrolls depicting the event were to be hung in the central hall of the temple during the ceremony. About forty copies of this manual remain today.[1]

In the *Mahāparinirvāṇa-sūtra* as well as in the resulting paintings, the number of mourning figures depicted around the Buddha (including his mother, Māyā) was set at fifty-two, and this also became the number of offerings performed during the parinirvāṇa ceremony. As we have seen, the ceremony took on an increasingly theatrical turn, especially after the monk Myōe (1173–1232) established his own liturgical rules for its observance in 1215.[2] Myōe's conception was more faithful to the details of the sūtra and differs on certain points from that of Genshin, who saw the cult of Śākyamuni as little more than an adjunct to the worship of Amida and the *Lotus Sūtra.* As is well known, Myōe even addressed a petition to the throne to denounce Hōnen (1133–1212) and the errors of the new Pure Land school, heirs to the cult of Amida advocated by Genshin.

NEW REPRESENTATIONS OF THE PARINIRVĀṆA

Traditional images of the parnirvāṇa show the Buddha lying on his right side, his head resting on his right hand. Representations of this scene can vary in size, from very small to colossal. Celebrated examples of the latter have been found in India, Sri Lanka, and at numerous sites in Southeast Asia and China, where the theme is popularly known as the Sleeping Buddha—the reference to nirvāṇa being thus euphemized. Let us note in passing that one of these representations was erected in the twentieth century on the archaeological site of the ancient city of Kuśinagara (Kushinagar, in present-day Uttar Pradesh), where the parinirvāṇa is said to have taken place. As icons, statues and paintings implied the real presence of the Buddha himself, at the center of the ceremony. Toward the eleventh century, paintings began to take precedence over statues in depicting the event, and they inherited the continental tradition, remaining close to the sculpture of Gandhāra.

Japanese representations of the parinirvāṇa fall into two primary types. The first, and the oldest, is dominated by a large image of the Buddha in the foreground, with the audience still quite small. In the second type, which became predominant in the thirteenth century, the Buddha's size is closer to normal, and the scene is occupied by many mourning figures—not only his followers but also bodhisattvas and gods, lay people and animals, and Queen Māyā descending from Trāyastriṃśa Heaven with her retinue (at the upper right).

Over time, the atmosphere of these paintings became overloaded with emotion. In his liturgical text, Genshin had already described with a luxury of detail, and in an overtly emotional style, the paroxysm of pain that captures all the witnesses of the parinirvāṇa. Nature itself, down to the smallest insects, joins in the concert of laments. The increasing number of animals in painted representations during the Kamakura period seems to reflect an influence from Myōe. In one of its versions, the *Mahāparinirvāṇa-sūtra* mentions lions, buffaloes, oxen, sheep, ducks and wild geese, and even bees, which, like the bodhisattvas and gods, give free rein to their grief over the extinction of the Buddha. To these, Myōe added snakes and scorpions, tigers, wild boars, deer, monkeys, and dogs. Mourning animals now take center stage. Predators and their prey, united in their laments, roll on the ground and forget their hostility for a while. The whole of nature is in mourning: the earth shakes, trees bloom out of season, and soon wither away.

PARODIC VERSIONS

Around the fourteenth century, representations of the death of eminent monks such as Saichō, Hōnen, and Nichiren began to take inspiration from depictions of the Buddha's parinirvāṇa. Hōnen, for example, is shown lying on his side with his head on his right arm; the landscape is reminiscent of Kuśinagara, and the five buddhas descending on a cloud are reminiscent of Māyā's descent from Trāyastriṃśa Heaven. In the Nichiren sect, the image of the founder, who was held to be the reincarnation of a bodhisattva named Jōgyō, came to supplant that of Śākyamuni, and Nichiren's nirvāṇa became the main object of worship at the Buddha's parinirvāṇa assemblies. For the most part, these latter-day depictions of the parinirvāṇa remain bound to conventional layouts and iconography, but they also include some radical innovations, starting with their main protagonist.

From the seventeenth century on, more or less parodic versions of the parinirvāṇa began to appear (see plate 7). Perhaps the best-known example is the *Vegetable Nirvāṇa* (*yasai nehan*) by Itō Jakuchū (1716–1800), a painted scroll preserved at the Kyoto National Museum, and dated about 1780 (fig. 16).[3] It represents the Buddha as a large forked radish (*daikon*) lying on a bed made of a farmer's satchel. He is surrounded by about sixty disciples, also represented by vegetables and fruits (turnips, radishes, pumpkins, gourds, mushrooms, eggplants, burdock roots, lotus, bamboo, melons, pears, and chestnuts). Cornstalks represent the sal trees (*sāla* tree, *Shorea robusta*) between which, according to tradition, the Buddha passed away. At the top left, a fruit in the middle of the cornstalks represents Māyā descending from Trāyastriṃśa Heaven. The scene, in its composition if not in its details, faithfully reproduces the classic theme of the parinirvāṇa. The possibility that this painting is a simple parody of the theme cannot be excluded, but given the Buddhist context, it could also be an allegorical representation of a doctrinal theme particularly popular in Japan, according to which "trees and grass become buddha" (*sōmoku jōbutsu*). The *Mahāparinirvāṇa-sūtra* had already affirmed the idea that all sentient beings possess a buddha-nature, and this notion was extended to plants, an idea that was deemed of sufficient interest to be staged in several plays written for the Nō theater. As for the radish, it was celebrated as the king of vegetables for various reasons, both culinary and symbolic, and it often appears in Zen paintings of the time.[4] Shimizu Yoshiaki interprets the radish motif primarily as a symbol of the buddhahood of vegetables and as an aesthetic theme borrowed by Buddhism from Chinese painting and literature, symbolizing the simplicity and poverty of the Zen ideal.[5] Attempting to place this painting in the biographical context of Jakuchū's life, Shimizu sees it as a "traditional act of piety in its spirit," intended to commemorate the death of Jakuchū's brother, but also to represent his own spiritual journey.[6] Without wanting to deny the validity of this interpretation, I will propose a complementary interpretation, to be considered for heuristic purposes. What Shimizu seems to ignore is the fundamental symbolic valence of the black radish (*daikon*) in premodern Japan, namely, its sexual connotations. It is well known that *daikon* is a slang term for the penis, while the forked form of the vegetable, such as the mandrake in the West, has often been used to symbolize the human body. The two interpretations are not mutually exclusive, however, given the polysemy of these representations.

Another version of the *Vegetable Nirvāna*, a little less known, is that of Shibata Zeshin (1807–1891). Apart from the paintings of Itō Jakuchū and Shibata Zeshin, parodic images of the parinirvāṇa were in vogue in secular circles, including kabuki actors and men of letters who were depicted lying on

FIGURE 16. Vegetable nirvāṇa, by Itō Jakuchū. 18th century. Japan. Hanging scroll, ink on paper. Kyoto National Museum (AK83).

their deathbed in the final posture of the Buddha, surrounded by their disciples or weeping admirers.[7]

We also see, from the seventeenth century on, parinirvāṇa parodies involving famous historical figures, such as the poets Ariwara no Narihira (825–880) and Matsuo Bashō (1644–1694). The parodic intention is particularly clear in the former case, a painting by Hanabusa Itchō (1652–1724), which replaces Śākyamuni with the erotomaniac Narihira, who was said to have slept with 3,733 women. He is depicted surrounded by a sample of them, of all ages and classes, mourning the death of their former lover.[8] We also have a parinirvāṇa depiction of the painter and Zen monk Sengai (1750–1837) by Saitō Shūhō (1769–1859). The *sāla* trees are painted here in the form of twisted pine trees. Sengai is lying with his back to the viewer, and he seems to be asleep. Around him are gathered about fifty people, some of them crying, while others look pleased. It does not seem to be a funeral wake, and there are no animals here, only plants—various types of vegetables.

Another significant example is a print of the mortuary portrait of the kabuki actor Ishikawa Danjurō VIII, with his father and two brothers behind him, and a group of grieving admirers in front of his deathbed, or, in a variant, other members of the Ishikawa family. As in the representations of the Buddha, the dead person is much larger than life in relation to the people around him. In a print dated 1854, an admirer holds one of the actor's enormous feet close to her, and a crying cat reminds us of the crying animals of the Buddhist parinirvāṇa. A 1903 tryptic depicting the death of Danjurō IX shows the same characteristics, except that the direction of the body is reversed, and an attempt has been made to erase the Buddhist references to suggest a Shintō ceremony. As is well known, Buddhism was suppressed by the Meiji government in favor of the new official religion, Shintō. But ironically, the Buddhist structure of the scene is preserved.[9]

A further example is the anticipatory depiction of Matsuura Takeshirō's "parinirvāṇa" painted in 1886 by Kawanabe Kōsai (1831–1889). Matsuura (1818–1888) was a noted explorer of Ezo (present-day Hokkaido) and a well-known collector. At his request, Kawanabe undertook to produce a nirvāṇa painting in which the Buddha would be replaced by Matsuura. But instead of dying between the *sāla* trees, he is depicted, in the words of the painting's title, as "napping under the pines." And he is surrounded not by mourning relatives but by the many objects he had collected during his life, together with a few friends. Completed in 1886, two years before Matsuura's death, the painting is not simply a parodic nirvāṇa painting, but rather a deliberate step in his conscious preparation for death.[10]

A Phallic Nirvāṇa

In the register of parodic nirvāṇa paintings, a kind of climax (or nadir) is reached toward the end of the Edo period with images in which sexual symbolism, already latent in the case of vegetables such as radishes, bursts upon the scene, literally becoming "ob-scene." In one of these images, which could be described as a "phallic nirvāṇa," the Buddha is represented naked, lying on his side in the conventional position associated with the parinirvāṇa (fig. 17).[11] His body is golden in color, and his head has the shape of a large *penis glans*. In front of him, his two main disciples, Ānanda and Mahākāśyapa, are prostrate on the ground. They too have phallic heads. A group of women with vulva-shaped faces crowd around his body. Behind them stand two gods: one of them, with three heads and eight arms (probably Brahmā), holds a dildo and other instruments of pleasure, while the other (Indra) joins hands in prayer. Paradoxically, these eminently male gods also have invaginated faces, and their hair, standing on their heads like that of Tantric deities, evokes pubic hair. In the foreground, several couples of rutting animals are visible (a rooster and hen, mandarin ducks, eels, etc.), as well as molluscs and plants (radishes, shallots, ginger, mushrooms) symbolizing sexual union, fecundity, and fertility. A copy of this work, recently put on sale on the Internet, was accompanied by a comment that it is not a malicious parody but a representation whose motivations are perhaps (as in the case of the *Vegetable Nirvāṇa*) of a religious nature. This argument is too clearly self-serving not to appear suspicious. Yet it may not be entirely devoid of pertinence. We recall that Ānanda showed the Buddha's genitalia to women at the time of the parinirvāṇa. If, as some have argued, phallic cults constitute one of the sources, or even the foundation, of religion, could we not see there—in the wake of the medieval parinirvāṇas mentioned above—a return in force of a quasi-Rabelaisian grotesque, inspired by the fecundating powers of the earth?[12]

The interpretation of this type of image is obviously delicate. One can clearly see in it a singular anticlerical parody, aiming at the major symbol of Buddhism, the Buddha himself, who is usually presented as a renouncer.[13] But one can also detect a more serious theme, a response to death by fertility, which gives to this representation a character, if not religious, at least magical. This is suggested, for example, by details such as the roots of the various plants littering the ground, intertwined to evoke the sexual act. In Japanese religion, representations of the sexual act often have an apotropaic nature and are aimed at defeating demonic forces as well as death itself. In popular cults such as that of the crossroads deities (*dōsojin*), the staging of genitalia and the sexual act has been a way of symbolically overcoming death through procreation. In the primitive scene that gave birth to these deities, the goddess Izanami, outraged because her brother Izanagi, breaking the underworld's taboo, beheld her cadaveric form, tells him that she will kill a thousand people a day; to which Izanami replies that he will give birth to 1,500 people a day in return.[14] This exchange recalls the scene in medieval Japanese mythology that pits a

FIGURE 17. Phallic nirvāṇa. 19th century. Japan. Hanging scroll, ink, colors and gold on silk. British Museum (2011, 3012.1).

pestilence god named Gozu Tennō (the Ox-Headed Heavenly King) against the Buddha, and ends with the death of the latter. Before returning to this myth, let us remember that popular cults favor the sexual act and procreation over the sacrifice and death of the Buddha. Beyond its obviously anticlerical tone, this is perhaps the lesson to be learned from this phallic nirvāṇa.

14

THE BUDDHA AS SEEN BY HIS RIVALS

The image of the Buddha could not fail to influence (and be influenced by) the other religious currents in Asia: Hinduism, Jainism, Tibetan Bön, Chinese Daoism, and Japanese Shintō, to name only the major ones. In many Hindu texts, the Buddha is simply regarded as a manifestation or avatar of the god Vishnu: the ninth in the classic series of ten avatars.[1] In modern times, this conception was strongly criticized by B. R. Ambedkar, who rallied a large number of Hindu untouchables to Buddhism. Among the twenty-two vows he made converts recite, the fifth states: "I do not and will not believe that the Lord Buddha was an incarnation of Vishnu. I believe that this is pure folly and false propaganda."[2] In at least one Buddhist *Jātaka,* it is Rāma, the seventh avatar of Vishnu, who is presented as an incarnation of the Buddha in a past life.[3]

Unfortunately, there are few serious studies of the relationship between Buddhism and Jainism or of the links between their putative and contemporary founders, Śākyamuni and Mahāvīra. Biographies of the latter appeared as early as the third and second centuries BCE. They dwell on his extreme ascetic practices but say little about his birth and death. The god Indra is said to have given him a divine robe when he renounced the world. He had a difficult life and was subject to violence from householders and attacks by gods and wild beasts. He took little care of himself, lived naked, and spent long periods without eating or sleeping. Unlike the story of the Buddha, nowhere is it said that he had to suffer attacks from Māra. A Buddhist influence seems to be reflected in part of his life, however, unless the two stories are based on a common substratum. Thirteen years after renouncing the world, Mahāvīra is said to have awakened, attaining omniscience while crouched in a field meditating under the sun, after fasting for two and a half days—not, like the Buddha, sitting under a tree at night, not far from a river, after interrupting his fast. He began to preach before a crowd of ascetics and lay people in the temple of a tree spirit in the city of Campā, joined by gods who had descended from their heavenly abode for the occasion. His body, like that of the Buddha, was thought to correspond perfectly to the model of the *cakravartin* king,[4] and he was regarded as the last of the twenty-four "ford makers" (*tīrthaṅkaras*). In spite of the obvious parallelism between their stories, there is no hint of antagonism between the two figures, such as can be found, for example, between the Buddha and the founders of Chinese Daoism and Tibetan Bön.

Around the second century CE, a theory appeared in China that Buddhism was nothing more than the doctrine preached by the sage Laozi to "convert the barbarians" (*huahu*). This theory was based on the legend that Laozi, toward the end of his life, left China and headed west. He was said to have gone to Kashmir first, which he converted to his doctrine, and then to India. According to the *Internal Section of the Deep Mystery* (*Xuanmiao neipian*): "The consort of the king of that country was called Qingmiao. Laozi, taking advantage of the fact that she was taking a nap, used the essence of the sun to enter her mouth. On the eighth of the fourth month of the following year, at midnight, he tore her right armpit and was born. As soon as he touched the ground, he took seven steps and raised his hand toward heaven. . . . From that moment on, Buddhism flourished."[5] The theory of the conversion of barbarians does not seem to have been originally directed against Buddhists. Toward the beginning of the fourth century, however, it took a distinctly polemical turn. In the Scripture on Laozi's *Conversion of the Barbarians* (*Laozi huahu jing*), Laozi now orders the barbarians to practice asceticism not only to break their cruel and violent nature, but to put an end to their "rebellious seed." It is no longer a question of saving them, but of humiliating, weakening, and even exterminating them by preventing them from reproducing. The Buddhist counterattack was not long in coming: Laozi, far from being the founder of Buddhism, is now said to be in fact a manifestation or a disciple of Śākyamuni, sent by him to the east to propagate an inferior teaching that was to serve nonetheless to prepare the ground for the Buddhist revelation. Moreover, the circumstances of Laozi's birth borrow certain traits from that of the Buddha: he preaches a sūtra while still residing in the womb and is twice (sic) born from the left (not right) side of his mother.[6]

In Tibet, there also were anti-Buddhas who were almost as Buddhist as the Buddha himself. Such was the case with Shenrab Miwo (Tonpa Shenrab), the alleged founder of the Tibetan religion known as Bön. He occupies a very similar position in Bön to that of Śākyamuni in Buddhism, but the lack of sources about his origins, life, and teaching contrasts with the wealth of reported data about Śākyamuni. The main biographical sources are *terma* (hidden scriptures) discovered in the tenth and eleventh centuries CE. According to tradition, Shenrab Miwo lived long before Śākyamuni, about twenty-three thousand years ago, and thus long before Padmasambhava, the legendary patriarch of Tibetan Buddhism, revered by some as a "second Buddha." Like Śākyamuni, Shenrab was a prince by birth, but he is said to have renounced the throne at the age of thirty-one to seek awakening. He practiced austerities for many years and, after reaching awakening, went to the Zhangzhung region, which is usually identified with Mount Kailash, the sacred mountain of Tibet.

The Life of Shenrab is illustrated in many narrative paintings or *thangka*. They show Shenrab contemplating the world from atop Mount Meru, the cosmic mountain, to determine in which country he will be reborn in human form (just as the Buddha did from Tuṣita Heaven). He turns into a cuckoo, the king of birds, and from the top of a stūpa, which his mother-to-be is circumambulating, he announces his upcoming birth. That night, two rays of light, one white, the other red, descend, respectively, on the heads of his future parents. Nine months later, he is born from his mother's right side. At the age of twelve, after the death of his parents, Shenrab begins to propagate his doctrine (in three hundred sixty languages!). He invokes the earth goddess, who emerges from the ground and offers him a vase filled with nectar. He then emits luminous rays from the thirty-three principal marks of his body (one more than the Buddha). At the age of fifteen, he converts several kings and marries a princess, who soon gives him two sons and a daughter. He then leaves to spread his doctrine on the four continents. He marries a second princess, who in turn gives birth to two sons and a daughter. Then he goes to Trāyastriṃśa Heaven to preach to the gods. The goddess of the Ganges offers him her younger sister as his wife. Shenrab then routs the army of the demon king. The latter orders his four ministers to carry out "perverse" rites and to propagate a counterfeit Buddhist Law throughout the continent of Jambudvīpa (one of four continents, south of Mount Meru). After preaching his doctrine and performing numerous miracles, Shenrab renounces his princely life and is ordained, motivated by the compassion for every being that he felt after contemplating the four rivers of birth, old age, sickness, and death. (Again we meet the Buddhist theme of the four encounters.)[7] Shenrab pursues ascetic practices for three years, first in the manner of birds, then in the manner of monkeys, and lastly in the manner of humans. Impressed by the power of his asceticism, the demon king himself ends up converting. After ordaining many monks and nuns, Shenrab withdraws into solitude and enters parinirvāṇa at the age of seventy-five.

Despite the obvious similarities to the Life of the Buddha, the Life of Shenrab differs from it in a number of respects—in particular, by the importance given to animal transformations, which introduce us to a universe with strong shamanic resonances. As Per Kvaerne notes, the Bön tradition has an ambivalent attitude toward the Buddha, and a frankly negative attitude toward Buddhism.[8] For Bönpo authors, Buddhism is a perverse doctrine propagated by demons. These authors used various strategies to assert the (symbolic) superiority of their religion—notably by appropriating the character of Śākyamuni to make him a simple disciple of Shenrab. Several legends mention a bodhisattva who, on Shenrab's orders, was reborn in this world into the Śākya family, under the name of Śākyamuni, to reform this doctrine. However, this Śākyamuni is not the Buddha of the present kalpa, but a mere bodhisattva.

His doctrine is actually the Bön, and he is merely continuing the work of Shenrab.

We have seen some of the developments to which the parinirvāṇa gave rise in Japanese Buddhism. Still to be described is a very different account of the death of the Buddha that was widespread in medieval times in certain circles hostile to Buddhism. It is the myth of Gozu Tennō, a powerful pestilence deity. In the most common version of the myth, this Asian minotaur—who paradoxically became the protector of Jetavana, the Buddha's monastery near Śrāvastī—swore revenge on a householder named Kotan, who had once refused him hospitality when he was a visitor passing through the area. Returning a few years later, Gozu Tennō keeps his promise and destroys Kotan's household.[9] A variant of the myth contains a surprising episode, that of the fatal interview between Gozu Tennō and the Buddha, which can only be summarized here.[10]

Kotan is presented as a lay Buddhist who refuses hospitality to Gozu Tennō because the latter is a demon. When Gozu Tennō returns for revenge, Kotan asks the Buddha for help. Despite the rites of protection performed by the Buddha's disciples, Kotan and his family are massacred to the last man. The Buddha then resolves—a little late—to confront the demon in person. A dialogue ensues that recalls the one between Śākyamuni and Māra in the Indian legend. But Gozu Tennō, wiser than Māra, attacks the Buddha at his Achilles' heel, compassion. He declares to him that he will kill ten thousand of his disciples every day unless the Buddha agrees to sacrifice himself in their place. The Buddha accepts what looks very much like a fool's bargain, and Gozu Tennō, in his most virulent—viral—form, enters the Buddha's body through one of his fingers. On the first of the second lunar month, the disease spreads throughout the Buddha's body, and at the dawn of the fifteenth of the second month (the traditional date of the parinirvāṇa), the Buddha dies. His disciples, men and animals alike, lament, just as in the canonical scene of the parinirvāṇa. The body is then cremated, and Gozu Tennō exults, boasting that he has overcome Śākyamuni.[11] The crushing victory of Gozu Tennō over Śākyamuni is quite unique in the Buddhist annals, and there is nothing like it in the polemical texts of rival traditions such as Hinduism, Tibetan Bön, Daoism, or Shintō. In fact, it was in a tradition close to Buddhism, that of medieval Onmyōdō, that this story was born, even if it was just a development of latent tendencies in that tradition.

In this strange myth, one may also note the structural kinship with an episode, admittedly secondary, in the Life of Śākyamuni: namely, the destruction of the Śākya clan by the king of Koṣala, Viruḍhāka. André Bareau wanted to see in this episode an attempt to explain why, one century after the parinirvāṇa, the city of Kapilavastu, the cradle of the future Buddha, a holy place famous for its splendor, had disappeared from the face of the earth, giving way to a poor countryside where the very name of the Śākya clan no longer evoked anything of its past greatness.[12] One can wonder, as Bareau did—although for other reasons—about the historicity of this episode. The parallelism between the destruction of Kotan's family and that of the Śākya clan is striking. In both cases, they are Buddhist clans ravaged by a sworn enemy's desire for revenge (perhaps serving as a proxy for karmic retribution).

The story, in broad outline, is as follows. The young prince Viruḍhāka, having been insulted in his youth by the Śākya—who had called him a "son of a slave"—swore to take his revenge and destroy all the members of this clan (except Śākyamuni himself, whom he respects). Just like Gozu Tennō, Viruḍhāka intends to exact in blood the injury done to him, and the Buddha proves unable to prevent the carnage. Commentators have sought to justify his impotence as the result of the inexorable karma of the victims, who in this view are already guilty. Viruḍhāka nevertheless decides to spare those who do not belong to the Śākya clan. In order to be recognized and get out of the city safely, they will have to use insignia made of reeds.[13]

In both stories, people who do not belong to the cursed family are spared, thanks to a kind of safe-conduct that allows them to leave the place before the total destruction begins. Their salvation depends on a sign, as in the biblical legend. In the myth of Gozu Tennō, the pestilence god decides to spare the descendants of Somin Shōrai, Kotan's poor brother, who had offered him hospitality. He gives him as a sign of gratitude a wheel made of braided reed stems, which will serve as a talisman for them. The vegetal symbolism is not very clear, but it can be noted that reeds play an important role in China and Japan in rites conducted to expel epidemics (especially in the festival of Tsushima Shrine, near Nagoya, which is centered on Gozu Tennō).[14]

This motif, at first glance peculiar in the chronicle of the Śākya, stems from the cults of epidemic deities that took root in Asia. The sudden decline of the Śākya could certainly have been explained by an epidemic, but in traditional India the epidemic as punishment would involve a god or demon of the type of Gozu Tennō, a solution that was not acceptable to early Buddhist storytellers. It was therefore more seemly to transform a god of epidemics into a bloodthirsty warrior and to situate the revenge episode on a purely secular level. Viruḍhāka is, moreover, explicitly compared to a demon. However, unlike Gozu Tennō, who, as a divine scourge, can commit his criminal act with impunity, Viruḍhāka dies and falls into hell seven days after the massacre of the Śākya. Karmic justice is saved. Although it is impossible to establish a filiation between the two stories, the resemblance of certain details stands out as significant. Admittedly, a complex legend cannot be reduced to a single element, however important it may be, and the legend of the Śākya massacre is quite different from the myth of Gozu Tennō. In any case, the link between the two makes more sense from a structural standpoint than from a historicist one. The parallelism suggests that in both cases we are dealing with a narrative developed in circles hostile to Buddhism.

As all these stories show, the rival religions of Buddhism have sought, to varying degrees, to demean the Buddha, but they have in turn been deeply influenced by Buddhist legend. The Life of the Buddha provided a biographical paradigm to which the authors of the biographies of the founders of the other religions conformed, without always realizing it. The only case where the influence seems to have been reciprocal is that of Jainism, which is also the religion least critical of Buddhism and its spiritual ancestor.

15

JAPANESE BIOGRAPHIES AND CRITICISMS

The influence of the pictorial versions of the Life of the Buddha from the Edo period (1600–1868) can be seen even on orthodox biographies of the master. Some Buddhists sought to respond to the excesses of imagination in popular culture by advocating a return to the canonical view. One of the most significant voices in this regard was that of the Buddhist nun Kōgetsu Sōgi (1756–1833), a disciple of the reformer Jiun Onkō (1718–1805). In her *Light of the Three Ages* (*Miyo no hikari*), Kōgetsu presented a biography of the Buddha scrupulously based on canonical sources—in effect, a denial of the many more or less fantastic Lives of the Buddha then in vogue. One theory in particular caused her to marshal her resources: the notion that the jealousy of Mahāprajāpatī Gautamī toward her sister Māyā was the cause of the latter's untimely death. To combat this idea, Kōgetsu reintroduces the episode in which Mahāprajāpatī demands ordination from the Buddha and ends up obtaining it, though not without difficulty, thus becoming the first nun and the founder of the feminine order. This episode, although found in Chinese Lives of the Buddha, had disappeared from the Japanese Lives produced in medieval times. Another forgotten episode that reappears thanks to Kōgetsu is that of the massacre of the Śākya clan.[1]

Kōgetsu was not the only one to feel frustrated by the illustrated Lives of the Buddha of the Edo period. Another ardent defender of the orthodox account was a monk of the Pure Land school, Gentei (ca. 1621–1705), who scrutinized the presumed dates of the historical Buddha. After noting, for instance, five contradictory dates assigned to the parinirvāṇa, he chose the fifteenth day of the second lunar month, not because it is solidly based on scriptural sources, but because it marks the spring renewal.[2] In 1882, a Zen monk of the Sōtō sect, Tokumitsu Shōryū, published a *True Biography of the Venerable Śākyamuni* (*Shakuson shinjitsu denki*), which he claimed had been strictly confined to reliable sources. This book is not exactly a biography in the literal sense, however, since it begins with the formation of the universe and ends after the Buddha's parinirvāṇa with the compilation of the first Buddhist canon by his disciples.[3]

But the traditional Life of the Buddha came under threat from still another quarter with the sometimes cruel denials advanced by historical research, first Japanese, then Western. Soon a new type of intellectual, who accepted neither local innovation nor scriptural authorities, attacked the traditional story. Even before the discovery of Western historiography, it was the contradictions of Buddhist doctrinal sources that allowed Japanese textual criticism to be exercised. We owe to a young prodigy, Tominaga Nakamoto (1715–1746), the first proper historical and philological criticism of Buddhism and specifically of the accounts of its founder's life. His work, *Remarks upon Emerging from Meditation* (*Shutsujō kōgo*), became the locus classicus for this form of argumentation. In particular, he demonstrates that the first Buddhist texts are very much later than the Buddha, and that their content does not necessarily reflect the Buddha's thought (or his life), but is rather the result of struggles for influence within the new religion.[4]

HIRATA ATSUTANE

The scholar and Shintō ideologue Hirata Atsutane (1776–1843) took up Tominaga's title in his *Ironic Remarks upon Emerging from Meditation* (*Shutsujō shōgo*), compiled in 1811 but printed in 1849. Inspired by Tominaga's methodology, he developed a fierce criticism of Buddhism and its founder, which he continued in an incomplete work, *Notes on India* (*Indo zōshi,* ca. 1820–1826).[5] Hirata saw in the Life of the Buddha a series of fabrications that were full of contradictions, which he took a malicious pleasure in underlining.[6] Ironically, despite his polemical cast of thought, he was, after Tominaga, one of the first Japanese scholars to behave as a pure historian—a kind of Buddhist Foucher. He explains, for example, that the Vinaya of the Mūlasarvāstivādin, compiled four centuries after the Buddha's death, cannot faithfully reflect the master's words. As a man of his time, however, he believed in the reality of the Buddha's supernormal powers even though he condemned their use as vulgar.

Although he is not usually considered to be one of the Buddha's biographers, Hirata exerted an important influence on Japanese perceptions of the Buddha. He describes the Life of the Buddha as a work of pure imagination, and a late one at that. The Buddha appears in his work as a kind of charlatan, albeit endowed with supernormal powers. Hirata makes extensive reference to canonical sources, although he tries to prove that these are largely later than the parinirvāṇa. On this point, he agrees with current historians, and disagrees with the Buddhist tradition that credits Ānanda with the recitation of the sūtras during the First Council. But he does not limit himself to showing the contradictions within the scriptures; he expands on Tominaga's claim that they are, on the whole, a tissue of lies, strewn with a few true facts. Again, his approach anticipates the stance of Western historians except that, in his case, the anti-Buddhist bias is clearly displayed.

After tracing Śākyamuni's princely genealogy through a long line of kings, Hirata ignores the subsequent legends about the conception of the Bodhisattva and criticizes the miraculous events bound up with his birth as later additions. He claims that Māyā's death was the result of childbirth, an interpretation that had already appeared in *bunraku* plays. He also questions the characterization of the young prince's prodigious talents, together with the description of the four encounters, underlining in particular the contradiction between the supposed omniscience of the Bodhisattva at birth and the ignorance he shows in his youth toward the elementary realities of life. In fact, Śākyamuni seems to have adapted so well to the pleasures of palace life that the gods must repeatedly call him to order. Hirata ridicules the efforts of Buddhist commentators to demonstrate that Śākyamuni had no sexual desire. In passing, he also wonders why a bodhisattva should give up the pleasures of the flesh. As is well known, this was no longer required in the form of Tantric Buddhism that flourished in medieval Japan. The texts affirm, moreover, that Śākyamuni had three wives and three children. Hirata concludes that the third son, Sunákṣatra, must have been conceived after the great departure, proving that Śākyamuni returned to the palace to impregnate Yaśodharā, thus breaking his renunciatory vows. Like Tominaga, Hirata derides those who claim that Śākyamuni reuctantly had sex with her to prove his manhood to the rest of the world.

In the long period of asceticism pursued by the Bodhisattva, Hirata sees only a form of masochism. In the end, Śākyamuni had to admit defeat and realize that no one escapes the cycle of life and death. According to legend, of course, the Bodhisattva ended his mortifications for a different reason, but Hirata sees this as a pretext and accuses Śākyamuni of hypocrisy: why not admit that, as a result of his fasting, the Bodhisattva was hungry?[7] Furthermore, the Buddha's victory over Māra is not even worthy of mention, in Hirata's opinion. As for his teaching, Hirata points out that it is borrowed from Brahmanism, and that the doctrine of the Four Truths, in particular, was above all a way for the Buddha to "subdue" his five former disciples. Indeed, all of the Buddha's sermons aim to persuade his listeners that he is truly awakened. Likewise, his description of karma and the hellish sorrows that await sinners is only a way to frighten his listeners into conversion. As for his so-called miracles, it was nothing more than simple magic, exploited to triumph over his rivals and impress the audience. Hirata further criticizes the Buddha's forced conversions of family members, starting with his own son Rāhula and half brother Nanda. One recalls that in both cases the Buddha used a type of skillful means that may indeed seem a bit questionable. Finally, Hirata denies any value to the account of the parinirvāṇa. In his view, the Buddha's death was not voluntary, nor was it a deployment of skillful means to save beings. No, he simply died from food poisoning.[8] All these legends cannot hide the fact that Śākyamuni was a mere mortal, and that he never attained a transcendent awakening.

As might be expected, Hirata's work caused an outcry among the Buddhist clergy. The monks denounced its author as a servant of Māra, but they failed to come up with an adequate response to his polemical verve, even as (and especially when) they sought to maintain a spiritual plane. To give just one example: Ryōgetsu (d.u.), the abbot of a Sōtō Zen temple in the suburbs of Kameoka, produced a text entitled *The Flywhisk* (*Tsuiyō-barae*) in which he repeatedly characterizes Hirata as a bothersome fly, using the formula "The fly says that . . ." to introduce his citations. Yet his attempts at refutation prove weak.[9] Paradoxically, some monks began to take Hirata's side. In the late 1840s, two Zen monks of the Sōtō school, Saian Urin (d. 1845), abbot of the Sōtō headquarters at Eiheiji, and Kakugan Jitsumyō (1793–1857), co-authored a glowing preface to Hirata's *Notes on India,* where they compare him to the legendary layman Vimalakīrti and the famous Chinese poet Su Dongpo (a.k.a. Su Shi, 1037–1101), and even to "the light of the sun and the moon, which dispels the darkness of past and present illusions."[10]

NEW EVALUATIONS

Buddhist biographers soon found themselves confronted with other disturbing criticisms, this time from Christian missionaries and their Japanese emulators.[11] Some tried to respond to a pamphlet by the English missionary Joseph Edkins (1823–1905), *Correcting the Errors of the Buddhists,* published in China in 1857 and discovered in Japan around 1865. Although this pamphlet mainly attacks Buddhist doctrine, it also contains a study of the Life of the Buddha, that makes Śākyamuni a purely human character whose features have been distorted by legend. For Japanese Buddhists, calling the Life of the Buddha a "legend" might have seemed almost as insulting as seeing it, with Hirata, as the product of sectarian "fabrications." Thus Fujishima Ryōon (1852–1918), a monk of the Shinshū sect, published a study entitled "The Legendary Śākyamuni" (Shōsetsuteku Shakuson) in which he paradoxically restates arguments used by European critics of Émile Senart to denounce the mythological reading of the Life of the Buddha.[12]

Yet other Japanese intellectuals found nothing to object to in a literary reading of the Life of the Buddha. Interest in the character Śākyamuni, already evident in the many fictionalized accounts throughout the Edo period, increased in the last decades of the nineteenth century. Efforts were then made to publish a Life of the Buddha that could serve as a common denominator for all Japanese Buddhist sects. Critical biographies also appeared during the Meiji era (1868–1912), written by historians such as Inoue Tetsujirō (1855–1944).[13] In fact, this revival was influenced by Western Orientalist discourse. But it also reflected the spiritual quest of Japanese Buddhists like Shaku Sōen (1860–1919)—a Zen priest who went on pilgrimage to the Indian sources of

Buddhism. In the last years of the nineteenth century, Japanese translations of several Western biographies of the Buddha appeared.[14] Through them, the Japanese considered the possibility that the story of the Buddha's Life might not be simply a lie, but rather had literary value as a fictional narrative.[15] Also around this time, inspired by the art historian and critic Okakura Kakuzō (1862–1913), a new artistic trend called "Japanese painting" (Nihonga) emerged, aiming to depict a more human Buddha through a more realistic style.[16]

THE BUDDHA AS A POET

In this historical and literary context, I cannot resist the pleasure of quoting from "Venomous Coral Lips," a short text by the Japanese writer Kōda Rohan (1867–1947).[17] This work shows that a true novelist can take liberties with the Life of the Buddha without trivializing it. The narrator, having heard that a strange young woman is living alone on the banks of a river, decides to go and see what it's all about. He takes with him a carafe of wine to loosen her tongue, but she doesn't need it. Once the ice is (very quickly) broken, she confesses that she leads this eremitical existence because she has fallen in love with the Buddha, whom she considers above all to be a poet: "I learned by heart the whole life of the Buddha. And I thought: 'What a great poet in the world, what a sublime being, what a trustworthy person, what a refined and sincere man.' If he were here now, I would like to be cuddled, to be pampered by this gentleman. Is that so unreasonable?"[18] To which the narrator replies:

> In my opinion, Shakyamuni is a great liar, a pedlar of seeds for novels. The cunning ones who bought them and made them bear fruit are the novelists of old from China and Japan. For those who hold the Buddhist rosary, he is a providential theologian. For those who lean on the Daoist staff, he is only good to feed to Peking dogs. By declaring the Buddha is a great poet, you risk angering the zazen practitioners full of hemorrhoids and plastered with illusions who accumulate their years of asceticism like fools, or the so-called venerable ones who preach the uselessness of words but never notice the futility of their own kōans.[19]

The young woman then launches into a long and passionate tirade, from which I retain only the essential passages:

> So this lovely gentleman called Shakyamuni is, as you know, the son of a king of India. According to the gossip on the Celestial High Plain, he is the retarded elder son of a great chief. . . . Whether his father was a great chief or a prison guard, this child was endowed from birth with an

> exceptional temperament. He had little eczema, because he had been given potions of *makuri* seaweed. And since he was growing up healthy, he did not consume breast milk excessively and therefore had no mental illness. So, his natural intelligence, like everyone else's, was awakening day by day. But the fact that he had spent three years, three months, and I don't know how many days and hours in his mother's womb, and that he came out dancing through her ribs, must be a joke that I can't make heads or tails of! . . . Still, he grew little by little and realized for the first time that human beings are mortal. And he never once complained, in his little voice, that life is ephemeral and that a flower, once gone, can never blossom again.[20]
>
> When he reached a marriageable age, Shakyamuni found himself enlivened by elegant songs accompanied by Indian lutes with lascivious overtones. . . . At banquets, the white sleeves of the young girls twirled, and their red crepe belts created a striking contrast. "Magnificent! Splendid!" he might have exclaimed, giving himself up to the allure of this floating world. But, as perceptive as he was, he knew he would have ended up invading the neighboring countries and kidnapping one or two dazzling princesses so they could sweep the dust from his bedroom. He would have consumed the eighty years of his life in performing such base acts. But the phoenix never argues with chickens over food! . . . He did not hate the princess [Yaśodharā] for being immersed in her beautiful illusions. She tried to please him by putting makeup on and seeing to her clothes. But a feeling of pity filled his heart whenever she brushed her eyelashes, unaware, poor thing, that her last hour with him might come that very evening. So, naturally, how could they agree in the privacy of their bedroom? There was between their loves the difference between a lantern that illuminates a momentary space around itself and the moon eternally illuminating the whole universe.[21]

After leaving the palace, the Bodhisattva set out in search of the Way:

> He went knocking on the doors of the scholars of the time but found only futile prayers, blind faith, and lame theories. Never a true connoisseur able to unravel the complexity of the floating world. So he withdrew to a solitary mountain where he remained dark and pensive. He was like a young virgin in love who perceives before her eyes the ghostly image of her lover. . . . From then on, he pursued a life of asceticism. His face, tracked with tears day after day, finally gave him the scowling head and prominent forehead of an awakened one.[22]

Finally awakened, Śākyamuni begins to preach the Law:

> He then gave sermons for forty years. And how did this man end his life? With a smile, it is said, but to tell the truth, he died like a dog on the banks of the Ajiravati River, poisoned by mushrooms that he had greedily swallowed, crying out all the tears in his sullen head. . . .[23]

After this glimpse into the Buddha's life, the young woman attacks the misconceptions that circulate about his doctrine:

> Originally, the Buddha had broken with every attachment. After acquiring the first degree of wisdom, he gradually became like a withered tree, like a rock. He untied the sequence of all the fundamental causes and accessory factors behind his thoughts and feelings since the beginning of time. And finally, he entered parinirvāṇa perfectly clear and limpid like a jewel. Blind people have always seen in the Buddha what they wanted to see: a being who is no longer human. . . . .
>
> The origin of this misunderstanding is a confusion between reason and feelings. Being entirely bound by their doctrines, some people get bogged down in the words of Shakyamuni's songs and start to quibble: here is the reason for the three times, here is the explanation of the four elements, the twelve causal links that obey such logic, the two views of extinction or permanence are erroneous because of this or that. They explain each page by tearing it to pieces with their reasoning, like those fools who read the commentaries on Shakespeare's works. Nothing could be more normal than that they fail to grasp the spirit of the whole or to understand its purpose. A horsefly may bang its head against a paper wall and buzz like mad for a hundred years, but it will never get through. . . .
>
> They teach in a strangely complicated way the arrangement of the charcoal or the handling of the rag, and completely forgetting the good taste of the master who matched tea with white rice, they proclaim that it is imperative to have sweet bean paste in spring or a buckwheat pastry for the tea jar opening ceremony in winter. Yet the most annoying thing is that they end up measuring everything with a teaspoon. In short, they consider Shakyamuni the king of the theorists, which is perfectly ridiculous![24]

In reality, as she sees it, the Buddha is not a boring philosopher, he is a passionate, lively being, a poet:

> Gautama is entirely consumed by the flames of compassion. . . . He is certainly not a slacker like the shrewd monks or arrivist saints who succeeded him. His poems sound like icy theories in their filthy ears. But since when does he sound like a cold theorist? . . . They are so stupid they

have never noticed the great love he radiates. They only see the coldness and bitterness of his poems and embrace Shakyamuni like a potion of bear liver. . . . Isn't this the reason all sorts of wild theories about the Buddha's life have been developed?

He himself takes no notice because he is brimming over with burning tears of love. Else, how could he have traveled around the country for ten thousand and five or six hundred days, never worrying about the scorching sun despite all the big drops of holy sweat, never sparing the rambling speeches that inflamed his tongue, just to sell everyone, children, adults, and even shepherds, on the appropriate remedy? And if he had not been driven all his life by such an ardent passion, if he had been an eccentric, a charlatan manipulating cold theories, he would never have bothered to go out of his way to amuse children with the leaf of a tree that he passed off as gold. On the contrary, he would have grabbed hold of the leaders of the ninety-six heretical sects to engage in a duel of earthworms over the non-annihilated annihilation of thought.[25]

The first truth discovered by the Buddha, that of the impermanence of things, is here reinterpreted as a typically Japanese poetic feeling of *mono no aware,* and the Buddha becomes at the same time a poet consumed by compassion toward all beings, with whom one can fall in love. In spite of its strongly idiosyncratic character, I like this vision better than that of Western historians: for who could fall in love with the rather banal philosopher they attempted to turn the Buddha into? In any case, this vision is hardly more fictional than its scholarly counterpart.

16

THE INDIAN BUDDHA AS SEEN FROM THE WEST

The West did not wait for the "Edifying and Curious Letters" of the Jesuit missionaries in the eighteenth century, nor the rediscovery of Buddhism in the nineteenth century, to learn of the Buddha and his doctrine. The West's first contact with Buddhism dates back to Alexander's expedition in the third century BCE, and the first mentions of Indian "gymnosophists" appear among Greek and Christian authors around the same time. But it was above all through the intermediary of Arab culture, which had early contact with India, that Buddhism acquired its credentials in the Christian West. A few words about the Arab perception of Buddhism are therefore in order.

PERSIAN AND ARABIC LIVES

The term buddha (*budd*) appears in Arabic sources, but it does not always seem to refer to the Buddha Śākyamuni.[1] Certain episodes in the Life of the Buddha, however, are mentioned in a number of sources. According to the Persian philosopher as-Sahrastānī (1086–1153), for example: "The first *budd* who appeared in the world was called Šâkman [Śākyamuni], which means 'the noble lord.' From the time of his appearance until the time of the Hegira was five thousand years. Below the rank of the *budd,* they say, is the *bûdîsfiyya* [bodhisattva]: they mean the man who seeks the path of truth."[2] Going further, this text also gives a fairly accurate statement of Buddhist morality.

The figure of the Bodhisattva appears among medieval Muslim authors under the name Būdāsf, who became a fabulous character in the early days of antiquity, even before Adam. But he is also described as a false prophet who is said to have preached the religion of the Sabians (worshipers of the stars), a religion with a philosophical character but also a cult of idols. His disciples, the Sumaniyya [Skt. *śrāmana,* or Buddhist monk], are essentially idolaters, who believe in transmigration: "They admit that a human soul passes into a dog, and a dog's soul passes into a man. They claim that whoever commits a sin in one body suffers the punishment for that sin in another body. They say the same about reward."[3] Nothing is said about the four noble truths or the Life of the Buddha, and there seems to be no link between Būdāsf and *al-budd*.

A fragment of the *Universal History* (*Jāmi' al-Tavārīkh*), a work by the Persian scholar Rashid al-Dīn (1247–1318), contains illustrations of the life of Śākyamuni under the title "The Life and Teaching of the Buddha," based on the account of a Kashmiri Buddhist priest named Kamalashri.[4] It is a rather idiosyncratic illustrated story, combining Kashmiri and Mongolian influences. The author describes a kind of Arabic Buddhism, stating that before accepting Islam, "the inhabitants of Mecca and Medina were Buddhists, and in the Ka'ba they worshipped idols resembling the Buddha, which Mohammed then ordered to be destroyed."[5] The Buddha is described as a prophet, and Māra is called Iblis or Shaitan (Satan).

One of the illustrations shows Śākyamuni offering fruit to the demon Iblis/Shaitan (a.k.a. Māra). When Śākyamuni puts an end to his asceticism, a young girl prepares him a dish consisting of milk from one hundred cows, rice, and sugar. All her friends do the same. Śākyamuni pretends to appreciate all their offerings, but retains only the girl's offering. He gives the other girls' food to the demon. Then he throws his bowl into the waters of the Ganges and vows that if he is destined to become a guide to men, the bowl will float. The scene derives from an act of truth in the Buddha's Life, but the presence of the demon completely transforms its meaning. Māra obsequiously reaches out his hand toward the fruit that a majestic Śākyamuni offers him. Both are dressed in Persian or Muslim fashion, but a Chinese influence can also be felt in the composition of the landscape.

A second illustration represents the park of the Jetavana, but the Buddha does not appear there.[6] The third illustration shows the city of Kuśinagara as the theater of the parinirvāṇa. The Buddha descends by air, avoiding the mountain that blocks the entrance: "And in this city a dome-shaped building made of pure crystal rose. Śākyamuni entered it and slept there like a lion. And from the outside people could see him inside thanks to the transparency of the crystal. However, there was no entrance and the doors that had been open earlier were now closed. And suddenly people could see a bright light in the shape of a pillar rising from the top of the dome."[7] The illustration shows a kind of Persian mausoleum, but the Buddha, instead of being inside, is sitting on its right side. The story and its iconography have evidently taken ample liberties with the Buddhist tradition.

Another iconographic example can be found in the *Collection of Chronicles* (*Majma' al-tavārīkh*) by the historian Hafiz-i Abru (d. 1430), which is a sequel to the *Universal History* by Rashid al-Dīn.[8] It is a history of the world from Adam to the present time—in this case, the year 1425. The first scene depicts the birth of the future Buddha; it describes the dream of Queen Māyā, in which she swallows the sun and moon, drinks the sea in one gulp, and takes Mount Qaf as her pillow. Soothsayers interpret this dream as meaning that she will give birth to a child who will become a king or a buddha. Then she goes to a garden outside the city of Mahābodhi, clutches the branch of a tree, and gives birth while standing. The artist has departed from the text, embellishing the scene with details from the chapter on the birth of Maitreya: here Mahābodhi, the place of awakening, is mistaken for Lumbinī. Māyā is in a Persian garden, wearing a Muslim robe. The style also reflects a Persian inspiration. In the next scene, Śākyamuni welcomes a Brahmin (a hermit or Persian dervish) named Vasiṣta, who practices a strict asceticism in the hope of reaching paradise. Śākyamuni tells him that his asceticism cannot lead him to the truth, because it generates feelings of anger and hatred. Vasiṣta then asks that he teach him the true path. The Buddha wears a turban, the ascetic holds a fly swatter.[9] The third scene is that of the parinirvāṇa. This time, Śākyamuni is shown inside the crystal dome without an entrance, and people outside (on either side) are gazing at him (see plate 10). The text says that Śākyamuni appeared to onlookers three days after his death, which reminds one of Christ. This scene may stem from a Chinese version of the Buddha preaching to his mother.

There are important differences between the fragments from the *Universal History* and the *Collection of Chronicles*. The illustrator of the first work took liberties with the text, the second remained more faithful to it. The former work, based on the account of the monk Kamalashri, already shows important variations from the canonical legend of the Buddha. Emanating from the Kashmiri tradition, it perhaps reflects the syncretism of a border region, or the eclecticism that prevailed in Iran before the Mongol conquest.

Finally, it is worth mentioning the *Story of Bilawhar and Būdāsf* (*Kitāb Bilawhar wa Būdāsf*), which has been presented as a translation of the *Lalitavistara,* and that gave rise to the Christian legend of Barlaam and Josaphat—as found in the *Golden Legend.*[10] Daniel Gimaret, for his part, believes that by its content as well as by its style, it is "completely foreign to Buddhism and the Indian world" and is rather close to a Christian and Syrian tradition.[11] The main character is not Būdāsf, but his tutor, the sage Bilawhar, and the tutor's eschatological teaching seems incompatible with belief in *saṃsāra,* as does his heavenly kingdom with nirvāṇa. What remains of the Buddha's legend, according to Gimaret, is only a vague and very distorted "romanesque" framework: "One has the very clear impression that the Buddhist legend was only used here as a prop for an edifying book, whose source is quite different."[12]

Let us summarize in a few words the history of Būdāsf. It begins with a dream of the consort of King Ganaysar, a tyrant who supports idolaters and persecutes the "people of religion": "She saw in her dream a white elephant flying through the air that approached her and landed on her belly without doing her any harm. In the morning she told her dream to the king, who thereupon summoned his interpreters and told them the dream. And they told the king the good news that a boy would be born to him."[13] Astrologers agree that the prince will be more powerful than any other king of India. Only one of them, an old man, predicts that Būdāsf will be "a guide in religion and asceticism." The now troubled king evacuates the city and surrounds his son with trusted people who are instructed never to speak to him about death or illness. As he grows, the prince tries to understand why he is sequestered and eventually learns of the prediction that hangs over him. He asks the king to let him out of the palace. One day, he meets two beggars: one has a tumor and the other is blind. On another day, he meets an old man. He is troubled. Finally, his tutor informs him of the prior existence of ascetics, who were hunted and exterminated by order of the king. He learns of the existence of the ascetic Bilawhar, who comes to him at Sabilābatt [Kapilavastu] and begins his instruction. The king encourages Būdāsf to enjoy the pleasures of the gynaeceum, but a vision of the abject character of the sleeping women diverts him from carnal pleasures.

All these elements are unquestionably borrowed from the legend of the Buddha. Other elements, however, are original: the persecution of the ascetics and the coming of Bilawhar. The prince decides to leave despite those who try to hold him back: a young prince, then his *wazīr* (Candaka), and finally his horse itself, which God has endowed with speech for the occasion. He entrusts to his *wazīr* his clothes and jewels, and leaves by himself. Four angels lift him up to heaven and give him the knowledge of all things. After some time, he returns to Šawilābatt (Kapilavastu) and there he preaches the "religion of God," converting the entire population. Finally he leaves, after entrusting the government to his uncle. After long peregrinations, he arrives in Qasmir (an error for Kuśinagara), where he dies, lying on his side, head to the north, face to the east, after imparting his final instructions to his disciple.[14]

In the *Story of Bilawhar and Būdāsf,* the term *budd* does not refer to the prince Būdāsf but to the founder of the ancient religion of King Ganaysar. For Būdāsf, this religion of idolaters is a falsification of the *budd*'s original doctrine, whose truth he wants to re-establish. For Ganaysar, the *budd* preached a morality founded in generosity and worldly life; but for Būdāsf, he essentially preached renunciation, and his true servants are the ascetics whom the king persecutes. At any rate, the *budd* in question no longer has much of a Buddhist character.

These sources, which confirm the mediating role played by Arab culture between India and Europe, also suggest a revision of the classical pattern showing an exclusive transmission of Buddhism from India to the East. As we have seen, Buddhism was also transmitted to the West, through southwest Asia and the Near East. However, unlike East Asian cultures, Persian and Arabic cultures do not seem to have provided a breeding ground for independent development of the Buddhist legend. This relative infertility is consistent with the fact that one of the main reasons for the decline of Buddhism in India was the Arab invasions from the eighth century onward.

The Life of the Buddha was known in Europe long before the nineteenth century, but this Buddha, when he appeared under his true identity, took for a time an increasingly exotic and fantastic turn before being cut back to more human dimensions by historians. The first mention, still rather sober, appears in Saint Jerome in connection with a sect of gymnosophists or "naked sages," a term perhaps more appropriate to Jain ascetics than to Buddhist monks: "It is . . . a tradition among the gymnosophists of India that Buddha, the founder of their doctrine, was born of a virgin and came out from her side."[15] Thus, notes Foucher, "it is a Church Father, setting an example by himself, who invites us to bring the legend of the Buddha closer to that of Christ."[16]

A (NOT SO) CHRISTIAN LIFE

Yet it was above all through the *Golden Legend* of James of Voragine (ca. 1228–1298), itself influenced by Arab legend, that the Life of the Buddha surreptitiously entered the imagination of the Christian West. In the chapter "New Works on Buddhism" in his *New Studies on Religious History,* Renan wrote: "The narrative of the *Lalitavistara* seemed so beautiful to Eastern Christians that they made of it the Lives of Saints Barlaam and Josaphat, which for centuries has been read in the Church with edification. When the Buddhist Gospel was first translated into French by Mr. Foucaux, all people of taste read it with extreme pleasure and thought they were dealing with a fabulous legend rather than with a myth devoid of reality."[17]

Foucher, in turn, wrote: "The novel of the youth of the Buddha, passed from Sanskrit into Greek through Syriac, entered Christian patrology under the authority of St. John Damascene, and the Bodhisattva, barely disguised under the name of Josaphat, took his place in the Roman and Greek martyrology."[18] Thus, "on the authority of the pious novel of the Syrian John Damascene, Pope Sixtus V inscribed him in the Roman martyrology under the date of November 27."[19] This legend has had distant echoes, since relics of Saint Josaphat have been found (or rather invented) as far away as Belgium. These relics, a bone and a portion of the spinal column of Josaphat (therefore of the Buddha!), had been given in 1571 by the Doge Luigi Mocenigo to the Portuguese king Sebastian and had, after many adventures, washed up in Bruges, in the cloister of Saint-Sauveur. They don't seem to be there today.[20]

The Latin translation of the legend of Barlaam and Josaphat was preceded by three consecutive translations, into Arabic, Georgian, and Greek. There are in fact several Arabic versions. The richest and probably the oldest is known as the Syrian text or the Ismaili Arabic version, because it was preserved by the Ismaili community. Despite its monotheistic character, it is probably the closest to the original Buddhist tradition, and it contains many details that were expunged from the later Christian version. In fact, it is presented as being representative of the true teaching of the *Budd.* According to this text, which seems to echo the Arabic texts mentioned above, there are two traditions that claim to be faithful to the *Budd,* one polytheistic ("idolatrous") and hedonistic, the other monotheistic and ascetic. The author of course presents the second as the only authentic tradition, and he exhorts the rival stream to return to its sources. The *Budd* brought God's message to mankind, just as other messengers have done in other times. He was simply "a servant of God and a physician of souls." The Georgian version, more literary, eliminates the long developments of the Arabic version. The Greek version seems to date from the beginning of the eleventh century and is the source, through its Latin translations, of the Christian legend. It adds a number of materials to the Georgian version: elements of Christian doctrine, sermons, prayers, and biblical quotations. "Idolatry" is much more hateful here than in earlier versions, and the theological reasons for this hatred are clearly stated.

The story, in its main lines, is as follows: a proud and powerful king persecutes the ascetics who live in his kingdom. Being himself an idolater, he despises their renunciation and their monotheistic faith. When a boy (Josaphat) is born to him, he rejoices that his legacy is now assured. But astrologers predict a possible double future for the child: he could become a great king, but he could also renounce the world for a less earthly glory. Worried by this portent, the king sequesters the boy inside the palace. Josaphat, growing up, nevertheless has three encounters that disturb him. In the meantime, he has received a visit from the ascetic Barlaam (the monk of the Buddhist legend), who tells him that if the king prevents him from leaving the palace, it is for fear that he will convert to Christianity. It is thus no longer a question of hiding from Josaphat the harsh realities of existence, as in the case of the Bodhisattva, but of hiding the word of God. From that point on, Josaphat has only one desire: to find God. Barlaam instructs him in the monotheistic faith and in asceticism. Josaphat eventually leaves the palace and pursues an ascetic existence, but before that he must undergo a series of trials and even accept dominion over the kingdom for a time. Finally, having found Barlaam again, he lives and dies in the odor of sanctity, sure that he has earned his place in the Kingdom of Heaven.[21]

If at first glance this legend seems to be a mere replica of the Buddha's Life, its meaning is actually quite different, inasmuch as it leads to salvation through faith.[22] Josaphat's spiritual quest is an effect of divine grace and not the result of free choice, as was the case with the Bodhisattva (although he received a lot of help from the gods). Moreover, while renunciation and asceticism are common to both figures, the climax of the Buddha's Life, the awakening, is absent in the legend of Josaphat. However, the details associated with the Buddha's awakening have not entirely disappeared; they have simply been reinterpreted in a monotheistic way. When Josaphat approaches the marvelous tree, four angels lift him up into the air and reveal all things to him. But this vision is granted to him by divine messengers, not obtained through meditation. The family background of the two characters is also very different. Josaphat's mother is not mentioned, but his father is violent and dishonest; he threatens, tortures, maims, and burns his opponents. What strikes a modern reader most in this legend, as in most of the stories in the *Golden Legend,* is its atmosphere of violence. On the other hand, the flaw that sums up all the others for a premodern Christian author is that the king is an idolater. In any case, one comes to miss King Śuddhodana, whose only (well-forgivable) fault was to want his son to succeed him. It is Barlaam, the Christian anchorite, who plays the role of spiritual father for Josaphat. For the latter, it is not so much a question of practicing asceticism, but of denying his biological father and his father's religion, of rejecting evil for the good.[23]

AN EXOTIC BUDDHA

Later, the Buddha is mentioned again, under the name Sogomon Barchan, in the work of the Venetian traveler Marco Polo (1271–1295). However, despite the theological virtues of Śākyamuni, Marco Polo does not go so far as to identify him with Josaphat and simply says that he would have been a great saint if he had been born among Christians. Yet he describes in detail the life of the Bodhisattva in the palace:

> He was the son of a king of the island, who devoted himself to an ascetic life, refusing to accept kingdoms or any other worldly possessions, although his father endeavoured, by the allurements of women, and every other imaginable gratification, to divert him from the resolution he had adopted. Every attempt to dissuade him was in vain, and the young man fled privately to this lofty mountain [the so-called Peak of Adam, on the island of Zeilan, that is, Ceylon], where, in the observance of celibacy and strict abstinence, he at length terminated his mortal career.[24]

Marco Polo thus follows the Buddhist tradition quite faithfully in his description of the palace, but he is careful not to compare the court of the great khan, with its harem, to that of King Avennir (the Abenner of the *Golden Legend,* the Christian counterpart of Śuddhodana), whom the Bodhisattva wanted to flee. He mentions only two encounters (out of the four in the Buddhist legend) that led Śākyamuni to go in search of "The One Who Doesn't Die." He also reverses their order: first the corpse, then the old man.[25] Unfortunately, he does not mention the career of the Buddha after his awakening, and simply says that (Buddhist) "idolatry" began with the temple built by the father for his dead son. The connection that Marco Polo drew between Josaphat and the Bodhisattva went almost unnoticed, and it was not until three centuries later that the parallels, and then the identity, between the two Lives were rediscovered.[26] It was perhaps difficult to see what should have been obvious, namely, that as long as the Buddha remained an exotic monster, it would have been sacrilegious for anyone but the author of the *Book of Wonders* to compare him to a Christian saint.

The Buddha in the Classical Age

It is in the classical age that the Buddha took on truly fantastic dimensions. Simon de La Loubère (1642–1729), member of the third diplomatic mission sent by Louis XIV to the court of the king of Siam in 1687, gives a rather detailed account of the Life of the Buddha, which he calls Sommona-codom. I quote the passage almost in extenso, to give an idea of his style:

> 'Tis no fault of mine that they gave me not the life of *Sommona-Codom* translated from their books, but not being able to obtain it, I will here relate what was told me thereof. No matter how wonderful they claim his birth was, they still give him a father and a mother. His mother, whose name can be found in one of their Bali [Pāli] books, was called, they say, Mahà Maria [Mahā Māyā], which seems to mean the Great Mary, because Mahà means great.[27]

De La Loubère confuses the account of the last human life of the Buddha with that of his previous lives, in the form of Prince Vessantara and of King Śibi:

> 'Tis said, that he bestowed all his estate in alms, and that his charity not being yet satisfied, he pluck'd out his eyes, and slew his wife and children, to give them to the *Talapoins* of his age to eat. A strange contrariety of ideas in this people, who prohibit nothing so much as to kill, and who relate the most execrable parricides, as the most meritorious works of *Sommona-Codom.*[28]

The French diplomat then mentions the encounter of the Buddha with Māra, in whom he sees only a human rival:

> *Sommona-Codom,* having freed himself by the alms I have said, from all the attachments of life, devoted himself to fasting, prayer, and other practices of the perfect life: but since these practices are reserved to the *Talapoins,* he embraced the profession of *Talapoin;* and when he had completed his good deeds, . . . he found himself endowed with such great strength that he defeated in a single combat another man of consummate virtue, whom they call *Préa Soüane* [Māra?], and who, doubting the perfection which *Sommona-Codom* had achieved, challenged him to test his strength, and was defeated.[29]

The author establishes a curious causal relationship between the Buddha's victory over Māra (presented here as murder) and the fact that he lived only eighty years. We recall that, in the Buddhist legend, it is Māra who, after repeated attempts, convinces the Buddha to renounce life. In de La Loubère's account, Māra's name, along with that of his horde, becomes "Man":

> Although *Préa Pouti Tcháou* [Sommona-Codom] had reached such high virtue, this did not prevent him from killing a *Mar,* or a *Man* . . . ; and as punishment for this great sin, his life only lasted eighty years, after which he died, suddenly *disappearing* like a spark vanishes in the air. . . . The *Man* were the enemies of *Sommona-Codom,* and [the Siamese] call their king *Payà Man* [Māra Papiyan]; and because they suppose that these people were the enemies of such a holy man, they see them like monstrous people, with broad faces, horribly large teeth, and snakes on their heads instead of hair.

This distorted version of the Buddha's victory over Māra leads de La Loubère to attribute the Buddha's death to indigestion from eating pork:

> One day, therefore, when *Préa Poutì Tcháou* ate pig flesh, he had a colic which killed him: an admirable end for such an abstemious man: but he had to be killed by a pig, because they think that the soul of the *Man* he killed was not then in the body of a *Man,* but in that of a pig.[30]

This allows the author to discuss the animal rebirths of the Bodhisattva:

> And when they say that *Sommona-Codom* was a king, they say it as they say he was a monkey and a pig. They suppose that in the various transmigrations of his soul he was all things, and always excellent in each species, that is to say, that he was the most loosest of all pigs, as the most loosest of all the kings.[31]

But perhaps the most interesting innovation is the relationship the author establishes between Devadatta and Christ, based on a false etymology between Māyā and Maria (Mary):

> At any rate, this attracted the Missionaries' attention, and it perhaps led the Siamese to believe that Jesus, being son of Mary, was the brother of *Sommona-Codom;* and that having been crucified, he was this scelerat brother, whom they give to *Sommona-Codom* under the name of *Thevetat,* and whom they say is punished in hell with a torture that has something to do with that of the Cross.[32]

According to de La Loubère, the invention of Thevetat (Devadatta) parallels that of the Buddha—in which, from a narrative point of view, he may not be entirely wrong, as the following passage suggests:

> Since they tell nothing but fables about their *Sommona-Codom* . . . one can doubt, it seems to me, that there ever was such a man. He seems to have been invented gratuitously to express the idea of a man which virtue, as they conceive it, made happy. . . . And because they believed it necessary to express at the same time the opposite idea, that of a man which his wickedness subjected to great pains, they apparently invented this *Thevetat,* whom they suppose was the brother of *Sommona-Codom* and his enemy.[33]

The Siamese tradition concerning the damnation of Thevetat and the torture of the cross to which he was subjected suggested to de La Loubère that in reality we are dealing here with a tradition about Christ, whose Passion the Thai, by making him the enemy of the Buddha, transform into a well-deserved infernal punishment. This leads the author to add a long appendix on the life of Thevetat at the end of his work.[34]

One finds more or less the same description of the Buddha and his religion in the *Journal du voyage au Siam* written in 1685–1686 by François Timoléon, Abbé de Choisy (1644–1724) and great transvestite before the Lord:

> Their last god is called Ckodom; some call him Somono-Ckdom, in other words the great Ckdom. They say that he died 2229 years ago; that he passed through the bodies of five hundred animals of different species; that while he was a Talapoin, another Talapoin came from the eastern lands wanting to approach him very closely, and that suddenly by his command the earth opened, and the wicked Talapoin was thrown into hell, bound in chains, and in a posture quite similar to a crucified man. This fable gives them some distance from the Cross. They add that although Ckdom was annihilated, and therefore they have no God at this time, his remains are among the Talapoin, and that in a few centuries an angel will come to make himself Talapoin, and then God, and by his great merits he will deserve to be annihilated, and that his law will last a hundred million years.[35]

The style and rhetoric of these texts might make us smile if we fail to remember that we are basically in the same situation as their authors, and continue to judge Buddhism and its presumed founder by our hopes and fears. After all, the facts and legends that these early observers collected were real, and only their interpretation was wrong, unaware of its ideological and cultural assumptions. This situation was not going to improve, far from it, with the European expansion in Asia.

The Jesuit Buddha

In the West, the main source of information about the Buddha remained the Society of Jesus, thanks in particular to the *New Memoirs on the Present State of China* by the Jesuit missionary Louis Le Comte (1655–1729), whose account of the Buddhist legend is succinct but very nearly right:

> No body can well tell where this Idol *Fo* [Chinese reading for "Buddha"], of whom I speak, was born; (I call him an Idol and not a Man, because some think it was an Apparition from Hell) those who with more likelihood say he was a Man, make him born above a thousand years before JESUS CHRIST, in a Kingdom of the *Indies* near the Line, perhaps a little above *Bengala*. They say he was a King's Son. He was at first call'd *Che-Kia* [Śākya]; but at thirty years of Age he took the name of *Fo*. His Mother who brought him into the World thro her right side, died in Childbirth; she had a fancy in her Dream that she swallow'd an Elephant, and for this reason it is that the *Indian* Kings pay such honour to white Elephants: for the loss of which, or gaining some others they often make bitter Wars.[36]

From these rudiments of legend, Le Comte quickly drifts toward a deistic reading that will allow him to accuse the founder of the rival religion of heresy:

> When this Monster was first born he had strength enough to stand alone, and he made seven steps, and pointed with one hand to Heaven, and the other to the Earth. He did also speak, but in such a manner as shew'd what Spirit he was possess'd withal. *In Heaven or on Earth,* says he, *I am the only Person who deserve to be honoured.* At seventeen he married, and had a Son, which he forsook as he did all the rest of the World, to retire in a Solitude with three or four *Indian* Philosophers, whom he took along with him to teach. But at thirty he was on a sudden possess'd, and as it were fullfill'd with the Divinity, who gave him an universal knowledge of all things. From that time he became a God, and began by a vast number of seeming Miracles, to gain the Peoples admiration. The number of his Disciples is very great, and it is by their means that all the *Indies* have been poysoned with his pernicious Doctrine. Those of *Siam* call them *Talapoins,* the Tartars call them *Lamas* or *Lama-sem,* the Japoners *Bonzes,* and the Chinese *Hocham* [Ch. *heshang*].[37]

The teaching of this false God can be summed up for Le Comte in three words: idolatry, atheism, and nihilism:

> But this Chimerical God found at last that he was a Man as well as others. He died at 79 years of Age; and to give the finishing stroke to his

> Impiety, he endeavored to persuade his Followers to Atheism at his Death, as he had persuaded them to Idolatry in his Life time. Then he declared to his Followers that all which he had hither told them was enigmatical; and that they would be mistaken if they thought there was another first Principle of things beside nothing; *It was,* said he, *from this nothing that all things sprang, and it is into this nothing that all things must return. This is the Abyss where all our hopes must end.*
>
> Since this Impostor confessed that he had abused the World in his life, it is but reasonable that he should not be believed at his death. Yet as Impiety has always more Champions than Virtue, there were among the *Bonzes* a particular Sect of Atheists, formed from the last words of their Master. The rest who found it troublesome to part with their former prejudices, kept close to their first Errors. A third sort endeavoured to reconcile these Parties together, by compiling a body of Doctrine, in which there is a twofold Law, an interior and an exterior. One ought to prepare the mind for the reception of the other. It is, they say, the mould which supports the materials 'till the Arch be made, and is then taken away as useless.[38]

After Le Comte, Adriano di St. Thecla (1667–1765), in his *Short Treatise on Sects among the Chinese and Tonkinese* (*Opusculum de Sectis apud Sinenses et Tunkinenses*), tells us that the founder of the worshipers of Phat (Fo) was—

> a very famous man, named Thich Ca [Śākya] by the Annamites, and that he was born in India. His father was King Tinh Phan (Jing Fan), his mother was Mada, his wife Da Thi (Ye Shi), his concubine Nhu La (Ruo Luo). . . . When his father refrained for three years from paying the annual tribute he owed to King Li Ho (Li Hu), the latter threatened to punish him. When Tinh Phan resolved to pay the tribute, his ministers, fearing reprisals, shirked, and his son was sent. He was so diplomatic that all was restored to normal. His father rewarded him with a palace, but he preferred to retreat to the mountains. On the road, he met two demons, A la la (Aluoluo) and Hac la la (Heiluoluo), who introduced him to their doctrine. He then transmitted this doctrine to the members of his sect, who gave him a new name, Thich Ca Mau Ni Phat [Śākyamuni Buddha]. He also accepted this new name from two figures named Di Da (Mituo = Amitābha) and Di Lac (Milei = Maitreya). Sitting between these two demons, who served as his instructors, he listened to their instructions and wrote them in forty-two treatises.[39]

This story has little to do with the Buddha's story except for a few names. The asceticism in the mountain becomes an initiation, or rather two successive initiations by two couples of "demons," the Brahmins of the Buddhist legend first, and then the bodhisattvas, who represent the two aspects—exoteric (Hīnayāna) and esoteric (Mahāyāna)—of Buddhism.

In Japan, the Jesuit missionaries encountered a strong Buddhist presence. In spite of the initial interest of Francis-Xavier (1506–1552) in Buddhism, which seemed to him to be an intellectually profound doctrine (an opinion that the Jesuits of China were far from sharing), the knowledge that the missionaries managed to gather about the rival religion remained superficial. The Japanese convert Anjirō told them about the life of "Sciacca," who, only three months after his birth, had taken three steps, pointed to heaven and earth, and declared: "In Heaven and on Earth, I am the only Venerable One." When the king his father ordered him to marry one of his relatives, Sciacca fled to the mountains, where he lived in penance for seven years. Then he began to preach a new religion and eventually gathered around him no fewer than eight thousand disciples."[40] Anjirō's account, which betrays the influence of the Japanese Lives of the Buddha, had a great influence on the perception of Buddhism by Francis-Xavier and his successors.

For Juan Fernandez, Francis-Xavier's interpreter, Shaka or Yaca (Śākyamuni) is no longer a retarded apostle of Christianity, as Anjirō had portrayed him, but rather an impostor and blasphemer who, at the age of seven, dared to declare that he was the only Venerable One in the world. When he spoke of "ancient saints" like Amida, Shaka claimed that one could be transformed by praying to them, and he wrote many books in this vein. But at the age of forty-nine, Fernandez tells us, he suddenly changed his mind, declaring that he had been ignorant until then. He had just realized that salvation cannot be obtained through scripture, veneration, or prayer, but only through meditation. Shaka's sudden reversal is interpreted as hypocrisy by Fernandez and his disciple Cosme de Torres.[41]

Alessandro Valignano (1539–1606), who succeeded Francis-Xavier in Japan in 1571, distinguished the Japanese gods (*kami*) from the buddhas (*hotoke*), whom he counts as coming from Thailand: "Those, called *Hotoke,* are Chinese deities, themselves coming from Siam, and the main ones are called, one Amida, the other Shaka." This does not prevent Valignano from insisting on the human character of Śākyamuni:

> Shaka was a philosopher, a master of perversity, a stranger to things from above, ambitious, skillful. Wishing to make his name illustrious and famous in this world, because he knew little about the other, simulating a life of holiness and great penance, he began to preach Amida to the Siamese (a great and rich kingdom close to China), exalting Amida by giving him divine attributes and honors, and making him the principle from which all things are born and the end to which all things tend. . . . Shaka wrote a great number of books, or, perhaps more accurately, his disciples wrote down in these books the doctrine he preached to the people. These

> writings have as much credit and authority as the text of the Bible. But because Shaka was skillful, he preached in such a way that it can be interpreted in many ways.[42]

The often extravagant speculations of the Jesuit missionaries died hard, because those who landed in Japan after Valignano faced brutal repression by the Japanese government and did not have the time to study the sacred history of their rivals more closely. Martin Scorsese's recent film *The Silence,* based on a novel of the same title by the Japanese (and Catholic) writer Endō Shusaku, recounts their tragic history—but Buddhism appears only briefly in it, in a rather caricatured form. In the West, Jesuit theories were eventually refuted by early philological and historical studies of the Buddha's life and doctrine. However, one had to wait for this until the romantic impulse of the "Eastern Renaissance" of the first half of the nineteenth century slowed down a little.[43]

Also worth mentioning is another tenacious tradition regarding the negroid character of the Buddha.[44] This theory of an African or Ethiopian Buddha—at any rate, one of the negroid type—was rejected by the sinologist Jean-Pierre Abel-Rémusat (1788–1832), one of the founders of the Société Asiatique.[45] But the predominant thesis was that the Buddha is a Hindu god.[46] A century after de La Loubère and the Abbé de Choisy, Sir William Jones (1746–1794), an eminent Indianist of the East India Company, declared: "[We] may fix the time of *Buddha,* or the *ninth* great incarnation of Vishnu, in the year *one thousand and fourteen* before the birth of Christ."[47] But soon, in order to explain the ambivalence of Hindu sources with regard to this character who was sometimes presented as an avatar of Vishnu, sometimes as a heretic, Jones came to postulate a second Buddha, a thousand years later than the first, to whom he also attributed African origins. None of his informants had apparently explained to him the reason the Buddha was considered an avatar of Vishnu: obviously the Hindu god took on the features of a heretic in order to better damn his followers.[48]

Christian Prejudices

In the nineteenth century, Christian missionaries—mostly Protestant after the suppression of the Society of Jesus in 1773—had no better opinion of the Buddha and his doctrine than their Jesuit predecessors. Even though they now had better access to sources, they were too often blinded by their religious and orientalist prejudices. Toward the end of the century, the trend seems to have been reversed with the official recognition of the religions of Asia at the World Parliament of Religions in 1893 and the enthusiastic reception given to "The Light of Asia" (1879), the famous poem by Edwin Arnold (1832–1904) on the Life of the Buddha. This romantic work, abundantly translated and republished, aimed at adapting the Buddhist message to a Western audience by presenting the Buddha as a kind of Eastern Christ.[49]

In response, the English missionary John L. Atkinson dedicated to young Christians his English translation of the *Shaka hassō monogatari* (Tale of Śākyamuni's eight acts), which he entitled *Prince Siddhārtha, the Japanese Buddha*. In his dedication, he expresses "the sincere hope that its perusal may make clear to them the *vital difference* there is between the Light of Asia and the Light of the world." He hopes, in doing so, to turn to Christ "those millions of beings throughout the East who are now accepting the depressing and gloomy teachings of the Buddha."[50] The preface by Francis E. Clark sets the tone:

> No one can compare the grotesque account of the birth of Buddha with the noble and dignified story of the birth of Christ to the advantage of the former. The quarrel of Māyā and Kyodomi [Māyā/Gotamī] contrasts most unfavorably with the loving greetings of Mary and Elizabeth. . . . In fact, this book is an excellent foil to the Gospels. . . . If Buddhism has nothing better to offer the world than the life of Prince Siddartha [sic], the religion of Christ need not tremble.[51]

In addition to his translation, Atkinson provides a chapter on Buddha's paradise and its ten delights (illustrated), then another on the awakening (quoting Edwin Arnold) and the parinirvāṇa. He contrasts Buddhism and Christianity in these terms: "The teachings of the one represent chill and gloom, depression, darkness, despair, and irremediable death. The teachings of the other represent hope, cheer, light, life, and everlasting joy."[52] Atkinson points to the moon and sun to emphasize the contrast, the moon symbolizing the Buddha, the "Light of Asia," while the sun corresponds to Christ, the "Light of the world."[53]

In a number of authors, such as the philosopher Jules Barthélémy-Saint-Hilaire, a characteristically Christian prejudice against a quietist or nihilist Buddha—a kind of Asian Spinoza—makes itself known. This prejudice died hard, since it still appears at the beginning of the twentieth century—under the pen of Paul Claudel (1868–1955), for example.[54] In *Connaissance de l'Est* (1900), Claudel writes:

> But these blinded eyes refused to recognize the unconditional being, and to the one called the Buddha it was given to perfect the pagan blasphemy. . . . [To] break the dreadful circle of Vanity, you did not hesitate, Buddha, to embrace the Void. Rather than explain something by its outward use, he sought its intrinsic principle within himself and found nothing but the Void, and so his doctrine taught a monstrous communion. The method is that the Sage, having made the idea of form, and pure space, and the very idea of the idea, successively vanish from his mind, finally arrives at the Void, and *then* enters Parinirvāṇa. And

> people were astonished by this word. For me, I find the idea of *jouissance* added there, to the idea of the Void. And this is the last and Satanic mystery, the silence of the creature entrenched in its complete refusal, the incestuous quietude of the soul sitting on its essential difference.[55]

But Claudel's polemical text represented a rearguard struggle, and the Buddhism to which it addressed itself was already outdated. It was a new Buddha who became the darling of the West, and his image is reflected in the most diverse mirrors.

17

THE MODERN BUDDHA

Toward the middle of the nineteenth century, a real turnaround occurred, and the Buddha became the exemplar of an eminently rationalist mind, an incomparable philosopher.[1] With one more step came the affirmation that his teaching, free of all dogma and based on experience alone, is perfectly compatible with the scientific method. But as Donald Lopez points out, this "scientific Buddha" is in fact a "young buddha, born in the nineteenth century, not in the royal city of Kapilavastu, but in the republican city of Paris. From there he travelled to Sri Lanka and then to other parts of Asia."[2] But, Lopez wonders, "what happens to the old Buddha when a new Buddha appears on the scene, a Buddha whose coming had not been announced?" He concludes: "This scientific Buddha is a pale reflection of the Buddha born in Asia, a buddha who entered our world in order to destroy it. This buddha has no interest in being compatible with science."[3]

The notion of a scientific Buddha is still in vogue today, perhaps even more so than ever. To those who believe that the Buddhist doctrine is a prefiguration of quantum physics, Lopez, with a dry wit, replies: "If the Buddha had sought to alleviate only the most superficial form of suffering, then, endowed with both omniscience and deep compassion for all sentient beings, he would have taught something more compatible with modern science. Rather than teaching something that, to the ears of some, sounds vaguely like the theory of relativity, the Buddha would have provided a cure for suffering as science understands it; two millenia ago, he would have set forth the *Indoor Plumbing Sutra* and the *Lotus of Good Dental Hygiene*. But he did not."[4]

With the humanist Buddha discovered by Eugène Burnouf and the scientific Buddha invented by his successors, we are almost back to our starting point, the opposition between Senart's mythological Buddha and Oldenberg's historical and rationalist Buddha. The formative phase of the scientific study of Buddhism has been the subject of several studies, to which I can only refer.[5] The literary (or pseudo-literary) echoes raised by the Life of the Buddha, on the other hand, have yet to be explored, and it is to them that we turn in the following pages.

ROMANTIC AND "ROMANESQUE" VISIONS

Caroline Rhys Davids

One of the strangest contributions to the literary Life of the Buddha is undoubtedly that of Caroline Augusta Foley (C. A. F.) Rhys Davids (1857–1942), well remembered for the role she and her husband, Thomas Rhys Davids, played in the development of studies of the Pāli Buddhist canon. After the death of her son at the front in 1917, Caroline Rhys Davids sought refuge in spiritualism. Although her interpretation of Buddhism deviated from orthodoxy, she became, after her husband's death in 1922, president of the Pāli Text Society and remained so until her death in 1942. It was during this last period of her life that she set out in search of an "original Buddhism," with which her spiritualist convictions were increasingly mixed. Thus, in 1940, she reports having been in contact with the spirit of her late son. Her influence has nevertheless been important in the field of Buddhist studies, not only through her tireless activity in translating and publishing Pāli texts, but also through her interpretation of Buddhism as a psychology.[6]

In *Gotama The Man* (1928), a book halfway between biography (I hardly dare say autobiography) and novel, Caroline Rhys Davids makes the Buddha, who has returned from the beyond, address an English audience—or, more precisely, she is able to "communicate with him." The strange metaphysics of the voice that emerges is borrowed from the spiritualism of the time, its style also very dated (as is its psychology). The outdated character of the work becomes obvious when the Buddha praises magnetism, "which still awaits man's greater discoveries on it."[7] In any case, by making the Buddha speak in this way, the author endows him with a new, strongly individualistic personality. If the Buddha then undertakes to tell his own life story, it is above all to put an end to the legends invented and peddled by monks about him:

> I am the man who is called the Buddha, Sakyamuni, Bhagavat. I am the man Siddhattha Gotama. I have a mandate for the earth. The "man" is my theme.
>
> I am very man. I am not anything of the nature of a wonder-being. In the books that were written in Ceylon fom the oldest memorized sayings, I am spoken of in some ways worthily, but in the way of truth as to myself the telling is often worthless.[8]

This Buddha would therefore be above all a humanist thinker, an ardent supporter of man, but also a defender of the cause of women. The story of his life, stripped of all wonder, differs in many ways from traditional biographies. He expresses himself as an English gentleman, a reformer who was a proponent of feminism *avant la lettre,* and his movement aimed to give women "a new, freer life."[9] He is therefore opposed to the misogynistic reading that insists on his unwillingness to accept women within his monastic order. He further states that his mandate consists of a message centered on social activism that stands opposed to the monastic ideal of renunciation and the concomitant depreciation of life and body.[10] Māra, his old enemy, is reduced to a psychological type: "[He] was no devil or a mysterious wraith, as the books make out. When we used the term 'mara,' it was to speak of this man as a very type of will-worsener, either as a sceptic or as an encourager of low desires."[11] "Long after," he continues, "the monks came to give the idea real personality, personifying the things they most feared:—death, failure, seduction, the attraction of the world. . . . Māra is not a very devil himself or demon, but just a man who wills evil."[12]

We also learn that at the time of the parinirvāṇa, the Buddha, out of his body (as in the spiritualist testimonials concerning out-of-the-body experiences), could see his disciples crying around his remains. They did not realize that he was still there, ready to talk to them: they saw only the object, not the *real man,* the *pudgala* (a.k.a. the "individual"). This is a very unorthodox conception, as is the rest of the book, but we know that orthodoxy, in the author's view, is the monastic sin that the Buddha rejects in the name of a superior humanism. In service of the same humanism, he rejects the idea that man can be reborn in animal form.[13] He also praises secularism and regrets that the monks' negative values have prevailed. In the path he preached, "Much was there on the man, little the monk. But the later books are all of them by the monk and for monks."[14]

The Buddha subsequently launches into a diatribe against the monks who betrayed his message: "Thus the teaching came to be shaped by the monk's ideal, and that was not mine. The monk saw life as ill. I saw it as growing in the better. The monk saw man as the worse for his mind and body. I saw man as growing by means of his use of mind and body."[15] And in an ironic twist, he shows an anticlericalism that is very much in the spirit of the nineteenth century: "Monks are the very bats of the cult they call after me. They set store by the night. They prefer to have the mind dark on all that can be made of life. They are haters of the light."[16]

In a true piece of bravery, the Buddha then recounts his passage into the afterlife, the moment when he saw the buddhas of the past come to meet him: "In a moment I was with them, among them, one of them, no more a dying old man, but in a new body, as it seemed, a young body, a young mind, in the health of youth. Vanished was the old husk!"[17]

In his last message, the Buddha reaffirms his humanism: "What is it that I hold, now as of old, most precious upon earth? It is the men, the women, whose thoughts are upon both worlds, this and the next."[18]

In an appendix, Caroline Rhys Davids justifies her book by saying that if a person "came to us from the dead," she would probably correct a lot of things in her biography. This is precisely the testimony she gives us in these pages: "The one thing that can justify such a book as this, without further explanation, is the aim to get nearer the truth about the life and work of its subject [the Buddha]."[19] She concludes: "The one thing that most of all matters is that [the reader] sees the very Man—the 'man-in-man,'—who uses but is not body or mind—speaking to the man-in-man in each reader."[20]

In spite (or because) of these laudable intentions, the book quickly fell into oblivion, and I quote passages from it certainly not for their literary qualities, but because they reflect the spirit of an era that saw the Buddha rise from the abyss of time. Better than her contemporaries, Caroline Rhys Davids understood that the historical Buddha is a ghost, and that historians are spiritualists.

Victor Segalen

Another testimonial reflecting the zeitgeist, more literary this time, is that of the poet (but also doctor, novelist, sinologist, and archaeologist) Victor Segalen (1878–1919). Like so many others, Segalen makes a clear distinction between the pure doctrine of the Buddha and later Buddhism, which, in his view, was led astray by popular superstition. After a visit to Mount Wutai (a stronghold of Chinese Buddhism), Segalen offers this heartfelt appeal in a short text entitled "To the Hindu Buddha":

> Delivered One, you who left your immense memory in the hearts of more men than any saviour ever did—would you return to this mountain to witness the perjury done in your name?
>
> What have they done with you and your teachings! You taught us the denial of idols, and they fashion them like a sow her calves: all ugly and all alike. . . . Do not return, O Delivered One![21]

During a stay of a few months in Ceylon (Sri Lanka) in 1904, Segalen met a Buddhist monk and deepened his knowledge of the Buddha's life in books and paintings. It is then that he began to write the first of five acts of a drama entitled *Siddhârtha*. In "Roadmaps," written nearly twenty years later during an archaeological mission in China, he noted to himself: "Rewrite in the form of a comic and satirical drama,—against *Buddhism,* of course, my Siddhârtha Gautama (which would thus have, like a feigned Temptation, its two versions, one of a youthful 'naivety,' the other of an ironic maturity)."[22]

Segalen finished *Siddhârtha* in 1907, two years after his return to France. According to the interpretation given by Christian Doumet, *Siddhârtha* is the story of a man, a hero, marked at birth by a handicap: he refuses to open his eyes and see the world around him. Segalen conceives of the Bodhisattva's life as a drama of vision, an inability to see reality exacerbated by an entourage that seeks to protect him by preventing him from discovering the afflictions of human life: illness, old age, and death. The Buddhist theme, "thanks to the complex of visibility and invisibility that it implies, illustrates for him the exacerbation of a scopic drive on which an ideology and metaphysics of seeing is based. . . ."[23]

The prologue of *Siddhârtha* takes place one week after the birth of the Bodhisattva. The king despairs because the newborn has not yet opened his eyes, but a soothsayer predicts that the child "will be the Lord of the world and King of the Four Kingdoms . . . if he does not see—even with the eyes of a child—the Three Horrors . . . an old man—a sick man—a dead man." Hearing this, the king dismisses the old soothsayer and the villagers who have come with gifts, as well as Queen Māyā, who is feeling sick. The unfortunate mother will not have time to see her son's eyes. But this drama of sight, and the blindness that precedes it, also suggests that hearing and the ability to hear are at the origin of awakening.

Siddhârtha's quest begins with a misunderstanding. When his son is just born, his cousin Krisha says to him, "A son is born—here is the delivered one—The son is born—Where is the spouse?"

A startled Siddhârtha answers: "Delivered? Delivered! . . . She has thrown an omen clear as a dawn. . . . Delivered from doubts and delivered from sorrows. . . . She has sung as if through a prophetic breath.—Don't look any further: I have found myself through your voice . . . I have found myself . . . Krisha!"[24]

Siddhârtha discovers a meaning literally unheard of in the innocent words of his cousin. Krisha, through her singing, opens for Siddhârtha a path to himself. The misunderstanding, the equivocation, the misinterpretation provoke a totally new and unsuspected understanding by the very person who triggered this revelation.

In the same way Segalen gives a new but erroneous interpretation, according to the Buddhist tradition, of the Buddha's awakening. Once again Krisha is the intermediary, the one who guides Siddhârtha to a new understanding:

> Siddhârtha.—. . . Where to look?
> Krisha.—Deep inside you.
> Siddhârtha.—I can't see anything! . . .
> Krisha.—Listen too. Listen: there are voices that are never heard and that sing: there are unheard voices.

First of all, Siddhârtha finds it difficult to hear, but these voices that "sing ineffable things" delight him by revealing to him that "pain is not himself."[25] Thus Segalen makes the process of awakening a gradual disengagement from the fixation on sight. To see well, to discover like Siddhârtha the illusion of the world, one must first learn to hear well, to hear the unheard. This emphasis, the very personal importance given to hearing in Segalen's *Siddhârtha,* is undoubtedly its most original characteristic.

On hearing Debussy's music in *Pelléas et Mélisande,* a music of the unspoken, Segalen wished to complete his synesthesia, the sonic and visual illumination of his *Siddhârtha,* by bringing Debussy's music into it. He had perceived that there was still an empty place in his drama for the unspeakable and sensed that Debussy's music was the sound illumination that would complete his work. On April 27, 1906, Segalen met Debussy for the first time and spoke to him about his *Siddhârtha.* The composer did not immediately reject a possible collaboration. Segalen therefore sent him a first version of *Siddhârtha* from Brest. During a second interview, on September 11, 1906, Debussy asked him a question that Segalen found "unexpected and very beautiful": "Why not leave your manuscript as it is? Buddhism teaches the vanity and uselessness of all things." Segalen refused to listen to the unsaid in that question, through which Debussy was expressing his reservations about the possibility of making *Siddhârtha* an opera. On August 4, 1907, he sent Debussy a complete version of *Siddhârtha,* assuring him once again that it was a work "entirely plastic, malleable according to [his] own desires."[26] Then he wrote to him again to clarify a few points:

> Only one thing is definitive: the very fabric of the drama: Visions—Renunciation—Asceticism—Despair. It is not mine. It is the very progression of this admirable crisis of the legendary Siddhârtha (very close to being historical, which is not important to us), but, for sure, very close, very intimate to us.
>
> The Evolution, to be complete, would include, I told you, a fifth act or even an epilogue: the Nirvāṇa. But the drama ceases, in my opinion, with this cessation of Desire, this appeasement of the Thirst for life, of the Buddhist Tanhà, the only possible definitions of the Nirvanic state. From this moment, moreover, the Buddha is no longer man (*nor is he God either*). From then on, he is indifferent to us. I thus thought to do well by sticking to his poignant humanity.[27]

On August 26, 1907, Debussy finally gave his answer to Segalen: "It is a prodigious dream! Only, in its present form, I know of no music capable of penetrating this abyss!" His refusal was full of delicacy but nevertheless firm: "Note that I do not claim an impossibility, very simply . . . it frightens me. If I were to ask you to bring your dream back to more normal dimensions, I would have the impression of awkwardly destroying the effort of a part of your life."[28]

Debussy could only have imagined music for illustration, not an opera. The text seemed to him too long, and the drama too static to be represented on stage. He advised Segalen to rework the text by replacing the Buddha with Orpheus—which, by the way, shows the generic, ideal-typical character of this "historical" Buddha. Segalen then embarked on an Orphic cycle, without abandoning the idea of setting the Buddha's life to music. The same year, Debussy wrote an *Image* for piano entitled "And the moon descends on the temple" (Et la lune descend sur le temple), the manuscript of which has been preserved under the title "Buddha" in the Pierpont Morgan Library in New York. This *Image* with a hidden name could just as well have been entitled "Siddhârtha." Debussy had refused Segalen's "Buddha" to write his own Buddha. In secret, he had kept the base of Segalen's drama and inscribed his *Image* and music on it.

The story of this failed encounter condemned the Life of the Buddha to remain essentially textual, not musical. But Segalen's failure may have deeper reasons. One might think that his intuition of the "unspoken" would have opened the doors of the Buddhist legend for him. Unfortunately, by sticking resolutely to his perception of a purely human Buddha, he condemned himself to making his character a pale reflection of the Buddha of tradition and a copy of the Buddha of historiography.

Hermann Hesse

The romantic and literary career of the Buddha continued but without giving rise to the masterpieces one might have hoped for. Let us mention in passing a drama with Shakespearian accents, "The Buddha" (in three acts and four interludes), composed by Paul Carus (1852–1919), an author best known for his *Gospel of the Buddha.* After the 1893 World Parliament of Religions, Carus had welcomed the young D. T. Suzuki to the United States and exerted a certain influence on the man who would herald the arrival of Zen Buddhism in the new world. All the same, it was actually through a novel by a Swiss writer of German origin, Hermann Hesse (1877–1962), that a romantic and fictional vision of the Buddha was established in the West. This book, published in 1922, bears the same title as Segalen's play, *Siddhartha.* In translation, it became very popular in the '60s and '80s, and it is no exaggeration to say that it was through Hesse's *Siddhartha* that a whole generation (if not more) discovered Buddhism.

Hesse splits the person (and the name) of the Buddha into two protagonists: Siddhartha, a young Brahmin who goes in search of the truth and pursues ascetic practice for several years with his faithful companion Govinda; and Gotama, the Buddha, whom Siddhartha meets in the Jetavana Park. But unlike Govinda, Siddhartha refuses to enter the orders, and he explains to the Buddha that he must follow his own path. This meeting, however, produces in him a first realization that paradoxically leads him to return to the world. He abandons his path of renunciation and crosses a river, symbolizing his return to the world he had left behind. He then becomes the disciple of a courtesan, Kamala, who teaches him the ways of love; and of Kamaswami, a rich merchant, who teaches him the business of trade. He spends several years in accumulating pleasures and riches until he is satiated and then disgusted. He abandons Kamala even though she is pregnant with his child (as Yaśodharā had been of the Bodhisattva, his namesake). His footsteps leading him back to the river, he thinks for a moment about drowning himself in it. Finally he takes refuge with the old ferryman Vasudeva, who had accommodated him in the past. By the river, he finally understands that the ceaseless flow of things, like the river's flow, does not exist. He meets Kamala again, a new convert to Buddhism, when she comes to the river with their son, intending to cross it to attend the funeral of the Buddha. In this meeting, he discovers paternal love but immediately has to part with his son, who insists—just as he did—that he must follow his own destiny. The river helps him to overcome his despair once again, revealing itself as the ultimate reality encompassing all things. When he finds his old companion Govinda, whom the monastic life has not led to deliverance, he gives him, as a parting gift, a foretaste of the awakened state he now shares with the Buddha and with his friend and master, the ferryman Vasudeva (who is actually a god). In the last scene, where Siddhartha's enigmatic smile reveals to his friend the mystery of the cycle of life and death, Siddhartha is reunited with his alter ego (or rather non-ego, since his idea of himself has disappeared), the Buddha.

The life of Siddhartha replicates that of the Buddha while modifying the sequence somewhat. Siddhartha abandons the mother of his child, as did the Buddha. He also finds truth on the banks of a river even though he does not have to suffer Māra's assaults in the process. Hesse, however, contrasts the two "Awakened Ones": unlike the Buddha, Siddhartha renounces the world before he has tasted its pleasures, only to rediscover them later. After his awakening, he does not preach or found a community. Two variants, then, but an underlying unity. As Govinda points out, Siddhartha's teaching seems very different from the simpler teaching of the Buddha, but both masters have reached the same truth. In fact, the Buddha's teaching, at least as it was reported in early Buddhism, is what later Mahāyāna Buddhists will call the exoteric truth. Siddhartha thus comes to represent the truth of *esoteric* Buddhism.[29]

With the success of Hesse's novel, the influence of the Life of the Buddha, indirectly borne by the counterculture of the 1960s and '70s, probably reached its peak in the West.[30] Although Hesse's Siddhartha does not represent the Buddha's teaching, the rise of Neo-Buddhism in our time cannot be understood without him.[31]

THE BUDDHA IN *MANGA* AND FILM

Surprisingly, the most complete, and most openly romanticized, Life of the Buddha is in fact a *manga* series simply entitled *Buddha.* It is one of the masterpieces of Tezuka Osamu (1928–1989), the most popular Japanese author of comics (*manga*) and graphic novels.[32] The drawing may seem a little outdated to us today, but it is more alive than that of many sophisticated comics, and it does not shrink from expressing moral and religious concerns amid a highly contemporary world view. As Tezuka himself says, it is not an "exact illustrated adaptation of the Buddhist scriptures. . . . There are many versions of the life of Śākyamuni, and much of it is ambiguous." But Tezuka remains very close to the spirit of the Buddhist tradition even though he has been criticized for taking too many liberties with it. Obviously, some of his characters do not appear in the canonical legend. Several other lives, just as rich in color, cross that of the Buddha, all forming a rich brocade, a human comedy where destinies are often tragic. The style is in some ways reminiscent of the romanticized life of the Buddha by Ōga Mantei, illustrated by Utagawa Kuniyoshi (1797–1861). But Tezuka's Buddha also derives in a direct line from the Western conception of a historical Buddha, as it was affirmed from the nineteenth century on. The supernatural elements of the legend are either ignored or skillfully reinterpreted. Thus, after the Buddha's birth, instead of the conventional image of the child taking seven steps to assert his authority over the world, we see the newborn, sleeping like a blessed one in his cradle, pointing his little hands up and down in his sleep. Śākyamuni also remains very human in his doubts and weaknesses, even after becoming the Buddha. This realistic description of his career will certainly displease both Buddhist devotees and critics of historicism, but it is no less moving. By stepping back from tradition and introducing comic anachronisms and other visual jokes, Tezuka manages to avoid the pitfall of hagiographic heavy-handedness. Whatever one may think of his interpretation, he succeeds in bringing Buddhist values to a wide audience without trivializing them.

Tezuka divides the Life of the Buddha into six major periods, but unlike the traditional narrative, centered on the eight acts of the Buddha, the periods chosen shift the story to characters other than the Buddha: Chaprah, Tatta, Devadatta, Ānanda, Prince Ajataśatru (Ajase), Virūdhaka (Prince Luly), and Angulimāla (Yatara). Let's look briefly at the first period, starting with Siddhārtha's youth. The young prince is moping among the splendors of the palace, and he is in poor health. His adoptive mother, Mahāprajāpatī, blames herself, but the king tells her that it has nothing to do with her. If the child is weak, it's because his biological mother, Māyā, was sick and had a difficult delivery, from which she died. A little later, while playing in the park with children who want to introduce him to hunting, Siddhārtha is mortified when they kill a young hare. Immediately afterward, one of the children drowns in a pond. The two sudden deaths, echoing each other, affect the prince deeply, but no one can answer his questions about death.

Contrary to the legend that gives us a young Siddhārtha who excels in all sports, Tezuka shows him unfit for archery, which earns him the contempt of his coach, Bandhaka. He then meets a wise old man—actually the god Brahmā in disguise—who makes him experience death through a meditation in which he identifies with the hare pierced by Bandhaka's arrow. Later, during the Festival of the Ploughmen, while meditating under a jambu tree, Siddhārtha relives the whole life of a bird, until the last moments. When he tells his parents about his experience, they are struck by the strangeness of what they take for a dream.

During a first attempt to escape from the royal castle, the prince falls in love with a young outcaste girl, Migaila, who will be blinded by order of the king.

The episode of the four encounters has been considerably reworked: the wise old man reappears and takes Siddhārtha to a ruined tower, asking him to choose one of the four gates that will determine his fate. The first gate leads him to a sick man, the second to an old man, the third to a corpse. Since he refuses each of these destinies, he has only one choice left: to become a monk. After the departure of the Bodhisattva, his young wife Yaśodharā rejects the advances of Bhandhaka, to whom the king has just ceded the throne in the face of the threatened invasion by the neighboring kingdom of Kosala. Bandhaka hates Siddhārtha, and before dying on the battlefield, he fathers a child with another woman whom he names Devadatta. This boy's destiny is to avenge the wrongs done to his father by Siddhārtha. By splitting the character of Devadatta and aligning his evil nature with Bandhaka, Tezuka is able to present a much more nuanced and sometimes even touching depiction of Devadatta.

This partial overview of the first of the eight volumes of Tezuka's Life of the Buddha should suffice to show how complex and full of twists and turns it is. Tezuka follows the legend in its broad outline, and although he innovates unabashedly on many occasions, he strives to keep the spirit of the legend. Understandably, the transformation of the Buddha into a very human and at the same time very romantic character has displeased some people. Also noteworthy is the subliminal eroticism, the constant presence around the Buddha of half-naked young women with opulent forms and generous breasts, whose advances he must resist on several occasions. His only intimate contact with the female body takes place when Migaila, his childhood sweetheart, who has become the wife of his friend and disciple Tatta, falls seriously ill, and he treats her by sucking pus from her wounds. As Tezuka notes in one of the mischievous comments sprinkled throughout the *manga* (often placed in the mouth of his alter ego, a small figure wearing an artist's beret): "Don't have any naughty thoughts." While there is nothing here to offend the self-righteous, it does not prevent the Buddha's rigorist disciple Depa, deceived by appearances, from denouncing him to the community.

Despite its flaws, the *Buddha* series probably had more impact on the Japanese public, young and old, than the orthodox version of the Buddha's Life. It combines a modernist conception of Buddhism with a traditional taste for the marvelous, and a sense of humor too often lacking in devotees (but hopefully abundant in the Buddha himself, whatever his historicity). Perhaps the Buddhist truth should be sought elsewhere than in orthodox Buddhism.

The Life of the Buddha has been the subject of several Indian comics, but they generally constitute a purely educational venture, whose sometimes sumptuous graphics leave little room for originality—unlike those of Tezuka.[33] It has also had a predictable success with New Age followers. One of the main architects of this success is Dipak Chopra, to whom we owe a romanticized "timeless" Life of the Buddha. Chopra claims to present the Buddha as he was—an energetic, curious, and friendly prince who for many years was protected, by order of his father the king, from the realities of the outside world. The birth of Siddhārtha is presented as quite ordinary, and Chopra even feels authorized to add "realistic" details—such as the advice her maids give to Māyā after his birth: expose your breasts to moonlight to increase lactation, as a popular recipe recommends. But this is once again a humanistic reading of the legend, one that makes surreptitious appeals to the imagination while bearing witness to a rather impoverished imaginary.[34]

The Life of the Buddha has been brought to the screen on various occasions, with very mixed success.[35] Let us first mention the animated film based on Tezuka's *manga, The Great Departure,* directed by Kōzō Morishita (known especially for his *Dragon Ball* series). This film takes liberties, not only with the canonical biography of the Buddha, but with the *manga,* and it appears to be on the verge of establishing itself as a new canon in some circles. The "guardians of the Dharma"—this is the title some critics have given themselves—have not failed to criticize it.

But on the whole it is undoubtedly necessary to give the award for kitsch to Bernardo Bertolucci's *Little Buddha* (1994), with Keanu Reeves in the role of the Buddha (well before his Christic role in *Matrix* in 1999). This mawkish movie is a web of naiveties and misinterpretations. Thus the great seduction scene, where the daughters of Māra dance or rather gesticulate in front of the Buddha, is perfectly ridiculous. Māra himself appears in the form of a double of the Bodhisattva, whom he asks to become his god. The Bodhisattva, of course, refuses and takes the earth as his witness, although the necessity of such a testimony is not explained, since the movie fails to mention Māra's assaults. Despite the rather grotesque nature of the scene, this filmic innovation is ultimately just another example of how, over the centuries, the central myth of the Life of the Buddha has been constantly reinterpreted. It is precisely in this sense that Michael Nichols defines Māra as "malleable," and explains the fascination he continues to exercise.[36]

A SCIENCE-FICTIONAL BUDDHA

An interesting development has taken place in science fiction over the last forty years. There are several books in which characters inspired by the Buddhist legend are involved, but the most interesting one is undoubtedly *Lord of Light* by the prolific Roger Zelazny.[37] It's a strange novel, unclassifiable, mixing fantasy, science fiction, crime, and Indian mythology. The action takes place on a planet colonized by humans exiled from Earth. Deceiving the local populations with their superior technology, they pretend to be the great gods of Indian mythology and maintain themselves at the top of a social hierarchy based on the Hindu caste system. They suppress all technological advances that could challenge their power. The hero, Sam (an abbreviation of Mahāsamatman, "Sam the Great Soul"), was originally one of these gods (or rather "augmented humans"), but he rebelled against his fellow humans by posing as the Buddha. The author retains only certain features of the Buddhist legend, and he is influenced by the Western vision of the Buddha as a reformer of the caste system. He describes Sam as a proponent of progress, a kind of Asian Prometheus, who believes that technology should be accessible to the masses, and that reincarnation should not be controlled by an elite. He thus protests against the Hindu conception of karma: "The definition of bad karma is anything our friends the gods don't like."[38]

Sam explains to Yama, the god of death, why he went to war with the gods: "I decided that mankind could live better without gods. If I disposed of them all, people could start having can openers and cans to open again, and things like that, without fearing the wrath of Heaven. We've stepped on these poor fools enough. I wanted to give them a chance to be free, to build what they wanted."[39] Here we have the relations between the historical Buddha and the Brahmins, transposed into the future: "The local Brahmins did not approve of the antiritualistic teachings of the Buddha, but his presence filled their coffers to overflowing; so they learned to live in his squat shadow, never voicing the word *tirthika,* heretic."[40]

Sam is presented as a kind of divine trickster. Here is how one goddess describes him: "Sam was the greatest charlatan in the memory of god or man. He was also the worthiest opponent Trimurti ever faced. . . . You know that he stole the fabric of his doctrine, path and attainment, the whole robe, from prehistorical forbidden sources. It was a weapon, nothing more. His greatest strength was his insincerity."[41] A number of anachronisms make the text very funny sometimes. Sam is an inveterate smoker. In the middle of the final battle, he asks Yama: "Then what do we do now?"—"Cultivate patience and smoke cigarettes."[42] Cigarettes are not his only human weakness. When a hotelier who holds him in high esteem offers him burgundy, Sam asks a pianist to play "The Blue Danube," a tune forbidden on this planet.[43] Sam and Yama, old accomplices, are enemies for a time, but Yama becomes Sam's ally again in the final battle against the gods.

Sam is finally defeated, but the victory of the gods is Pyrrhic: "'The Buddha has gone to Nirvāṇa,' said Brahma. 'Preach it in the Temples! Sing it in the streets. Glorious was his passing! He has reformed the old religion, and we are better now than ever before!' . . . The demons were free. . . . And elsewhere in the world there were those who remembered bifocal glasses and toilets that flushed, petroleum chemistry and internal combustion engines. . . . Vishnu was heard to say that the wilderness had come into the City at last."[44]

Zelazny gives us, in the parodic mode that he enjoys, a particularly imaginative reinvention of the Life of the Buddha. It would seem difficult to go much further in that register. But when it comes to literature, the die is never cast. What matters in the end is that this Life of the Buddha, as in the past, still stimulates our imaginations in the postmodern and perhaps transhuman era. This fact bodes well for many more posthuman avatars of the Buddha.

A NEW AVATAR?

In the news, it is a more classic avatar that has recently attracted media attention. At the end of 2005, the Nepalese media relayed a news item that very quickly inflamed the international press: a Nepalese youth of about fifteen years of age, Ram Bahadur Bomjon, has been meditating in the jungle without eating or drinking for more than six months, sitting in the lotus position in the hollow of a pipal fig tree (*ficus religiosa*), the same type of tree under which the Buddha was awakened. This youth has been engaged in ascetic practice expected to consume up to six years in order to obtain the same realization as the Buddha. Of Tamang ethnicity, a Tibeto-Burmese speaking community practicing Tibetan Buddhism, he has settled not far from his village. Every day thousands of pilgrims arrive from within Nepal, but also from India and sometimes even from the West to meet the one that some already call a "reincarnation of the Buddha." This title given by the pilgrims and echoed by the media was quickly contested by local scholars, monks, and lay people, who contend that the Buddha, fully awakened, has left the cycle of life and death and therefore cannot be reincarnated.[45]

Ram Bahadur was born on April 9, 1990, in a village in southern Nepal not far from the Indian border, in the district of Bara, to a poor Tamang farming family. His mother's name is Māyā Devi, and he is the third of nine children. Legend has already embraced him, nourished by the statements of his relatives. As a child, we are told, his cries were like music. He often displayed very unusual behavior: he worshiped every pipal fig tree, maintained a pensive and solitary existence, and seemed fascinated by the monks he met. He never fought, spoke little, but smiled a lot. His mother said that he never ate fish or meat or drank alcohol. After studying for a few years in a local school, Ram Bahadur entered a monastery, where he stayed for two years. He was given the religious name Palden Dorje. Then he went to Lumbinī, the presumed birthplace of the Buddha, for a ceremony performed by a priest of the Sakyapa order, whom he then accompanied to his monastery in Deradhun (Uttarakhand, India). After two years of studies, he returned to his village. On May 16, 2005, he began his long asceticism. Disturbed by youths in the area, he withdrew into deeper solitude, but he was discovered a few days later. In March 2006 he disappeared, and a large search operation was carried out, but without result. He was found eight months later in the middle of the jungle. Disappearing again in March 2007, he was found two weeks later and asked for a place underground where he could meditate. He stayed there for a few months before beginning, in August 2007, to preach before several thousand people while continuing to meditate. Since 2008, his statements have appeared on websites under the name of Maitriya Guru Mahā Sambodhi Dharma Sangha (Benevolent Master [of] the Sangha of the Law of Great Perfect Awakening). In teachings given in November 2008, he presented himself as a *guru*, a spiritual master, who has come to liberate all beings from suffering under the spiritual guidance of the future Buddha, Maitreya, from whom he is said to have received visions (*darṣan*) during his long meditation. The same websites tell us that he was awakened in Bodh Gaya in 2008, the place where legend places the awakening of the Buddha. On May 15, 2011, a ceremony in which—according to *Paris Match*—thousands of people participated was held in the forest to celebrate his awakening. It is then, we are told, that he decided to put an end to his asceticism and to start eating again.

Ram Bahadur's spiritual path has some similarities with that of the Buddha, to whom he constantly refers: his birth not far from Lumbinī, from a mother who bears the same name as the Buddha's mother; his years of asceticism under a pipal fig tree, recalling the Buddha's six years of asceticism and his awakening under a pipal (or "Bodhi") tree. His abilities are certainly out of the ordinary for a youth of his age: he has remained absolutely motionless for days on end, for several months, under the gaze of pilgrims and cameras. The cult that has developed around him has taken in not only his emulation of the Buddha Śākyamuni, but also his references to the future Buddha Maitreya, heralding a new golden age. All these elements could only seize the imagination of a population that has a high regard for mystical experiences and has experienced nothing but political instability and conflict during the "People's War" led by the Maoists from 1996 to 2006. Moreover, to the local residents, Ram Bahadur's position in the religious field is legitimized by the monastic education he received in the Tibetan Sakyapa school.

At a time when the Western media have become infatuated with a reincarnation of the bodhisattva Avalokiteśvara (Tib. Chenrezig) in the person of the fourteenth Dalai Lama, a figure whose charisma has more to do with his monastic credentials and his jovial nature than with his ascetic prowess, an emulation of the traditional Life of the Buddha seems to have difficulty gaining traction in the West. This is not what has occurred in Nepal or India, where extreme manifestations of religiosity merit significant concern.[46] It remains to be seen what will become of Ram Bahadur now that his ascetic tour de force is behind him. What is important for our purposes is that a seeming paradigm of the Life of the Buddha remains alive and resistant to the winds and tides of modernity and postmodernity, forming, so to speak, a conservative counterpart to the science-fictional Buddha.

EPILOGUE

Each generation of scholars has sought to interpret the Life of the Buddha by its own yardstick. For ancient comparative mythology, the legend was merely a transcription of beliefs about natural phenomena. For the advocates of historicism, it was to be reduced to a biography that would explain the origins of Buddhism, once it was rid of its dross. For the proponents of structuralism, it was the transposition or expression of deep, mythical (or ideological) structures. Dumézil's structural analysis setting out the three functions of Indo-European ideology, for example, applies to certain aspects of the legend—such as the courtesan and the "colored" lords who come to bring their offerings to the Buddha, or the offering of four bowls made by the four heavenly kings. But it does not apply to the legend as a whole, and Dumézil did not seek to do for the Buddhist Golden Legend what he had done for an Indian epic like the *Mahābhārata.* One can also, in a more fragmentary way, see in the Life of the Buddha a mine of socio-cultural information on the morals and ideals of one or several periods; or one can approach it in hermeneutical fashion, seeking in it a purely philosophical or spiritual meaning. I myself sought to find in it the paradigm of the religious practices and beliefs of the Buddhists. But in any domain, this effort is always about reducing one type of discourse (hagiographic) to another (historicist, structuralist, functionalist, etc.).

One of the arguments in this book is that all developments in the Buddha's legend, even outside India, are worthy of note, as they contribute to the creativity of the Buddhist tradition. Faced with the impoverishing vision of a kind of historicism, which reduces the Buddha's life to a banal *curriculum vitae,* it was necessary to choose the opposite bias, which consists in deploying the range of possibilities and considering the *Lives* of the Buddha, in their unfolding, as a tribute to the creativity of men, traditions, and cultures. In this sense, it seemed logical to integrate Lives that are critical, or episodes based on Buddhist hagiography that sometimes divert it in a polemical sense. However, certain limits must also be respected. Indeed, the enrichment that comes from variety can, on the contrary, become an impoverishment when anecdotes relating to the Buddha aim too clearly at denigrating the character and reflect only the prejudices of those who peddle them. Such is the case with certain accounts by Christian missionaries, whose inventiveness cannot be denied: we have seen that some went so far as to make the Buddha a frizzy-haired African, raising a question as to how far one can go before it's too far. Not that I am worried about offending sensitive souls. But at what point, when one chooses to open wide the floodgates of imagination, can one say that one is going outside the Buddhist tradition? Can we, by analogy, consider that Monty Python's "Life of Brian" is a variant of the Life of Christ? The same question might be asked about the "phallic nirvāṇa" or the first Western accounts of the Life of the Buddha. The cases of the Buddha in *manga* or science fiction are less extreme, and probably different—if it is the intention that counts. Any interpretation, as we know after Jacques Derrida, is context dependent, and contexts vary indefinitely. Still, it is true—and Derrida was the first to recognize this—that some interpretations are better than others. Perhaps the rule in this matter is one of pragmatism: an interpretation should be judged by its fruitfulness.

To be sure, the Life of the Buddha seems perfectly teleological, inasmuch as it is oriented toward a goal, awakening—and not only that of the Buddha, but that of all beings. To that end, it stages a grandiose forward march, that of humankind toward what is perhaps post-humanity, but if so, an entirely spiritual post-humanity, not the one prepared for us by a naturalist science. At the same time, the Buddha's legend overflows all methodological frameworks, founded on so many Procrustean beds. Despite its kaleidoscopic appearance, it is not just the result of the interplay of certain deep structures (mythological or otherwise). While many *Jātakas* are didactic and moralizing, or seek to justify the Bodhisattva's acquisition of moral perfections and the marks distinguishing his perfect body, the meaning of some remains opaque, their narrative thrust seemingly without specific purpose. All fables are not moral, with all due respect to La Fontaine. The pedagogical moralization of tales is very often nothing more than their domestication. Behind all these attempts at interpretation remains the metaphor of the core: no longer the historical core, but the core of meaning that one hopes to reach after peeling through all the layers of nonsense. But could it be that this core, if it exists, is precisely a jewel of pure nonsense, the ineffable pleasure of the narrative? Indeed, the narrative resists, something in it remains opaque to clarification, to any total or even partial explanation. Is it possible to avoid all reductionism and preserve its "disturbing strangeness"? Can we simply savor it rather than hasten to interpret it? Its flavor is perhaps what remains when all the interpretations have been exhausted, and we simply let ourselves be carried by the word, the text, or the image.

At the end of the journey, the Life of the Buddha closes (or opens) on a mystery.

NOTES

Introduction

1. Admittedly, the historicist (or at least historical critical) approach has some credentials, since it can be seen in the canonical tradition itself. See for instance this (unwittingly) amusing discussion about the Buddha's excrement in the *Kathavatthu* 18, 4: "Controverted Point.—That [even] the excreta of the Exalted Buddha excelled all other odorous things. . . . This would imply that the Exalted One fed on perfumes. But you admit only that he fed on rice gruel. Hence your proposition is untenable. Moreover, if your proposition were true, some would have used them for the toilet, gathering, saving them in basket and box, exposing them in the bazaar, making cosmetics with them. But nothing of the sort was done." See Aung and Rhys Davids 2001: 326.
2. Baltrušaitis 2008: 10.
3. On this point, see Ray 1999: 111–123.
4. See, for example, Saintyves 1987; and Eliade 1975.

Part One: Myth And History

Chapter 1: The Legend of the Buddha between History and Myth

1. One of the few authors to have noted this point is Guillaume Ducœur (2011).
2. Tāranātha 2003: 483–484.
3. Ibid., 484–485.
4. See for example Ambedkar 2011.
5. Cited in Renan 1992: 403–404.
6. Thomas 1996: 28.
7. Ibid., 235.
8. Oldenberg 1997: 90.
9. Foucher 1949: 34–35.
10. Couture 1988: 25.
11. Senart 1882: xi-xii.
12. See on this point Ray 1999: 141.
13. Couture 1988: 24.
14. Strickmann 1996: 19.
15. Oldenberg 1997: 101. See also Schumann 2003.
16. Mettanando and von Hinüber 2000: 110.

17. T. W. and C. A. F. Rhys Davids 1910: 1. See also S. Shaw 2010: 17; and Woodward 1997: 42.
18. Tambiah 1984: 7.
19. See Latour 2010: 22. "[We] shall use the label factish for the robust certainty that allows practice to pass into action without the practitioner ever believing in the difference between construction and reality, immanence and transcendence."
20. Borges 1964: 13.
21. Bareau 1985: 34.
22. Strong 2001: 4–5.
23. Lamotte 1949–1980, 1: 22.
24. Paradoxically, however, it seems that the account of the Buddha's previous existences (*Jātakas*) developed before that of the events of his last earthly existence.
25. The most complete form of this trend is a series of online Japanese articles that seek to determine what the Buddha's schedule was, almost day by day. ("A Study of the Biography of Sakya-muni Based on the Early Buddhist Scriptural Sources," www.sakya-muni). As Shōji Mori explains, "We have, as far as possible, collected all the passages in the earliest Scriptures describing the places where the Buddha spent the rainy season or where we can be fairly certain that he did so." See also the article by Shogo Iwai on the same site. For a more balanced approach, see Nitta 2008.
26. See Barthes 1989: 141–148.
27. Foucher 1949: 270.
28. Lamotte 1949–1980, 1: 547.
29. Lévi and Chavannes 1916.
30. See Jayawickrama 1978.
31. Certeau 1988: 270.

Chapter 2: A Bit of Historiography

1. The first biography of the Buddha in English, by Paul Ambroise Bigandet (1866), is contemporary to the *Introduction to the History of Indian Buddhism* by Eugène Burnouf (1844), but is based on a non-Indian (Thai) source.
2. See Burnouf 1844; Barthélémy Saint-Hilaire 1862.
3. Max-Müller 1872: 298.
4. Foucher 1949: 11.
5. Senart 1882: xiii
6. Ibid., xii–xiii.
7. Lopez 2013: 221.
8. Ibid.
9. Senart 1882: 442–444.
10. Ibid., xxv.
11. Schopen 2004.
12. Senart 1882: 435.
13. Renan 1992: 404–405.
14. La Vallée Poussin 1925a: 217.
15. Ibid., 218

16. A more recent attempt—but unfortunately too punctual—is that of Georges Dumézil, who examined certain episodes of the Buddhist legend in light of his theory of the three Indo-European functions. See Dumézil 1984.
17. Oldenberg 1997: 71.
18. Ibid., 73.
19. Ibid., 72.
20. Ibid., 89–90. *Edda* is a collection of Nordic mythology dating from the early 13th century, and its mention in the present context is an easy pun rather than an allusion to the Indo-European ideology dear to Dumézil.
21. Ibid., 86
22. Ibid., 73.
23. Ibid., 109.
24. Ibid., 112.
25. La Vallée Poussin 1925a: 87–88.
26. On this question, see Snodgrass 2007.
27. T. W. Rhys Davids 1956: xvii-xviii.
28. Ibid., 17
29. T. W. Rhys Davids 1907: 88–89.
30. Balbir 2009: 110–111.
31. Ibid., 108.
32. Ibid., 109.
33. Couture 1988: 23.
34. Foucher 1949: 343.
35. Ibid., 11–12.
36. Ibid.
37. Ibid., 10–11.
38. Ibid., 185.
39. Ibid., 16.
40. Balbir 2009: 113.
41. Ibid.
42. Balbir 2009: 114; Foucher 1955: 76.
43. Foucher 1955: 272.
44. Foucher 1949: 73.
45. Balbir 2009: 115.
46. Foucher 1949: 13.
47. Ibid., 23.
48. Foucher, quoted in Strong 2001: 3.
49. Foucher 1949: 13.
50. Ibid., 72
51. Ibid., 70–71.
52. Couture 1988: 25.
53. Foucher 1949: 347.
54. Ibid., 9.
55. Ibid., 16.
56. Ibid., 10.
57. Ibid., 347.

58. See Foucher 1949: 13; and Strong 2001: 3.
59. Strong 2001: 3.
60. Bareau 1985: 15.
61. Couture 1988: 22.
62. Bareau 1974b: 283.
63. Bareau 1974a: 266.
64. Bareau 1985: 22
65. Bareau 1974a: 270.
66. Bareau 1985: 20.
67. Ibid., 232.
68. Ibid., 239, and 233n.
69. Ibid., 150–151.
70. Ibid., 22.
71. On this issue, see in particular Fiordalis 2008.
72. Gombrich 2003: 14.
73. Ibid.
74. Gombrich 1990: 9–12.
75. Collins 2016: 11.
76. Penner 2009: 135–136.
77. Ibid., 124.
78. Ibid., 133.
79. Ibid., 141.
80. Strong 2011: 2.
81. See Strong 1998 and 2004.

Chapter 3: An Unfindable Biography

1. Ketelaar 2006: 79.
2. See Durt 1989; and Ketelaar 2006.
3. Ketelaar 2006: 66–67.
4. Ibid., 72.
5. Ibid., 73.
6. Ibid., 75.
7. Prebish 2008: 2; see also Bechert 1991–1997; Bechert 1995; Durt 1989 and 1994; Gombrich 1992; Narain 1994 and 2003.
8. Norman, in Bechert 1991–1997, 1: 302–303.
9. G. Obeyesekere 1991: 182.
10. Bareau 1985: 14–15.
11. With one exception, that of Hans Penner. See Penner 2009.
12. Lamotte 1958: 707.
13. Quoted in Penner 2009: 126.
14. On this notion, see Assmann 2010.
15. See James 2000.
16. Foucher 1949: 15.
17. Bareau 1955: 306–308.
18. Bareau 1993: 27.
19. Schopen 2004.

20. Foucault 1972: 138–139.
21. Lamotte 1949–1980, 2: 714.
22. Strong 2001: 4–5.
23. See Cowell and Neil 1990 (1895); Johnston 1972 (1936); Olivelle 2008; Willemen 2009; and Steiner 2010.
24. This school, whose founder is unknown, is a transition between the Buddhism of the Nikāya (Hīnayāna) and the Mahāyāna.
25. See Foucaux 1988 (1884–1892). See also Khosla 1991; Mitra 1882; and Krom 1926.
26. See Senart 1882–1897. See also Jones 1949–1956.
27. On the *Shishi yuanlu,* see Wieger 1951; and Lesbre 2002.
28. Burnouf 1852: 234.
29. Ibid., 352.
30. T. W. Rhys Davids, cited in Woodward 1997: 41.
31. Lamotte 1949–1980, 4: 2004–2005.
32. Ibid., 714.
33. Ibid., 713–714.
34. Ibid., 716.
35. Ibid., 717–718.
36. Certeau 1988: 280.
37. Foucher 1949: 18.
38. Ibid., 245.
39. Ibid., 121
40. Ibid., 123.
41. Ibid., 124–125.
42. Penner 2009: 124–125.
43. Schopen 2004: 398.
44. Ibid., 400.
45. Ibid., 400–401.
46. Ibid., 401.
47. Oldenberg 1997: 77–78.
48. Edward Conze, cited in Woodward 1997: 42.
49. Max Weber, quoted in Woodward 1997: 43.
50. Serres 2006: 31.
51. Some recent illustrated Korean biographies contain several hundred, or even several thousand, illustrations. A case in point is the *Daebul chon* (Complete biography of the Buddha) with 2,400 illustrations painted in a realistic style with vivid colors by the painter Kim Sanho. The work was commissioned by a Korean publisher, the Society for the Promotion of Buddhism, and published in three volumes in 1996.
52. See Reynolds 1997.
53. Collins 1992: 242–243.
54. On this text, see Rotman 2008.
55. See Wieger 1951.
56. See Vendova 2020.
57. See Marin 1978.
58. Certeau 1988: 89.
59. See Snellgrove 1973.

60. See Saintyves 1987.
61. See Strawson 2004.
62. Muñoz-Molina 2016: 322–323.

Part Two: The Life of the Buddha as Narrative and Paradigm

Chapter 4: The Life of the Buddha in Acts

1. See Skilling 2004: 348; and Griswold 1965.
2. On this episode, see Durt 1982; and Vendova 2020.
3. See Chavannes 1903; Julien 1857; Meuwese 1968; and Li 1996.
4. See Chavannes 1903.
5. On this figure, see Parlier 1991.
6. Chavannes 1903: 410–411.
7. Ibid., 414.
8. Ibid., 428.
9. Ibid., 418–429.
10. See Ohnuma 2007, chap. 1; and Li 1996: 86–87.
11. See Barrett 1990; and Eckel 1990 and 1994.
12. On the birth of the future Buddha, see Cueppers, Deeg, and Durt 2010.
13. Foucaux 1988: 33.
14. Tāranātha 2003: 38–39.
15. On the meaning of this change of pattern, see Deeg 2010b.
16. Foucher 1949: 37.
17. Ibid., 40.
18. Renan 1992: 355.
19. See Strong 2001: 38.
20. Foucher 1949: 45.
21. Bloch 1950: 157.
22. Tāranātha 2003: 43.
23. Dihle 1965: 38.
24. Lamotte 1949–1980, 1: 6.
25. See Silk 2003: 864.
26. Foucher 1949: 53. Surprisingly, Foucher failed to note that the name of the Buddha's cousin and nemesis, Devadatta, could be translated into French as "Dieudonné" (God-given)!
27. Foucaux 1988: 100.
28. See Willemen 2009: 14.
29. See Senart 1882: xx–xxi.
30. See Strong 2001: 69.
31. Lamotte 1949–1980, 1: 227–228.
32. In Japan, this episode gave rise to the conviction that one can ritually become a Buddha by making one's way through a sacred landscape to the place of awakening (e.g., Mount Kinpu in the Shugendō tradition, centered on practice in the mountains). Hence the importance of the characters (the cowherd Sujātā, the *nāga,* the grass merchant) that the Bodhisattva encounters on his way: they are, ritually speaking, the guardians of the threshold.

33. Senart 1882: 215. However, it is difficult to follow Senart when he sees there an "inexorable connection that belongs only to natural phenomena disguised under the legendary garment."
34. Senart 1882: 163.
35. Ibid., 166. Temptation is not entirely absent from the episode, however, as Māra's daughters seek to seduce the Bodhisattva. I give here the description given by Flaubert in another famous *Temptation:* "Then he sent me his daughters—beautiful, well-attired with golden girdles, teeth white as the jasmine, and limbs round as an elephant's trunk. Some of them stretched up their arms when they yawned to display the dimples in their elbows; others blinked their eyes; others began to laugh and others unfastened one another's garments. Amongst them were blushing virgins, matrons full of pride, and queens with great trains of baggage and attendants." See Flaubert 1904: 99.
36. Senart 1882–1897: 224.
37. Ibid.
38. Ibid., 371.
39. Ibid., 281, quoted in Senart 1882: xxix.
40. Senart 1882–1897: 345; also in Senart 1882, xxxiii.
41. See Berkwitz 2007.
42. Foucher 1949: 184. In the *Thūpavamsa,* the daughters of Māra each take turns assuming six hundred different forms to seduce the Bodhisattva, but to no avail. See Berkwitz 2007.
43. See Guthrie 2004; and Likhitpreechakul 2011.
44. Dumézil 1984: 42–43.
45. Ibid., 43–44.
46. Foucher 1949: 144.
47. See *Hōbōgirin,* s.v. "Daitsūchishō nyorai" (Hubert Durt), fasc. 6: 1087–1092. See also the *Recorded Sayings* of the Chan master Linji Yixuan (*Linji lu,* 9th cent.): "The Great Universal Wisdom Excellence Buddha sat in the place of practice for ten kalpas, but the Dharma of the buddhas did not appear before him and he was unable to complete the Buddha Way." See Watson 1993b: 71.
48. Lamotte 1949–1980, 1: 418–419. In fact, the life of this Buddha is only a transposition of that of Śākyamuni, with a few variations.
49. Ibid., 419.
50. Ibid., 421.
51. Dumézil 1984: 38.
52. Anālayo 2015b: 22.
53. Ibid., 24.
54. Ibid., 25.
55. For a structural interpretation of this episode, see Dumézil 1984, 186–187.
56. The images showing the Buddha making the symbolic gesture (*mudrā*) of "setting in motion the wheel of the law" refer to this event. This image, which symbolizes the Buddha's teaching, is widespread throughout Asia.
57. Foucaux 1988: 212–213.
58. Senart 1882–1897: 324–326.
59. Karetzky 1992: 155–156.
60. Bareau 1985: 234. See also Przylusky 1920.

61. Foucher 1963: 231. See also Waley 1932.
62. On this question, see Waley 1932; and Wasson 1982.
63. Bareau 1985: 239–240.
64. Lamotte 1949–1980, 1: 88–89.
65. Bareau 1985: 275
66. Bareau 1974b: 281.
67. Nagoya shiritsu hakubutsukan 1997.
68. Bareau 1975: 155.

Chapter 5: Secondary Episodes

1. Foucaux 1988: 154.
2. Ibid., 160.
3. Ibid., 163.
4. Bareau 1974a: 202.
5. Ibid., 231.
6. Ibid., 226–227.
7. The Buddha recalls: "I went continually to meditate in the gardens. The shadows of the trees used to move; but the shadow of the one that sheltered me did not move." See Flaubert 1904: 98.
8. On this question, see Vendova 2020.
9. In China and Japan, the theme of the four encounters develops in a slightly different way. In Dunhuang's "transformation texts" (*bianwen*), for example, the four encounters, corresponding to the four gates of the palace, the four cardinal points (east, south, west, north) and the four seasons (spring, summer, autumn, and winter) are related to the four phases of life (birth, old age, illness, and death). In the Chinese theory of the five elements, in fact, the east corresponds to birth. As a result, the encounter with the ascetic, which in the Indian tradition took place at the north gate, is the subject of a separate account.
10. See Silk 2003.
11. Ibid.
12. Bays 1983: 312–313.
13. This scene inspired the ascetic practices known collectively as the "contemplation of impurity," which often took a decomposing female body as a morbid object of concentration. See Wilson 1996.
14. Tāranātha 2003: 72.
15. See Senart 1882: xxiii.
16. Foucher 1949: 138.
17. As reported in the *Mahāvastu:* "During the six years of penance, Māra never stopped following in his footsteps to find the opportunity to take him over, but without success. It was not the first time." And the text mentions various *Jātakās* where the Bodhisattva, in animal form (bird, turtle, monkey, antelope), escaped the traps set for him by Māra. See Senart 1882: xxiv–xxvi.
18. Lamotte 1949–1980, 2: 906–907.
19. Soymié 1984: 99.
20. Strong 2001: 274
21. Ibid., 112–117.

22. Bareau 1985: 103.
23. The story seems to have been popular, since there is a Chinese version of it among the manuscripts found in the oasis of Dunhuang, on the Silk Road.
24. Lamotte 1949–1980, 1: 474.
25. Ibid., 476–477.
26. Ciurtin 2009: 83.
27. Ibid.
28. Lamotte 1949–1980, 1: 549. About the Grotto of the Buddha's Shadow, see also Chavannes 1903: 428.
29. Lamotte 1949–1980, 1: 553.
30. According to Foucher 1949: 218–219.
31. Bareau 1985: 85.

Chapter 6: Previous Lives

1. Foucher 1949: 27.
2. Skilling 2009: 127.
3. See Collins 1998: 257–267, cited in S. Shaw 2010: 32.
4. Strong 2001: 17.
5. Ibid., 19.
6. Chavannes 1910–1934. See also Terral 1958.
7. See Skilling 2009.
8. Strong 2001: 68–69.
9. La Vallée Poussin, quoted in Lubac 1951: 17.
10. Cited in Osier 2010: 18.
11. Strong 2001: 26–27.
12. See Ohnuma 2000; and Lopez 2004: 159–171.
13. Skilling 2009: 135
14. The six perfections are generosity (*dāna*), morality (*śīla*), patience (*kṣānti*), effort (*virya*), concentration (*samādhi*), and wisdom (*prajñā*); to which are added skillful means (*upāya*), the aspiration to save all beings (*praṇidhāna*), spiritual powers (*bala*), and gnosis (*jñāna*).
15. Foucher 1949: 28.
16. See *Brāhmana-jātaka,* in Khoroche 1989: 84–87.
17. Powers 2009: 9–10.
18. Senart 1882: 87–124.
19. Strong 2001: 39; see also Duroiselle 1904.
20. See Vendova 2020.
21. See on this point Ohnuma 2007.
22. Nichols 2010: 199; and Vendova 2020.
23. Lamotte 1949–1980, 1: 252–255.
24. Ibid., 255.
25. On this question, see Banerjea 1930.
26. Lamotte 1949–1980, 1: 273–274.
27. See Kamens 1988: 101.
28. Brown 1990: 98.
29. Senart 1882: 143–144.

30. Lamotte 1949–1980, 1: 462.
31. Ibid., 457.
32. Ibid., 275.
33. Ibid., 274–275.
34. See Yamabe 1999: 379.
35. See T. Rhys Davids 1880: 90.
36. See Foucher 1955: 77. On this question, see also Vendova 2020.
37. Flaubert 1904: 100.
38. Lamotte 1949–1980, 1: 259–260.
39. T. 12, 365: 691–693.
40. Max-Müller 1872: xi. See also Speyer 1895.
41. On this question, see Ohnuma 2007 and Benn 2016.
42. Collins 2016: 6. The success of a recent Thai film about Vessantara attests to the ever-growing popularity of this legend. The *Vessantara-jātaka is* regularly shown on Thai television, and the tale can be found in comics and various artistic adaptations.
43. Osier 2010: 181.
44. Ibid., 187.
45. Ibid., 200.
46. Ibid., 53.
47. Ciurtin 2009.
48. See Ladwig 2016. See also Leclère 1902.
49. See Lienhard 1978; and Emmrich 2016.
50. See Durt 1999.
51. Ibid.
52. *Milindapañha* IV, 8, 1. See T. Rhys Davids 1894: 114; and Osier 2010: 68.
53. Gabaude 1991.
54. Osier 2010: 52.
55. Ibid., 49.
56. Ibid., 50.
57. Ibid., 51.
58. Ibid., 52.
59. See Collins 2016.
60. See Osier 2010.
61. Ibid., 43.
62. Ibid., 55.
63. Ibid., 56.
64. Ibid., 59.
65. Ibid., 60. See also Collins 2016.
66. Osier 2010: 75.
67. *Mahāpadāna* I: 246–247, quoted in S. Shaw 2010: 32.
68. Lamotte 1949–1980, 1: 508–517. See also Levitt 2009.
69. Lamotte 1949–1980, 2: 897–898.
70. See Horner 1969, 1: 290.
71. Cited in Walters 1990.
72. For a table of the acts in question, see Strong 2001: 33. On this question, see also Lamotte's excellent clarification, from which I borrow some of the data.

73. In other words, the nine misdeeds committed during his previous lives. See Lamotte 1949–1980, 1: 507.
74. Ibid., 4: 1756.
75. Ibid., 1: 513–515.
76. On Vimalakīrti's illness, see Lamotte 1949–1980, 1: 516; and Lamotte 1987.
77. Lamotte 1949–1980, 4: 1779–1780.
78. Ibid., 1: 509–510.

Chapter 7: Dramatis Personae

1. On these characters, cf. Strong 1997.
2. I borrow the expression from Hubert Durt.
3. See Dehejia 1997; and Foucher 1934.
4. Yet some critics of Buddhism have not failed to point out the implausibilities. Thus Hirata Atsutane, in his *Remarks upon Emerging from Meditation* (*Shutsujō shōgo,* 1811), wrote: "It is false to say that he was born from his mother's right side. In any case, his mother died as a result of a difficult childbirth."
5. Foucher 1949: 65.
6. See *Mohemoye jing,* T. 383. This text, probably apocryphal, is said to have been translated into Chinese by the monk Tanjing (ca. 479–502). It has been studied by Hubert Durt, on whose work I rely here. There is also a *Sūtra of the Buddha's Mother* and a *Sūtra of the Buddha's Ascension to Trāyastriṃśa Heaven to Preach the Law to His Mother.* See T. 815; Pelliot manuscript P 4576 (Bibliothèque nationale de France); and Durt 2008: 24.
7. See Lopez 2004: 132–133.
8. T. 815; see Durt 2008: 24.
9. Durt 1996: 1–2.
10. Ibid.
11. Wilson 1996: 64–65.
12. Lamotte 1949–1980, 1: 228.
13. Ibid., 1: 228–229.
14. This episode is a counterpoint to the famous apologue of the Prodigal Son in the *Lotus Sūtra,* where the son, reduced to begging, and having forgotten all his princely dignity, returns home and must be gradually cured of his amnesia before being re-installed on the throne.
15. The text adds that the four deva kings asked to carry the coffin and the Buddha allowed them to do so. See *Konjaku monogatarishū* 2.1, in Dykstra 1986, 1: 155–157, and Ury 1985: 40.
16. See for example Faure 1993.
17. Walters 1994: 378.
18. See Bareau 1982. See also Péri 1918; Strong 1997; Tatelman 1999; and Deeg 2010a.
19. Bareau 1982: 57. See also R. Obeyesekere 2009.
20. See Péri 1918.
21. See Jones 1949–1956, 3: 18.
22. M. Shaw 1994: 143. Tantric Buddhism, which developed from the sixth century onward, emphasizes sexual techniques for awakening.

23. Ibid., 143. The marital relations of the Bodhisattva and Yaśodharā before the great departure are sometimes used to justify the relations of Buddhist monks with women. For example, in the *Tale of the Whispering Bamboo* (*Sasayakitake monogatari*), a monk of Kurama temple (north of Kyoto) states that if Śākyamuni, before awakening, had sexual intercourse with Yaśodharā, he may well be having an affair with the woman he himself is in love with.
24. La Vallée Poussin 1925a: 407.
25. Couture 1988: 14.
26. See Cowell and Neil 1886; Tatelman 2005; and Rotman 2008.
27. See Strong 1995: 21; and Lewis 2000.
28. *Mahāvastu* 2.162. See Jones 1949–1956: 122; and Senart, xvii–xviii.
29. Lamotte 1949–1980, 2: 1002–1007.
30. Ibid., 1004–1005.
31. Quoted in Péri 1918: 6–8. See also Lamotte, 1949–1980, 2: 1009.
32. Péri 1918: 5–6. Despite the negative judgments made of her by an often misogynistic tradition, Yaśodharā has remained a model for Indian women, as evidenced by the *Ode to Yaśodharā* by a modern poet, Hira Bansode, a woman belonging to the Dalit (outcaste) community of Mahārashtra. See R. Obeyesekere 2009: 95–96.
33. Strong 1995: 10.
34. Ibid.
35. Jones 1949–1956, 3: 246–254.
36. *Konjaku monogatarishū* 3.30, in Yamada et al. 1963, 1: 255–257; translated in Dykstra 1986, 2: 63–65.
37. Vinaya 1:43, quoted in Wijayaratna 1990a: 90.
38. Wilson 1996: 29.
39. Chavannes 1910–1934, 1: 312.
40. See Lamotte 1949–1980, 2: 873–875.
41. Ibid., 1: 407.
42. On Ajātaśatru, see Radich 2011.
43. Lamotte 1949–1980, 2: 872; see also Durt 1997; and Tāranātha 2003: 309–310.
44. On this question, see Bareau 1991a.
45. Yampolsky 1990: 88.
46. The story was well known in Japan, as shown in a poem from the *Ryōjin hishō:* "Devadatta the evildoer, / his name stained with the five vices: / in truth he was this same seer, Asita, / who taught Śākyamuni the Lotus Sutra." See Kim 1994: 79.
47. See Watson 1993a: 184.
48. Foucher 1949: 286.
49. See Bareau 1991a.
50. On this point, see Deeg 1999.
51. See de La Loubère 1700: 413–421; and Lopez 2013: 81–87.

Chapter 8: Māra, the Fallen Demon King

1. See Windisch 1895; and Ling 1962.
2. Ling 1962.
3. Boyd 1975: 75.
4. On this question, see Boyd 1975; and Doniger 1976.

5. Strong 2001: 70.
6. Foucher 1949: 152.
7. Ibid.
8. Ibid., 153.
9. *Milindapañha* IV, 6, 10. See T. Rhys Davids 1894: 50–51.
10. Lamotte 1949–1980, 1: 605.
11. Foucher 1949: 151–152.
12. Nichols 2010: 97–98.
13. Lamotte 1949–1980, 1: 340.
14. Ibid., 345–346.
15. Nichols 2010: 79.
16. Yampolsky 1990: 259.
17. Ibid.
18. Lamotte 1949–1980, 1: 228–229.
19. Nichols 2010: 106.
20. Ibid., 113–114.
21. Ibid., 107.
22. See Bareau 1985: 239
23. Lamotte 1949–1980, 1: 239.
24. Ibid., 236.
25. Ibid., 179 and 193.
26. Strong 1992: 100–101.
27. See Strong 1992: 110–111; and Duroiselle, 1904.
28. Strong 1992: 201.
29. Lévi and Chavannes 1966: 203–204.
30. See Lamotte 1987: 259; and Watson 2000: 81.
31. See McCullough 1959.
32. See Morrell 1985.

Chapter 9: The Life of the Buddha as a Paradigm

1. Ray 1999: 61.
2. *Shintō taikei,* Ronsetsu-hen 16: Onmyōdō, 62.
3. Ibid., 62–63.
4. See Beal 1879.
5. Swearer 2010: 46–47. See also Turpie 2001.
6. Manuscript Stein 2440, in Demiéville 1971: 130.
7. See translations of this scene by Drège in Faxian 2013: 7; and in Legge 1965 (1886). See also Yang 1984: 46–47 and 196; and Wong 2012.
8. Martin 2002: 100.
9. Ibid.
10. On the bath of the infant Buddha, cf. Rhi 2010.
11. Ibid., 332.
12. Kamens 1988: 260–261.
13. Yamabe 2010a.
14. Ibid.
15. Rhi 2010: 328

16. Kamens 1988: 312.
17. On this question, see Schopen 2014. The first images of the Buddha appear at the beginning of our era. It is not known exactly when and why this ban on depicting the Buddha was lifted. Much has been written about the alleged aniconism of early Buddhism. See in particular Huntington 1990. According to Paul Mus, "The aniconism of the Buddha reveals its transcendence." See Mus 1935b: 63.
18. See Martin 2002: 76.
19. Ibid., 84.
20. Ibid., 99.
21. Ibid.
22. On this question, see Faure 1991.
23. Martin 2002: 100.
24. Ibid., 101.
25. Nolot 1992: 123. See also Horner 1969, 1: 104.
26. Strong 2001: 51.
27. Ibid., 59.
28. See Swearer 2010: 55; and Strong 2001: 83.
29. See Brinker 1973: 23.
30. See Schopen 2007.
31. See Bizot 1994; see also Strong 2004: 221; and Schopen 2007: 64.
32. In Hinduism, the *dakṣinā* is the offering made to the priest for service rendered.
33. Swearer 2010: 34.
34. DeCaroli 2004: 108.
35. Ibid., 110–111.
36. Ibid., 112.
37. Ibid., 114–116.
38. *Keiran shūyōshū,* T. 76, 2410: 729.
39. Guthrie 2004: 88.
40. See Formoso 1996: 58; and Coedès 1968.

Chapter 10: New Conceptions of the Buddha

1. See Guang 2005.
2. On this question, cf. Lévi and Chavannes 1916.
3. Strong 2004: 228.
4. These relics were sent by the British to King Chulalongkorn, who deposited them at Wat Saket in Bangkok. The Thais distributed some of them to the Sinhalese, Burmese, and Japanese Buddhists (in 1901). Then, in 1935, some were given to the American Buddhists, and in 2009, to the Buddhist Union of France. The latter are now in the great pagoda of Bois de Vincennes, the former Cameroonian pavilion of the 1931 International Colonial Exhibition. John Strong, personal communication.
5. Strong 2004: 187.
6. Ibid., 150.
7. Lamotte 1949–1980, 1: 600.
8. See Lévi and Chavannes 1916.
9. See Wang-Toutain 1994; and Strong 2004: 211. On the Buddha's robe, see Strong 2004: 216–218; and *Hōbōgirin,* s.v. "Den'e."

10. See Lamotte 1949–1980, 1: 192.
11. On this question, see Faure 1989.
12. On this question, see Dumézil 1985; and Zürcher 2006: 29.
13. Strong 1992: 28–29.
14. See Grousset 1971: 102–103; and Strong 1992: 29–30.
15. See Bizot 1971.
16. See *Hōbōgirin,* s.v. "Bussokuseki," fasc. 2–3: 187–190; and Miller 1975.
17. See Nitta 2008.
18. *Kathāvatthu* 18, 4, in Aung and Rhys Davids 2001: 326.
19. A term borrowed from Christianity, from the Greek *dokesis,* the doctrine that Christ did not die on the Cross, but simply created an illusion.
20. Lamotte 1949–1980, 4: 1941.
21. See ibid., 1: 20.
22. Ibid., 1: 179.
23. Ibid., 4: 1940.
24. Watson 1993: 225.
25. Ibid., 229.
26. *Treatise;* see Lamotte 1949–1980, 1: 418.
27. Renan 1992: 352.
28. See Kamens 1988: 102.
29. See *Hōbōgirin,* s.v. "Busshin," 174–185.
30. *Hōbōgirin,* 1: 175.
31. Stein 1991: 120.

Part Three: The Unending Story

1. The bibliography is long. I will just mention Skilling 2010, Strong 2001 and 2004, and Swearer 2010.
2. See, for example, Roerich 1976: 17–22; and Tāranātha 2003.

Chapter 11: Chinese Lives of the Buddha

1. *Weishu;* see Hurvitz 1956.
2. Another *bianwen,* the *Taizi chengdao bianwen,* shows a clumsy effort to reconcile the Indian and Chinese theories: the Bodhisattva sees birth *and* old age at the east gate, illness at the south gate, death at the west gate, and deliverance symbolized by the monk at the north gate. See Stein manuscript 3096 (British Library).
3. The symbolism of the four gates is found in the funerary ritual of cremation, where it corresponds to the four traditional phases of Buddhist practice: production of the thought of awakening (*bodhicitta*), cultivation, awakening, and nirvāna. On this question, see Faure 1991: 191–203.
4. A second edition, dated 1486, contains 400 sections. See Vermeersch 2011.
5. Two versions exist, entitled *Historical Facts about the Original Metamorphoses of Śākyamuni* (*Shijia rulai yinghua shiji*) and *Recording of the Manifestations of the Buddha Śākyamuni* (*Shijia rulai yinghua lu*). It is the latter that Léon Wieger, S.J. (1856–1933) translated in 1913 under the title *Récit de l'apparition sur terre du Bouddha des Śākya* (republished in 1951 under the title *Les Vies chinoises du Bouddha*),

containing a summary of the text and selected scenes reproduced in a rather poor quality monochrome.

6. A revised edition of the book, the *Shishi yuanliu yinhua shiji* (Kor. *Sokshi wonlyu unghwa sajok*), dated 1631, was published in Korea in 1673. The book was republished in 1996 in a modern Korean translation by Yi Gwang-u. A Korean Life of the Buddha, the *Wol'in Sokpo* (1459), also had a great influence. It focuses on the eight acts based on a slightly modified list that was to become particularly important in Japan. A representation of these acts in eight sumptuous paintings has been preserved in a great Korean monastery, the Tongdosa.

Chapter 12: Japanese Lives

1. See Brinker 2011.
2. See for example *Yōtenki* (ca. 1223), in *Shintō taikei,* Tendai shintō.
3. *Ryōjin hishō* 411, in Kim 1994: 92–93.
4. Girard 1990: 118.
5. Ibid., 138. In a Nō play entitled *The Dragon God of Kasuga* (*Kasuga ryūjin*), Myōe receives an oracle telling him to give up his trip to India, because Mount Misaka is actually the Vulture Peak where the Buddha preached, and Kasuga is the place described in the *Lotus Sūtra* as the Buddha's abode after his parinirvāṇa. Kasuga is therefore the Pure Land of Śākyamuni. In the same play, the dragon king of Kasuga appears to Myōe in a dream and describes the events of the Buddha's life to him. Myōe is thus able to fulfill his inner pilgrimage, and is transported to Vulture Peak, where he can fulfill his dearest wish, to see and worship the Buddha.
6. Girard 1990: 77.
7. Ibid., 75.
8. See ibid., 17–18; and Tanabe 1992: 70.
9. Girard 1990: 91 and 106.
10. See Glassman 2007: 315.
11. See Derris 2000.
12. *Kakuzenshō,* in *Dai Nihon bukkyō zensho,* 6: 140; and Kurobe 1989: 112.
13. *Ryōjin hishō* 207, in Kim 1994: 63 (slightly modified).
14. *Ryōjin hishō* 219, in Kim 1994: 64.
15. See Kamens 1988: 149–157.
16. See Kurobe 1989: 486.
17. The story appears in a *Jātaka* from the *Nirvāna-sūtra,* T. 12, 365: 691–693.
18. See Brisset and Griolet 2010.
19. See for example the legend of Chūjōhime, in ten Grotenhuis 1992: 180–200.
20. See "Shaka no honji," in Yokoyama and Matsumoto 1979: 144.
21. Ibid., 144–146.
22. See "Shaka no gohonji," in Yokoyama and Fujiwara 1936: 190.
23. Ibid., 194.
24. While in the canonical texts the Bodhisattva transforms himself into an elephant or descends from Tuṣita Heaven on the back of an elephant to enter the side of Māyā, in the *Sangoku denki* he rides an elephant and enters through her mouth, while in the *Honkai denki* he descends on the back of a bird.

25. Atkinson chastely translates: "Buddha again became enshrined in her person and a clear and radiant light shone forth from his resting place." See Atkinson 1893: 38–39.
26. Auerback 2016: 75–76.
27. On this question, see Auerback 2016, to whom I am indebted for most of the materials below.
28. Kichijō(ten) is the name of a Japanese goddess of fortune, derived from the Indian goddess Śrī or Lakśmī, who plays an important role in premodern Japanese Buddhism.
29. Chikamatsu Monzaemon, "Shaka nyorai tanjō-e," in Chikamatsu zenshū kankōkai 1988: 533. Cited in Auerback 2016: 89.

Chapter 13: The Illustrated Nirvāṇa

1. This narrative also formed the basis for simpler narratives, the so-called "Nirvana narratives" (*Nehan monogatari,* an example of which can be found in the *Tales of Times Now Past* [*Konjaku monogatarishū,* ca. 1274]. This theme was soon taken up again for famous people, e.g., the poet Bashō, for whom a "Parinirvāṇa of Bashō" (*Bashō nehan*) was conceived.
2. Girard 1990: 91–92.
3. See Shimizu 1992: 202.
4. Ibid., 216–223.
5. Ibid., 223
6. Ibid., 232.
7. See Moerman 2007–2008; and Smith 2014.
8. See the "Parinirvāṇa of Narihira" (Narihira *nehan-zu*), by Hanabusa Itchō (1652–1724), at the National Museum of Tokyo, cited in Moerman 2012.
9. See Moerman 2012.
10. See Smith 2014.
11. See the exhibition catalog Clark et al. 2013: 110–111. This image is reminiscent of an engraving by Vivant Denon, also in the British Museum, which is part of his *Priapic Works* (*Oeuvres Priapiques*). It shows a giant phallus, surrounded by small figures, bringing to mind a stranded whale. See also, in the same catalog, an engraving by Terasawa Masatsugu (d. 1790) showing a couple of figures whose genitals and faces are inverted.
12. See Derrida 2001; and Atlan 2014.
13. However, the importance of the Buddha's penis in the Buddhist tradition is well known. On this question, see Yamabe 1999: 379. Furthermore, the episode of the procreation of Siddhārtha's son, Rāhula, plays an important role in some accounts of the great departure.
14. See Philippi 1968.

Chapter 14: The Buddha as Seen by His Rivals

1. On this issue, see Saindon 2004.
2. Quoted in Ucko 2000: 101.
3. See Fausbøll 1871.
4. See Dundas 2002: 39.
5. Zürcher 2006: 301.

6. Ibid., 94.
7. Kvaerne 1986: 72.
8. Kvaerne 1989: 33.
9. *Hoki naiden,* in *Shintō taikei, Ronsetsu-hen 16:* Onmyōdō.
10. See Yamamoto 2003, 2: 546.
11. Ibid.
12. Bareau 1979: 71–73.
13. Bareau 1979: 59.
14. On this question, see Yamamoto 2003, 2: 275–344.

Chapter 15: Japanese Biographies and Criticisms

1. On this nun, see Auerback 2016: 103–117.
2. Ibid., 99–101.
3. Ibid., 116–117.
4. See Tominaga 1990; Katō 1967; and Durt 1994.
5. See Auerback 2016: 119–122. My discussion of Hirata's criticism is based on this book.
6. Ibid.
7. Ibid., 139–141.
8. Ibid., 142.
9. Ibid., 160–161.
10. Ibid., 153–154.
11. Ibid., 153–172.
12. Ibid., 191.
13. Cf. for example Inoue 1897 and 1902.
14. These include Sir Edwin Arnold's *The Light of Asia* (1874) and Paul Carus's *The Gospel of Buddha* (1894), translated as early as 1895 by Sōen Shaku's disciple Suzuki Daisetsu (D. T. Suzuki).
15. Auerback 2016: 192.
16. Okakura is best known in the West for his essay entitled *The Book of Tea;* see Okakura 1930. His "realistic" description of the Life of the Buddha was inspired by Paul Carus's *The Gospel of the Buddha,* published in 1894; see Carus 1985.
17. See Mollard 2007.
18. Ibid., 72.
19. Ibid., 73.
20. Ibid., 74.
21. Ibid., 77.
22. Ibid., 79–80.
23. Ibid., 78.
24. Ibid., 84–85.
25. Ibid., 86.

Chapter 16: The Indian Buddha as Seen from the West

1. According to Daniel Gimaret, the term *al-Budd* is used as a common name meaning "idol." Thus, speaking of the "Sabians" of India, Sā'id al-Andalusī (1029–1070)

writes: "They worship the stars, representing them in forms that resemble them. . . . They give each of these forms the name of *budd.*" See Gimaret 1969: 274–275.

2. Ibid., 277.
3. See al-Bagdādī, quoted in Gimaret 1969: 297.
4. Canby 1993: 300–301.
5. Ibid., 301.
6. Ibid., 301–302.
7. Ibid., 305.
8. Ibid., 305–306.
9. Ibid., 307.
10. The oldest fragments of this text, dating from the tenth century, were discovered in Turfan in the Chinese province of Xinjiang. See Gimaret 1971; Mahé and Mahé 1993; and Zotenberg 1886.
11. Gimaret 1969: 282.
12. Ibid., 283.
13. Ibid., 283.
14. Ibid., 283–285.
15. Foucher 1949: 46.
16. Ibid., 46.
17. Renan 1992: 403.
18. Foucher 1949: 21.
19. Ibid., 113.
20. Information collected online at Tibeto-Logic, http://tibeto-logic.blogspot.fr/2010/01.
21. Foucher 1949: 147.
22. Ibid., 150.
23. Ibid., 160.
24. Marco Polo 1908: 373
25. Foucher 1949: 113.
26. The Portuguese traveler Diogo de Couto (1542–1616), when he visited Ceylon in the second half of the sixteenth century, heard about the Buddha's legend and wondered if the local tradition did not in fact preserve the memory of Saint Josaphat. See Mahé and Mahé 1993: 17–18.
27. De La Loubère 1700: 413.
28. See Lopez 2013: 50. According to Wikipedia, the term "talapoin," which also designates a small cercopithecus from West Africa, with forehead hair raised in short tufts, is the name given to Buddhist monks from Thailand and Burma by Europeans in the 17th–18th centuries.
29. De La Loubère 1700: 416.
30. Ibid., 419.
31. Ibid., 421. The Jesuit Louis Le Comte sees stories about the past lives of Buddha in animal form as evidence of the bestial (and therefore demonic) character of Buddhism: "Thus the Devil making use of Mens Folly and Malice for their destruction, endeavours to erase out of the minds of some those excellent ideas of God which are so deeply ingraved there, and to imprime in the minds of others the Worship of false Gods under the shapes of a multitude of different Creatures, for they did not stop at the Worship of this Idol. The Ape, the Elephant, the Dragon have been worshipped in several places, under pretence perhaps that the God *Fo*

had successively been transmigrated into these Creatures." See Le Comte 1698: 321–322.

32. De La Loubère 1700: 413.
33. Ibid., 420.
34. The idea appears in Alexandre, Chevalier de Chaumont (1640–1710), leader of the first mission sent by Louis XIV to the Court of Siam in 1685, who wrote: 'The last of these three *Talapoins* is the greatest God called Nacodon, because he has been in five thousand bodies; in one of these Transmigrations, of *Talapoin* he became a Cow, his brother would have killed him several times; but there needs a great book to describe the miracles, which they say, Nature, and not God wrought for his preservation. In short, his Brother was thrown into Hell for his great sins, where Nacodon caused him to be crucified; and for this foolish reason they abominate the Image of Christ on the Cross, saying we adore the image of this Brother of their God, who was crucified for his Crimes." Quoted in Lopez 2013: 85. The idea was taken up by the Jesuit Guy Tachard (1651–1712), a member of the second mission. It is undoubtedly from the latter that de La Loubère, in charge of the third mission, took his information and interest in this alleged figure of the crucified Christ, which led him to have the Thais compile a short work on Thevetat in Pāli. Voltaire echoes this in his *Dictionnaire philosophique.* See Lopez 2016: 72, 98–99, 146–148, and 188–189. On Tachard, see also Lopez 2013: 85–94.
35. See Choisy 1993: 245.
36. Le Comte 1698: 320.
37. Ibid., 320–321.
38. Ibid., 321.
39. See Dror 2002: 184–185.
40. See App 2014: 12.
41. Ibid., 28–30. Note that in these Jesuit biographies, Śākyamuni is often confused with the Chan patriarch Bodhidharma.
42. Valignano 1990: 84–85.
43. See Schwab 1984.
44. See Almond 1988: 20–22.
45. Abel Rémusat 1825.
46. On this question, see Almond 1988: 15–17.
47. Jones 1801, 1: 425, quoted in Lopez 2013: 150.
48. Jones 1801, 2: 145.
49. See Arnold 1890. Recently, the former Indian minister Jairam Ramesh declared: "For long I have been struck by why and how 'The Light of Asia,' which was a milestone in Buddhist historiography, got translated into over thirty languages, impacted so many public personalities in different countries, inspired movements for social equality and incarnated itself in music, dance, drama, painting and film" (*The Indian Express,* December 16, 2020). Among artistic adaptations, Dudley Buck's oratorio *The Light of Asia,* first performed in London in 1887, and Franz Osten and Himansu Rai's film *Prem Sanyas* (The light of Asia), 1925, should be mentioned. On the reception of *The Light of Asia,* see Ober 2020.
50. Atkinson 1893: 3.
51. Ibid., 6.
52. Ibid., 306.

53. The contrast between the two "Lights" quickly became a topos. See, for instance, Kellog 1885.
54. See Barthélémy Saint Hilaire 1862.
55. See Claudel 1974.

Chapter 17: The Modern Buddha

1. See Lopez 2012.
2. Ibid., 120.
3. Ibid., 123.
4. Ibid., 109.
5. See Welbon 1968; Droit 2004; App 2014; and Lopez 2012.
6. For more details, see Neal 2014.
7. Ibid., 190.
8. Ibid., 9.
9. C. A. F. Rhys Davids 1928: 29.
10. Ibid., 119.
11. Ibid.. 126.
12. Ibid., 127.
13. Ibid., 165.
14. Ibid., 206.
15. Ibid., 235.
16. Ibid., 281.
17. Ibid., 251.
18. Ibid., 288.
19. Ibid., 292.
20. Ibid., 292.
21. Segalen 1995, 1: 869. The same rejection of Buddhist devotion to the glorified image of the Buddha can be found in the literary critic René Etiemble (1909–2002), who should have been more charitable toward the naive beliefs of garbage collectors: "Devotion to the Buddha's hair irritates me. But as soon as I evoke the society that the Buddha was trying to convert, a world where ritual and the caste system controlled all life, I forget Gautama's teeth, bones, and hair, to remember only one thing: thanks to him, Brahmins like Śāriputra, Mahākāśyapa or Maudgalyāyana became simple monks who consorted in good conscience with craftsmen, farmers, whiteners, and garbage collectors. See Etiemble 1968: 19–20.
22. Segalen 1995, 1: 1003.
23. Doumet 1993: 111.
24. Segalen 1995, 1: 584.
25. Ibid., 613.
26. Joly-Segalen and Schaeffner 1962: 64–65.
27. Segalen 1995, 1: 619.
28. Joly-Segalen and Schaeffner 1962: 66–67.
29. In Conrad Rooks's film *Siddhārtha* (1972), based on Hesse's novel, the meeting between Siddhārtha and the Buddha is shown from the latter's viewpoint (identified with that of the viewer). When the young Siddhārtha explains that he will not join the Buddhist community, we see (as it were from within) the Buddha's hand reaching

out to him to give him a flower—a variant on the theme of the Dharma transmission to Mahākāśyapa, as reported in the Chan (Zen) tradition.

30. This vogue went hand in hand with that of Zen and psychoanalysis, particularly in its Jungian version. On this subject see Liard 2005.
31. See Castañeda 1985.
32. On Tezuka, see MacWilliams 2000.
33. Let us mention the *Legend of the Buddha* by Ohm Rachavate (Amarin Publishing, 2014), with its splendid graphics (sometimes with a strong eroticism, especially in the passages concerning Māya and Yaśodharā). The same tendency can be found in the fascicle devoted to Yaśodharā (*The Sacrificer,* 2013), where we see Siddhārtha tenderly hugging his young wife.
34. Following the success of his book, Chopra has embarked on the creation of a new six-part graphic. For a time he became president of Virgin Comics, a publishing company created in 2006, which closed its doors in 2008. Four volumes of the Life of the Buddha in comics had been projected, but they do not seem to have seen the light of day. One of them, however, was published by a new company, Liquid Comics, in 2010. Chopra hoped to make a film out of it. There has been a lot of publicity in India about this book, which has very modern graphics and a rather pompous title: *Deepak Chopra's Buddha: A History of Enlightenment.* We are still waiting for its release.
35. The first silent movie on the life of Buddha was *Buddhadev* (English title: *Lord Buddha*), in 1923, by the director Dadasaheb Phalke (1870–1944). It was closely followed by another silent movie entitled *The Light of Asia* (1925), like Edwin Arnold's long poem, by the German director Franz Osten (1875–1956). In fact, the content of the film is quite different from Arnold's poem, and gives a rather romantic idea of the Buddha's life. Incidentally, this film was banned in Ceylon (present-day Sri Lanka) and in the Malaysian states (present-day Malaysia) on the pretext that a human actor should not be used to personify the Buddha.

    In 1952 a Japanese film by Teinosuke Kinugasa (1896–1982) was nominated for the Cannes Film Festival. In 1957, the Indian government produced another movie, directed by Bimal Roy and entitled *Gotama the Buddha,* as part of the celebration of the 2500th anniversary of the Buddha's birth. This film received an honorable mention at the Cannes Film Festival the same year.

    In 1961, the Japanese director Kenji Misumi shot another movie entitled *Shaka* (Śākyamuni), which was shown in the United States in 1963 under the title *Buddha.* Then it was the turn of the Koreans, who in 1964 presented a film also entitled *Śākyamuni* (in Korean: *Seokgamoni*). In 1997, a long film in five DVDs, entitled *Buddha,* was produced by the Indian director Sheshagiri Rao. It was never released in theaters. In 2008, another Indian film entitled *Tathāgata Buddha* was produced by K. Raja Sekhar. Several animated films have also been made, among them a Nepalese *Buddha* and two Japanese films (2011 and 2014) based on the *manga* series of Tezuka Osamu.
36. Nichols 2010: 273–274. The "naive" approach is also well represented by Martin Meissonnier's recent documentary film *The Life of Buddha* (2001), whose trailer states that, rather than adopting the hagiographic approach, he seeks to find "who the Buddha really was." It emerges that the Buddha was an anarchist visionary who tried to undermine the Indian caste system, which forbids his followers to make representations of him. He is said to have invented the law of cause and effect, a law recently

rediscovered by scientists. As we can see, the myth of the "demystified" Buddha has a hard life.

37. Zelazny 2009.
38. Ibid., 82.
39. Ibid., 301.
40. Ibid., 120.
41. Ibid., 18–19.
42. Ibid., 387.
43. Ibid., 67.
44. Ibid., 337–338.
45. See Buffetrille 2020.
46. The case of Ram Bahadur forms a contrast with that of another Nepalese, the Newari poet Chittaram Hrdaya (1906–1982), who, during his stay in prison from 1941 to 1945, wrote an epic poem on the Life of the Buddha that advocates Newari resistance. I am indebted to John Strong for this information.

BIBLIOGRAPHY

Abbreviations

BEFEO	*Bulletin de l'École Française d'Extrême-Orient*
JIABS	*Journal of the International Association of Buddhist Studies*
JICABS	*Journal of the International College for Advanced Buddhist Studies*
T.	*Taishō shinshū daizōkyō*. Edited by Takakusu Junjirō and Watanabe Kaigyoku. 85 vols. Tokyo: Issaikyō kankōkai and Daizō shuppan, 1924–1932.

Primary Sources

CHINESE TEXTS TRANSLATED FROM THE SANSKRIT

Beihua jing (*Karunāpuṇḍarīka-sūtra*, J. *Hikekyō*). T. 3, 157; T. 12, 380.

Chang ahan jing (*Dīrghāgama*). Translated by Buddhayaśas and Zhu Fonian, T. 1, 1.

Daban niepan jing (*Mahāparinirvāṇa-sūtra*). "Northern tradition," T. 12, 374–375.

Daban niyuan jing (*Mahāparinirvāṇa-sūtra*). Translated by Bai Fazhu, T. 1, 5; translated by Buddhayaśas, T. 1, 6; translated by Faxian, T. 1, 7.

Dazhidulun. T. 25.

Fahua jing (*Saddharmapuṇḍarika-sūtra;* J. *Hokekyō*). See *Miaofa lianhua jing*.

Fobenxing ji jing. Translated by Jñanagupta, T. 3, 190.

Fobenxing jing. Translated by Baoyun, T. 4, 193.

Foshuo shier yu jing. Translated by Jialutuojia, T. 4, 195.

Fo suoxing zan, by Aśvaghoṣa. Translated by Tan Wuchen (Dharmakṣema), T. 4, 192.

Genben shuo yiqie youbu pinaiye (*Mūlasarvāstivāda Vinaya*). Translated by Yijing, T. 24, 1442.

Guanfo sanmei hai jing. Translated by Buddhabhadra, T. 15, 643.

Guoqu xianzai yinguo jing. Translated by Guṇabhadra (444–453), T. 3, 189.

Miaofa lianhua jing. Translated by Kumārajīva, T. 9, 262.

Mohe moye jing. Translated by Danjing, T. 12, 383.

Puyao jing (*Lalitavistara*). Translated by Zhu Fahou (Dharmarakṣa), T. 3, 186.

Shisong lü (*Sarvāstivāda Vinaya*). Translated by Puṇyatāra and Kumārajīva, T. 23, 1435.

Sifen lü (*Dharmaguptaka Vinaya*). Translated by Buddhayaśas and Zhu Fonian, T. 22, 1428.

Taizi ruiying benqi jing. Translated by Zhi Qian, T. 3, 185.

Weicengyou yinyuan jing. Translated by Danjing. T. 17, 754.

Weimojie jing (*Vimalakīrti-nirdeśa*). Translated by Shi Qian, T. 14, 474.
Weimojie suoshuo jing (*Vimalakīrti-nirdeśa*). Translated by Kumārajīva, T. 14, 475.
Xiuxing benqi jing. Translated by Zhu Dali and Kang Mengxiang. T. 3, 184.
Yichu pusa benqi jing. Translated by Nie Daozhen. T. 3, 188.
Za ahan jing (*Samyuktāgama*). Translated by Guṇabhadra, T. 2, 99.
Zengyi ahan jing (*Ekottarāgama*). Translated by Zhu Fonian. T. 2, 125.
Zhong ahan jing (*Madhyamāgama*). Translated by Gautama Samghadeva, T. 1, 26.
Zhong benqi jing. Translated by Tan Guo and Kang Mengxiang, T. 4, 196.

Chinese sources

Jinglü yixiang, by Baochang. T. 53, 2121.
Lidai sanbao ji, by Fei Changfang (597). T. 49, 2034.
Shijiapu, by Seng'you (502–518). T. 50, 2040.
Shijiashi pu, by Daoxuan (665). T. 50, 2041.
Shishi yuanliu (1425). Two versions: *Shijia rulai yinghua shiji;* and *Shijia rulai yinghua lu,* translated in Wieger 1951 (1913), and Chandra and Lohia 2010.

Japanese sources

Hoki naiden. In *Shintō taikei,* Ronsetsu-hen 16: Onmyōdō.
Kakuzenshō, by Kakuzen. In *Dai Nihon bukkyō zensho,* edited by Suzuki Gakujutsudan, vols. 44–51. Tokyo: Suzuki Gakujutsu Zaidan, 1970–1973.
Keiran shūyōshū, by Kōshū. T. 76, 2410.
Shintō taikei. Edited by Shintō taikei hensankai. 123 vols. Tokyo: Shintō taikei hensankai, 1977–1994.

Translations into Western languages

Anguttara-nikāya. Bodhi 2012.
Avadāna-jātaka. Feer 1891.
Buddhacarita. Beal 1884; Cowell 1977 (1894); Johnston 1972 (1936); Olivelle 2008; Willemen 2009.
Dasaratha-jātaka. Fausbøll 1871.
Datang Xiyu ji, by Xuanzang. French: Julien 1857. English: Beal 1884; Li 1996.
Dazhidulun. French: Lamotte 1949–1980.
Dīgha Nikāya. French: Wijayaratna 2010. English: T. and C. Rhys Davids 1899.
Divyāvadāna. Cowell and Neil 1886; Tatelman 2005; Rotman 2008.
Foguo ji, by Faxian. Legge 1886 (1965).
Fo suoxing zan (*Buddhacarita*). Beal 1879.
Jātakas. French: Chavannes 1910–1934. English: Cowell 1977 (1895); Fausbøll 1877–1896; T. Rhys Davids 1880; S. Shaw 2007.
Jātaka-nidāna. Jayawickrama 1978.
Konjaku monogatarishū. French: Frank 1987. English: Dykstra 2014.
Lalitavistara. French: Foucaux 1998 (1884–1892). English: Mitra 1882.
Mahāparinirvāna-sūtra. Blum 2013.
Mahāvastu. French: Senart 1882–1897. English: Jones 1949–1956.
Majjhima-nikāya. Ñānamoli and Bodhi 1995.
Milinda-pañha. French: Finot 1992 (1923); Nolot 1992.

Nidānakathā. T. Rhys Davids (1880).
Saddharmapuṇḍarika-sūtra (*Lotus Sūtra*): French: Burnouf 1852; Robert 1997. English: Kern 1884; Watson 1993.
Samyutta-nikāya. Bodhi 2000.
Sanbō ekotoba. Kamens 1988.
Shishi yuanliu (*Shijia rulai chengdao yinghua shiji*). French: Wieger 1951 (1913). English: Chandra and Lohia 2012.
Vimalakīrti-nirdeśa. French: Lamotte 1987 (1962). English: Thurman 1992 (1976); Watson 2000.

Secondary Sources

Abel Rémusat, Jean-Pierre. 1825. "Sur quelques épithètes descriptives de Bouddha qui font voir que Bouddha n'appartenait pas à la race nègre." In *Mélanges asiatiques*, edited by Jean-Pierre Abel Rémusat, vol. 1, 100–128. Paris: Librairie Orientale de Dondey-Dupré Père et Fils.
Abe Yasurō and Yamazaki Makoto, eds. 2000. *Chūsei butsuden shū*. Tokyo: Rinsen shoten.
Alexandre, Chevalier de Chaumont. 1687. *A Relation of the Late Embassy of Monsr. de Chaumont, Knt. to the Court of the King of Siam with an Account of the Government, State, Manners, Religion and Commerce of That Kingdom*. London.
Almond, Philip. 1988. *The British Discovery of Buddhism*. Cambridge: Cambridge University Press.
Ambedkar, Bhimrao. 2011. *The Buddha and His Dhamma*. London: Oxford University Press.
An, Yang-Gyu. 2003. *The Buddha's Last Days: Buddhagosa's Commentary on the Mahāparinibbāna Sutta*. London: Pāli Text Society.
Anālayo, Bhikkhu. 2015a. "The Buddha's Past Life as a Princess in the Ekottarika-āgama." *Journal of Buddhist Ethics* 22.
———. 2015b. *Compassion and Emptiness in Early Buddhist Meditation*. Cambridge: Windhorse Publications.
App, Urs. 2014. *The Cult of Emptiness: The Western Discovery of Buddhist Thought and the Invention of Oriental Philosophy*. Rorschach, Switzerland: UniversityMedia.
Appleton, Naomi. 2010. *Jātaka Stories in Theravāda Buddhism: Narrating the Bodhisattva Path*. Farnham, Surrey: Ashgate.
Arnold, Edwin. 1890. *The Light of Asia: Being the Life and Teaching of Gotama, Prince of India and Founder of Buddhism*. Chicago: Rand, McNally. First published 1879.
Assmann, Jan. 2010. *La mémoire culturelle: Écriture, souvenir et imaginaire politique dans les civilisations antiques*. Paris: Aubier.
Atkinson, Jon L. 1893. *Prince Siddhartha: The Japanese Buddha*. Boston: Congregational Sunday-School and Publishing Society.
Atlan, Henri. 2014. *Croyances: Comment expliquer le monde*. Paris: Autrement.
Auboyer, Jeannine. 1983. *Buddha: A Pictorial History of His Life and Legacy*. New Delhi: Roli Books International.
Auerback, Micah L. 2016. *A Storied Sage: Canon and Creation in the Making of a Japanese Buddha*. Chicago: University of Chicago Press.
Aung, Shwe Zan, and Caroline A. F. Rhys Davids, trans. 2001. *Points of Controversy, or Subjects of Discourse: Being a translation from the Kathā-vatthu from the Abhidhamma-piṭaka*. Oxford: Pāli Text Society. First published 1915.

Babbit, Helen C., trans. 2015. *Jātaka Tales.* CreateSpace Independent Publishing Platform.

Balbir, Nalini. 2009. "Les vies antérieures du Bouddha et les recherches sur les Jātaka." In *Bouddhismes d'Asie: Monuments et littératures,* edited by Pierre-Sylvain Filliozat and Jean Leclant. Paris: Académie des Inscriptions et Belles-Lettres.

Baltrušaitis, Jurgis. 2008. *Les perspectives dépravées: tome 1: Aberrations, essai sur la légende des formes.* Paris: Flammarion.

Banerjea, Jitendra Nath. 1930. "The 'Webbed Fingers' of Buddha." *Indian Historical Quarterly* 6, no. 4: 717–727.

Bareau, André. 1969. "The Superhuman Personality of the Buddha and Its Symbolism in the *Mahāparinirvāṇasūtra* of the Dharmaguptaka." In *Myths and Symbols: Studies in Honor of Mircea Eliade,* edited by Joseph M. Kitagawa and Charles Long, 9–21. Chicago: University of Chicago Press.

———. 1971–1995. *Recherches sur la biographie du Buddha dans les Sūtrapiṭaka et les Vinayapiṭaka anciens.* 3 vols. Paris: Presses de l'École Française d'Extrême-Orient.

———. 1974a. "La jeunesse du Buddha dans les *sūtrapiṭaka* et les *vinayapiṭaka* anciens." *BEFEO* 61: 199–274.

———. 1974b. "Le Parinirvāṇa du Buddha et la naissance de la religion bouddhique." *BEFEO* 61: 275–299.

———. 1975. "Les récits canoniques des funérailles du Bouddha et leurs anomalies: nouvel essai d'interprétation." *BEFEO* 62: 151–189.

———. 1979. "Le massacre des Śākya: Essai d'interprétation." *BEFEO* 64: 45–103.

———. 1982. "Un personnage bien mystérieux: l'épouse du Buddha." In *Indological and Buddhist Studies in Honour of Professor J. W. De Jong on His Sixtieth Birthday,* edited by L.A. Hercus et al., 31–59. Delhi: Satguru Publications.

———. 1985. *En suivant Bouddha.* Paris: Philippe Lebaud.

———. 1987. "Lumbinī et la naissance du futur Buddha." *BEFEO* 76: 69–81.

———. 1988. "Les débuts de la prédication du Buddha selon l'*Ekottara-Āgama.*" *BEFEO* 77: 69–96.

———. 1991a. "Les agissements de Devadatta selon les chapitres relatifs au schisme dans les divers Vinayapiṭaka." *BEFEO* 78: 87–132.

———. 1991b. "Quelques considérations sur le problème posé par la date du Parinirvāṇa du Buddha." In Bechert, *The Dating of the Historical Buddha,* vol. 1, 211–221.

———. 1993. "Le Bouddha et les rois." *BEFEO* 80: 15–39.

Barrett, Timothy H. 1990. "Explanatory Observations on Some Weeping Pilgrims." *Buddhist Studies Forum* 1: 99–110.

Barthélémy-Saint-Hilaire, Jules. 1855. *Du bouddhisme.* Paris: Benjamin Duprat.

———. 1862. *Le Bouddha et sa religion.* Paris: Didier. Reprint, Los Angeles: Hardpress Publishing, 2013.

Barthes, Roland. 1989. *The Rustle of Language.* Translated by Richard Howard. Berkeley: University of California Press.

Bautze-Picron, Claudine. 1995–1996. "Śākyamuni in Eastern India and Tibet in the 11th to the 13th Centuries." *Silk Road Art and Archeology* 4: 255–408.

Bays, Gwendolyn, trans. 1983. *The Lalitavistara Sutra: The Voice of the Buddha.* Berkeley, CA: Dharma Publishing.

Beal, Samuel, trans. 1875. *The Romantic Legend of Śākya Buddha: A Translation of the Chinese Version of the Abhiniṣkramaṇasūtra.* London: Trübner & Co. Reprint, Delhi: Motilal Banarsidass, 1985.

———, trans. 1879. *The Fo-sho-hing-tsan-king: A Life of the Buddha by Asvaghosha Bodhisattva.* Vol. 19 of Sacred Books of the East. Oxford: Clarendon Press.

———, trans. 1884. *Si-Yu-Ki: Buddhist Records of the Western World.* London: Trübner & Co.

Bechert, Heinz, ed. 1991–1997. *The Dating of the Historical Buddha.* 3 vols. Göttingen: Vandenhoeck & Ruprecht.

———. 1995. *When Did the Buddha Live? The Controversy on the Dating of the Historical Buddha.* Delhi: Sri Satguru Publications, 1995.

Bell, Alexander Peter. 2000. *Didactic Narration: Jātaka Iconography in Dunhuang with a Catalogue of Jataka Representations in China.* Münster: LIT Verlag.

Benn, James A. 2016. *Burning for the Buddha: Self-Immolation in Chinese Buddhism.* Honolulu: University of Hawai'i Press.

Berkwitz, Stephen C. 2007. *The History of the Buddha's Relic Shrine: A Translation of the Sinhala Thūpavaṃsa.* Oxford: Oxford University Press.

Bigandet, Paul Ambrose. 1866. *The Life, or Legend of Gaudama, the Buddha of the Burmese.* 2 vols. Rangoon: American Mission Press. Reprint, Delhi: Bharatiya Publishing House, 1979.

Bizot, François. 1971. "La figuration des pieds du Buddha au Cambodge." *Études Asiatiques* 25: 407–439.

———. 1994. "La consécration des statues et le culte des morts." In *Recherches nouvelles sur le Cambodge,* 101–139. Paris: EFEO.

Bloch, Jules. 1950. *Les Inscriptions d'Aśoka.* Paris: Les Belles Lettres.

Bloss, Lowell W. 1973. "The Buddha and the Nāga: A Study in Buddhist Folk Religiosity." *History of Religions* 13, no. 1: 36–53.

Blum, Mark L., trans. 2013. *The Nirvana Sutra (Mahāparinirvāna-sūtra).* Berkeley, CA: Bukkyo Dendo Kyokai America.

Bodhi, Bhikkhu, trans. 2000. *Connected Discourses of the Buddha: A Translation of the Samyutta Nikāya.* Somerville, MA: Wisdom Publications.

———, trans. 2012. *The Numerical Discourses of the Buddha: A Translation of the Anguttara Nikāya.* Boston: Wisdom Publications.

Bokenkamp, Stephen R., trans. 1997. *Early Daoist Scriptures.* Berkeley: University of California Press.

———. 2006. "The *Viśvantara-jātaka* in Buddhist and Daoist Translation." In *Daoism in History: Essays in Honour of Professor Liu Ts'un-yan,* edited by Benjamin Penny, 56–73. London: Routledge.

Borges, Jorge Luis. 1964. *Labyrinths.* New York: New Directions.

Boyd, James W. 1975. *Satan and Māra: Christian and Buddhist Symbols of Evil.* Leyden: E. J. Brill.

Brewster, Earl. 1926. *The Life of Gotama the Buddha.* London: Routledge & Kegan Paul. Reprint, 2000.

Brinker, Helmut. 1973. "Shussan Shaka in Sung and Yüan Painting." *Ars Orientalis* 9: 21–40.

———. 2011. *Secrets of the Sacred: Empowering Buddhist Images in Clear, in Code, and in Cache.* Lawrence: Spencer Museum of Art, University of Kansas.

Brisset, Claire-Akiko. 2010. "De Siddhartha à Shitta: Une Vie du Buddha dans le Japon du XVIe siècle." In Brisset and Griolet 2010, 57–68.

Brisset, Claire-Akiko, and Pascal Griolet, eds. and trans. 2010. *Shaka no honji: La Vie du Buddha racontée et illustrée au Japon.* Paris: Presses Universitaires de France.

Brown, Robert L. 1984. "The Śrāvastī Miracles in the Art of India and Dvāravatī." *Archives of Asian Art* 37: 79–95.

———. 1990. "God on Earth: The Walking Buddha in the Art of South and Southeast Asia," *Artibus Asiae* 50, nos. 1–2: 73–107.

———. 1997. "Narrative as Icon: The *Jātaka* Stories in Ancient Indian and Southeast Asian Architecture." In Schober, *Sacred Biographies*, 64–109.

Buffetrille, Katia. 2020. "Ram Bahadur Bomjon: A New Buddha in the Making (Nepal)?" In *On a Day of a Month in the Fire Bird Year: Festschrift for Peter Schwieger on the Occasion of His 65th Birthday*, edited by Jeannine Bischoff, Peter Maurer, and Charles Ramble, 71–74. Lumbini: Lumbini International Research Institute.

Burlingame, Eugene Watson. 1921. *Buddhist Legends*. 3 vols. Cambridge, MA: Harvard University Press, 1921. Reprint, London: Pāli Text Society, 1971.

Burnouf, Eugène. 1852. *Le Lotus de la Bonne Loi*. Paris: Imprimerie Nationale. Reprint, 2007.

———. 2010 (1844). *Introduction to the History of Indian Buddhism*. Translated by Katia Buffetrille and Donald S. Lopez Jr. Chicago: University of Chicago Press.

Buswell, Robert E., Jr. 2004. *Encyclopedia of Buddhism*. New York: Macmillan.

Calabrese, Michael. 1997. "Between Despair and Ecstasy: Marco Polo's Life of the Buddha." *Exemplaria* 9, no. 1: 189–229.

Canby, Sheila R. 1993. "Depictions of Buddha Śākyamuni in the Jamiʿ al-Tavarikh and the Majmaʿ al-Tavarikh." In *Essays in Honor of Oleg Grabar*, edited by Sheila Blair et al., 299–310. Muqarnas, vol. 10. Leiden: Brill.

Carr, Kevin G. 2012. *Plotting the Prince: Shōtoku Cults and the Mapping of Medieval Japanese Buddhism*. Honolulu: University of Hawaiʻi Press.

Carrithers, Michael. 1996. *The Buddha*. Oxford: Oxford University Press.

Carter, Martha L. 1990. *The Mystery of the Udayana Buddha*. Naples: Istituto Universitario Orientale.

Carus, Paul. 1911. *The Buddha: A Drama in Three Acts and Four Interludes*. Chicago: Open Court.

———. 1985. *L'Évangile du Bouddha*. Paris: Aquarius.

Castañeda, Carlos. 1985. *Les enseignements d'un sorcier Yaqui*. Paris: Éditions Gallimard.

Cata, Isabelle. 1991. "Segalen's *Siddhartha*." *Literary Studies East and West* 5: 155–160.

———. 2008. *Le "Siddhārtha" de Victor Segalen: une dés-orientation*. Paris: L'Harmattan.

———. n.d. "La musique inouïe de Victor Segalen: son Siddhārtha et le Bouddha de Debussy." Grand Valley State University, Allendale, Michigan.

Celli, Nicoletta. 2010. "The Birth of the Buddha and Related Episodes as Represented in Chinese Art." In Cueppers, Deeg, and Durt, *The Birth of the Buddha*, 305–320.

Certeau, Michel de. 1988. *The Writing of History*. Translated by Tom Conley. New York: Columbia University Press.

Chandra, Lokesh, and Sushama Lohia. 2010. *Life of Lord Buddha Compiled by Monk Pao-ch'eng from Chinese Sutras and Illustrated in Woodcuts in the Ming Period*. New Delhi: Aditya Prakashan.

Chavannes, Édouard. 1903. "Le Voyage de Song Yun dans l'Udyāna et le Gandhāra." *BEFEO* 3, no. 1: 379–441.

———. 1910–1934. *Cinq cents contes et apologues extraits du Tripiṭaka chinois*. 4 vols. Paris: Leroux.

Chikamatsu zenshū kankōkai, ed. 1988. *Chikamatsu zenshū*. Tokyo: Iwanami shoten.

Choisy, François-Timoléon (Abbé) de. 1993. *Journal of a Voyage to Siam, 1685–1686.* Translated by Michael Smithies. Kuala Lumpur: Oxford University Press. Originally published as *Journal du Voyage de Siam fait en 1665 et 1686* (Paris: Édition du Chartres & Van Buggenhoudt, 1930).

Chopra, Deepak. 2008. *Buddha: A Story of Enlightenment*. HarperCollins e-books.

Ciurtin, E. 2009. "The Buddha's Earthquakes [I]: On Water: Earthquakes and Seaquakes in Buddhist Cosmology and Meditation." *Studia Asiatica* 10: 59–123.

Clark, Timothy, et al. 2013. *Shunga: Sex and Pleasure in Japanese Art.* London: British Museum.

Claudel, Paul. 1974. *Connaissance de l'Est: suivi de L'oiseau noir dans le soleil levant.* Paris: Éditions Gallimard. First published 1900.

Coedès, George. 1968. "Une vie indochinoise du Buddha: La *Pathamasambodhi.*" In *Publications de l'Institut de Civilisation Indienne,* vol. 28, 217–227. Paris: Éditions E. de Boccard. Reprinted in *The Pathamasambodhi,* edited by George Cœdès and Jacqueline Filliozat (Oxford: Pāli Text Society, 2003).

Cogan, Thomas G., trans. 1987. *The Tale of the Soga Brothers.* Tokyo: University of Tokyo Press.

Collins, Steven. 1990. "On the Very Idea of the Pāli Canon." *Journal of the Pāli Text Society* 15: 90–126.

———. 1992. "Nirvāna, Time and Narrative." *History of Religions* 31, no. 3: 215–246.

———. 1998. *Nirvāna and Other Buddhist Felicities: Utopias of the Pali Imaginaire.* Cambridge: Cambridge University Press.

———. 2010. *Nirvāna: Concept, Imagery, Narrative.* Cambridge: Cambridge University Press.

———, ed. 2016. *Readings of the Vessantara Jātaka.* New York: Columbia University Press.

Cone, Margaret, and Richard Gombrich. 1977. *The Perfect Generosity of Prince Vessantara.* Oxford: Clarendon Press.

Conze, Edward. 1967. "Recent Progress in Buddhist Studies." In *Thirty Years of Buddhist Studies.* San Francisco: Wheelwright Press.

Coomaraswamy, Ananda. 1927. "The Origin of the Buddha Image." *Art Bulletin* 9, no. 4: 287–329.

Corrao, Francesca Maria. 2010. "Indian and Buddhist Influences in Islamic Anecdotes." *Tōyō tetsugaku kenkyūjo kiyō,* 159–169.

Couture, André. 1988. "Revue de la littérature française concernant l'hagiographie du bouddhisme indien ancien." In *Monks and Magicians: Religious Biographies in Asia,* edited by Phyllis Granoff and Koichi Shinohara, 9–44. Oakville, Ontario: Mosaic Press.

Covill, Linda. 2010. "Handsome Is as Handsome Does": Aśvaghoṣa's Story of the Buddha's Younger Brother." In Covill, Roesler, and Shaw, *Lives Lived, Lives Imagined,* 123–138.

Covill, Linda, Ulrike Roesler, and Sarah Shaw, eds. 2010. *Lives Lived, Lives Imagined: Biography in the Buddhist Tradition.* Boston: Wisdom Publications.

Cowell, Edward B. 1977. *The Buddha-carita, or Life of Buddha, by Asvaghosha.* New Delhi: Cosmo Publications. First published 1894.

Cowell, Edward B., and Robert A. Neil, eds. 1886. *The Divyāvadāna: A Collection of Early Buddhist Legends.* Cambridge: Cambridge University Press.

———, eds. 1990. *The Jātaka, or Stories of the Buddha's Former Births.* New Delhi: Munshiram Manoharlal. First published 1895 by Pali Text Society (London).
Cueppers, Christoph, Max Deeg, and Hubert Durt, eds. 2010. *The Birth of the Buddha: Proceedings of the Seminar Held in Lumbini, Nepal, October 2004.* Lumbini: Lumbini International Research Institute.
Cummings, Mary. 1982. *The Lives of the Buddha in the Art and Literature of Asia.* Ann Arbor: University of Michigan Press.
DeCaroli, Robert. 2004. *Haunting the Buddha: Indian Popular Religions and the Formation of Buddhism.* Oxford: Oxford University Press.
Deeg, Max. 1999. "The Sangha of Devadatta: Fiction and History of a Heresy in the Buddhist Tradition." *Journal of the International College for Postgraduate Buddhist Studies* 2: 183–219.
———. 2010a. "Chips from a Biographical Workshop—Early Chinese Biographies of the Buddha: The Late Birth of Rāhula and Yaśodharā's Extended Pregnancy." In Covill, Roesler, and Shaw, *Lives Lived, Lives Imagined,* 49–88.
———. 2010b. " 'Why Is the Buddha Riding on an Elephant?' The Bodhisattva's Conception and the Change of Motive." In Cueppers, Deeg, and Durt, *The Birth of the Buddha,* 93–128.
Dehejia, Vidya. 1990. "On Modes of Visual Narration in Early Buddhist Art." *Art Bulletin* 72, no. 3: 374–392.
———. 1997. *Discourse in Early Buddhist Art: Visual Narrative of India.* Delhi: Munshira Manoharlal Publishers.
De La Loubère, Simon. 1700. *Description du royaume de Siam.* Amsterdam.
Demiéville, Paul, trans. 1971. *Airs de Touen-houang (Touen-houang k'iu): Textes à chanter des VIIIe-Xe siècles.* Paris: CNRS.
Derrida, Jacques. 2001. *Acts of Religion.* Edited by Gil Anidjar. London: Routledge.
Derris, Karen. 2000. "Virtue and Relationships in a Theravādin Biography of the Buddha: A Study of the *Sotaṭṭhakīnimahānidāna.*" PhD diss., Harvard University.
Dihle, Albrecht. 1965. *Buddha und Hieronymus.* Mittelatteinishes Jahrbuch 2: 38–41.
Doniger, Wendy. 1976. *The Origins of Evil in Hindu Mythology.* Berkeley: University of California Press.
Doumet, Christian. 1993. *Victor Segalen: L'origine et la distance.* Paris: Champ Vallon.
Droit, Roger-Pol. 2009. *The Cult of Nothingness: The Philosophers and the Buddha.* New Delhi: Munshiram Manoharlal.
Dror, Olga, trans. 2002. *A Small Treatise on the Sects among the Chinese and Tonkinese: A Study of Religion in China and North Vietnam in the Eighteenth Century.* Ithaca, NY: Cornell Southeast Asia Program.
Ducœur, Guillaume. 2011. *Initiation au bouddhisme.* Paris: Ellipses Marketing.
Dumézil, Georges. 1984. *La courtisane et les seigneurs colorés. Esquisses de mythologie.* Paris: Éditions Gallimard.
———. 1985. "D'une coupe à quatre, de quatre bols à un." In *L'Oubli de l'homme et l'honneur des dieux,* 192–210. Paris: Éditions Gallimard.
Dundas, Paul. 2002. *The Jains.* London: Routledge.
Duroiselle, Charles. 1904. "Upagutta and Mâra." *BEFEO* 4: 414–428.
Durt, Hubert. 1982. "La 'visite aux laboureurs' et la 'méditation sous l'arbre Jambu' dans les biographies sanskrites et chinoises du Buddha." In *Indological and Buddhist*

Studies: Volume in Honour of Professor J. W. De Jong, edited by L. A. Hercus et al., 95–120. Delhi: Satguru Publications.

———. 1989. "La date du Buddha en Corée et au Japon." In *The Dating of the Historical Buddha,* edited by Heinz Bechert, 458–489. Göttingen: Vendenhoeck & Ruprecht.

———. 1994. *Problems of Chronology and Eschatology. Four Lectures on the "Essay on Buddhism" by Tominaga Nakamoto (1715–1746).* Occasional Papers 4. Kyoto: Scuola Italiana di Studi sull' Asia Orientale.

———. 1996. "L'apparition du Buddha à sa mère après son nirvâna dans le *Sûtra de Mahâmâyâ* (T. 383) et dans le *Sûtra de la Mère du Buddha* (T. 2919). In *De Dunhuang au Japon, études chinoises et bouddhiques offertes à Michel Soymié,* edited by Jean-Pierre Drège, 1–24. Paris: Droz.

———. 1997. "Quelques aspects de la légende du Roi Ajase (Ajātaśatru) dans la tradition canonique bouddhique." *Ebisu* 15: 13–27.

———. 1999. "The Offering of the Children of Prince Viśvantara/Sudāna in the Chinese Tradition." *Journal of the International College for Postgraduate Buddhist Studies* 2: 147–182.

———. 2000. "The Casting-off of Madrī in the Northern Buddhist Literary Tradition." *JICABS* 3: 133–158.

———. 2002. "On the Pregnancy of Māyā I: The Five Uncontrollable Longings (*dohada*). *JICABS* 5: 43–66.

———. 2003. "On the Pregnancy of Māyā II: Māyā as Healer." *JICABS* 6: 43–62.

———. 2004. "On the Pregnancy of Māyā III: Late Episodes." *JICABS* 7: 55–64.

———. 2006. "The *Shijiapu* of Sengyou: The First Chinese Attempt to Produce a Critical Biography of the Buddha." *JICABS* 10: 51–86.

———. 2007–2008. "The Post-Nirvāṇa Meeting of the Buddha with Māyā in the Trāyastriṃśa Heaven: Examination of the *Mahāmāya Sūtra* and Its Quotations in the *Shijiapu.*" Pts. 1 and 2. *JICABS* 11: 44–66; 12: 1–25.

———. 2010. "The Birth of the Buddha in the Chinese Anthologies of the Early Sixth Century." In Cueppers, Deeg, and Durt, *The Birth of the Buddha,* 277–304.

Dykstra, Yoshiko Kurata, trans. 1986. *The Konjaku Tales. Indian Section: From a Medieval Japanese Collection.* Osaka: Intercultural Research Institute, Kansai Gaidai University.

———, trans. 1994. *The Konjaku Tales. Chinese Section: From a Medieval Japanese Collection.* Osaka: Intercultural Research Institute, Kansai Gaidai University.

———, trans. 1998–2003. *The Konjaku Tales. Japanese Section: From a Medieval Japanese Collection.* Osaka: Intercultural Research Institute, Kansai Gaidai University.

———. 2014. *Buddhist Tales of India, China, and Japan: A Complete Translation of the Konjaku monogatarishū.* 3 vols. Honolulu: Kanji Press.

Ebert, Jorinda. 1985. *Parinirvāṇa: Untersuchungen zur ikonographischen Entwicklung von den Anfängen bis nach China.* Wiesbaden: Steiner.

Eckel, David. 1990. "The Power of the Buddha's Absence: On the Foundations of Mahāyāna Buddhist Ritual." *Journal of Ritual Studies* 4, no. 2: 61–95.

———. 1994. *To See the Buddha: A Philosopher's Quest for the Meaning of Emptiness.* Princeton, NJ: Princeton University Press.

Ehrhard, Franz-Karl. 2010. "The Narrative of the Birth of the Buddha as Told by Bskal-bzang Chos-kyi Rgya-mtsho (15th century)." In Cueppers, Deeg, and Durt, *The Birth of the Buddha,* 355–376.

Eliade, Mircea. 1975. *Myth and Reality.* New York: Harper & Row.
Emmrich, Christoph. 2016. "Vessantara Opts Out: Newar Versions of the Tale of the Generous Prince." In Collins, *Readings of the Vessantara Jātaka,* 183–210.
Etiemble, René. 1968. "Introduction." In *L'Inde du Bouddha vue par des pèlerins chinois sous la dynastie Tang (VIIe siècle),* edited by Catherine Meuwese, 7–23. Paris: Calmann-Levy.
Faure, Bernard. 1986. "Bodhidharma as Textual and Religious Paradigm." *History of Religions* 25, no. 3: 187–198.
———. 1989. *Le bouddhisme Ch'an en mal d'histoire: Genèse d'une tradition religieuse dans la Chine des T'ang.* Paris: Adrien-Maisonneuve.
———. 1991. *The Rhetoric of Immediacy: A Cultural Critique of Chan/Zen Buddhism.* Princeton, NJ: Princeton University Press.
———. 1993. *Chan Insights and Oversights: An Epistemological Critique of the Chan Tradition.* Princeton, NJ: Princeton University Press.
———. 1998. *The Red Thread: Buddhist Approaches to Sexuality.* Princeton, NJ: Princeton University Press.
Fausbøll, Michael Viggo. 1871. *The Dasaratha Jātaka, Being the Buddhist Story of King Rāma.* Copenhagen: Kopenhagen Hagerup.
———. 1877–1896. *The Jātaka, Together with Its Commentary.* 6 vols. London: Trübner & Co.
Faxian. 2013. *Mémoire sur les pays bouddhiques.* Translated by Jean-Pierre Drège. Paris: Les Belles Lettres.
Feer, Léon. 1891. *Le Livre des cent légendes: Avadâna-Çataka.* Paris: Ernest Leroux.
Finot, Louis, trans. 1992. *Milinda-pañha: Les questions de Milinda.* Connaissance de l'Orient. Paris: Éditions Gallimard. First published 1923.
Fiordalis, David V. 2008. "Miracles and Superhuman Powers in South Asian Buddhist Literature." PhD diss., University of Michigan.
Flaubert, Gustave. 1904. *The Temptation of St. Anthony: Or, A Revelation of the Soul.* Dodo Press.
Fleet, J. F. 1907. "The Tradition about the Corporeal Relics of the Buddha." *Journal of the Royal Asiatic Society* 39, no. 2: 341–363.
Formoso, Bernard. 1996. "La cosmologie des T'aï et l'empreinte du bouddhisme." *Diogène* 174: 53–71.
Foucault, Michel. 1972. *The Archaeology of Knowledge: and the Discourse on Language.* Translated by A. M. Sheridan Smith. New York: Pantheon Books.
Foucaux, Philippe-Édouard. 1988. *Le Lalitavistara: L'histoire traditionnelle de la vie du Bouddha Çakyamuni.* 2 vols. Paris: Les Deux Océans. First published 1884–1892, Annales du Musée Guimet, vols. 6 and 19.
Foucher, Alfred. 1900. *Étude sur l'iconographie bouddhique de l'Inde d'après des documents nouveaux.* Paris: Ernest Leroux.
———. 1917. *The Beginnings of Buddhist Art.* Paris: Paul Geuthner.
———. 1934. On the Iconography of the Buddha's Nativity." *Memoirs of the Archaeological Survey of India* 46.
———. 1949. *La vie du Bouddha d'après les textes et monuments de l'Inde.* Paris: Adrien Maisonneuve.
———. 1951. *L'Art gréco-bouddhique du Gandhara: Étude sur les origines de l'influence classique dans l'art bouddhique de l'Inde et de l'Extrême-Orient.* Vol. 2. Paris: Imprimerie Nationale.

———. 1955. *Les vies antérieures du Buddha.* Paris: Presses Universitaires de France.

———. 1963. *The Life of the Buddha according to the Ancient Texts and Monuments of India.* Abridged translation by Simone Brangier Boas. Middletown, CT: Wesleyan University Press.

Frank, Bernard, trans. 1987. *Histoires qui sont maintenant du passé.* Paris: Éditions Gallimard.

Frauwallner, Erich. 1956. *The Earliest Vinaya and the Beginnings of Buddhist Literature.* Rome: Istituto Italiano per il Medio ed Estremo Oriente.

Frédéric, Louis. 1994. *Bouddha en son temps.* Paris: Éditions du Félin.

Frye, Stanley, trans. 1981. *The Sūtra of the Wise and the Foolish (mdo bdzans blun); or The Ocean of Narratives (üliger-ün dalai).* Dharamsala: Library of Tibetan Works & Archives.

Gabaude, Louis. 1991. "Controverses modernes autour du *Vessantara-Jātaka.*" *Cahiers de l'Asie du Sud-Est* 29–30, no. 1: 51–73.

Geiger, Wilhelm. 1912. *The Mahāvaṃsa, or the Great Chronicle of Ceylon.* London: Pāli Text Society. Reprint, 2001.

Gerstle, Andrew, ed. 2005. *Kabuki Heroes on the Osaka Stage, 1780–1830.* Honolulu: University of Hawai'i Press.

Gimaret, Daniel. 1969. "Bouddha et les bouddhistes dans la tradition musulmane." *Journal Asiatique* 258: 273–316.

———. 1971. *Le Livre de Bilawhar et Būdāsf: selon la version arabe ismaélienne.* Genève: Librairie Droz.

Girard, Frédéric. 1990. *Un moine de la secte Kegon à l'époque de Kamakura: Myōe (1173–1232) et le "Journal de ses rêves."* Paris: École Française d'Extrême-Orient.

Glassman, Hank. 2007. "*Shaka no honji:* Preaching, Intertextuality, and Popular Hagiography." *Monumenta Nipponica* 62, no. 3: 299–321.

Gombrich, Richard F. 1980. "The Significance of Former Buddhas in the Theravādin Tradition." In *Buddhist Studies in Honour of Walpola Rahula,* edited by Somaratna et al., 62–72. London: Gordon Fraser.

———. 1990. "Recovering the Buddha's Message." *The Buddhist Forum* 1: 5–20.

———. 1992. "Dating the Buddha: A Red Herring Revealed." In Bechert, *The Dating of the Historical Buddha,* vol. 2, 237–259.

———. 1997. *How Buddhism Began: The Conditioned Genesis of the Early Teachings.* New Delhi: Munshiram Manoharlal.

———. 2003. "'Obsession with Origins': Attitudes to Buddhist Studies in the Old World and the New." In *Approaching the Dhamma: Buddhist Texts and Practices in South and Southeast Asia,* edited by Anne M. Blackburn and Jeffrey Samuels, 3–15. Seattle: BPS Pariyatti Editions.

Grimm, Martin. 1967. *Das Leben Buddhas: ein chinesisches Holzschnitt-fragment.* Leipzig: Insel-Verlag.

Griswold, A. B. 1965. "The Holy Land Transported: Replicas of the Mahābodhi Shrine in Siam and Elsewhere." In *Paranavitana Felicitation Volume on Art and Architecture and Oriental Studies,* edited by N. A. Jayawickrama, 173–222. Colombo: M .D. Gunasena.

Grousset, René. 1971. *In the Footsteps of the Buddha.* Translated by J. A. Underwood. New York: Grossman Publishers.

Guang Xing. 2005. *The Concept of the Buddha: Its Evolution from Early Buddhism to the Trikaya Theory.* London: RoutledgeCurzon.

Guthrie, Elizabeth. 2004. "The History and Cult of the Buddhist Earth Deity in Mainland Southeast Asia." PhD diss., University of Canterbury, Christchurch (New Zealand).

Hallisey, Charles. 1995. "Roads Taken and Not Taken in the Study of Theravāda Buddhism." In *Curators of the Buddha: The Study of Buddhism under Colonialism,* edited by Donald S. Lopez Jr., 31–61. Chicago: University of Chicago Press.

Hardy, Spence R. 1874. *Christianity and Buddhism Compared.* Colombo: Wesleyan Mission Press.

Hayashi, Masahiko. 2008. "A Research Paper on Buddhist Narrative and Pictures in Asia: Referring to the Pictures of 'The Life of Buddha' in East and Southeast Asia." *Meiji daigaku jinbun kagaku kenkyūjo kiyō* 63: 1–28.

Hesse, Hermann. 1982. *Siddhartha: A Novel.* New York: Bantam.

Hinüber, Oskar von. 2009a. "Cremated like a King: The Funeral of the Buddha within the Ancient Indian Context." *Journal of the International College of Postgraduate Buddhist Studies* 13: 33–66.

———. 2009b. "La légende de la vie du Bouddha, Quelques pensées sur les recherches d'Alfred Foucher, Résultats acquis et progrès entamés." In *Bouddhismes d'Asie: Monuments et littératures,* edited by Pierre-Sylvain Filliozat and Jean Leclant, 141–151. Paris: Académie des Inscriptions et Belles Lettres.

Hōbōgirin; dictionnaire encyclopédique du bouddhisme d'après les sources chinoises et japonaises. 1927–. Paris: Adrien Maisonneuve.

Horner, I. B., trans. 1969. *Milinda's Questions.* 2 vols. London: Luzac and Company.

Howard, Angela. 1981. "The Imagery of the 'Cosmological Buddha.'" PhD diss., New York University.

Huntington, Susan L. 1990. "Early Buddhist Art and the Theory of Aniconism." *Art Journal* 49: 401–408.

Hurvitz, Leon, trans. 1956. *Treatise on Buddhism and Taoism: An English Translation of the Original Chinese Text of Wei-shu CXIV and the Japanese Annotation of Tsukamoto Zenryū.* Reprinted from *Yün-kang, the Buddhist Cave-Temples of the Fifth Century A.D. in North China,* vol. 16, supplement. Kyoto: Kyoto University.

Inoue, Tetsujirō. 1897. *Shaka shuzokuron.* Tokyo: Tetsugaku shoin.

———. 1902. *Shakamuni den.* Tokyo: Bunmeidō.

Irwin, John. 1981. "The Mystery of the (Future) Buddha's First Words." *Annali del Istituto Universitario Orientale* 41: 623–653.

Iwai, Shogo. n.d. "Verifying Traditions Concerning the Locations of Sakyamuni's Rainy Season Retreats." In "A Study of the Biography of Sakya-muni Based on the Early Buddhist Scriptural Sources." http://sakya-muni.jp/monograph/06/5/1-3.html.

Iyanaga, Nobumi. 1996–1997. "Le Roi Māra du Sixième Ciel et le mythe médiéval de la création du Japon." *Cahiers d'Extrême-Asie* 9: 323–397.

Jaffe, Richard. 2004. "Seeking Śākyamuni: Travels and the Reconstruction of Japanese Buddhism." *Journal of Japanese Studies* 30, no. 1: 65–96.

James, William. 2000. *Pragmatism and Other Writings.* New York: Penguin Classics.

Jayawickrama, N. A., trans. 1978. *The Sheaf of Garlands of the Epochs of the Conqueror.* Oxford: Pāli Text Society.

———. 1990. *The Story of Gotama Buddha (Jātaka-nidāna).* Oxford: Pāli Text Society.

Johnston, E. H. 1972. *The Buddhacarita, or Acts of the Buddha.* Delhi: Motilal Banarsidass. First published 1936.

Joly-Segalen, Annie, and André Schaeffner, eds. 1962. *Segalen et Debussy.* Monaco: Éditions du Rocher.

Jones, J. J., trans. 1949–1956. *The Mahāvastu.* 3 vols. Sacred Books of the Buddhists. London: Luzac.

Jones, William. 1801. Asiatick Researches, or Transactions of the Society, Instituted in Bengal, for Inquiring into the History and Antiquities, the Arts, Sciences, and Literature of Asia. 2 vols. London. Reprint of the original Calcutta edition.

Jong, J. W de. 1954. "L'épisode d'Asita dans le *Lalitavistara.*" In *Asiatica: Festschrift Friedrich Weller,* 312–325. Leipzig: O. Harrassowitz.

Jory, Patrick. 2002. "The *Vessantara Jataka,* Barami, and the Bodhisattva Kings: The Origin and Spread of a Thai Concept of Power." *Crossroads: An Interdisciplinary Journal of Southeast Asian Studies* 16, no. 2: 36–78.

Julien, Stanislas, trans. 1857. *Mémoires sur les contrées occidentales.* Paris: Imprimerie impériale.

Kalupahana, David J., and Indrani Kalupahana. 1982. *The Way of Siddhārtha: A Life of the Buddha.* Boulder: Shambhala.

Kamens, Edward, trans. 1988. *The Three Jewels: A Study and Translation of Minamoto Tamenori's Sanbōe.* Ann Arbor: Center for Japanese Studies, University of Michigan.

Karetzky, Patricia E. 1992. *The Life of the Buddha: Ancient Scriptural and Pictorial Traditions.* Lanham, MD: University Press of America.

———. 2000. *Early Buddhist Narrative Art: Illustrations of the Life of the Buddha from Central Asia to China, Korea and Japan.* Lanham, MD: University Press of America.

Katō Shūichi. 1967. "Tominaga Nakamoto, 1715–46: A Tokugawa Iconoclast." *Monumenta Nipponica* 22, nos. 1–2: 177–193.

Kellog, S. H. 1885. *The Light of Asia and the Light of the World: A Comparison of the Legend, the Doctrine, & the Ethics of the Buddha with the Story, the Doctrine, & the Ethics of Christ.* London: MacMillan and Co.

Kern, Hendrik. 1884. *Saddharma-pundarīka, or The Lotus of the True Law.* Oxford: Clarendon Press.

Ketelaar, James. 2006. "The Non-Modern Confronts the Modern: Dating the Buddha in Japan." *History and Theory* 45: 62–79.

Khoroche, Peter, trans. 1989. *Once the Buddha Was a Monkey: Ārya Śūra's Jātakamālā.* Chicago: University of Chicago Press.

———, trans. 2017. *Once a Peacock, Once an Actress: Twenty-Four Lives of the Bodhisattva from Haribhaṭṭa's* Jātakamālā. Chicago: University of Chicago Press

Khosla, Sarla. 1991. *Lalitavistara and the Evolution of the Buddha Legend.* New Delhi: Galaxy Publications.

Kim, Yung-hee. 1994. *Songs to Make the Dust Dance: The Ryōjin hishō of Twelfth-century Japan.* Berkeley: University of California Press.

Klimburg-Salter, Deborah E. 1988. "The Life of the Buddha in Western Himalayan Monastic Art and Its Indian Origins: Act One." *East and West* 38, nos. 1–4: 189–214.

Krom, Nicolas Johannes, ed. 1926. *The Life of Buddha on the Stūpa of Barabudur according to the Lalitavistara Text.* The Hague: Nijhoff.

Kurobe, Michiyoshi. 1989. *Nihon butsuden bungaku no kenkyū.* Osaka: Izumi shoin.

Kvaerne, Per. 1986. "Peintures tibétaines de la vie de sTon-pa-gçen-rab." *Arts asiatiques* 41: 36–81.

———. 1989. "Śākyamuni in the Bon Religion. *Temenos* 25: 33–40.

Lachaud, François. 2006. *La jeune fille et la mort. Misogynie ascétique et représentations macabres du corps féminin dans le bouddhisme japonais.* Paris: Collège de France—Institut des Hautes Études Japonaises.

Ladwig, Patrice. 2016. "Emotions and Narrative: Excessive Giving and Ethical Ambivalence in the Lao *Vessantara-Jātaka.*" In Collins, *Readings of the Vessantara Jātaka,* 53–80.

Lai, Whalen. 1982. "The Search for the Historical Śākyamuni in Light of the Historical Jesus." *Buddhist-Christian Studies* 2: 77–91.

Lamotte, Étienne. 1947–1948. "La légende du Buddha." *Revue de l'Histoire des Religions* 134: 37–71.

———, trans. 1949–1980. *Le Traité de la grande vertu de sagesse.* 5 vols. Louvain: Institut Orientaliste.

———. 1958. *Histoire du bouddhisme indien: des origines à l'ère Śaka.* Louvain: Publications Universitaires. Translated as *History of Indian Buddhism from the Origins to the Śaka Era* (Louvain: Peeters, 1988).

———. 1966. "Vajrapāṇi en Inde." In *Mélanges de sinologie offerts à Monsieur Paul Demiéville,* vol. 1, 113–159. Paris: Institut des Hautes Études Chinoises.

———. 1970. "Le Buddha insulta-t-il Devadatta?" *Bulletin of the School of Oriental and African Studies* 33: 107–115.

———, trans. 1987. *L'enseignement de Vimalakīrti.* Louvain-la-Neuve: Institut Orientaliste. First published 1962.

Latour, Bruno. 2010. *On the Modern Cult of the Factish Gods.* Durham: Duke University Press.

La Vallée Poussin, Louis de. 1925a. *Bouddhisme: Opinions sur l'histoire de la dogmatique.* Paris: Gabriel Beauchesne.

———. 1925b. *Nirvāna.* Paris: Gabriel Beauchesne.

———. 1929. "Les neuf kalpas qu'a franchis Śākyamuni pour devancer Maitreya." *T'oung Pao* 26: 17–24.

Leashko, Janice. 1993–1994. "Scenes of the Buddha's Life in Pāla-Period Art." *Silk Road Art and Archeology* 3: 251–76.

Leclère, Adhémar. 1902. *Le livre de Vesandâr, le roi charitable.* Paris: Ernest Leroux.

———. 1907. *La crémation et les rites funéraires au Cambodge.* Hanoi.

Le Comte, Louis. 1698. *Nouveaux mémoires sur l'état présent de la Chine.* 2 vols. Paris. Reprinted as *Un jésuite à Pékin: Nouveaux mémoires sur l'état présent de la Chine, 1687–1692* (Paris: Editions Phébus, 1990).

Lee, Junghee. 1993. "The Origins and Development of the Pensive Bodhisattva Images of Asia." *Artibus Asiae* 53, nos. 3–4: 311–357.

Lee, Sonya S. 2010. *Surviving Nirvāna: Death of the Buddha in Chinese Visual Culture.* Hong Kong: Hong Kong University Press.

Legge, James, trans. 1965. *A Record of Buddhistic Kingdoms.* New York: Paragon Books Reprint Corp. First published 1886.

Legittimo, Elsa I. 2005–2006. "Synoptic Presentation of the *Pusa chi tai jing* (PCJ), the *Bodhisattva Womb Sūtra.*" Pts. 1 and 2. *Sengokuyama Journal of Buddhist Studies* 2: 1–111; 3: 1–177.

Lesbre, Emannuelle. 2002. “Une vie illustrée du Buddha (*Shishi yuanliu,* 1425), modèle pour les peintures murales d’un monastère du XVe s. (Jueyuan *si,* Sichuan oriental).” *Arts Asiatiques* 57: 69–101.

Lévi, Sylvain. 1925. “Le Soutra du sage et du fou dans la littérature de l’Asie centrale.” *Journal Asiatique* 207: 305–332.

———. 1996. “Les Jātaka: Étapes du Bouddha sur la voie des transmigrations.” In *Mémorial Sylvain Lévi.* New Delhi: Motolal Banarsidass.

Lévi, Sylvain, and Édouard Chavannes. 1916. “Les Seize Arhat protecteurs de la Loi.” *Journal Asiatique* 11, no. 8: 5–50 and 189–293.

Levitt, Stephan H. 2009. *Explanations of Misfortune in the Buddha’s Life: The Buddha’s Misdeeds in His Former Human Lives and Their Remnants.* New York: Buddhist Literature Society.

Lewis, Todd. 2000. *Popular Buddhist Texts from Nepal.* Albany: State University of New York Press, 2000.

Liard, Véronique. 2005. “Le Siddhartha de Hermann Hesse: une intégration jungienne de l’Orient.” In Sharon Fuller, *Les écrivains en voyage: nouveaux mondes, nouvelles idées?,* 293–309. Paris: L’Harmattan.

Lienhard, Siegfried. 1978. “La légende du prince Viśvantara dans la tradition népalaise.” *Arts Asiatiques* 34: 139–156.

Likhitpreechakul, Paisarn. 2011. “The Legend of the Earth Goddess and the Buddha. *Journal of the Oxford Centre for Buddhist Studies* 1: 108–113.

Ling, Trevor. 1962. *Buddhism and the Mythology of Evil: A Study in Theravāda Buddhism.* London: Allen & Unwin.

Li Rongxi, trans. 1996. *The Great Tang Dynasty Record of the Western Regions.* Berkeley, CA: Numata Center for Buddhist Translation and Research.

Lopez, Donald S., Jr., ed. 2004. *Buddhist Scriptures.* London: Penguin Books.

———. 2005. “Buddha.” In *Critical Terms for the Study of Buddhism,* 13–36. Chicago: University of Chicago Press.

———. 2012. *The Scientific Buddha: His Short and Happy Life.* New Haven, CT: Yale University Press.

———. 2013. *From Stone to Flesh: A Short History of the Buddha.* Chicago: University of Chicago Press.

———, ed. 2016. *Strange Tales of an Oriental Idol: An Anthology of Early European Portrayals of the Buddha.* Chicago: University of Chicago Press.

Lopez, Donald S., Jr., and Peggy McCracken. 2014. *In Search of the Christian Buddha: How an Asian Sage Became a Medieval Saint.* New York: W.W. Norton.

Lubac, Henri de, S.J. 1951. *Aspects du Bouddhisme.* Paris: Éditions du Seuil.

Luczanits, Christian. 2010. “Prior to Birth: The Tuṣita Episodes in Indian Buddhist Literature and Art.” In Cueppers, Deeg, and Durt, *The Birth of the Buddha,* 41–92.

MacQueen, Graeme. 1998. “Changing Master Narratives in Midstream: *Barlaam and Josaphat* and the Growth of Religious Intolerance in the Buddhalegend’s [sic] Westward Journey.” *Journal of Buddhist Ethics* 5: 144–166.

———. 2002. “The Killing Test: The Kinship of Living Beings and the Buddha Legend’s First Journey to the West.” *Journal of Buddhist Ethics* 9: 109–148.

MacWilliams, Mark W. 2000. “Japanese Comic Books and Religion: Osamu Tezuka’s Story of the Buddha.” In *Japan Pop! Inside the World of Japanese Popular Culture,* edited by Timothy Craig, 109–137. New York: M. E. Sharpe.

Mahé, Annie, and Jean-Pierre Mahé, trans. 1993. *La sagesse de Balahvar: Une vie christianisée du Bouddha.* Paris: Éditions Gallimard.

Marco Polo. 1908. *The Travels of Marco Polo the Venitian.* London: J. M. Dent.

———. 2010. *The Description of the World.* Translated by A. C. Moule and Paul Pelliot. Tokyo: Ishi Press.

Marin, Louis. 1978. *Le Récit est un piège.* Paris: Éditions de Minuit.

Martin, François. 2002. "Les 'quatre portes de la ville': Pratique bouddhique et jeu poétique sous les Six Dynasties." In *Bouddhisme et lettrés dans la Chine médiévale,* edited by Catherine Despeux, 67–102. Paris-Louvain: Peeters.

Mather, Richard. 1987. "The Life of the Buddha and the Buddhist Life: Wang Jung's (468–93) 'Songs of Religious Joy' (Fa-le tz'u)." *Journal of the American Oriental Society* 107, no. 1: 31–38.

Max-Müller, Friedrich. 1872. *Essais sur l'histoire des religions.* Paris: Didier et Cie.

McCullough, Helen Craig. 1959. *The Taiheiki: A Chronicle of Medieval Japan.* New York: Columbia University Press.

Mettanando, Bhikkhu, and Oskar von Hinüber. 2000. "The Cause of the Buddha's Death." *Journal of the Pāli Text Society* 26: 105–117.

Meuwese, Catherine. 1968. *L'Inde du Buddha vue par les pélerins chinois sous la dynastie T'ang* (VIIe siècle). Paris: Calmann-Lévy.

Miller, Roy Andrew. 1975. *"The Footprints of the Buddha": An Eighth-century Old Japanese Poetic Sequence.* New Haven, CT: American Oriental Society.

Mitra, Rajendralala, trans. 1882. *The Lalita-Vistara, or Memoirs of the Early Life of Sakya Siñha.* Calcutta: J. W. Thomas.

Moerman, D. Max. 2007–2008. "Dying Like the Buddha: Intervisuality and the Cultic Image." *Impressions* 29: 28–49.

Mollard, Nicolas. 2007. "Construction d'une identité littéraire moderne à travers la relecture d'une esthétique traditionnelle: Fūryū dans les écrits de Kōda Rohan autour de 1890." PhD diss., Université de Genève, 2007.

Mori Shōji et al. n.d. "A Study of the Biography of Sakya-muni Based on the Early Buddhist Scriptural Sources." http://sakya-muni.jp.

Morrell, Robert. 1985. *Sand and Pebbles (Shasekishū): The Tales of Mujū Ichien, A Voice for Pluralism in Kamakura Buddhism.* Albany: State University of New York Press.

Muñoz-Molina, Antonio. 2016. *L'ombre qui s'en va.* Paris: Éditions du Seuil.

Murray Julia K. 2000. "The Evolution of Pictorial Hagiography in Chinese Art: Common Themes and Forms." *Arts asiatiques* 55: 81–97.

Mus, Paul. 1928. "Le Buddha paré. Son origine indienne, Çākyamuni dans le Mahāyānisme moyen." *BEFEO* 28, nos. 1–2: 153–278.

———. 1935a. "Alfred Foucher: On the Iconography of the Buddha's Nativity." *BEFEO* 35: 397–404.

———. 1935b. *Barabudur: Esquisse d'une histoire du bouddhisme fondée sur la critique archéologique des textes.* Hanoi: Imprimerie d'Extrême-Orient.

Nagoya shiritsu hakubutsukan, ed. 1997. *Nehan-zu.* Nagoya: Nagoya shiritsu hakubutsukan.

Nakamura Hajime. 1977. *Gotama Buddha.* Los Angeles: Buddhist Books International.

Ñānamoli, Bhikkhu, trans. 1972. *The Life of the Buddha, as It Appears in the Pāli Canon.* Kandy: Buddhist Publication Society.

Ñāṇamoli, Bhikkhu, and Bhikkhu Bodhi, trans. 1995. *The Middle Length Discourses of the Buddha: A New Translation of the Majjhima Nikāya.* Kandy: Buddhist Publication Society.

Narain, Abhod Kishor. 1994. "An Independent and Definitive Evidence on the Date of the Historical Buddha." *Indian Journal of Buddhist Studies* 6: 43–58.

———. 2002. "The Exact Spot of Birth of Siddhārtha Gautama, the Śākyamuni Buddha." *Indian International Journal of Buddhist Studies* 3: 169–179.

———, ed. 2003. *The Date of the Historical Śākyamuni Buddha.* Delhi: B. R. Publishing Corporation.

Neal, Dawn. 2014. "The Life and Contribution of CAF Rhys Davids." *The Sati Journal* 2: 15–32.

Nichols, Michael David. 2010. "Malleable Mara: Buddhism's 'Evil One' in Conversation and Contestation with Vedic Religion, Brahmanism, and Hinduism." PhD diss., University of Illinois, Evanston.

Nitta Tomomichi. 2008. "On the 'Deification' of the Historical Buddha in the Studies of the Buddha's Life Story." *Hōrin* 15: 43–53.

Nolot, Edith, trans. 1992. *Milinda-pañha: Les questions de Milinda.* Paris: Éditions Gallimard.

Nyanaponika, Thera, and Hellmuth Hecker. 1997. *Great Disciples of the Buddha.* Boston: Wisdom Publications.

Ober, Douglas. 2020. "Translating the Buddha: Edwin Arnold's *Light of Asia* and Its Indian Publics." *Humanities* 10, no. 1: 1–18. https://doi.org/10.3390/h10010003.

Obermiller, E., trans. 1931. *History of Buddhism (Chos-hbyung) by Bu-ston.* Heidelberg: O. Harrassowitz.

Obeyesekere, Gananath. 1991. "Myth, History and Numerology in the Buddhist Chronicles." In Bechert, *The Dating of the Historical Buddha,* vol. 1, 152–182.

———. 2003. "The Death of the Buddha: A Restorative Interpretation." In *Approaching the Dharma: Buddhist Texts and Practices in South and Southeast Asia,* edited by Anne M. Blackburn and Jeffrey Samuels, 17–45. Seattle: BPS Pariyatti Editions.

Obeyesekere, Ranjini. 2009. *Yaśodharā, the Wife of the Bodhisattva.* Albany: State University of New York Press.

Obry, Jean-Baptiste. 2016. *Du Nirvâna bouddique: En réponse à M. Barthélémy Saint-Hilaire.* Paris: Hachette Livre BNF. First published 1863.

Ohnuma, Reiko. 2000. "The Story of Rūpavatī: A Female Past Birth of the Buddha." *JIABS* 23: 103–145.

———. 2007. *Head, Eyes, Flesh, and Blood: Giving Away the Body in Indian Buddhist Literature.* New York: Columbia University Press.

Okakura Kakuzō. (1906) 1930. *The Book of Tea.* New York: Duffield.

Oldenberg, Hermann. 1997. *Buddha: His Life, His Doctrine, His Order.* Translated by William Hoey. Delhi: Motilal Banarsidass.

Olivelle, Patrick. 2008. *The Life of the Buddha.* New York: New York University Press.

Osier, Jean-Pierre. 2010. *Le "Vessantara jātaka" ou l'avant-dernière incarnation du Bouddha Gotama.* Paris: Éditions du Cerf.

Pai, Anant. 1982. *Tales of the Buddha.* Bombay: Indian House Education Trust.

Pal, Pratapaditya. 1984. *Light of Asia: Buddha Śākyamuni in Asian Art.* Seattle: University of Washington Press.

Panglung, Jampa Losang. 1981. *Die Erzählstoffe des Mūlasarvāstivāda-vinaya analysiert auf Grund der tibetischen Übersetzung.* Tokyo: Reiyukai Library.
Parimoo, Ratan. 1980. *Life of Buddha in Indian Sculpture (Aṣṭa-Mahā-Pratihārya).* New Delhi: D. K. Printworld.
Parlier, Edith. 1991. "La légende du roi des Śibi: du sacrifice brahmanique au don du corps bouddhique." *Bulletin d'études indiennes* 9: 133–160.
Penner, Hans. 2009. *Rediscovering the Buddha: Legends of the Buddha and Their Interpretation.* London: Oxford University Press.
Péri, Noël. 1915. "Un conte hindou au Japon." *BEFEO* 15: 1–15.
———. 1917. "Hārītī la mère-de-démons." *BEFEO* 17: 1–102.
———. 1918. "Les femmes de Śākya-muni." *BEFEO* 18: 1–37.
Philippi, Donald. 1968. *Kojiki.* Tokyo: University of Tokyo Press.
Pleyte, C. M. 1901. *Die Buddha-Legende in den Skulpturen des Tempels von Bôrô-Budur.* Amsterdam: J. H. De Bussy.
Poppe, Nicholas. 1964. "The Mongolian Versions of the *Vessantarajātaka.*" Societas Orientalis Fennica (Helsinki), Studia Orientalia, vol. 30, 2–14, 74–92.
———. 1967. *The Twelve Deeds of Buddha.* Wiesbaden: O. Harrassowitz.
Powers, John. 2009. *A Bull of a Man: Images of Masculinity, Sex, and the Body in Indian Buddhism.* Cambridge, MA: Harvard University Press.
Prebish, Charles S. 2008. "Cooking the Buddhist Books: The Implications of the New Dating of the Buddha for the History of Early Indian Buddhism." *Journal of Buddhist Ethics* 15: 1–21.
Przylusky, Jean. 1920. *Le parinirvāṇa et les funérailles du Buddha.* Paris: Librairie Orientaliste Paul Geuthner.
———. 1935–1936. "Le partage des reliques du Buddha." *Mélanges chinois et bouddhiques* 4: 341–367.
Radich, Michael. 2011. *How Ajātaśatru Was Reformed: The Domestication of "Ajase" and Stories in Buddhist History.* Tokyo: International Institute for Buddhist Studies.
Rahula, Walpola. 1974. *What the Buddha Taught.* New York: Grove Press.
Ray, Reginald A. 1999. *Buddhist Saints in India: A Study in Buddhist Values and Orientations.* New York: Oxford University Press.
Renan, Ernest. 1992. *Études d'histoire religieuse. Nouvelles études d'histoire religieuse.* Paris: Éditions Gallimard.
Reynolds, Frank E. 1976. "The Many Lives of the Buddha." In *The Biographical Process,* edited by Frank E. Reynolds and Donald Capps, 37–61. The Hague: Mouton.
———. 1997. "Rebirth Traditions and Lineages of Gotama: A Study in Theravāda Buddhology." In Schober, *Sacred Biographies,* 19–39.
Rhi, Juhyung. 2010. "The Birth of the Buddha in Korean Buddhism: Infant Buddha Images and the Ritual Bathing." In Cueppers, Deeg, and Durt, *The Birth of the Buddha,* 321–344.
Rhys Davids, Caroline Augusta Foley. 1928. *Gotama the Man.* London: Luzac & Co.
Rhys Davids, Thomas W. 1880. *Buddhist Birth Stories, or Jātaka Tales.* London: Trübner and Co. Reprinted as *Buddhist Birth-Stories (Jataka Tales): The Commentarial Introduction Entitled Nidana-Katha, the Story of the Lineage* (London: Forgotten Books, 2017).
———. 1894. *The Questions of King Milinda.* 2 vols. Oxford: Clarendon Press.
———. 1907. *Buddhism: Its History and Literature.* New York: G.P. Putnam and Sons.

———. 1956 (1899). *Dialogues of the Buddha: Translated from the Pāli.* Vol. 2. London: Luzac & Company.
Rhys Davids, T. W., and Caroline A. F. Rhys Davids, trans. 1899–1921. *Dialogues of the Buddha: Translated from the Digha Nikaya.* 3 vols. Oxford: Pāli Text Society.
Rockhill, William Woodville. 1884. *The Life of Buddha and the Early History of His Order, Derived from Tibetan Works.* London: Kegan Paul.
Roerich, George N., trans. 1976. *The Blue Annals.* New Delhi: Motilal Banarsidass.
Ronkin, Noa. 2003. "Once upon a Rebirth: The Buddha's (Anti)Biography." Paper presented at the Stanford Center for Buddhist Studies.
Rotermund, Hartmut, trans. 1979. *Collection de sable et de pierres. Shasekishū.* Paris: Éditions Gallimard.
Rotman, Andy. 2008. *Divine Stories: Divyāvadāna, Part I.* Boston: Wisdom Publications.
Saindon, Marcelle. 2004. "Le Buddha comme avatāra de Viṣṇu et le mythe de Raji." *Indo-Iranian Journal* 47, no. 1: 17–44.
Saintyves, Pierre. 1987. *Les Contes de Perrault; En marge de la Légende Dorée; Les reliques et les images légendaires.* Edited by Francis Lacassin. Paris: Robert Laffont.
Sanford, James H., William R. LaFleur, and Masatoshi Nagatomi, eds. 1992. *Flowing Traces: Buddhism in the Literary and Visual Arts of Japan.* Princeton, NJ: Princeton University Press.
Schober, Juliane, ed. 1997. *Sacred Biographies in the Buddhist Tradition of South and Southeast Asia.* University of Hawai'i Press.
Schopen, Gregory. 1991. "Archeology and Protestant Presuppositions in the Study of Indian Buddhism." *History of Religions* 31, no. 1: 1–23.
———. 2004. "If You Can't Remember, How to Make it Up: Some Monastic Rules for Redacting Canonical Texts." In *Buddhist Monks and Business Matters,* 395–407. Honolulu: University of Hawai'i Press.
———. 2005. "Taking the Bodhisattva into Town: More Texts on the Image of 'the Bodhisattva' and Image Processions in the *Mūlasarvāstivāda-vinaya.*" *East and West* 55, nos. 1–4: 299–311.
———. 2007. "Cross-Dressing with the Dead: Asceticism, Ambivalence, and Institutional Values in an Indian Monastic Code." In *The Buddhist Dead: Practices, Discourses, Representations,* edited by B. Cuevas and J. Stone, 60–104. Honolulu: University of Hawai'i Press.
———. 2014. *Buddhist Monks, Nuns, and Other Worldly Matters: Recent Papers on Monastic Buddhism in India.* Honolulu: University of Hawai'i Press.
Schumann, Hans Wolfgang. 2003. *The Historical Buddha: The Times, Life, and Teachings of the Founder of Buddhism.* Delhi: Motilal Banarsidass.
Schwab, Raymond. 1984. *The Oriental Renaissance: Europe's Rediscovery of India and the East, 1680–1880.* New York: Columbia University Press.
Segalen, Victor. 1995. *Oeuvres complètes.* Edited by Henri Bouillier. 2 vols. Paris: Laffont.
Senart, Émile. 1882. *Essai sur la légende du Buddha, son caractère et ses origines.* Paris: Ernest Leroux.
———. 1882–1897. *Le Mahāvastu.* 3 vols. Paris: Imprimerie Nationale.
Serres, Michel. 2006. *Récits d'humanisme.* Paris: Éditions Le Pommier.
Seth, Ved. 1992. *Study of Biographies of the Buddha.* New Delhi: Akay Book Corporation.
Shaw, Miranda. 1994. *Passionate Enlightenment: Women in Tantric Buddhism.* Princeton, NJ: Princeton University Press.

Shaw, Sarah. 2007. *The Jātakas: The Birth Stories of the Bodhisattva.* New Delhi: Penguin.
———. 2010. "And That Was I: How the Buddha Himself Creates a Path between Biography and Autobiography." In Covill, Roesler, and Shaw, *Lives Lived, Lives Imagined,* 15–47.
Shimizu, Yoshiami. 1992. "Multiple Commemorations: *The Vegetable Nehan* of Itō Jakuchū." In Sanford, Lafleur, and Nagatomi, *Flowing Traces: Buddhism in the Literary and Visual Arts of Japan,* 201–233.
Silk, Jonathan. 2003. "The Fruits of Paradox: On the Religious Architecture of the Buddha's Life Story." *Journal of the American Academy of Religion* 71, no. 4: 863–881.
Skilling, Peter. 2004. "Lumbinī: Liturgy and Devotion." In Cueppers, Deeg, and Durt, *The Birth of the Buddha,* 345–354.
———. 2008. "New Discoveries from South India: The Life of the Buddha at Phanigiri, Andhra Pradesh." *Arts asiatiques* 63: 96–118.
———. 2009. "Quatre vies de Śākyamuni: À l'aube de sa carrière de Bodhisattva." In *Bouddhismes d'Asie: Monuments et littératures,* edited by Pierre-Sylvain Filliozat and Jean Leclant, 125–139. Paris: Académie des Inscriptions et Belles Lettres.
———. 2010. *Buddhism and Buddhist Literature of South-East Asia: Selected Papers.* Lumbini: Lumbini International Research Institute.
———. 2012. "Did the Buddhists Believe Their Narratives? Desultory Remarks on the Very Idea of Buddhist Mythology." In *Studies on Buddhist Myths: Texts, Pictures, Traditions and History,* edited by Wang Bangwei. Shanghai: Zhongxi shuju.
———. 2016a. "La Vie du Bouddha: Traditions et histoires." *Religion* 8: 18–23.
———. 2016b. "Le Jâtaka: Vies antérieures and Perfections du Bouddha." *Religion* 8: 52–57.
Skilling, Peter, and Justin McDaniel, eds. 2012. *Buddhist Narrative in Asia and Beyond.* 2 vols. Bangkok: Institute of Thai Studies, Chulalongkorn University.
Smith, Henri. 2014. "The Stuff of Dreams: Kawanabe Kyōsai's Nirvāna Painting of Matsuura Takeshirō." *Impressions* 35: 96–135.
Snellgrove, David. 1973. "Śākyamuni's Final 'Nirvāna.'" *Bulletin of the School of Oriental and African Studies* 36, no. 2: 399–411.
Snodgrass, Judith. 2007. "Defining Modern Buddhism: Mr. and Mrs. Rhys Davids and the Pāli Text Society." *Comparative Studies of South Asia, Africa and the Middle East* 27, no. 1: 186–202.
Soymié, Michel. 1984. "Quelques représentations de statues miraculeuses dans les grottes de Touen-houang." In *Contributions aux études de Touen-houang III,* edited by Michel Soymié. Paris: École Française d'Extrême-Orient.
Speyer, J. S., trans. 1895. *Jātakamālā, or Garland of Birth-Stories.* Vol. 1 of Sacred Books of the Buddhists. London: Henry Frowde. Reprint, Kindle edition, 2018.
Stein, Rolf A. 1991. "Buddhist Mythology." In *Asian Mythologies,* edited by Yves Bonnefoy, translated by Wendy Doniger, 119–121. Chicago: University of Chicago Press.
Steiner, Roland. 2010. "Truth under the Guise of Poetry: Aśvaghoṣa's 'Life of the Buddha.'" In Covill, Roesler, and Shaw, *Lives Lived, Lives Imagined,* 89–122.
Strawson, Galen. 2004. "Against Narrativity." *Ratio* 17, no. 4: 428–452.
Strickmann, Michel. 1996. *Mantras et mandarins: Le bouddhisme tantrique en Chine.* Paris: Éditions Gallimard.
Strong, John S. 1979. "The Legend of the Lion-Roarer: A Study of the Buddhist Arhat Piṇḍola Bhāradvāja." *Numen* 26: 50–88.

———. 1985. "The Buddhist Avadānists and the Elder Upagupta." In *Tantric and Taoist Studies in Honour of R. A. Stein,* edited by Michel Strickmann, vol. 3, 862–881. Bruxelles: Institut Belge des Hautes Études Chinoises.
———. 1992. *The Legend and Cult of Upagupta.* Princeton, NJ: Princeton University Press.
———. 1995. *The Experience of Buddhism: Sources and Interpretations.* Belmont, CA: Wadsworth Publishing.
———. 1997. "A Family's Quest: The Buddha, Yaśodharā, and Rāhula in the Mūlasarvāstivāda Vinaya." In Schober, *Sacred Biographies,* 113–128.
———. 1998. "Les reliques des cheveux du Bouddha au Shwe Dagon de Rangoon." *Aséanie* 2: 79–107.
———. 2001. *The Buddha: A Short Biography.* Oxford: Oneworld Publications.
———. 2004. *Relics of the Buddha.* Princeton, NJ: Princeton University Press.
———. 2007a. "The Buddha's Funerals." In *The Buddhist Dead: Practices, Discourses, Representations,* edited by Bryan J. Cuevas and Jacqueline I. Stone, 32–59. Honolulu: University of Hawai'i Press.
———. 2007b. "Two Buddha Relic Traditions." *Religion Compass* 1, no. 3: 341–352.
———. 2011. *The Buddha: A Beginner's Guide.* Oxford: Oneworld Publications.
Swearer, Donald K. 2010. *The Buddhist World of Southeast Asia.* Albany: State University of New York Press.
Tambiah, Stanley. 1984. *The Buddhist Saints of the Forest and the Cult of Amulets.* Cambridge: Cambridge University Press.
Tāranātha. 2003. *Le Soleil de la confiance: La vie du Buddha.* Translated by Comité de traduction Padmakara. Saint-Léon-sur-Vézère: Éditions Padmakara.
Tatelman, Joel. 1998. "The Trials of Yaśodharā and the Birth of Rāhula: A Synopsis of *Bhadrakalpāvadāna* II–IX." *Buddhist Studies Review* 15, no. 2: 1–42.
———. 1999. "The Trials of Yaśodharā: The Legend of the Buddha's Wife in the *Bhadrakalpāvadāna.*" *Buddhist Literature* 1: 176–261.
———, trans. 2005. *The Heavenly Exploits: Buddhist Biographies from the Dívyavadána.* New York: New York University Press.
Tauer, Felix. 1959. *Cinq opuscules de Hāfiz-i Abru concernant l'histoire de l'Iran au temps de Tamerlan.* Prague: Académie tchécoslovaque des sciences.
ten Grotenhuis, Elizabeth. 1992. "Chūjōhime: The Weaving of her Legend." In Sanford, Lafleur, and Nagatomi, *Flowing Traces: Buddhism in the Literary and Visual Arts of Japan,* 180–200.
Terral, Ginette, trans. 1958. *Choix de Jâtaka: Extraits des vies antérieures du Bouddha.* Connaissance de l'Orient. Paris: Unesco / Éditions Gallimard.
Thomas, Edward J. 1996. *The Life of Buddha As Legend and History.* London: Routledge.
Thurman, Robert A. F. 1992. *The Holy Teaching of Vimalakīrti: A Mahāyāna Scripture.* University Park: Pennsylvania State University Press. First published 1976.
———. 1996. *Essential Tibetan Buddhism.* New York: HarperOne.
Tominaga, Nakamoto. 1990. *Emerging from Meditation.* Translated by Michael Pye. Honolulu: University of Hawai'i Press.
Turpie, David. 2001. "*Wesak* and the Re-Creation of Buddhist Tradition." Montreal Religious Site Project, October 2001. https://fr.slideshare.net/anthony_morgan/wesak.
Ucko, Hans. 2000. *The People and the People of God: Minjung and Dalit Theology in Interaction.* Münster: LIT Verlag.

Ury, Marian, trans. 1985. *Tales of Times Now Past: Sixty-two Stories from a Medieval Japanese Collection.* Berkeley: University of California Press.

Valignano, Alexandre. 1990. *Les jésuites au Japon: Relation missionnaire (1583).* Paris: Desclée de Brouwer.

Vaudeville, Charlotte. 1964. "La légende de Sundara et les funérailles du Buddha dans l'Avadānaśataka." *BEFEO* 52: 73–91.

Vendova, Dessislava. 2020. "The Great Life of the Body of the Buddha: Re-examination and Re-assessment of the Images and Narratives of the Life of Buddha Shakyamuni." PhD diss., Columbia University.

Vermeersch, Sem. 2011. "An Early Korean Version of the Buddha's Biography." *Journal of the Oxford Centre for Buddhist Studies* 1: 197–211.

Waley, Arthur. 1932. "Did the Buddha Die of Eating Pork: With a Note on Buddha's Image." *Mélanges chinois et bouddhiques* 1: 343–354.

Walshe, Maurice, trans. 1987. *The Long Discourses of the Buddha: A Translation of the Dīgha Nikāya.* Boston: Wisdom Publications.

Walters, Jonathan S. 1990. "The Buddha's Bad Karma: A Problem in the History of Theravāda Buddhism." *Numen* 37, no. 1: 70–95.

———. 1994. "A Voice from the Silence: The Buddha's Mother's Story." *History of Religions* 33: 358–379.

———. 1997. "Stūpa, Story, and Empire: Constructions of the Buddha Biography in Early Post-Aśokan India." In Schober, *Sacred Biographies in the Buddhist Tradition of South and Southeast Asia,* 160–192.

Wang-Toutain, Françoise. 1994. "Le bol du Buddha: Propagation du bouddhisme et légitimité politique." *BEFEO* 81: 59–82.

Wasson, R. Gordon. 1982. "The Last Meal of the Buddha." *Journal of the American Oriental Society* 102: 591–603.

Watanabe, Masako. 1996. "A Preliminary Study of the 'Life of Buddha' in Medieval Japan: The Metropolitan Museum Paintings." *Orientations* 27, no. 8: 46-56..

Watanabe Satoshi. 2012. *Butsuden zu ronkō.* Tokyo: Chūōkōron bijutsu shuppan.

Watson, Burton, trans. 1993a. *The Lotus Sutra.* New York: Columbia University Press.

———, trans. 1993b. *The Zen Teachings of Master Lin-chi,* Boston: Shambhala.

———, trans. 2000. *The Vimalakīrti Sūtra.* New York: Columbia University Press.

Wayman, Alex. 1997. *Untying the Knots in Buddhism: Selected Essays.* New Delhi: Motilal Banarsidass.

Weber, Max. 2006. *Sociologie des religions.* Paris: Éditions Gallimard.

———. 2015. *Hindouisme et bouddhisme.* Paris: Flammarion.

Welbon, Guy Richard. 1968. *The Buddhist Nirvāna and its Western Interpreters.* Chicago: University of Chicago Press.

Wieger, Léon. 1951. *Les vies chinoises du Buddha.* Paris: Cathasia. First published 1913.

Wijayaratna, Mohan. 1990a. *Buddhist Monastic Life: According to the Texts of the Theravāda Tradition.* Cambridge: Cambridge University Press.

———. 1990b. *Le Bouddha et ses disciples.* Paris: Éditions du Cerf.

———. 1998. *Le dernier voyage du Bouddha: avec la traduction intégrale du Mahā-parinibbāna-Sutta.* Paris: Éditions Lis.

Willemen, Charles. 2009. *Buddhacarita: In Praise of Buddha's Acts.* Berkeley, CA: Numata Center for Buddhist Translation and Research.

———. 2011. "Selected Materials for the Study of the Life of Buddha Śākyamuni." *Pacific World,* 3rd ser., 13: 67–80.

Willford, Francis. 1811. "An Essay on the Sacred Isles in the West, with Other Essays Connected with That Work." *Asiatick Researches* 10: 94–95.

Wilson, Liz. 1996. *Charming Cadavers: Horrific Figurations of the Feminine in Indian Buddhist Hagiographic Literature.* Chicago: University of Chicago Press.

Wiltshire, Martin G. 1990. *Ascetic Figures before and in Early Buddhism: The Emergence of Gautama as the Buddha.* Berlin: Mouton de Gruyter.

Windisch, Ernst. 1895. *Māra und Buddha.* Leipzig: B. G. Teubner.

———. 1908. *Buddhas Geburt und die Lehre von der Seelen-wanderung.* Leipzig: B. G. Teubner.

Wong, Po Yee. 2012. "Acculturation as Seen through the Buddha's Birthday: Parades in Northern Wei Luoyang; A Micro-perspective on the Making of Buddhism as World Religion." PhD diss., University of the West.

Woodward, Mark R. 1997. "The Biographical Imperative in Theravāda Buddhism." In Schober, *Sacred Biographies in the Buddhist Tradition of South and Southeast Asia,* 40–61.

Wray, Elizabeth, Clare Rosenfield, and Dorothy Baily. 1996. *Ten Lives of the Buddha: Siamese Temple Paintings and Jātaka Tales.* Tokyo: Weatherhill.

Yamabe, Nobuyoshi. 1999. "The Sūtra on the Ocean-Like Samādhi of the Visualization of the Buddha: The Interfusion of the Chinese and Indian Cultures in Central Asia as Reflected in a Fifth-Century Apocryphal Sūtra." PhD diss., Yale University.

———. 2010a. "Visionary Consecration: A Meditative Reenactment of the Buddha's Birth." In Cueppers, Deeg, and Durt, *The Birth of the Buddha,* 239–276.

———. 2010b. "The *Ocean Sūtra* as a Cross-Cultural Product: An Analysis of Some Stories on the Buddha's 'Hidden Organ.'" In *"The Way of Buddha" 2003: The 100th Anniversary of the Otani Mission and the 50th of the Research Society for Central Asian Cultures,* edited by Irisawa Takashi. Kyoto: Ryukoku University.

———. 2014. "Indian Myth Transformed into Chinese Apocryphal Text: Two Stories on the Buddha's Hidden Organ." In *India in the Chinese Imagination: Myth, Religion, and Thought,* edited by John Kieschnick and Meir Shahar, 51–70. Philadelphia: University of Pennsylvania Press.

Yamada Yoshio, Yamada Tadao, Yamada Hideo, and Yamada Toshio, eds. 1963. *Konjaku monogatarishū.* 5 vols. Nihon koten bungaku taikei 22–26. Tokyo: Iwanami shoten.

Yamamoto, Hiroko. 2003. *Ijin: Chūsei Nihon no hikyōteki sekai.* Tokyo: Heibonsha.

Yampolsky, Philip, trans. 1990. *Selected Writings of Nichiren.* New York: Columbia University Press.

Yang Hsüan-chih. 1984. *A Record of Buddhist Monasteries in Lo-yang.* Translated by Yi-t'ung Wang. Princeton, NJ: Princeton University Press.

Yokoyama Shigeru and Fujiwara Hiroshi, eds. 1936. *Sekkyōbushi shōhonshū.* Tokyo: Okayama shoten.

Yokoyama Shigeru and Matsumoto Ryūshin, eds. 1979. *Muromachi jidai monogatari taisei.* Tokyo: Kadokawa shoten.

Zafiropoulo, Ghiorgo. 1993. *L'Illumination du Buddha: Essais de chronologie relative et de stratigraphie textuelle.* Innsbrück: Institut für Sprachwissenschaft.

Zelazny, Roger. 2009. *Lord of Light.* New York: Harper.

Zin, Monica. 2006. "About Two Rocks in the Buddha's Life Story." *East and West* 56, no. 4: 329–358.

Zotenberg, Hermann 1886. *Notice sur le Livre de Barlaam et Joasaph.* Paris: Imprimerie Nationale.

Zürcher, Erik. 1982. "Prince Moonlight: Messianism and Eschatology in Early Medieval Chinese Buddhism." *T'oung Pao* 68, no. 1: 1–75.

———. 2006. *The Buddhist Conquest of China. The Spread and Adaptation of Buddhism in Early Medieval China.* Leiden: E. J. Brill.

INDEX

ABOUT THE AUTHOR

Bernard Faure, who received his PhD (Doctorat d'Etat) from Paris University, is interested in various aspects of East Asian Buddhism, with an emphasis on Chan/Zen and Tantric or esoteric Buddhism. His work, influenced by anthropological history and cultural theory, has focused on topics such as the construction of orthodoxy and heterodoxy, the Buddhist cult of relics, iconography, sexuality, and gender. He has published a number of books in French and English. His English-language publications include: *The Rhetoric of Immediacy: A Cultural Critique of Chan/Zen Buddhism* (1991), *Chan Insights and Oversights: An Epistemological Critique of the Chan Tradition* (1993), *Visions of Power: Imagining Medieval Japanese Buddhism* (1996), *The Red Thread: Buddhist Approaches to Sexuality* (1998), *The Power of Denial: Buddhism, Purity, and Gender* (2003), *Double Exposure* (2004), and the four-volume *Gods of Medieval Japan* (2015–), which explores the mythico-ritual system of esoteric Buddhism and its relationships with medieval Japanese religion. He has taught at Cornell University and Stanford University and is presently Kao Professor in Japanese Religion at Columbia University.